IKE AND MONTY

IKE AND MONTY

Generals at War

Norman Gelb

Constable · London

First published in Great Britian 1994
by Constable and Company Limited
3 The Lanchesters, 162 Fulham Palace Road
London W6 9ER
Copyright © Norman Gelb 1994
Paperback edition 1996
ISBN 0 09 476700 9
The right of Norman Gelb to be
identified as the author of this work
has been asserted by him in accordance
with the Copyright, Designs and Patents Act 1988
Printed in Great Britain by
St Edmundsbury Press Ltd
Bury St Edmunds, Suffolk

A CIP catalogue record for this book
is available from the British Library

FOR MALLARY

CONTENTS

16. Overlord   304

17. Normandy   320

18. Generals at War   337

19. The Waning of the Chase   357

20. The Bulge   379

21. The Long Winter   399

22. Victory   416

23. In Conclusion   424

     Acknowledgments   444

     Endnotes   446

     Selected Bibliography   466

     Index   469

. . . it is precisely the essence of military genius that it does not consist in a single appropriate gift—courage, for example—while other qualities of mind or temperament are wanting or are not suited to war. Genius consists *in a harmonious combination of elements*, in which one or the other ability may predominate, but none may be in conflict with the rest.

CARL VON CLAUSEWITZ

By command I mean the general's qualities of wisdom, sincerity, humanity, courage and strictness.

SUN TZU

The greatest general is he who makes the fewest mistakes.

NAPOLEON BONAPARTE

Statues erected to honor the memories of General Dwight Eisenhower and Field Marshal Viscount Montgomery of Alamein stand across town from each other in central London. Eisenhower's is on a plinth at a corner of Grosvenor Square, near the American embassy; Montgomery's on Whitehall, in front of the Ministry of Defence.

Depicted in battle dress and wearing the tank soldier's beret for which he was famous, Montgomery looks the warrior, ready to command his men in battle. In contrast, a stern-visaged Eisenhower, in dress uniform, is portrayed as the more exalted commander, removed not only from actual combat but even from the combat zone by his more important duties in masterminding victory over Nazi Germany in the Second World War. To that extent, those images are accurate. But there were important singularities to both these men that their statues do not—perhaps cannot—capture.

Dwight David Eisenhower and Bernard Law Montgomery were the most eminent Allied military figures during the war—Eisenhower as Allied Supreme Commander and senior American general in Europe, Montgomery as the most celebrated

British field commander. Together, they and the forces they commanded crushed the German armies in North Africa and Western Europe and, with the Soviets, went on to demolish Adolf Hitler's Third Reich.

It was a monumental achievement and earned them much acclaim. But theirs was a troubled collaboration. Eisenhower was conditioned by the military traditions and military capabilities of the United States, Montgomery by Britain's very different traditions and capabilities. That they would sometimes disagree on fundamentals was to be expected. But their differences over strategy and tactics were compounded by personality and behavioral contrasts so profound that, though they spoke the same language, communication between them became an ordeal and their relationship grew strained almost to the point of rupture.

No great powers of perception were required to recognize how they differed in character and patterns of conduct. Eisenhower was open and gregarious. He had a ready, warm smile and a generally easy manner that charmed friends and strangers alike. He was modest, courteous, and straightforward.

"Ike" was personally liked by almost everyone with whom he dealt. "Damn it," he complained. "Montgomery's the only man in either army I can't get along with." It was no exaggeration. Montgomery's chief of staff, General Francis De Guingand, said of Eisenhower, "There are few cases in history where a Supreme Commander was so universally esteemed and honored. . . . He inspired love and unfailing loyalty."

In contrast to Eisenhower, Montgomery was arrogant, conceited, boastful, abrasive, tactless, and capable of gross boorishness. He saw criticism of himself only as confirmation of the ineptitude of his critics. His personal behavior was at times an embarrassment to many other British generals and even to Winston Churchill, who once called him "a little man on the make." Some of the Americans with whom he dealt came to abominate him.

Such a man could hardly have been expected to have made his way up through the British military hierarchy when many others less eccentric, and adhering to traditional codes of behavior, fell by the wayside. But Montgomery was a soldier with special qualities. He was an extraordinary leader of men, greatly respected by the officers who served under him and revered by his troops. He was known to possess, wrote the London *Times*, "to an exceptional degree that magnetic and mysterious power to inspire confidence" in his men.

Montgomery also had a superb grasp of tactics, as was demonstrated when he commanded the Allied invasion of Nazi-occupied Europe from across the English Channel, the most important single operation in the war. To his troops and to the British people generally, "Monty" was a heroic figure. He redeemed the battered reputation of the British Army and lifted the morale of the British people at a time when they were plagued by dread and despair.

His admirers endowed his slender, taut, five-foot-seven frame—"that intensely compacted hank of steel wire," George Bernard Shaw called him—with the dimensions of a titan. His often outlandish conduct, sometimes gleefully reported in the British press, was commonly regarded as the endearing eccentricity of a great man and a master of the battlefield. A general who served under him called him "the greatest field commander since Cromwell. Only Napoleon," he said, "was as good." Others expressed doubts about that, maintaining that Montgomery's achievements were vastly exaggerated, by himself as well as by others.

However, few extravagant claims were made about Eisenhower's qualities as the leader of men in battle. Having never previously held even a junior combat command, he came under intense pressure during the war well beyond his experience. Montgomery scorned his military talents, summing him up as "Nice chap; no general." The British High Command believed Eisenhower to be dangerously out of his depth as a commander of the Allied forces in the field. Even his friend, General Omar Bradley, who admired his achievements as chief executive officer of the most massive military campaign in history, doubted his ability to properly manage a battlefield in combat, a different matter altogether.

Nor was Eisenhower always as supremely confident as the

general in charge was meant to be. He was often deeply anxious about his performance as top soldier of the western Allies. He later confessed to a lifelong hope that he "wouldn't go into a blue funk" when required to make important yes-or-no decisions. One of his closest aides said he kept "poring over problems both real and imaginary as ants swarm over an anthill."

But no one, not even his critics, questioned Eisenhower's most momentous achievement in the war. As Supreme Allied Commander, he forged and managed the often-strained British-American military alliance and led it to victory over the armies of Nazi Germany. Churchill's chief military adviser, Lord Ismay, called him the only man who could have made it work.

But Montgomery, his senior British subordinate, was a painful enigma to Eisenhower. He found dealing with him exasperating and infuriating, while Montgomery found serving under Eisenhower endlessly bewildering and frustrating. As generals at war, each had important qualities the other lacked that, had the two men been able to work together in harmony, might have compensated considerably for their respective limitations. Their discord made that impossible, with costly consequences in the most devastating conflict in human history.

CHAPTER 2
Origins

Sahiwal, a city in central Pakistan, was once called Montgomery, after Field Marshal Montgomery's paternal grandfather, Sir Robert Montgomery. Sir Robert was a senior British official in the province of Punjab in the nineteenth century when Pakistan was still part of India. His act in disarming native troops at the start of the great Indian Mutiny against British colonial rule was credited with saving the metropolis of Lahore from the sort of massacres that occurred elsewhere in the Indian subcontinent at the time.

Bernard Law Montgomery's forebears on his mother's side could also claim eminence. In London, near Westminster Abbey, Dean Farrar Street, still so designated, was named after his maternal grandfather, Dean Frederic Farrar, a prominent nineteenth-century clergyman, educator, and writer.

No such illustrious figures featured in Eisenhower's genealogy. His forebears, who achieved neither fame nor influence, were originally from Germany. Their name was at first spelled "Eisenhauer," which means "hewer of iron." It indicates there may have been a blacksmith among the general's ancestors, though suggestions were made during the war that the name

"Eisenhauer" might instead have originally referred to a warrior, one who metaphorically hammered the enemy. However, as far back as can be traced, the Eisenhauers were pacifist Mennonites who had emigrated to what was to become the United States before the American Revolution.

The Mennonites were members of a Christian sect founded in the sixteenth century by a Menno Simons, a Dutch theologian who had once been a Catholic priest. Simons maintained that the Bible was the sole source of religious faith. He rejected the precepts of the predominant Christian churches and their religiously privileged priesthoods. He held that each individual was directly answerable to God. His influence spread to Switzerland, Germany, and other parts of Europe during the seventeenth and eighteenth centuries.

Persecuted as heretics in their native Rhineland, a group of Menno's followers, including the Eisenhauers, fled to Switzerland and then to Holland. From there, in 1741, Hans Nicholas Eisenhauer, his wife, and three sons made their way by ship to the Americas, where they settled in Lebanon County in the British colony of Pennsylvania. Other groups of Mennonites did the same. This was rich farmland where they believed with justification that they would be able to sustain themselves by working the soil and to practice their religion without being persecuted.

The Eisenhauers worked 120 acres of farmland, upon which they built a house and raised their families. Having carried their pacifist convictions with them from Europe, they and their offspring were unlikely to have participated in the fighting during the War of Independence. But details are sparse, and a man named Frederick Eisenhauer is recorded as having served in George Washington's army.

Some years after the United States gained its independence, Frederick Eisenhauer, grandson of Hans Nicholas, possibly the same Frederick who fought in the Revolution, moved to near Elizabethville in Pennsylvania. His son Jacob was born there in 1826. By then the spelling of the family name had been altered to "Eisenhower."

Jacob Eisenhower became a leading figure among the River

Brethren, a Mennonite sect so named because it favored river baptisms. Jacob was reputed to have been a magnificent orator. His sermons were said to have drawn large, appreciative congregations among the local communities of German origin, whose residents are still known collectively as the Pennsylvania Dutch. Ironically, the grandfather of the general who commanded Allied forces in the war against Germany a century later spoke and preached mostly in German, the predominant language in that part of Pennsylvania at the time.

In 1863, Jacob's wife, the former Rebecca Matter, gave birth to the first of the couple's fourteen children—a son, David, who was to be General Eisenhower's father. It was at the height of the Civil War, some of whose battles took place nearby— Gettysburg was not far away—but many Mennonites, Jacob among them, adhered to their pacifist principles and declined the call to the colors.

The Civil War marked a turning point in American history. Regional antagonisms would linger long afterward, but divisive influences that had threatened the cohesion of the United States were overwhelmed. However, large parts of the nation's heartland and its western regions remained sparsely populated. There was land out there to claim and fortunes to be made.

During the scandal-ridden post–Civil War administration of President Ulysses S. Grant, some of those fortunes were made through corrupt practices involving land grants and railroad construction. One effect was to vastly accelerate the pace at which railway lines were laid. That facilitated the migration westward of people who had settled in the East, as well as of new immigrants from Europe.

Circulars were widely distributed extolling the quality of life in the western territories, where, it was suggested, tracts of land could be cheaply acquired. For the River Brethren, anxious to insulate themselves from the baleful influences of the expanding, diversified population of Pennsylvania, the inducement was great. Exploratory visits fixed on Kansas as a promising venue in which to establish a new community safe from external intrusions. In 1878, a party of some 300 River Brethren under Jacob Eisenhower's leadership undertook a mass migration by rail to central Kansas. They settled not far south of Abilene, in Dickinson County.

Jacob bought 160 acres of rich alluvial farmland and built a house and a barn. His neighbors would gather at his farm for prayers and hymn-singing on Sundays. Things were good at the time. The economy of the country was strong. There was a ready market for the grain the River Brethren extracted from the earth. Others followed the pioneer party to Kansas and more land was acquired. They worked hard and prospered.

The Mennonite creed stressed the dignity of labor. But Jacob Eisenhower's eldest son David, fourteen years old at the time of the move to Kansas, was not much taken with the drudgery of sowing and harvesting. He wanted to go to college to become an engineer, and when he came of age his father reluctantly agreed to fund his attendance at Lane University in Lecompton, Kansas. He enrolled at Lane—which is now long defunct—in 1883, when he was twenty years old.

At the university David met Ida Elizabeth Stover, who was to be Dwight Eisenhower's mother. Her forebears had also emigrated to pre-Revolutionary America from Germany to escape religious persecution. They too were farmers. They had settled and raised children in a Mennonite community in Virginia, where Ida was born in 1862. Her parents died when she was still a young girl and she was raised by her maternal grandfather who, when she reached the age of twenty-one, gave her money that had been left to her by her father. With it she bought a train ticket to Kansas, where two of her older brothers, River Brethren like herself, had previously settled.

It was not common at the time for women to seek higher education, but Ida had too lively a mind to be denied further schooling. She used some of the money left from her inheritance to enroll at Lane, where she and David Eisenhower met. They were married in 1885 in the university chapel. The first of their sons was born the following year.

With the proceeds of substantial wedding gifts from his father—a farm property and money—David, who had by then abandoned his engineering aspirations, opened a general store with a partner in the town of Hope, north of Abilene. But lack of experience, poor business sense, and luck were against him. Times had turned bad, farmers could not pay their bills, and the partner absconded with some of the assets. More money was owed than could be found, and the business failed.

Jobs were hard to come by at the time. David went off in search of work while his wife, pregnant with their second child, stayed with friends in Kansas. He found employment at a machine shop run by the Cotton Belt Railroad in Denison, Texas. After Ida gave birth again, she and their two small sons joined him in Denison, where the family lived in poverty. David was earning the meager sum of ten dollars a week and could afford to rent only a small, dilapidated wood-frame house. David Dwight Eisenhower, their third son, was born there on October 14, 1890. To avoid confusion with his father, his given names were reversed in common usage to Dwight David. He may have been named after the popular evangelist Dwight Moody.

In 1891, the Eisenhower family moved back to Kansas. With the help of his family and the River Brethren, David Eisenhower had gotten a better but still low-paying job as a mechanic in the Belle Springs Creamery in Abilene, which was owned by the sect. In the following years, four other sons, one of whom died in infancy, were born to Ida and David.

Home for them and their six sons in Abilene was at first a one-story shack in a run-down section of town. However, in 1898, they were able to move into the more substantial dwelling of David's brother Abraham, who had decided to move west. It had no electricity or running water. An outhouse served as its toilet. It was still literally and figuratively on the wrong side of the tracks, in a district where the poorer people of Abilene, manual laborers and unskilled workers, lived. No sharply defined, European-style class prejudices existed. There was much mingling during the course of the day, particularly among youngsters. Nevertheless, people like the Eisenhowers tended to be looked down upon by the businessmen, bankers, and professionals of the town and their wives.

David Eisenhower continued working at the creamery, but Ida took to turning the property—the house was set on three acres of land—into a miniature working farm. They acquired a horse for plowing and cows for milking, and rabbits, pigs, chickens, and ducks. They grew vegetables and fruit to sell fresh or preserved. All worked hard, the young boys as well as Ida. The boys regularly also took outside jobs, even when at school, to help contribute to the family's upkeep.

Religion and standards of proper behavior played key roles in the Eisenhower household. Parents and sons knelt in prayer each morning and night. All took turns reading aloud from the Bible. But none of the boys was particularly religious; they all tended to fidget during Sunday services at the River Brethren meetinghouse. They were taught that cursing, smoking, drinking, and gambling were wicked and would not be tolerated. But it made no lasting impression. In later life Dwight Eisenhower, for example, smoked like a steam engine, cursed tolerably well, played a mean game of stud poker, and was not at all averse to the occasional snifter of alcoholic beverage.

Nevertheless, this was for the most part a tightly knit and loving family. Ida was central in its life; David, away at his job twelve hours a day, six days a week, was far less so. He had, in any case, become a moody, distant, largely incommunicative man, perhaps because of the poverty that had become so much a part of his life and the difficulties he had encountered in providing for his large family. When little, the boys often feared him. When they did something particularly mischievous, Ida, who normally punished them moderately for minor infractions, would inform David, who wielded the switch.

Abilene was at the time a quiet town of less than five thousand souls. In the 1860s it had been a booming, raucous cow town and western railhead.* It was there where the famous Marshal "Wild Bill" Hickok gunned down desperados. But by the time the Eisenhowers had settled there, the railroad had moved farther west. Cowboys no longer drove their herds of cattle there from Texas grazing land in order to ship them to markets east and north by train.

Tall tales about gunfights in the street and related excitements

---

*The menu of Abilene's venerable Texan Cafe still bears the legend "Last place for a full meal before heading West."

were all that was now left of those heady days. Abilene had settled down into a sober, stable community, abounding with churches, where very little out of the ordinary happened. Its citizens were mostly hardworking, law-abiding, deeply religious, and intensely patriotic. Despite their own distant origins, they tended to be suspicious of foreigners and foreign ideologies. There were few external cultural influences. Children were expected to be well-behaved and obedient, though a certain amount of harmless mischievousness was, albeit punishable, considered normal and even admirable among boys. At school, Eisenhower—called "Ike" even then; it was a convenient diminutive for his family name—was a popular if not a dedicated student, strong in sports. He was good at baseball and football.

There was nothing calculated or carefully considered about the direction his career took. He hoped to go to the U.S. Naval Academy at Annapolis after graduating from high school because a close friend would be going there. But he managed his way through a competitive examination to gain a place at West Point instead. Seeking a military education had nothing to do with his ambitions for later life. Money was still short and both Annapolis and West Point—it did not matter much to him which one he attended—offered a free college education as well as an opportunity to play football.

For many West Point cadets, the early period at the U.S. Military Academy was torment. It was marked by relentless drilling and cruel hazing by senior cadets. Every moment of their day was prescribed. But for Eisenhower, robust and used to hard work and long hours, the process was invigorating. Besides, he thought, "Where else could you get a college education without cost?" He was subjected to none of the questing or querying that is often part of a boy's passage to manhood. He was becoming an officer in the Army of the United States along well-established and clearly defined lines. Though he hadn't planned on it, he considered it a privilege to be given the opportunity.

He was not a particularly diligent cadet. In an atmosphere in which obedience was virtually sacred, he regularly committed far more than his share of transgressions, including such petty infractions as "Smoking in room during call to quarters," "Apparently making no reasonable effort to have his room properly cleaned," "Not writing two hundred words in Spanish composition . . . as required." An accumulation of demerits that might affect his class standing, and perhaps his career, did not appear to have alarmed him.

Having grown up in a large family, Eisenhower quickly adapted to and came to enjoy the camaraderie and community life of West Point. His gregariousness, ready smile, and, especially, his prowess on the football field made him popular with his fellow cadets. He made several close friends, some of whom would later serve under him in senior positions.

His greatest disappointment at West Point was sustaining a serious knee injury during a football game that was aggravated by a fall from a horse soon after. It put him on crutches for a month and spelled the end of his football career at the academy. As for his studies, he was no better than average. He did not greatly impress his instructors, graduating no higher than sixty-first in a class of 164. At the time, the prospect of pursuing a career as an officer in the army of the United States of America did not feature greatly in his calculations.

In contrast to Eisenhower's modest family background, it has been said that a warrior knight was the earliest known ancestor of Bernard Law Montgomery. Roger de Montgomeri came from Falaise, in Normandy, where his twentieth-century descendant would engage the enemy during the most important battle of the Second World War. Sir Roger was second in command to William the Conqueror when he crossed the English Channel to invade England and vanquish the English in 1066. During the Norman period in Britain, Montgomerys were lords of large estates on the Welsh border. In subsequent times, members of the clan settled in other parts of Britain, notably in Scotland, from which a branch of the family crossed over to Northern Ireland to colonize land.

Samuel Montgomery, who was born in 1723, was a prosperous wine merchant in the Northern Irish town of Londonderry. He acquired a huge estate at nearby New Park that he established as the Montgomery family seat. His son, also named Samuel, was a clergyman to whom was born Robert Montgomery, the field marshal's grandfather, the adventurous figure who was knighted by Queen Victoria and after whom the above-mentioned city in Pakistan was named.

Henry Montgomery, the field marshal's father, was Sir Robert's second son. In the tradition of the administrators of the British Empire, Sir Robert sent his sons back to England to be educated. Henry went to Harrow and then to Cambridge University. At the age of twenty-four he was ordained a vicar in the Anglican Church. He became curate at St. Margaret's Church in Westminister, London's most fashionable Anglican church. The rector there was Frederic Farrar, the aforementioned Dean Farrar after whom the London street is named.

In 1881, at the age of thirty-four, Henry married Maud Farrar, one of Dean Farrar's five daughters. She was sixteen at the time. Despite her youth, Maud proved a valuable partner for the dedicated cleric. She assisted him energetically in his parish duties, maintaining his church as a center of community activity, despite bearing three children in quick succession. On November 17, 1887, when Maud was still only twenty-two years old, she bore a fourth child, a boy, at her husband's vicarage in South London. They named him Bernard Law.

Two years later, Henry Montgomery was consecrated Bishop of Tasmania. It was an honor, though Tasmania was as remote a corner of the British Empire as could be imagined. Less dedicated clerics might have considered being dispatched to a distant, offshore corner of Australia, especially after having been energetically engaged at the London hub of the Victorian world, as equivalent to being sent into exile. But Henry, Maud, and their small children—there were now five of them—set off on the long sea voyage to his new posting with great anticipation of serving the Lord and the Anglican Church in that distant outpost.

Strangers from afar, exalted representatives of Mother England, speaking in a way most Tasmanians considered offensively posh, Bishop Montgomery and his family settled in with difficulty. The bishop was a busy man. He assiduously went about his duties. His diocese was huge, covering some 26,000 square miles. It included remote bush districts and lesser off-shore islands. His duties regularly took him away from home for long periods of time while he saw to the needs of his far-flung flock. It fell to Maud, though still only in her mid-twenties, to see to every household chore and care.

In this strange and not overly welcoming environment, she strove to draw the family protectively close around her. She knew no other way of doing so than through rigid discipline. It suited her temperament. She was a strong-willed, domineering woman. Bernard Montgomery's childhood in Tasmania—and particularly his difficult relationship with his mother there—molded his character.

Tutors were brought from England for the children so that they would not be contaminated by local teachers and their strange accents. Each day was meticulously organized for them, with every hour planned, including those designated as play-time. Disobedience or infraction of rules exposed the small culprits to punishment, to being sent to bed early, deprived of pocket money, or beaten.

Bernard rebelled against his mother's severe rule while still a young boy. He had inherited her willpower, stubbornness and self-regard rather than his father's benign, easygoing, charitable nature. He was regularly punished for persistent naughtiness and deliberate disobedience, behavior that had come to be expected of him. If his mother did not know where he was, she would tell one of the other children, "Go and find out what Bernard is doing and tell him to stop it." He and his mother were endlessly locked in quarrels and bickering. The punishment she administered for his insubordination served only to embitter him and strengthen his determination not to submit to her will. He later candidly described his childhood as unhappy because of the clashes of wills and temperament between his mother and himself from which she always emerged the victor.

Life in Tasmania wasn't all miserable for young Bernard. The out-of-doors aspects of life there suited him. He very much enjoyed country treks, camping, and related outdoor activity.

Despite his relentless conflict with his mother, family occasions were often enjoyable. He adored his father, who made few demands on him, was usually away, and whose punishment for his son's alleged transgressions was, to his wife's outrage, never more than a joint prayer session after which Bernard was invariably forgiven.

But his bitter, endlessly acrimonious relationship with his mother remained the most important experience of his childhood. His siblings were able to adjust with far less difficulty to the way the bishop's wife ran the family. "I was the bad boy of the family," he later wrote, "the rebellious one, and as a result I learnt to stand or fall on my own." Bernard emerged into adolescence convinced that life was a personal, perpetual struggle against unreasonable, unworthy authority. It made him defiant and egocentric. He would remain so for the rest of his life.

When Bernard was thirteen years old, Bishop Montgomery was recalled to London to become head of the Anglican Church's Society for the Propagation of the Gospel. The family moved into a big house in Chiswick, West London, and Bernard went off as a day boy to the elite St. Paul's School. Adjusting to this major change of social climate might have been difficult for a youngster. English schools had expectations, procedures, and pecking orders likely to cause a boy transplanted from Australia much anguish. Bullying was ingrained and habitual. But Bernard, lean and wiry, was good at sports. What was more, attitudes at the school were such that a strong-willed lad capable of administering as well as absorbing punishment could quickly gain leadership status among his peers. It compensated for Bernard's social failings and for his mediocrity as a scholar.

At home in London, he was subjected by his mother to the same oppressive restraints that had tormented him in Tasmania. He continued to rebel against discipline, even of the mildest sort. But school was for him a glorious escape. He was content at St. Paul's because, though his studies did not interest him greatly, away from classes he was often in charge. He became captain of the cricket and rugby teams, and through his un-

abashed assertiveness became the dominant figure in a group
of mischievous students.

"For the first time in my life," he said, "leadership and authority came my way; both were eagerly seized." He reveled in
the attention paid to him and in the experience of being on
display. According to his brother Donald, who was at St. Paul's
at the same time, he "developed a streak of showmanship he
never had before."

It was noticeable that when he was reduced to being just
another member of a team or group he was a troublemaker,
disputatious and hypercritical, winning arguments through
persistence while displaying indifference to the views and feelings of others. Despite his popularity and leadership, he made
no firm friends at St. Paul's.

His decision to consider an army career was made on his very
first day at the school. It appears to have been made casually,
without consideration of what it might mean in the future. Boys
at St. Paul's who thought they might aspire to a military career
or did not feel academically inclined could opt for the so-called
"Army Class," which would direct them along lines different
from those students intent on concentrating more intently on
academic studies. Montgomery's parents were distressed when
they learned of his choice. His mother was particularly upset
and angry, which made Montgomery determined to hold to his
decision, which in turn better prepared him, in his final year at
St. Paul's, for the competitive examination for a place at Sandhurst Royal Military College than might otherwise have been
the case. He passed, though not with distinction.

Sandhurst, which Montgomery entered in 1907 at the age of
twenty, had long been the preserve of the social elite. In the
British gentry it was traditional for one son to take on management of the family estate, for another to go into the church,
and for a third to go into the army or navy, given of course
there were enough sons to assume those various obligations.
One Sandhurst graduate complained, "There were some dread-
ful outsiders among us, as could hardly be prevented by open
examination." They were few in number and were not generally

accepted by their social superiors at the academy. In addition to absorbing the rudiments of soldiering at the college, most cadets had an agreeable time while there, drinking, gambling, and for most very likely experiencing their first sexual encounters.

Montgomery engaged in none of that. It didn't appear to interest him, though that may have been partly because, in contrast to almost all other cadets, he had no money to squander on such distractions. Pay for a British Army officer had never been enough to live on and would not be until the Second World War. A private income or allowance was almost essential. Even at Sandhurst some outside income was necessary. Despite his father's senior church position, the Montgomerys had little money to spare. Bernard was given an allowance by his parents of a mere two pounds a month, which even at that time was very little. He later recalled how envious he was of fellow cadets who could afford to buy the wristwatches that were then becoming popular.

At Sandhurst he at first attempted to lead the kind of life he had enjoyed at St. Paul's. While more or less keeping up with his studies and training, he was actively and successfully engaged in group sports, once more usually as a star performer. Also repeating a role he had played at school, he soon assumed leadership of a gang of mischievous cadets who engaged in pranks and sometimes dangerous practical jokes. In one incident, they tied up a cadet and Montgomery set fire to his clothes. The victim suffered serious burns and Montgomery might have been expelled from Sandhurst because of it. But he was spared that fate, possibly to save his distinguished father from scandal.

However, the incident had a salutary effect on Montgomery, who'd had no wish to inflict such injuries on the victim, and certainly not to expose himself to severe punishment. He subsequently toned down his extracurricular activities and took to concentrating, with the diligence of which he was capable, on what Sandhurst required of him. By the time his studies there were completed, he had made up much lost ground and was well equipped to begin his career as a British Army officer.

He wanted to be sent to India, then the jewel in the imperial crown. Under the procedures and practices of the British Empire, the Indian Army, though controlled, officered, and partly manned by the British, was administratively an independent entity. It was a popular posting for Sandhurst graduates, particularly for impecunious ones like Montgomery, because an officer in the Indian Army, unlike those posted almost everywhere else, was paid enough to live on his salary. So many Sandhurst cadets preferred an India posting that only those graduating near the top of their classes succeeded in their quest. Despite the improvement in his scholastic performance at the academy, Montgomery was not chosen. He was required to apply for posting to a regiment in Britain.

The choice was not as predetermined as it was for most other Sandhurst graduates. Unlike most of them, having spent so much of his young life abroad Montgomery had no county connections that would dispose him toward one regiment or another. He said later that he picked the Royal Warwickshire Regiment because he liked the looks of the cap badge its officers wore and, more likely, because it was known that Royal Warwickshire officers were not put under excessive financial pressure. In addition, some of the regiment was serving in India. That raised the possibility that before long he would be dispatched there as well.

Montgomery emerged from Sandhurst a well-trained aspiring young subaltern, but little had changed in his personality. Though generally comfortable with groups of other young men engaged in arduous activity or sports, provided none of them presumed to tell him what to do, he still lacked social polish. He remained unflinchingly assertive, opinionated, and argumentative, even in circumstances when he should have known better. Offended by his brashness, one of the officers told him upon his departure from the college that he would never get anywhere in the army.

Though only twenty-one years old, Montgomery had become an eccentric figure, unconcerned by the reaction of others to his often gauche behavior. He was also single-minded now. He maintained little contact with his family. He had no romantic interests. The army had become his life to the exclusion of everything else. It was his religion. Its daily observances were his sacraments, though he was developing radical ideas about how they should be administered and performed.

A military career for Dwight Eisenhower when he graduated from West Point in 1915 was by no means certain. The senior medical officer at the academy told him it was possible that the knee injury he had sustained playing football would trouble him for the rest of his life. He was likely to be denied an active-service commission because of it. The U.S. Army was not greatly interested in an officer who might soon be claiming a disability pension or who might be prevented by physical handicap from performing his duties to the full.

This did not particularly distress the twenty-four-year-old Eisenhower. Most of his fellow cadets were committed to following army careers, but he was not sure what he wanted to do next. Interest in developments in South America had become fashionable in the United States, and he contemplated setting off southward to see what life might be like there. "I was curious about the gauchos," he later said, "and Argentina sounded to me a little like the Old West."

Nevertheless, when it appeared that the infantry would accept him despite his knee injury, even if the cavalry he preferred would not, he applied for a commission. It seemed the simplest thing to do. Besides, since he had no independent resources, an army career might permit him to satisfy his craving to visit exotic places.

He listed the Philippines, then under American rule, as the place he favored for his first posting and bought uniforms for tropical wear in confident anticipation. To his disappointment and financial embarrassment, he was assigned instead to the 19th Infantry Regiment at Fort Sam Houston in San Antonio, Texas, near the Mexican border. Friction had developed between the United States and Mexico over Mexican political instability and U.S. intercession in that country's factional strife. But though Second Lieutenant Eisenhower hoped to see some action as compensation for missing out on a Philippines posting, the time he spent at Fort Sam was to be largely uneventful.

It proved, however, to be far more tolerable than he imagined duty in the state where he had been born could possibly be. The requirement that he immerse himself in endless drilling and the other dreary routines of peacetime military life was minimal. He had much leisure time and spent much of it playing poker and carousing with friends. With the approval of the camp commandant, he coached the football team of a local private military academy. Its success under his tutelage made him popular both with his fellow officers and the townsfolk. To his embarrassment, he was applauded and cheered at public occasions.

His popularity may have helped him in the pursuit of the girl he was to marry. Mary Geneva Doud, "Mamie" to her family and friends, was the daughter of a wealthy retired meat packer. She lived with her family in a large, comfortable house in a prosperous neighborhood in Denver, Colorado. To escape its severe winters, the Douds spent part of each year in San Antonio. Mamie had received a finishing-school education and normally associated only with people of her own social standing. She was a slender, not unattractive nineteen-year-old and could be expected to marry someone wealthy enough to permit her to continue enjoying the style of life to which she was accustomed. Second Lieutenant Eisenhower, whom she met while visiting the officers' club at Fort Sam, could not do that. But he was an interesting-looking, courteous, well-built, popular young man who courted her with great persistence. They were married in 1916.

That same year, the Mexican revolutionary Francisco "Pancho" Villa led a troop of Mexican irregulars on a raid into New Mexico. For officers in the peacetime U.S. Army, promotion was hard to come by. The quickest route was to engage in combat when the rare opportunity arose to do so. Eisenhower was among the officers who applied to be assigned to an expeditionary force that General John J. Pershing was to lead on a punitive operation into Mexico. He was not chosen, but was assigned instead to train a National Guard unit that was to be held in reserve in case Pershing needed reinforcements.

The slaughter of what was later to be called World War I had by then been in progress in Europe for two years. Though sympathizing with the Allies' struggle against the German-led Central Powers, the United States was neutral in the conflict and the American people wished their country to remain so. However, raids by German submarines on American shipping in the Atlantic tried the patience of the government in Washington. And on March 1, 1917, President Woodrow Wilson declared that Germany was engaging in impermissible action against the United States.

The British had intercepted and passed to the American government a secret message sent from the German foreign ministry in Berlin to the German ambassador to the United States. The "Zimmermann Telegram"—a reference to German Foreign Minister Arthur Zimmermann—stated that if America entered the war on the Allied side, Mexico should be persuaded to join the Central Powers. After the Allies had been defeated, Mexico would be rewarded with territory in Arizona, New Mexico, and Texas.

The entry of the United States into the war in Europe then became inevitable and imminent despite the fact that the U.S. Army was under-equipped and unprepared for a conflict of such proportions. On April 3, 1917, Eisenhower was appointed supply officer for the hastily created 57th Infantry Regiment.

Three days later, President Wilson announced America's declaration of war. General Pershing, appointed commander of the American Expeditionary Force that was to be deployed in Europe, called for one million troops to be sent to France. To his regret, Eisenhower, whose organizational talents were already recognized, was not to be among them.

In September, he was assigned to train officer candidates at Fort Oglethorpe in Georgia. Two months later, he was shifted to Fort Leavenworth in Kansas to train fledgling officers there. Three months after that, Eisenhower, having taken a course in tank warfare at Leavenworth, was assigned to a tank battalion that was training—without tanks—at Camp Meade, Maryland. The battalion was scheduled soon to be shipped to France. Mamie had given birth to a son—Doud, nicknamed "Icky"—a few months earlier, but, having previously seen his opportunity for active duty and accelerated promotion slip away, Eisenhower was elated at the prospect of finally getting his chance. However, though now a captain, he was disappointed once again. He was considered too useful as a training officer to be spared for service abroad. Instead of France, he was posted to Camp Colt at Gettysburg, Pennsylvania, to train the U.S. Army's first tank unit, ambitiously called a "tank corps" though it was yet to be equipped with tanks.

Wherever Eisenhower served, his superior officers filed favorable evaluation reports on his organizational and training skills and his capacity for getting on with whatever job he was assigned without excessive supervision. On his twenty-eighth birthday in October 1918, he finally received orders to go overseas. He was to take command of a tank unit serving against the Germans in France. But shortly before he was due to depart, the armistice was declared in Europe. The Great War was over and he had missed out on it.

Eisenhower felt thwarted. He had by then become a dedicated career soldier and the function of a soldier was to fight in defense of his country's interests, while advancement in the ranks was every soldier's ambition. Now the war to end all wars was history, and he believed he had "missed the boat."

It was the wrong time to be in the army. Americans were

asking what need the country had of men in uniform and, indeed, what good had come of the United States' involvement in shabby squabbles overseas. Demands were being made that it never happen again. Congress set about rapidly trimming the country's military budget. The nation forswore foreign entanglements and turned in on itself. Its concerns were domestic— labor strife, the Red Scare at home, and the flapper age. The military was an irrelevance. Many officers who had not seen action in France, and many who had, were compelled to return to civilian life. Still more cuts were in the pipeline; America's peacetime army was to be a fraction of its wartime size.

But while more than a hundred thousand officers were required to shed their uniforms, Eisenhower's position in the service proved secure. The glowing assessments that had been placed in his War Department file by the officers he had served under since leaving West Point shielded him from being numbered among the unwanted. Perhaps working even more to his advantage was the fact that the military services were obsessed with sports. His skill and zeal as an Army football coach in some of the places where he had been posted were well known.

For some military thinkers, it was a time for examination and review. Despite the slaughter at the Somme and elsewhere during the war, many remained convinced that committing great numbers of infantry to battle was the only the way to vanquish an enemy. But others realized a new era of military technology was dawning and that it would spawn a different kind of warfare. Some looked to air power as the wave of the future. (Eisenhower had himself once briefly contemplated transferring to the newly formed Army Aviation Section.) Others concluded that the time of mechanized land warfare had arrived. They included Charles de Gaulle in France, Heinz Guderian in Germany, and, to a lesser extent, Bernard Montgomery in Britain. They also included Dwight Eisenhower.

These men saw the lumbering tank, which had performed briefly and without great impact in World War I, being transformed into a much more effective battlefield weapon. "The Tank," Eisenhower wrote in *The Infantry Journal* in 1919, "is in its infancy and the great strides already made in its mechanical improvement only point to the greater ones still to come. The clumsy, awkward, snail-like pace of the old tanks must be forgotten, and in their place we must picture a speedy, reliable, and efficient engine of destruction."

That view was shared by Major George S. Patton, Jr. who was also at Camp Meade, at the Infantry Tank School to which Eisenhower, also now a major, had been assigned. Patton was rich and rambunctious. He was given to wandering about with ivory-handled pistols on a gunbelt around his waist and uttering obscenities at the slightest provocation. With his wealth, swaggering manner, and passion for polo, he and Eisenhower had little in common except the army, but they became good friends.

However, the opinions they shared about the future of mechanized warfare made no impact in Washington, where Congress was busily slashing rather than increasing funds for the military. Of greater immediate significance for the two of them was the army's attitude. The ideologues at the War Department still dismissed any suggestion that wars could be won by any other means than the efforts of hordes of infantrymen advancing across a battlefield with rifles ready and bayonets fixed. Eisenhower soon discovered he would be taking career risks if he continued to espouse contrary notions. "I was told that my ideas were not only wrong but dangerous and that henceforth I would keep them to myself. Particularly, I was not to publish anything incompatible with solid infantry doctrine. If I did, I would be hauled before a court-martial."

He did as he was told. He was not inclined to buck the system that had nurtured him and from which he could easily be put out into the cold. He was disgruntled but did not consider it his job to tell his superiors what they were doing wrong.

Tragedy, the most serious Eisenhower was ever to experience, struck while he was at Camp Meade. Icky, his beloved three-year-old son, was stricken with scarlet fever and soon succumbed to it. Eisenhower was emotionally shattered by the boy's death. He had never before known great grief. It injected into his personality a measure of hardness that hadn't been there before. The relationship between him and Mamie, for whom the loss was also devastating, was affected. Some measure of its warmth and intimacy was lost and never would be regained. For each, the bereavement was private and personal, something they had difficulty sharing with each other.

Between 1919 and 1940, Eisenhower held a succession of army positions in which he performed with what had become characteristic efficiency and resourcefulness and for which he continued to receive commendations from his superiors. His first major postwar assignment was as executive officer to General Fox Connor, who was commanding troops in the Panama Canal Zone to guard the waterway. An attack by an enemy power on the canal was unlikely, but routine precautions were considered necessary.

Panama was not a favored posting for either officers or troops. Most who were assigned there concentrated on avoiding exertion while trying to keep as cool and comfortable as possible in its torrid and debilitating climate. But that was not the kind of command General Connor, who had been Chief of Operations of the American Expeditionary Force in France in the First World War, intended to run. As far as he was concerned, it was the duty of soldiers on active duty always to be kept both alert and busy even if no enemy threat was in evidence. As Connor's executive officer, conditioned to act in accordance with the wishes of his superiors, Eisenhower devoted himself diligently to seeing that the general's wishes were complied with.

As a consequence, he was not much liked either by the troops or by the officers serving under him. He would not permit them to use the region's tropical climate as an excuse to laze about. In addition to conducting intensive training programs, he made certain the base was kept scrupulously policed at all times, the base lawns trimmed, and the base drives clear and neatly lined with white-painted rocks. He saw to it that the base buildings were maintained in good repair and the various other petty procedures of military housekeeping strictly adhered to.

Having to concentrate on such trivia might have been a tiresome experience. However, Eisenhower's time in Panama proved to be enormously rewarding for him. In contrast to most U.S. Army generals then—and probably most generals everywhere at the time—Fox Connor was a man of considerable intelligence, imagination, and foresight. Eisenhower had never before been exposed at close quarters and at length to an individual with a strong intellect and penetrating ideas. They spent much time together and examined strategy and tactics on a higher level than Eisenhower had ever done before. He found himself turning away from the potboiler Western novels that had long been his spare-time reading to studies of military theory and biographies of military figures.

Connor was delighted to have an executive officer who saw things his way about keeping the troops fully occupied, even in Panama's oppressive climate, and who, at the same time, was a receptive student for his wide-ranging catalogue of ideas and theories. In his official assessment of Eisenhower, he described him as "one of the most capable, efficient, and loyal officers I have ever met." In turn, Eisenhower was excited by the realm of thought to which Connor introduced him.

On the issue of basic American military strategy, Connor was convinced that expanding Japanese military might was a threat that the United States would soon have to confront. He also believed that the Versailles Treaty signed at the conclusion of the Great War had inflicted such severe penalties on Germany that another major conflict in Europe was likely within two decades and that the United States would again be drawn into it. He analyzed the deficiencies in the top command structure of the Allies in the Great War and sharply criticized its failure to override "nationalistic considerations in the conduct of campaigns." Eisenhower saw the logic of that judgment, not suspecting that he himself would one day have to resolve problems related to the separate and sometimes conflicting national interests and objectives of the military forces under his command.

Eisenhower's satisfaction with his life in the Canal Zone, his immersion in military theory, and the great amount of time he spent with Connor—often on camping trips they took alone together in the Panamanian Zone jungle—had somewhat chilled his relationship with Mamie, who hated the place. In the later stages of her second pregnancy, she fled the discomforts of the

climate and went to Denver to stay with her parents and have
her baby there. Eisenhower did not mind. But he was delighted
when his new son was born. Indeed, when Mamie returned to
Panama with baby John, the strained feelings between them
were much eased.

After two years in Panama, Eisenhower was sent to attend
the Command and General Staff School at Fort Leavenworth.
General Connor's backing had overridden obstructions set in
his way by the military bureaucracy in Washington. To attend
the school was to proceed along the path to the highest ranks
in the army. Men considered to be the brightest, most accomplished young officers were sent there to see how they could
survive a grueling ordeal of concentrated study. Students regularly stayed up long into the night absorbing what they were
taught and preparing for difficult examinations that could determine the course of their careers and lives. Nervous collapse
was not unknown among them, even the occasional suicide.
But Eisenhower had few difficulties there. He had been well
tutored by Connor during his time in Panama. He emerged at
the top of his class, evidently headed for a senior position in
the army.

However, his first posting upon leaving the college was a
disappointment. He was sent to command an infantry battalion
at Fort Benning, Georgia, with the understanding that he would
coach the fort's football team as well. Eisenhower still very
much enjoyed football, but he believed that as the best student
at the army's elite Command and General Staff School, he deserved better.

Connor came to his rescue once more. He recommended him
to General Pershing, who had been appointed head of the Battle
Monuments Commission. Eisenhower was given the task of
putting together a guide to European battlefields where American troops had fought during the Great War. It was not an
exciting chore, but it was obvious that association with "Black
Jack" Pershing could do an officer's career nothing but good.
With the help of his brother Milton, who had acquired considerable journalistic experience, Eisenhower handled his assignment with his usual efficiency and dispatch. Along with praise

for assisting Pershing in the compilation of his memoirs, it earned Eisenhower a posting to the Army War College in Washington, D.C. It was further evidence that high rank would be his further down the line. That was followed by a year in Paris on the Battle Monuments Commission (Mamie's preferrence when he was given the choice, rather than his own), and then a posting back in Washington at the office of the Assistant Secretary of War.

Though he was now at the nerve center of the American military services, much of what he had been doing since leaving the General Staff School was only marking time. Eisenhower had frustratingly remained fixed at his rank of major. But though promotions had remained hard to come by in America's miniaturized peacetime army, he had been marking that time in some of the right places with many of the right people.

Eisenhower arrived in Washington from Paris at the end of September 1929. Four weeks later Wall Street crashed, heralding the great depression of the 1930s. Tens of thousands of businesses collapsed. Factories closed across the nation. Millions were thrown out of work. In that climate of pain and despair, Eisenhower was given the task of drawing up a plan for organizing the country's industrial economy in case the United States was required to fight another major war. To an outside observer the job would have seemed absurd. It was not so much fiddling while Rome burnt as making a comprehensive real estate survey while the flames rose to the sky.

The chore was also no more than marking time, but Eisenhower's luck held. He got to know and deal with people outside the narrow horizons of the army, men who could make things happen—in Congress, in the various branches of the civil service, and in industry. In addition, the methodical nature with which he set about his task, and his diligence in getting it done, brought him to the attention of General Douglas MacArthur. Recognizing his talents, MacArthur, the newly appointed Army Chief of Staff, was soon calling on him to produce reports and write some of his speeches.

In 1933, Eisenhower was formally taken on as MacArthur's personal assistant. He was to remain in that role for the next six years, first in Washington until 1935, and then in Manila when MacArthur was made military adviser to the newly established Philippine Commonwealth and commissioned to prepare the Philippine Army for the country's eventual independence from the United States.

Eisenhower's experiences in Manila were frustrating. MacArthur, whom he had at first admired, was proving to be a fraud. He claimed to be successfully constructing and training a professional Philippine army on the cheap, one that would be able to defend the country from external aggressors after it was independent. Eisenhower knew that nothing of the sort was taking place and that insufficient resources were being expended on the job to get it done properly. But he was under strict orders from his chief not to file disheartening reports on "minimum of performance from a maximum of promise," or to make waves any other way.

By 1939, Fox Connor's prediction of another great conflagration had come true. Already having seized Austria and Czechoslovakia, Hitler sent his armies into Poland. Britain and France thereupon declared war on Germany. It was clear to many, including Eisenhower, that the United States would soon be drawn into the conflict and that the U.S. Army was nowhere near ready for it.

Under MacArthur, as under Pershing and in the various other staff jobs he had previously held, Lieutenant Colonel Eisenhower, as he now was, had continually longed to be involved in real soldiering. Now the opportunity appeared to have arisen. He asked MacArthur for release from his assignment in the Philippines so that he could return to the United States to take a field assignment. The general attempted to dissuade him, and the Philippine president, Manuel Quezon y Molina also asked him to stay on, telling him to name his own price on a new contract. But Eisenhower did not want to risk missing out on truly active duty.

At first it seemed that the danger of that happening still existed. He was named training officer for the 15th Infantry Regiment, based at Fort Lewis in Washington state. He threw himself with determination and vigor into the job of training troops for the combat to which he was convinced they would soon be exposed. The men were driven hard. Training was tough and discipline was stringently enforced. War clouds were gathering over the United States. Germany invaded Denmark and Norway, and then Belgium, Holland, and France. The British Expeditionary Force sent across the English Channel to bolster the French was driven by Hitler's armies into the sea at Dunkirk, and Britain itself was threatened with invasion. It was clear that the United States might soon to find that its own comparatively feeble armed forces were the first line of defense against an aggressive, resourceful, and victorious adversary ruled by a ruthless megalomaniac in Berlin.

The army was hastily gearing for war. Existing units were being expanded and a multitude of new ones was being created. As the need for additional officers of all ranks developed, promotions were finally coming through. Officers were being shifted around, sometimes remaining only briefly in new jobs before being assigned to others. In November 1940, Eisenhower was named Executive Officer of the 15th Regiment. The following June he was back at Fort Sam Houston in San Antonio as Third Army Chief of Staff.

Among other things, he was required to prepare the Third Army for maneuvers scheduled to start within two months. It was to invade Louisiana, which was to be defended by the Second Army. This was the most serious test Eisenhower had yet faced. He had no direct experience of large-scale war games. But he successfully met the challenge, coping calmly but expeditiously with the problems involved. At the same time, he made a point of not concealing or making excuses for the training and equipment deficiencies he observed among his troops. Despite those drawbacks, the Third Army executed a surprise mass-flanking movement and overwhelmed the mock defenders in Louisiana. It was a notable achievement for Eisenhower and was recognized as such at the War Department in Washington.

War news from Europe was now receiving wide press coverage across the United States. Newsmen had been assigned to cover the Louisiana maneuvers to report on how U.S. forces would be capable of performing in combat. Eisenhower impressed them with his plain talking, infectious smile, and success in the field. They wrote flatteringly about him in their newspapers, though not always spelling his name right.

On December 12, 1941, five days after the Japanese had bombed Pearl Harbor and the day after Nazi Germany and Fascist Italy had declared war on the United States, General George C. Marshall, the U.S. Army Chief of Staff, had Eisenhower summoned to Washington. The call came from Colonel Walter Bedell Smith, the General Staff secretary, who telephoned to tell him, "The Chief says for you to . . . get up here right away." Orders would follow. No explanation was offered, but it was obvious that the man from Abilene was about to climb a big step up the army's ladder.

CHAPTER 4
Sandhurst to Dunkirk

Unlike Eisenhower, who had contemplated other possibilities when he graduated from West Point, Second Lieutenant Bernard Montgomery, fresh out of Sandhurst Royal Military College, could imagine only a military career. The British Army offered greater opportunities than did its American equivalent to an ambitious young man. Rivalries among the European powers were considered to require the maintenance of permanently combat-ready armed forces. In addition, the far-flung British Empire had to be patrolled and policed. There would still not have been room for impecunious farmboys in the country's intensely class-conscious officer corps, but the offspring of a bishop had sufficient status to be eligible for a place in its ranks.

However, Montgomery was the proverbial square peg in a round hole. Most officers had substantial private incomes to supplement their meager pay. Montgomery had none and received no further allowance from his family once he was commissioned. It didn't matter as much as it would have for a different sort of young man. Montgomery had no interest in the social obligations, the gambling and boozing, that were a

customary part of an officer's life in peacetime. He was in the
army because he was interested in war as a profession. He
regularly irritated or bored his fellow officers by talking shop
in the officers' mess, a practice still frowned upon in the British
Army. He in turn had low regard for many of the men with
whom he served. To him, "A great number of these officers—
and the older officers at the top—were useless, quite useless."

When Montgomery left Sandhurst in 1908, his first posting
had been to a battalion of the Royal Warwickshire Regiment.
Almost immediately, the battalion was, as he had hoped, dispatched to British-ruled India, to Peshawar, on the Northwest
Frontier. Aside from dealing with occasional unrest among the
local population, there was little real soldiering to be done
there. Life for an officer on the Northwest Frontier could be
profoundly tedious, especially for someone who, like Montgomery, had no fondness for alcoholic beverages or the usual
officers'-mess fun and games. But it wasn't tedious for him. He
was incapable of engaging in anything with less than zeal and
determination to have things done in ways he considered
proper.

He spent far more time than was usual for a British officer
with the platoon of Indian soldiers under his command. He
quickly mastered their Hindustani language enough to be
able to issue commands they would immediately understand
and respond to. He drilled them rigorously, but they came to
esteem the officer who treated them as professional soldiers,
"as good material as anyone could want," rather than as just
another assortment of wogs, the way most other officers appeared to do.

Many of the officers frowned upon the unconventional behavior and persistent fractiousness of this undersized subaltern.
But some admired or at least were impressed by his enthusiasms and dedication. That he excelled at sports, notably cricket
and field hockey, in a place where sports were a prime distraction, enhanced the image of eagerness he projected. In sports
as in everything else, he was determined to come out on top.

Though he was not an accomplished horseman and not sol-
vent enough to afford a decent mount, the first point-to-point

race he entered not long after his arrival in Peshawar was a triumph for him. He fell off at the start, a humiliation that would have driven most other men out of the race and possibly into hiding. But Montgomery hastily remounted and drove the swaybacked creature he had acquired so hard that it carried him first over the finish line, whereupon he tumbled from the saddle again. It was hardly the most graceful of performances, but his spunk drew cheers from the onlookers. It is myth that Britons believe that how you play the game is more important than winning.

After two years on the Northwest Frontier, Montgomery, now a first lieutenant, was transferred southward with his battalion to the steamy environs of Bombay. There he was soon again demonstrating a readiness to act far more zealously than others in pursuit of his objectives. When the regimental quartermaster went home to Britain on extended leave, Montgomery applied to take on the man's job although, by prevailing standards, he was too junior and too young for it. He might have done his image serious damage by being more pushy than was deemed proper for a young officer. But his reputation for hard work already having been established, he received the appointment and brought to it the drive that was ingrained in his character.

Though some officers were content to have this energetic workhorse relieve them of tedious chores, others considered Montgomery boorishly over-assertive and thought he was conducting himself not quite the way a British officer should. But criticism didn't bother Montgomery or influence how he went about things. If some locally based British military and civilian mandarins looked askance and muttered disapprovingly when he chugged his way through the crowded streets of Bombay on the secondhand motorcycle he had acquired, he considered it (if their disapprobation registered on him at all) their problem, not his. He found concern for what he considered useless proprieties absurd, as was demonstrated in an incident involving the crew of the German battleship *Gneisenau* which visited Bombay during his service there.

As was often done in such circumstances, the British challenged the visitors to a friendly soccer game. The British Army team was highly skilled and Montgomery, who was officer in charge of sports, was advised by his commander to field only his second-string squad against the German sailors who, spending most of their time at sea, were unlikely to be very good at the game. To take advantage of the Germans' inferior skill on the soccer field would be embarrassing to both British and German officers and to other dignitaries who would be watching the match. But Montgomery chose to ignore the advice and fielded his best players. In a game where final scores rarely rise above single digits, the result was a 40–0 victory for the British. Asked to explain his perverse behavior, Montgomery explained, "I was not taking any risks with Germans." It was an attitude for which he would be reproached for other reasons during the Second World War when he was fighting them.

Montgomery's four years in India were greatly instructive. In the rarefied air of the Raj, he mastered the patterns and routines of active army service. But not until his battalion was rotated back to England in 1912, shortly before the eruption of World War I, did Montgomery, by then twenty-five years old, begin to go about grasping the finer points of the martial profession he had chosen.

Captain B. P. Lefroy, an officer who had been seconded to the British Army's Staff College for two years, returned to the Royal Warwickshire Regiment at that time. He and Montgomery had long talks "about the Army and what was wrong with it, and especially how one could get to real grips with the military art." They discussed strategic and tactical concepts, past battles, and future military prospects. For the first time, Montgomery's smoldering energy, assertiveness, and blossoming ambition were given a rational underpinning and direction. He concluded that something was fundamentally out of kilter in the British Army and decided that he would try to do what he could to put it right.

On June 28, 1914, when the fatal bullet fired at Austrian Archduke Ferdinand in Sarajevo proved to be the opening shot of the First World War, Montgomery's battalion was based at Shorncliffe in Kent. Within weeks it was shipped to France and was quickly thrown into combat against German troops. Montgomery was appalled that the battle was being fought by the British without prior reconnaissance, plan of attack, or covering fire. Dealing with the enemy that way made no sense.

The British Expeditionary Force was outnumbered by the German forces it faced. Its experience during the following months was largely of retreat and desperate, ultimately successful efforts to stabilize a defensive line. But the conflict amounted to slaughter on both sides. Men were cut down in horrific numbers contending for a few yards of barren ground between muddy trenches. The "ghosts of the Somme," as one English general later called them, would haunt British perceptions for a long time afterward and would strongly influence Montgomery's thinking when he became a senior commander in France in World War II.

He himself emerged a decorated hero from his early participation in battle. Armed only with his officer's sword during an attack, he spotted an enemy soldier aiming his rifle at him. Montgomery dropped the sword, leaped at the German, and kicked "as hard as I could in the lower part of the stomach." But he was soon one of the casualties of the Battle of the Somme. While bracing his troops for an attack, he was shot by a German sniper, the bullet lodging in his lung. A soldier who rushed to help him was shot also and fell dead on top of him. The soldier's body shielded him from several other enemy bullets, but one did hit him in the knee. He lay there slowly dying, unattended for three hours until nightfall, when troops could venture out and carry him back to have his wounds treated. By then he was considered so close to death that a grave was dug for him outside the makeshift casualty station to which he had been taken. However, the medics managed to save his life and he was sent back to England to recover—and learn that he had been promoted to the rank of captain and awarded the Distinguished Service Order for conspicuous gallantry.

It is tempting to suggest that this personal brush with death had a pronounced influence on Montgomery's personality and way of thinking. He was of course physically affected. The wounded lung would always trouble him. Yet he seemed to

have grown harder. There was an added sharpness to his attitude, voice, and gaze. His character appeared to have taken on
a severe, no-nonsense edge.

But he had long been developing along those lines. As a boy,
a youth, and a young man, Montgomery had rarely doubted
that he was right about the things that mattered to him. Now,
instead of mellowing under the impact of his near-death experience, he grew even more certain of himself, even more intoler-
ant of ideas and judgments he did not share. At twenty-eight,
Captain Montgomery was older than his age.

By 1916, Montgomery, his wounds healed, was back in
France, promoted to major with a temporary rank of lieutenant
colonel, serving as a senior brigade staff officer. This was a
different kind of soldiering from what he had experienced before. This was plotting and planning and passing word along
to others remote from him to act upon. There was now little
opportunity for him to satisfy his undiminished craving for
direct leadership. But he was able to fill an important gap in his
military training and understanding. Like everything connected
with war, it was all absorbed greedily by him, analyzed, and
judged.

It struck him as idiotic that so much staff planning was left
to chance. He was dismayed by procedures that denied rear
headquarters word of what was transpiring at the battlefront
quickly enough for effective use to be made of such intelligence.
He knew something was distinctly unsound with an army in
which the men doing the fighting never saw or directly heard
from their senior commanders. He was left with the impression
that, according to prevailing rear-area doctrine, the troops existed for the benefit of the higher staff when it should have
been the other way around.

He found it intolerable that senior officers had no idea of the
conditions under which their troops lived, fought, and died.
He was sharply critical of tactics responsible for the horrendous
level of casualties and contemptuous of officers who could have
done something about it. But he was neither a pacifist nor
greatly sensitive to human agony. Unlike many British officers,

his experiences in France did not make him recoil in horror
from the thought of war. Combat was his element. His objections were directed instead at how battlefield objectives could
be more efficiently achieved.

To his superiors, Montgomery's intelligence, efficiency, and
resourcefulness compensated for his increasing abrasiveness.
He was put in ever more responsible positions. When the war
ended, Montgomery, though only thirty-one years old, was
chief of staff to the 47th (London) Division. The next step in his
career should have been attendance at the army's Staff College,
through which young officers destined for high command were
expected to pass. He found, however, that he was not among
those selected for a place there.

Though disappointed, he did not react as officers so spurned
normally did. He refused to accept his rejection as the workings
of fate. He presumed to take the matter up with General Sir
William Robertson, commander-in-chief of the British Army of
Occupation in Germany, with which Montgomery was then
serving. The general, with whom Montgomery also took the
opportunity to discuss some of the opinions he had formed
during the war, was one of the few officers in the British Army
ever to have advanced through the ranks to so senior a position
exclusively on the basis of merit and without the benefit of high
social standing or wealth. Robertson was impressed with the
plucky young officer, and Montgomery's name was soon added
to the list that had already been issued of students accepted for
the next Staff College intake.

Montgomery's gratitude for such a dispensation did not curb
his assertiveness. Having seen the face of war, he scorned the
"nonsense" that, he maintained, made up the curriculum at
the college. He aroused much displeasure with his criticism
of much of what was being taught. He was not alone in his
judgments. Other students at the Staff College, like Montgomery veterans of the recent First World War slaughter, also were
dismayed that many of their instructors had not absorbed the
lessons that had been painfully taught on the battlefields of
France and Belgium. But none of the others was as openly

critical and relentlessly argumentative. He was thought of as "a bit of a bolshevik," not so much an ideologue as a nuisance and a troublemaker.

He did not do badly in his studies, and upon his graduation from Staff College in 1920 he was posted to the 17th Infantry Brigade, garrisoned in Cork, Ireland, as brigade major. Ireland was then still part of the United Kingdom, but would not be much longer if the Irish Republican Army had its way. Though the Easter uprising of the Irish in 1916 had been crushed, the revolutionaries had been led to believe their country would be awarded Home Rule by the British government as soon as the details could be worked out. But as the years passed with Home Rule still being debated in Parliament, frustration produced an explosion of IRA violence. Bombs were exploded, people were shot, policemen were kidnapped, property was destroyed, and large parts of Ireland were racked by mayhem and insecurity.

Though urban terrorism was not nearly as common then as it was later to become, it was anathema to any military officer assigned to deal with it. It meant coping with an enemy who did not stand up and fight, wore no uniform, might appear anywhere at any time and blend back into the surrounding environment just as quickly, and did not confine his attacks to military targets. Montgomery had to put aside his ideas about how battles should be fought. He turned his attention to a different dimension of combat, involving roadblocks against civilians, house-to-house searches, and swoops in the night on suspected IRA arms and explosives caches. He found such a war "thoroughly bad for officers and men." It was "degrading for us soldiers." He was relieved when Eire received its independence in 1922, the uprising came to an end (to be followed by the Irish Civil War), and his tour of duty in Ireland was completed.

During the next four years, Montgomery had various staff postings in England, with the 3rd Division in Plymouth, the 49th Division in Yorkshire, and then back to the Royal Warwicks. As in the United States, these were not the best of times for professional soldiers. After the slaughter of the previous war, their role aroused much general cynicism. Pacifism was popular. A Peace Pledge Union drew the support of countless Britons. Military budgets were cut. Units were retrenched. Many officers found themselves facing the unfamiliar, harsh realities of civilian life. For those remaining in uniform and not posted to restive imperial outposts around the world, army life could seem to be no more than time-serving. There was nothing but drilling and parading and the persistent worry about being next for the chop, with no guarantee of an adequate pension.

Constitutionally incapable of stumbling into that sort of demoralizing rut, the hyperactive Montgomery personally took to organizing and holding classes in tactics for junior officers. Though officers often informally established teacher-student relationships with subordinate officers, as was the case between Fox Connor and Eisenhower, doing such a thing in such a methodical way was unprecedented in the British Army. Montgomery, who didn't drink, wasn't married, and did not much socialize with officers who were his equal in rank, was already considered odd. Summoning junior officers to his lectures was deemed another of his eccentricities.

But those attending them were exhilarated by his zeal and by what he taught them. General Sir Frederick Morgan, who was exposed to Montgomery's special instructions when he was a young officer and who would later encounter him under different circumstances, recalled that he and others privileged to receive such attention were held "entranced. . . . Every minute of it was of the utmost value as we were instructed in every conceivable aspect of the whole art of war. It was inspiring beyond words to meet this single-minded zealot."

Like radical military thinkers in other countries, Montgomery was trying to get his country's army to break free of the dead hand of outdated battlefield tactics. During World War I set-piece battles were all of a kind. Heavy artillery barrages would be followed by frontal-assault surges of great numbers of men to seize defended, usually entrenched fixed positions. If an assault was repelled it would be repeated until it was successful or the level of casualties ruled out further attack.

Montgomery dismissed such tactics as senseless. The object of engaging in a battle was to win it. But so little attention was being paid to the importance of intelligence-gathering that, in combat, there was no way knowing if a frontal assault had any chance of success. It was blind guesswork and might again be grotesquely, needlessly, uselessly costly in lives.

In his lectures, Montgomery stressed that it was more important to outwit an enemy than to try to overwhelm him. The battle had to be exhaustively prepared. The battlefield had to be carefully reconnoitered and intelligence data had to be collated and meticulously examined before combat was joined. Weak points in the enemy's positions had to be pinpointed. Feints and other forms of deception had to be utilized to the maximum advantage. The troops had to be well trained, well equipped, highly motivated, and aware of what they were doing. Their strength had to be superior to that of the enemy, if not all along the line, then at the point where one intended to strike the decisive blow. The risk element had to be eliminated. Those were the doctrines Montgomery took with him when, in 1926, he was honored with a posting as instructor at the Staff College from which he had graduated six years earlier.

There had until then been no place for a wife or for intimate contact of any kind with a woman in Montgomery's scheme of things. It may have been a consequence of his difficult relationship with his mother or because of his dedicated commitment to army life and the science of warfare. He had lectured younger officers about the dangers of marriage. He told them, "You cannot marry and be an efficient officer. If you marry you must realize you will have to give up to your wife much of the time which you would otherwise need for the study of your profession." Whatever was responsible for his having developed such an attitude, not until he was thirty-seven years old did he show any interest in marriageable females, and probably then because he thought having a wife would improve his chances of career advancement.

There is nothing to indicate that he had ever regretted being deprived of the comforts of marriage. There were no known earlier romances. He had never loved and lost. Even as a young man, he had shown no signs of having a sexual appetite. But he now went about seeking a woman to marry. He did so as if going into battle, not easy for someone his age with no previous experience in that sort of campaign. He reconnoitered the terrain, first on vacation in the south of France, where he permitted himself to grow infatuated with a pretty seventeen-year-old English girl. It was a brief and strange courtship. On long walks along a beach, on which the girl's mother pressed her to accept his invitations to join him, he explained to her how he would command troops in battle, drawing diagrams in the sand with his walking stick to show how he would deploy men and tanks.

It was hardly the thing to sweep a young girl who was far more interested in popular music and dancing off her feet. She was bewildered and embarrassed by his attentions, and found his blunt declaration that he intended to marry her grotesque. When he realized that he was being rejected by her, he showed no signs of despair and immediately put the girl out of his thoughts. That battle had been lost, but the war was still to be won. He still intended to find a wife. The following year, on a skiing holiday in Switzerland, he met the forty-year-old widow of an officer who had been killed in the First World War and decided that she would make a suitable bride.

That he and Betty Carver found friendship together, not to mention love, is remarkable. Deprived by war of her husband and the father of her two children, she had developed pacifist leanings. She was gregarious and easygoing, and she numbered artists and writers, the kind of people Montgomery tended to shun, among her closest friends. She herself was an amateur painter and sculptor.

Over a period of more than a year, Montgomery wooed and won her. He was assisted in this pursuit by her two sons, who took quickly to this officer who had a car and who was fit enough and not too proud to engage in energetic games and activities with them. Recalling his admonition that "You cannot be a good soldier and a good husband," some officers jokingly sent Montgomery a telegram asking, "Which is it to be, the soldier or the husband?" He did not reply. He and Betty were married in London in July 1927.

The effect she had on this self-obsessed loner bewildered

those who knew him. The only wife imaginable for him should have been a shrinking figure who knew her place and served only the purpose of providing him with the comforts of home without making intolerable demands on his time or creating inexcusable distractions, thus permitting him to concentrate as before on the science of war. Instead, Betty Montgomery remained a lively, sociable woman, still interested in things that held no attraction for him, including art, music, and literature.

He often bullied her; that was his way. He was a difficult man. Montgomery's longtime acquaintance, the military historian and strategist Basil Liddell Hart, told him he bullied Betty "unmercifully, as you bullied everyone else!" But others who knew them said that he generally treated Betty with respect, care, and consideration. He not only tolerated her friends—he had virtually none of his own—but even sometimes enjoyed their company, provided they did not speak of military matters about which he was convinced they could not possibly know anything or have opinions of any value.

A year after their marriage, their son David was born. With his characteristic obsession for details, Montgomery had already taken charge of overall management of the household. He now also took upon himself the task of organizing care for the boy. That took more time and effort than he liked and led him to decide he didn't want another child because it required "too much staff work."

Marriage added a new dimension to his life without eliminating the previously existing ones. At work he was still abrasively outspoken and egocentric. He did not waver in his insistence that he was right about everything related to the military and that anyone who held ideas about it that differed from his own was useless. Though he continued to offend superiors, his skills, dedication, and enthusiasms could not be overlooked. In 1930, promoted to the rank of lieutenant colonel and put in command of a battalion of the Warwicks, he was shipped off to Palestine, which had been mandated to the British after the collapse of the Turkish Empire in 1918, and then to Alexandria.

Whether attempting to establish order between the feuding Jews and Arabs in Palestine, whose conflict had not yet assumed the proportions it later would, or trying to keep his men fully occupied in Egypt, where there was nothing to do, Montgomery was always a concern to his chiefs at British Army Middle East headquarters in Cairo. His way of doing things did not always coincide with those of his predecessors or his superiors. His problem—or rather the army's—was that regardless of existing procedures, he was determined to use his own judgment, even when it meant the employment of unconventional practices and procedures.

In Egypt he refused to be awed by the effect on the troops of having to serve in a peaceful, exotic location where non-military distractions were ever-present. Alexandria had traditionally been considered easy duty, as much a holiday as a posting. But Montgomery would not tolerate such an attitude among the men serving under him. Remote from home and far enough from Cairo not to be under close observation by his superiors, he had never before had such an opportunity to mold a battalion of troops in accordance with his own ideas.

He immediately set about deemphasizing the army's traditional spit-and-polish drilling. He was not concerned with how trimly the troops turned out. Instead he stressed their physical fitness and tactical preparedness. Night training out in the desert was high on his agenda. His officers and other ranks had other agendas. They had expected easy duty in Egypt and did not take well to his demands. There was much grumbling. Excelling in maneuvers provided a measure of satisfaction, but not enough to compensate for the tough regimen Montgomery imposed or for his unprecedented intrusion into the private lives of his men.

He issued new rules governing the permitted conduct of junior officers when off duty. He maintained that in a place like Alexandria, whose brothels and bars offered pernicious temptations, strict maintenance of personal-hygiene standards were necessary to make certain the men were fit for soldiering. He also decreed that summary punishment should be inflicted for comparatively minor trespasses. That he personally concerned himself with even trivial misdemeanors was considered absurd and provoked a chorus of protest. He ignored it.

His career might have seized up right there. His behavior seemed perverse. He was a nuisance of a newcomer, making waves where none had existed before. It appeared to serve no greatly useful purpose. Senior officers scurried over from headquarters in Cairo or from regimental headquarters in Ismailia from time to time to prevent rows that he had provoked from getting out of hand. However, no one could deny that the troops under Montgomery's command were being superbly trained. They did not cut much of a figure on parade, and that irked some officers and not a few sergeants who specialized in drilling soldiers for parade ground razzmatazz. But on maneuver, when it came to escaping the tedium of Montgomery-ruled garrison life and showing what sort of soldiers they would be in combat, they shone.

As a consequence, Montgomery shone too, regardless of the complaints about his overbearing, autocratic behavior. In time, his troops came to admire and even like him because unlike most other officers they had ever known he displayed no snobbish aloofness and was often present among them, clearly explaining his objectives in down-to-earth language and assuring them that if they ever were required to go into battle, what he was making them do would save their lives.

When he was posted away from Egypt in 1934, four years after his arrival in the Middle East, the assessment of him submitted by his commanding officer was that he was, "Definitely above the average of his rank and should attain high rank in the Army. He can only fail to do so if a certain high-handedness, which occasionally overtakes him, becomes too pronounced. . . . He has fertile and original thoughts which he expresses in the most inimitable way. He is really popular with his men whom he regards and treats as if they were his children."

His next posting was back in India. When he went there with his battalion, Montgomery acted with uncharacteristic reasonableness; he accepted that there was a difficulty he could not overcome. The Indian Army High Command was unshakably dedicated to the spit-and-polish and parade-ground smartness of troops that Montgomery scorned as demoralizing and worthless. Recognizing that he was still too junior in rank to win this battle, he applied for the two months' leave that was due him and went sightseeing with Betty in Japan, Hong Kong, and other points east.

His unusual act of prudence was rewarded. Instead of getting into trouble with his superiors over procedures and practices, he was promoted to full colonel upon his return to duty and appointed senior instructor at the Military Staff College at Quetta, in what is now Pakistan. For three years a succession of student officers were exposed to his ideas on how soldiers should be trained, how battles should be fought, and what previous procedures were to be shunned, no matter what other training officers might say, if disaster was to be avoided.

He drilled into his students the importance of reducing battle-field problems to the absolute essentials of outmatching and outwitting the enemy so as not to be distracted by peripheral matters. He stressed the significance of commanders insisting on reliable subordinates to whom they could confidently dele-gate sorting out details so that they themselves could concen-trate on the core aspects of the problems they faced. He emphasized the importance of morale; the troops, he said, had to know what they were doing and believe they were being led to the successful attainment of their objectives. He laid down the rules he himself was to follow when his moment of fame arrived.

The Japanese, having occupied Manchuria, were about to go on the march in China, and war was nearing again in Europe. But as far as Montgomery was concerned, much was right with the world. He was able to expand upon and develop his theol-ogy of combat, and it was being understood and appreciated. The young officers who were his students were fascinated, enthusiastic, and reverential.

Montgomery was now heading for the upper echelons of army command. In 1937, promoted to brigadier, he was posted back to England to take command of the Ninth Infantry Brigade at Portsmouth—and to be confronted with the greatest personal tragedy in his life.

On holiday on the beach at Burnham-on-Sea, his wife Betty was bitten on the leg by an insect. The wound became infected and the infection spread with astonishing rapidity. She was hospitalized, and Montgomery, who was supervising maneuvers on Salisbury Plain at the time, rushed to her side. The doctors said it was essential to amputate her leg to save her life. Montgomery gave his permission and set about planning the organization of her future needs—a special wheelchair, special furniture, possibly an artificial limb, servants. But the infection continued to spread. The doctors had no idea how to deal with what was happening. They were still pondering Betty's problem when she died of septicemia.

She and Montgomery had been married ten years. Her death was an emotional disaster to him. Whatever cold calculations might have led him to seek out and marry her, he had come to love her deeply and now she had been taken away. Never before—not even when he had tangled with his mother as a child—had he been so defeated. This was a judgment he could not contest, a force he could not challenge, an argument he could not win. There were no tears and few other outward signs of bereavement. Those around him, respecting the privacy of his grief, were reluctant to so much as offer condolences. No one but Betty had ever been able to penetrate his emotional defenses.

Not long before they had bought a large house in Portsmouth. There he stayed alone. His son, David, was at boarding school. To spare him the painful experience, his father had not permitted him to see Betty while she was dying or to attend his mother's funeral. The boy was subsequently farmed out to various friends and acquaintances. Montgomery had little to do with his upbringing anymore, except to pay for it. Much later, Montgomery said, "My married life was absolute bliss. The death of my wife was a shattering blow from which I recovered with great difficulty, and very slowly."

Taking little time off, he was soon back at his job. In maneuvers soon afterward, the troops under his command again outshone all others. But the loss of his wife had an important bearing on his character. She had provided something of a balance for his otherwise lopsided, narrow character. That balance was now lost. Much of the softness that married life had induced was gone. He again donned the loner's shroud that Betty had been helping him to shed. He reverted to being a driven character, obsessed with the science of combat.

Now that Montgomery was rising high in the ranks and was based at home, his conspicuously unconventional behavior was much talked about among his fellow officers. Brian Horrocks, who would later serve under him as a corps commander in North Africa and Europe, said, "He was probably the most discussed general in the British Army before the war, and—except with those who had served under him—not a popular figure. Regular armies in all countries tend to produce a standard type of officer, but Monty . . . didn't fit into the British pattern. His methods of training and command were unorthodox, always a deadly crime in military circles."

Lord Carver, who served under him during the war, said, "His vigorous and uncompromising methods of command, injecting a rigorous degree of realism into training, had made him enemies." This did not distress Montgomery. He observed that Napoleon was never liked by any officer in his army higher than the rank of captain.

In 1938, the year after his wife died, he was promoted to major general and put in command of the 8th Division, one of two sent to Palestine to do something about the Arab-Jewish riots that were erupting in the Holy Land with increasing frequency, and to deal as well with acts of sabotage committed by both sides. It was a delicate assignment, but for Montgomery delicacy was not the concern of soldiers, but of the politicians who were responsible for having permitted such a state of affairs to develop. He did not take sides in the Arab-Jewish conflict. His job was to stop the killing and prevent destruction. He instructed his troops to do that as quickly and efficiently as possible, regardless of who might initially have been at fault and regardless of what the politicians thought of how he went about his assignment.

Events of greater importance for Britain, indeed crucial to the country's survival, were happening elsewhere at the time. The fearful shadow of an aggressive, powerful Nazi Germany had risen over Europe. Prime Minister Neville Chamberlain had tried to neutralize the Nazi threat through negotiations with Hitler. But few responsible people believed his claim to have achieved peace with honor by appeasing the German dictator. An officer with Montgomery's credentials and skills was needed at home to help prepare the British Army for war. He was ordered to return to England in August 1939 to assume command of the 3rd Division, then part of Britain's Southern Command.

Shortly before his departure from Palestine to take on his new job, he fell seriously ill. The doctors were not certain, but thought he might have been stricken with diphtheria. He was sent for treatment to a military hospital near Haifa, where his condition continued to deteriorate, though he was still strong enough to insist on being shipped home. When he left Haifa by ship, he was so ill that it was believed he would not survive the journey. But he staged a remarkable recovery during the homeward cruise. By the time the ship reached the London port of Tilbury, he had almost completely recovered.

Because of his illness, other plans had been made by the War Office for the 3rd Division. Its commander, whom Montgomery had been scheduled to replace, was to stay on. Montgomery was ordered to join the pool of spare generals until another post could be found for him. That was asking too much of him. He was emotionally incapable of standing by, twiddling his thumbs. He badgered the War Office for an immediate posting, and the position he wanted was the promised command of the 3rd Division. The War Office finally succumbed to his nagging and he was given the job.

It was now October 1939. Germany had invaded Poland the month before. In response, Britain and France, honoring treaty obligations, had declared war on Germany. Europe was plunging into a replay of the Great War of a generation earlier, on a much expanded scale.

British politicians and generals sought to calm public concern by declaring that the British Army was as well-equipped and as combat-ready as any in the world. Montgomery knew it was not true and that to suggest such humbug was dangerous.

[T]he British Army [he later wrote] was totally unfit to fight a first class war on the continent of Europe. . . . In the years preceding the outbreak of war no large-scale exercises with troops had been held in England for some time. Indeed the Regular Army was unfit to take part in a realistic exercise. The Field Army had an inadequate signals system, no administrative backing, and no organisation for high command. . . . The transport was inadequate and was completed on mobilisation by vehicles requisitioned from civilian firms.

To deal with the enemy's tanks, Montgomery's 3rd Division, sent across the English Channel to take up defensive positions in France soon after he took command, was equipped only with two-pounder guns. When battle was joined, their shells could do no more than bounce off the armored skins of the German panzers.

Montgomery did not permit his determination to meet the challenge his country and his troops faced to be undermined by such a state of affairs. The nine-month-long Phoney War on the French-German border that followed the formal declaration of hostilities presented an excellent setting for him to bring his troops to the level of preparedness he knew was necessary if they were to have any chance of proving effective. The threat was real. The men were in the field. They faced an enemy who might attack at any moment. It was combat without the shooting.

Nine divisions of the British Expeditionary Force were deployed in northeastern France under Lord Gort, a general whom Montgomery thought worthy at best to command a regiment. Allied strategy was simple. Along the French-German border, the Maginot Line, a formidable fortified barrier built by France in the 1930s, would be manned and backed up by strong elements of the French Army. Two French armies would defend the area north of the Maginot Line facing the Ardennes Forest, which was considered impenetrable for a mechanized army attempting to advance at speed. Thus blocked, the Germans, when they finally launched their attack westward, were expected to lunge through neutral Belgium to outflank the Allied defenders in France. When that happened, the French First Army and the nine British divisions would rapidly pivot from their positions in northeastern France into Belgium, where they would stem and repel the German offensive.

Through the autumn, winter, and spring of 1939–1940, Montgomery prepared his troops for the role they would pay. He placed special emphasis on night exercises so that if called upon to deploy in darkness they would be ready by early light to meet any attack. He went among the men personally to speak with them, tell them what they would have to do when the moment came, show them they were part of a closely knit team, and display his confidence in their ability to deal with whatever situation might arise. Boredom was rife along the Allied line during the Phoney War, but morale remained high in the British 3rd Division.

As before, Montgomery scorned spit-and-polish, make-believe soldiering. The job of his troops was to fight when called upon to do so, not to parade. He was sufficiently confident in the headquarters staff he had chosen, and the clear instructions he gave its members, to continue going to bed at 9:30 each night. He was to be disturbed before his regular early morning wake-up time only if there was a crisis, a practice he maintained right through the war. Even at the worst of times, when panic or despair might have been understandable, an ordered calm prevailed at his headquarters.

Nevertheless, Montgomery almost found himself shunted off the road to glory even before the shooting began. When he discovered that some of his men had contracted venereal disease in France soon after arriving there, he issued a typically straightforward directive to deal with the problem. Instead of forbidding his men to consort with the prostitutes who flocked to the garrison area and making it a court-martial offense, which he knew would have undermined their morale and probably wouldn't have worked anyway, he ordered that arrangements be made for them to be able to purchase contraceptives and that facilities for early treatment of venereal disease be established in each company area.

Army chaplains and other guardians of the morals of the troops were outraged. They complained that rather than discouraging the troops from indulging wickedly in wanton sex, Montgomery was promoting lascivious behavior among them. So strong was the outcry that the matter was brought to the attention of Lord Gort, who, having little to do while waiting for the Germans to launch their offensive, considered the matter serious enough for action to be taken that might have nipped Montgomery's career in the bud.

The matter was put to General Alan Brooke, II Corps commander and Montgomery's immediate superior. Brooke, who had been a fellow instructor with Montgomery at the Staff College, thought highly of him and yet realized that he might be obliged to "withdraw Monty from his division and to send him home" because of the fuss. He considered him too good a commander to lose at that perilous moment. Instead of sending him home he reprimanded him, warning him that his position could not withstand "any further errors of this kind." Montgomery accepted Brooke's chastisement without making excuses. He uncharacteristically admitted to him that "he was apt to do foolish things" and thanked him fulsomely for coming to his aid. He realized how close he had come to being denied what he wanted most—the opportunity to command troops in battle again. Though convinced he had been right, he was prepared to humble himself when personal disaster threatened.

The incident proved to be the beginning of the most important relationship in Montgomery's career. Brooke was soon to become Chief of the Imperial General Staff and was to remain in that position throughout the war. He was to become and remain Montgomery's patron, protector, and confessor. He was one of the very few top-echelon officers Montgomery unqualifiedly admired and the only one from whom he willingly accepted criticism. Indeed, he sometimes wrote fondly of having received a "wigging from Brookie."

I had several more occasions during the war [Brooke later wrote] when I had to guard him against his own foolishness. In doing so, I inevitably had to adopt a most unpleasant attitude towards him. He never resented such reproof and always received every admonishment in the spirit in which it was intended. I could not have an easier or more pleasant commander to handle.

As had been planned, when Hitler unleashed his armies on the western front before dawn on May 10, 1940, the British Expeditionary Force in France and the French First Army shifted into neutral Belgium to block the expected major German thrust there. The Belgians were still unsure what they should do about it. When a Belgian customs official on the French border demanded an official permit from his government before allowing units of the 3rd division to cross into his country, Montgomery responded by sending a heavy truck crashing through the barrier and advancing as instructed.

The pivot of the Allied armies into Belgium to meet the anticipated German assault was executed smoothly and with precision. But the Germans had expected it to be and had based their own strategy around it. Their tanks raced instead through the supposedly impenetrable Ardennes Forest and smashed through the weakest point of the French lines, at Sedan. The Luftwaffe rapidly seized mastery of the skies over the combat area and provided close cover for Hitler's advancing panzers. Allied antitank weapons had little effect and nothing the Allies could field could withstand the impact of the German 88mm cannon. German infantry followed quickly through the holes punched by the armor. Allied communications proved unreliable where they existed at all after the launching of the enemy blitzkrieg.

The situation for the Allied forces, which were under overall French direction, was soon critical. The Germans were racing virtually unchecked toward the English Channel to cut off and trap them. It soon became evident that even where Allied troops were not directly engaged by the enemy, retreat was the only option if they were to avoid total catastrophe.

But they could not move fast enough. With their tanks thundering through northern France, the Germans were revolutionizing warfare. No army had ever moved so quickly. Within ten days of having launched its offensive, the 2nd Panzer Division had reached the English Channel coast near Abbeville. If it swooped up along the Channel to meet the German forces heading for the coast through Belgium, the Allied forces would be trapped. With the war just beginning, Britain would have lost its expeditionary force, which contained almost all its combat-ready troops. The British would have had no army with which to defend themselves against a Nazi invasion.

That might have happened had it not been for one of the great mysteries of the war. For reasons never fully explained or understood and to the despair of his panzer generals, Hitler ordered his tanks to halt in their tracks for two days before permitting them to proceed to close the trap around the retreating Allied forces. Perhaps it was to permit his infantry to catch up, or perhaps so that his cherished Luftwaffe could force the Allied forces to surrender; perhaps it was because his attention was now fixed instead on capturing the glamorous, vulnerable prize of Paris that was soon to fall to him.

Whatever the reason, in those two days Lord Gort was able to establish an effective perimeter defense line around the Channel coast port of Dunkirk. Over in England, the realization of how desperate the situation had become spurred High Command into action. Plans were hastily drawn up for a rescue armada to evacuate from Dunkirk as much as possible of the British Expeditionary Force. It was gloomily believed that only a fraction of the quarter of a million men falling back on the escape perimeter could be saved before the Germans slammed the trap shut around them.

Montgomery had established a set pattern to his day and maintained it even during this critical period of the staged withdrawal to the coast. After assessing the prevailing situation each evening, he issued clear, concise instructions to his staff and let them get on with the job of implementing them. He spent most of each day with the troops, seeing that their needs and the needs of the operation were met. As the retreat turned into a scramble back for most of the expeditionary force, rations proved increasingly hard to come by. As was traditional with

armies, the British soldiers took to living off the land and off
the civilians through whose villages and towns they streamed.
But few troops found themselves as certain of hot meals as
Montgomery's. He had his Service Corps confiscate grazing
beef cattle and drive them along to provide necessary suste-
nance.

Montgomery appeared to be no more under pressure or anxious than he had been when on a peacetime training exercise.
He required that his staff also respond calmly to the crisis. At
one point, he defused a potential row with a Belgian general in
an area where Montgomery's troops were to establish a temporary defense line by flatteringly offering to come under the
general's command. He actually had no intention of obeying
any orders the general might issue and simply took command
himself when the situation there turned critical.

On May 27 it seemed that the day-old evacuation from Dunkirk would have to be hastily wound up, though comparatively
few of the retreating British troops had yet been carried back to
England from France. King Leopold of Belgium announced that
his battered and bloodied army, which was holding part of the
shrinking line near the coast, would surrender to the Germans,
opening a hole in the line through which the Germans might
rush to force the evacuation to come to an abrupt halt.

General Brooke, whose II Corps was deployed in the area,
had no reserves with which to prevent that from happening.
He turned to Montgomery to cope with the situation. The 3rd
Division commander was to disengage his troops—no easy
task under the circumstances—and shift them behind the line
overnight to close the gap being created by the Belgian surrender. It was a complicated maneuver, "a task," Brooke wrote,
"that might well have shaken the stoutest of hearts, but for
Monty it might just have been a glorious picnic."

By morning, his troops were in place, having closed the gap
before the Germans could rush through. A considerable
achievement, it testified to how well his men had been trained
to do exactly as instructed, by night as well as day, efficiently,
expeditiously, and successfully. "I thanked heaven," Brooke

wrote, "to have a commander of his calibre to undertake this hazardous march."

It drew little attention at the time. All eyes were on the port and beaches of Dunkirk, where the Royal Navy, strongly supported by the Royal Air Force, was in the process of saving the British Army from virtual obliteration. Despite intensive German air attacks and artillery bombardments, more and more troops were ferried back across the Channel to England from Dunkirk's harbor and nearby beaches.

As the end neared for the British at Dunkirk, Brooke, who had been ordered back to England, appointed Montgomery to succeed him as II Corps commander though he was the junior divisional commander in the corps. That afternoon, Lord Gort also made preparations to return to England as ordered. He was instructed by London to choose a successor to command what remained of the British Expeditionary Force in France. He chose I Corps commander General Michael Barker, whose troops were to be evacuated last.

When Montgomery heard of the appointment, he asked for a word in private with Gort to tell him he was making a mistake. He told him what was needed for the wind-up in France was a calm, confident, clear-headed man and that Barker could by no means fit that description. He urged Gort to name 1st Division commander General Harold Alexander instead. He said it might then be possible to get practically all the troops away in the time remaining before the Germans finally closed in. It was a presumptuous intervention. Officers were not expected to openly pass critical judgment on those who outranked them. But Gort, who would also soon be the butt of Montgomery's outspoken criticism, agreed that what he suggested made sense and acted accordingly, assigning Alexander to superintend the final evacuation at Dunkirk.

It was just about all over. Almost all of the British troops who had fallen back on the city and its adjoining beaches had been rescued, though thousands of French troops were still to be taken off. On the night of May 30, Montgomery pulled his II Corps from the perimeter line back to the beaches. With his aide-de-camp, who was wounded that night by artillery fire, Montgomery walked five miles along the sands, reaching Dunkirk harbor at dawn. There they boarded one of the Royal Navy destroyers that had been shuttling back and forth for more than a week while executing the most remarkable military rescue operation in history, and were also brought home.

Though the British Expeditionary Force in France had been saved from what had appeared to be certain disaster, Britain found itself in crisis. The astonishing success of the Dunkirk operation was received with enormous relief and treated as a triumph over the enemy. But there was no concealing the fact that the British Army had been outfought by the Germans. It had been driven out of Europe, and it seemed likely that the victorious Hitler would order his armies to follow up their triumph by invading England. Many believed they had a good chance of succeeding.

With the shooting war less than a month old, the British had already sustained some 70,000 casualties. Most of its Army's hardware had been left scattered across the countryside of northern France and Belgium or on the beaches of Dunkirk. Only 22 of 704 tanks sent to France had been brought back, and most of the heavy guns had been abandoned there. There were not even enough rifles to go around, and in some places only a single machine gun was available for each mile of coastline. Home Guard volunteers drilled with pikes and farm tools to deal with expected enemy parachutists. Churchill warned the British people that if they failed to meet the challenge they now faced, ". . . the whole world, including the United States . . . will sink into the abyss of a new Dark Age." The country stood alone against an aggressive, resourceful, powerful enemy twenty miles away across the English Channel. Its struggle was now for survival as an independent nation.

The day after he was brought back to England from Dunkirk, Montgomery insisted on a private interview with General Sir John Dill, then Chief of the Imperial General Staff who, considering the circumstances, was a very busy man. Never one to mince words, he told Dill that a number of British generals responsible for the defense of the country were "useless." He named some of the those whose abilities he scorned.

At the time, morale was an especially precious commodity in Britain and Dill reacted sharply to such potentially destructive backbiting. He issued a warning to senior officers about "rather loose criticism going on among commanders . . . regarding the manner in which their seniors, their equals and their juniors conducted the recent operations in France and Belgium. . . . Any failings of commanders or staff officers should be submitted confidentially through the proper channels but on no account must they be discussed unofficially." Nevertheless, Montgomery observed that "one by one the useless generals disappeared."

The War Office did not require Montgomery's goading to undertake a thorough reexamination of the situation. Its carefully plotted war plans had become irrelevant. The Germans had not been halted as intended and thrust back in Belgium, which instead, like the Netherlands, had been overrun. France also was being overrun, its army proving to be far less than the mighty instrument it had been ballyhooed as being. Preparations had to be made by the British command to fight a different kind of war against an adversary who was already well ahead on points.

Montgomery had reverted to the command of the 3rd Division. Quickly regrouped and refitted after its evacuation from Dunkirk, it was to return to France to try to bolster the disintegrating French resistance to the rampaging Germans. But the French capitulated before it could be dispatched. Plans were then considered for it to secure the Azores to help guard the North Atlantic sea routes, to seize the Cape Verde Islands to secure the South Atlantic sea routes, or to seize Cork and Queenstown in Ireland for use as bases for antisubmarine operations in the Atlantic. None of those operations were undertaken. With the British homeland facing invasion, such operations would have been reckless luxuries.

As the War Office came to grips with the transformed situation, Montgomery's division was deployed in southeast England. He thought little of the coastal defense plans he inherited there. He saw little sense in establishing fixed positions from which to repel invaders. If such positions were overrun, a major enemy breakthrough would be difficult to prevent and the enemy would be able to establish a firm presence on British soil.

Montgomery insisted instead on a fluid defense that would permit his troops to plunge in and exploit the lapses and weaknesses of the invaders as they tried to secure a beachhead. Instead of having his men dig in where he believed their presence would serve little purpose, he wanted to establish a thin defense screen along the coast while drawing the bulk of his forces back in a position to counterattack where the enemy proved vulnerable. The battlefield, he insisted, was too fluid an environment for the situation to be controlled in any other way.

Very likely he would have ignored War Office and corps instructions to the contrary or maneuvered around them if he had been able to. But he had not been supplied with sufficient transport to prepare for a fluid defense. Practically all of the British Army's trucks had been left in France and few others were yet available. Building tanks and aircraft had higher priority at the war-production factories.

But Montgomery knew where the transport he wanted could be obtained. When Churchill came down to inspect his troops, he went over the heads of his superiors and buttonholed the prime minister to tell him there were thousands of buses in England that could be put to effective war use. "[L]et them give me some," he said, "and release me from this static role so that I [can] practice a mobile counter-attack role." Churchill was impressed and gave instructions for the appropriate steps to be taken.

I was disturbed [Churchill told War Minister Anthony Eden] to find the 3rd Division spread along thirty miles of coast, instead of being, as I had imagined, held back concentrated in reserve, ready to move against any serious head of invasion. But much more astonishing was the fact that the infantry of this division, which is otherwise fully mobile, are not provided with the buses necessary to move them to the point of action. This provision of buses, waiting always ready and close at hand, is essential to all mobile units, and to none more than the 3rd Division while spread about the coast.

Britain needed more than buses. Among other things, fresh ideas were necessary, and some were soon provided. The elderly General Sir Edmund Ironside was replaced as Home Forces Commander-in-Chief by Brooke, who would soon succeed Dill as Chief of the Imperial General Staff. Brooke knew that skilled commanders were in too short supply for Montgomery to be confined to a division. He had him promoted to the rank of lieutenant general and elevated to the command of V Corps, guarding the Hampshire and Dorset coasts in southern England. That was in July 1940. Eight months later, he took command of XII Corps in Kent, the corner of southeastern England most vulnerable to a German assault.

Hitler had endorsed plans for an invasion of England within days of the fall of Dunkirk. Germany's Operation Sealion was to be undertaken with a pre-invasion aerial softening-up of selected coastal targets and with strong Luftwaffe cover for the invading troops. The German dictator had ordered plans to be drawn for the occupation of Britain, including the rapid establishment of a military occupation government and the arrest and elimination of individuals the Nazis considered undesirables.

However, few operational details for an actual assault on the British homeland were produced. More realistic German generals and admirals knew it was highly unlikely that one would take place. But the British continued to fear otherwise, and some among them favored an attempt to reach a peace settlement, even if concessions to Hitler had to be made. However, the voices of unwavering defiance predominated in the land. Churchill even contemplated the use of poison gas against enemy troops if they dared to come ashore in England.

Despite the prime minister's support for a fluid defense, Montgomery's tactics aroused much controversy. His decision to hold the bulk of his forces back from the coast in order to hammer the invaders at their weakest point implied, at least temporarily, surrender of some land to the Germans when they landed in force. He required the evacuation of sections of the region so his troops would have room to maneuver and prepare to meet the enemy. The criticism of those who refused to concede that a single inch of precious English soil be surrendered to the Nazis, even if only for tactical purposes, left him unmoved.

Local officials wanted to discuss their own ideas with him, but he was not interested. They could make whatever plans they wanted. He knew exactly how he intended to deal with the problems presented by a probable German attack and needed no advice from people who, he believed, were unlikely to have any idea what they were talking about. If their objections had any value, he was certain he had already taken them into consideration, so consultations would be a waste of time. He had no intention of abandoning the region to the enemy. But he insisted on retaining mobility and flexibility, challenging the invaders where they were weakest until they were vanquished or driven off.

All his life he had come across people who could not comprehend how logical his views were. He was neither surprised nor fazed to run into a new assortment of them. He did not need the support of Churchill or Brooke for reassurance, though it was essential now as well as agreeable to have them on his side. He did not deign to apologize for ruffling feathers or for not presenting his case to local factotums and critics who did not have the power to obstruct him. He was content, if pressed, to inform those who disagreed with him that they were simply incapable of understanding the situation.

Montgomery demanded absolute obedience from his own officers, but he had no qualms about disregarding and slighting his own superiors. As XII Corps commander he was under the command of the highly regarded General Claude Auchinleck, who was commander-in-chief in southern England. But when he took exception to a decision made by Auchinleck's headquarters concerning the transfer of troops, he brought his objections directly to the War Office in London without troubling to consult with or inform Auchinleck's staff, as would have been proper. Auchenlick sent him a letter sharply reprimanding him for such insubordination and discourtesy. He received no reply, much less an apology. Shortly afterward, Montgomery added to the insult by repeating the transgression.

Under other circumstances, his undisguised insubordination might have led to his being relieved of his command and relegated to an obscure post, with little hope of further advancement in his army career. But aside from the fact that he was a protégé of the recently elevated Brooke, Montgomery's reputation as a superb tactician and training commander had by then become widely known. Britain, with its back to the wall, could not afford to dispense with the services of one of its few generals who had performed notably well in recent action against the enemy on the field of battle.

CHAPTER 5
Testing Time in Washington

S ummoned to Washington from Texas in December 1941, Brigadier General Eisenhower arrived by train in the capital exactly a week after the Japanese had bombed Pearl Harbor, plunging the United States into a war for which it was prepared neither militarily nor emotionally. Eisenhower found the atmosphere in the capital grim.

Nazi Germany and Fascist Italy had declared war on America three days before, aligning themselves with Japan. But the challenge from Europe was for the moment of little significance compared to what was happening in the Pacific. Details of the damage done by the Japanese raid on the U.S. fleet in Hawaii and also on the U.S. Army's Clark Airfield near Manila in the Philippines a few hours later was still being assessed. Word was still coming in of the fall of Guam and of Japanese troop landings in the Philippines, Hong Kong, Malaya, and Thailand.

Upon his arrival in Washington, Eisenhower went directly from Union Station to report to General Marshall at the chief of staff's War Department office in the Munitions Building on Constitution Avenue. The construction of the Pentagon, then in progress, would not be completed for another three years.

Marshall was a stern, forthright, no-nonsense, almost forbidding figure, greatly admired by the officers who served under him, by President Roosevelt, and even by members of Congress who—the pointlessness of the First World War's slaughter and expense still fresh in their minds—otherwise generally had little regard for the skills or value of military men. Marshall had served with distinction in the earlier conflict and was considered to have a brilliant military mind. He was also a paragon of integrity who made it a point of honor never to laugh at any joke Roosevelt told. It was not clear whether he was, as one of his subordinates said, genuinely "a cold fish" or whether he shunned informality even with the people he dealt with most closely to prevent intimacy from clouding his judgment. He was one of the few men with whom Eisenhower worked closely during his military career who, apparently considering nicknames undignified, refrained from calling him "Ike."

Prodded during the preceding months by the events in Europe and the growing Japanese menace, Congress and the president had authorized a buildup of America's armed forces. But Marshall remained keenly aware of how unprepared the United States still was to fight a war, especially one on two major fronts half a world apart.

America's allies in the conflict could offer little encouragement. Britain was braced for a German invasion that its military leaders feared might succeed. In the Soviet Union, the Red Army had been beaten back clear across a two-thousand-mile front, Leningrad was under siege, and German forces appeared poised to move on Moscow and the oil fields of the Caucasus. China was a bleeding, impotent dragon, vanquished and ravaged.

These were dismal realities over which the War Department's War Plans Division was agonizing when Eisenhower was shown into Marshall's office. The chief of staff knew that this fifty-one-year-old brigadier general's file contained nothing but commendations. A decade earlier, he had himself offered Eisenhower a position on his staff at Fort Benning, which Eisenhower had been unable to accept because of a prior assignment. He had, in short, long before been spotted by Marshall as a man likely to be capable of coping with great responsibility in the army. Besides, Eisenhower had spent four years in the Philippines during the late 1930s trying to whip the Philippine Army into shape, and now the Filipinos, and the American troops serving alongside them, were under attack.

Marshall quickly briefed him on developments in the Pacific, as far as they were known in Washington. He told him about the damage done at Pearl Harbor and at Clark Airfield, about the attacks on Midway and Wake islands, on Hong Kong and Singapore and the Dutch East Indies. He outlined where it was believed further threats might materialize in the region. He provided a general idea of the military resources available to the United States for action in that part of the world, to the extent that they were known to exist after the initial Japanese onslaught. He then asked Eisenhower how he thought Japan's challenge to the American presence in the Pacific should be met.

The question shook Eisenhower. He knew he had developed a reputation in the army as an ideas man. But he realized that the country's highest-ranking soldier hadn't summoned him from Texas because he himself and his War Plans Division were bereft of ideas of their own. He was obviously being tested for a job, probably at the War Department itself.

Having only just been made aware of how critical the American military position was, he did not feel capable of offering Marshall an off-the-cuff response. He asked for a few hours to absorb and consider what he had learned before suggesting a course of action. He was given permission to withdraw to a desk in the War Plans Division to mull over the options.

An American retreat from forward positions in the Pacific to form a less vulnerable defensive line further back was out of the question. It would devastate morale, both among Americans and the allies they had suddenly acquired. But Eisenhower knew from personal experience that the Filipinos, even buttressed by the few thousand U.S. troops then stationed in the Philippines, were likely to be quickly vanquished if the Japanese invading force was as strong as reports indicated. It was obvious that the question Marshall had in effect put to him could be narrowed down to, "What do you think we should do about the Philippines?"

It was, he realized, as much a political as a military question. Militarily, the loss of the Philippines, so close to Japan and if invaded by superior forces, was inevitable. But that incipient nation was an American protectorate, heading for promised independence. To abandon it would send a defeatist message across the United States and throughout the world. Eisenhower concluded that a great effort had to be made to support resistance in the Philippines, hopeless though it was. The Americans had to demonstrate that they recognized and would fulfill their responsibilities. Their allies, he said, "may excuse failure but they will not excuse abandonment." Besides, if the Japanese were not tied down in the Philippines, no matter how briefly, the forces they were committing there could be shifted to other targets before Allied defenses in the region could be strengthened.

"We must take great risks," Eisenhower told Marshall, "and spend any amount of money required." He told him that a Pacific base of operations should be established in Australia, which was itself under threat, and support for the defenders of the Philippines should be channeled through that base as soon as possible. The chief of staff agreed, told him, "Do your best to save them," and appointed him deputy chief of the War Plans Division, with special responsibility for its Pacific and Far East Section.

Eisenhower's new job was to be even more of a test. Marshall made it plain that he was not happy with the way the War Plans Division was being run by its chief, Eisenhower's old friend Brigadier General Leonard Gerow. He didn't want the division simply to provide him with information and analyses, as it had been doing, leaving it to him to draw conclusions on what should be done. He wanted it to make the necessary decisions and to implement them. He told Eisenhower, "I must have assistants who will solve their own problems and tell me later what they have done." That was what Eisenhower was expected to do.

Trying to bolster resistance to the Japanese in the Philippines
proved no less daunting than had been expected. A week after
Eisenhower's arrival in Washington, Japanese forces landed at
Lingayen Gulf on Luzon Island, not far from Manila. Four days
later, General MacArthur declared the Philippine capital an
open city. He would soon feel obliged to order his outgunned
19,000 American troops and 12,000 Philippine Scouts to fall
back on Bataan Peninsula to continue a hopeless resistance.

Eisenhower tried to arrange for supplies to be shipped
through to them. But the Japanese had established mastery of
the air and sea in the region and the United States did not
yet have the ships or planes to challenge them. Having no
alternative, he arranged for free-lance sailors, many of them
pirates who normally worked the waters of the southwest Pacific, to be hired at great expense to run the blockade. It had
little effect on the situation.

While that was happening, Eisenhower, with no home in
Washington and no time to look for one, accepted the hospitality of his brother Milton and his family at their home in Falls
Church, Virginia, just outside the capital. He was able to spend
little time with them; he was at work before dawn and still there
well after dark, usually seeing daylight only through his office
windows. On December 31, he wrote to an army friend who
was also being summoned to work in Washington and prepared
him for what he might expect when he got there.

Just to give you an inkling of the kind of mad house you are
getting into—it is now eight o'clock New Year's Eve. I have
a couple of hours' work ahead of me, and tomorrow will be
no different from today. I have been here about three weeks
and this noon I had my first luncheon outside of the office.
Usually it is a hot-dog sandwich and a glass of milk. I have
had one evening meal in the whole period.

Eisenhower soon had to accept that the troops in the Philippines could neither be helped very much nor saved, and that
any effort made on their behalf was futile. Their continued
resistance was important, yet Eisenhower saw no alternative

but to inform MacArthur that he would have to fight on only with the limited resources already at his disposal.

Eisenhower had long before lost whatever admiration he had first felt for the man under whom he had served in the Philippines. MacArthur was considered responsible for having done nothing about America's B-17 bombers lined up in neat rows on the ground at Clark Airfield, where they were easily destroyed by Japanese aircraft hours after Pearl Harbor had been attacked, when a raid on the air base might have been expected. Eisenhower also believed MacArthur could have done a better job of obstructing the Japanese landing at Lingayen Gulf. Having little regard for his generalship or pomposity, he had no doubt that MacArthur was the wrong man for the difficult task that now was his.

Unable to do anything to help him, he grew contemptuous of MacArthur's complaints and his lack of understanding of how limited Allied options were. MacArthur refused to accept that supplies and reinforcements could not be sent to him. He was convinced that his former deputy, whom he now concluded had tried to undermine him when they were together in the Philippines, was still trying to do so.

MacArthur's shortcomings were not publicly known. Eisenhower thought it ironic that the general was being turned by press reports into a hero—the gallant, beleaguered defender of a key American outpost in the Pacific. The War Department was flabbergasted when MacArthur, though instructed to tie down the Japanese as long as possible, appeared not to take exception to a proposal by Philippine President Quezon that the Philippines be declared a neutral zone, which would thereby effectively hand it over to Japanese control. MacArthur was firmly told that whatever the Filipinos did, the American troops on Bataan were to fight on. "In many ways," Eisenhower wrote in his diary, "MacArthur is as big a baby as ever. But we've got to keep him fighting."

The dispatch ordering MacArthur to fight on stung him. He angrily cabled back that he had never had any intention of surrendering, that he would retreat to the island of Corregidor if necessary, and would personally maintain resistance to the last. Marshall thought that would be a mistake—MacArthur was too much of a hero to the American public by then, and his death or capture would be a blow to public morale. He was ordered to escape to Australia to take command of U.S. forces in the southwest Pacific. He left Bataan by speedboat under the cover of darkness and was transported to Australia. His deputy, General Jonathan Wainwright, assumed command in his place with instructions to hold out as long as possible.

The first weeks after America's entry into the war were a torment for Eisenhower. American servicemen were dying in the Pacific. Allied positions in the region were being overrun. As new deputy chief of the War Plans Division, he was supposed to find ways to cope with what was happening. But there was little he could do. The United States was still in the process of gearing up for global war.

Marshall had summoned Eisenhower to Washington because of his reputation for making the right decisions and accepting responsibility for them. But with comparatively few resources yet at his disposal, he was not making much of a show of it. He was also frustrated by the limits of his ability to coordinate operations with the U.S. Navy. Unwilling to risk the rest of its fleet in the Pacific until it had begun rebuilding its strength, the navy was not interested in joint consultations on how to fight the Japanese. It had little regard for its army brothers-in-arms, and was determined to get even with the enemy on its own and in its own time. "What a gang to work with," Eisenhower moaned. He mused that the war might be more easily won if someone shot Admiral Ernest King, the Chief of Naval Operations.

The previous summer, Roosevelt and Churchill had conferred in Canada on strategic prospects. Britain had been at war with Germany for almost two years at the time, but the United States was still officially neutral. At that meeting, Roosevelt had assured Churchill that if the United States was drawn into the war, Germany's defeat would be America's top priority. But the British feared that Japan's attack on Pearl Harbor might have changed U.S. strategic attitudes, and would leave Britain without the American assistance they badly needed in the war against Hitler.

Two weeks after Pearl Harbor, and a week after Eisenhower had been transferred to Washington, Churchill therefore arrived in the American capital with a high-powered British delegation to consult with Roosevelt and American military leaders. At that conference—code-named Arcadia—the British were relieved to see that despite the American reverses in the Pacific, Roosevelt and the War Department still considered Nazi Germany the more dangerous adversary.

Eisenhower attended high-level military meetings during the Arcadia talks. But being of comparatively low rank among this galaxy of top-level generals and admirals, it was mostly his lot to listen rather than to contribute to the British-American consultations. It was a difficult time for the British. They had experienced virtually nothing but defeat since the war began. Their army had been forcefully expelled from Europe. Their attempt to stop the Germans in Norway had turned into a fiasco. They had been driven out of Greece and their forces on the island of Crete had been overwhelmed by German paratroops half their own numbers. They were suffering setbacks in the North African desert. Their merchant marine was being savaged by German submarine wolf packs. And now their imperial outposts in the Far East were either already lost or under severe attack by the Japanese.

Churchill's forceful personality partly obscured the fact that the British had, in effect, come to Washington as supplicants. As the prime minister himself put it, without American aid, "nothing but ruin faced the world." Thus, for the senior military men who had accompanied him to confer with their American counterparts, the situation was awkward. They were heirs to a proud military history and it was difficult for them not to think of the Americans as upstarts. "They are difficult to talk to," Eisenhower found, "apparently afraid someone is trying to tell them what to do and how to do it."

Some of the other American generals feared the reverse, that in the formulation of concerted Allied strategy, the British would try to force through their own ideas.

We were more or less babes in the woods in this planning
and joint business with the British [said General Thomas
Handy of the War Plans Division]. They'd been doing it for
years. They were experts at it and we were just starting. . . .
The British were always ready. They would have a paper
ready and they'd looked into most contingencies. . . . These
British planners were just smarter than hell. . . . Apparently
they had that technique, unless you registered an objection,
you accept it. . . . [W]e had hardly caught our breath after
Pearl Harbor.

Some of the Americans were scathing in their assessment of
British plans and achievements. General Stanley Embick, one
of the War Department's most respected strategists, dismissed
British proposals for an invasion of French North Africa as
fantastic. General Leslie McNair, unimpressed with British wartime performance thus far, seemed to want to have nothing
whatsoever to do with them. But whatever Eisenhower's
thoughts about the attitude of the British visitors, he got along
well with them, offering intelligent comments when required
to say something, always with a friendly smile.

However, he differed with them, and with his own superiors,
on fundemantal strategy. Deeply troubled by his inability to do
anything to halt the Japanese rampage in the Pacific, he believed that concentrating first on defeating Germany as planned
and now reaffirmed was a mistake. Churchill had managed to
persuade Roosevelt that the first major Allied offensive operation in the war should be against French North Africa. The
capture of Morocco, Algeria, and Tunisia, combined with British operations against Hitler's Afrika Korps in Egypt and Libya,
would expose the soft underbelly of Nazi-occupied Europe. It
would initiate a process of closing and tightening a ring around
Hitler's Fortress Europe before plunging in for the kill.

But Eisenhower believed instead that it was essential to "drop
everything else" and "scrape up everything, everybody" to
salvage the Allied position in the Pacific. He had been appointed by Marshall to take on that task and, good soldier that
he was, he focused his attention on it to the exclusion of other

considerations. He was able to divert some shipping that had been earmarked for the Atlantic run to Australia, where he believed it was more badly needed, and wrote in his diary that every ship sent across the Atlantic instead would be regretted.

But it was increasingly evident that whatever slight hope there might be of driving the Japanese back at that point would be lost unless all of America's resources then available were thrown into the struggle against them. That was not going to happen. Roosevelt and Marshall remained unshakable in their conviction that Nazi Germany, whose influence was already being felt in Latin America, was the more dangerous foe. As Eisenhower grew more familiar with global strategy and more frustrated with his impotence in the Pacific, he was won over by their logic and reluctantly forced to conclude that the war in the Pacific would have to be a holding operation for the time being.

It seemed possible that the battered Russians would be forced out of the war and that Britain, the last European buffer state between rampant Germany and the United States, would continue losing on every front where its forces were committed. The consequences would be grave for the United States. The decision practically made itself.

> [I]f we should decide to go full out immediately against Japan [Eisenhower later explained] we would leave the Allies divided, with two members risking defeat or, at the best, struggling indecisively against the great European fortress. Meanwhile America, carrying the war alone to Japan, would always be faced with the necessity, after a Pacific victory, of undertaking the conquest of Hitler's empire with prostrated or badly weakened Allies.

In his job, Eisenhower was required to confer each day with streams of officers, congressmen, war-production managers, and various others. He impressed them with his intelligence, grasp of the problems with which he had to deal, composure, and amiability. Having proved himself to Marshall's satisfaction, he was promoted to head the Operations Division, as the War Plans Division was renamed, taking over in February 1942, less than two months after his arrival in Washington. Gerow, his predecessor, who would later serve under him in the invasion of France, was assigned to the command of a division.

Marshall told Eisenhower he was likely to be stuck in Washington for the duration of the war. He told him not to expect promotion because, unlike what had happened in the previous war, the men who did the fighting would this time have first crack at gaining advancement. Eisenhower told him he didn't care about whether he was promoted or not. Marshall was unlikely to have been taken in by such nonsense but, contrary to his warning, he soon afterward had his new chief of operations elevated to the rank of major general.

However, Washington was not where Eisenhower wanted to be. He found the atmosphere unnerving. "Tempers are short!" he observed in his dairy. "There are lots of amateur strategists on the job—and prima donnas everywhere. I'd give anything to be back in the field." The idea that he would have to spend the war behind a desk far from the front, rather than where the action was and honor to be found, was infuriating. He told Patton it had been "a personal disappointment" for him to have come to Washington.

His wife had joined him there early in February. He and Mamie took an apartment at the Wardman Park Hotel, which had become something of a dormitory for officers and their wives. He kept working at the exhausting pace he had established when he first arrived. When his father died on March 10, he deeply mourned his passing but did not feel he could take time off to attend the funeral in Abilene. He "shut off all business and visitors for thirty minutes, to have that much time, by myself, to think of him." Mamie was worried by how tired and drawn Ike looked. He was depressed by the continuing Allied setbacks and losses and his inability to do anything about them.

The devastating German advance into the Soviet Union had been halted during the winter but appeared certain to resume when spring arrived. If there was any repeat of the enormous advances the Wehrmacht had made the previous year, Russia could be knocked out of the war within months. If that happened, the 200 divisions Hitler had sent against the Soviets would be freed to engage in other exploits. German armies might cross the Middle East and Persia to link up with the Japanese, turning the war into even more of a nightmare for the Allies than it already was. Secretary of War Henry Stimson and General Marshall agreed that Germany had to be driven onto the defensive as soon as possible through an invasion of occupied France.

A devout convert to that strategy, Eisenhower agreed emphatically. "We've got to go to Europe and fight," he said, "and we've got to stop wasting resources all over the world—and still worse—wasting time. If we're going to keep Russia in, save the Middle East, India and Burma, we've got to begin slugging with air at West Europe, to be followed by a land attack as soon as possible."

He, like Marshall, envisioned an attack on German-occupied France from England to be mounted across the English Channel, the shortest possible route. There would thus be a minimum strain on shipping, which was still in frighteningly short supply and likely to remain so for a long time. Lines of communication across the English Channel could be more easily maintained than anywhere else. Air cover for a cross-Channel invasion could be most easily provided and maintained. Under direct threat, Germany would be compelled to ease its pressure on the Soviet Union, eliminating the fear that the Soviet ally would be forced out of the war.

A plan presented by Eisenhower's Operations Division suggested three operations to enable the Western Allies to seize the initiative from the Germans. Operation Bolero would be a massive American buildup in Britain to prepare for an American-British invasion of northern France across the English Channel. The invasion itself, Operation Roundup, would take place the following spring, with April 1, 1943, as the target date. The third suggested operation—Sledgehammer—was for contingency purposes only. It was to be implemented within the next few months if the German offensive in the east threatened to defeat the Russians.

All of that ran sharply counter to the strategy the British had proposed. They still were anxious to close a ring around Hitler's European fortress before making a frontal assault on it. But Roosevelt was impressed by the War Department's more ambitious plan and dispatched his confidant and adviser Harry Hopkins, along with Marshall, to London to present it personally to the British and gain their approval.

This placed Churchill, his War Cabinet, and his chiefs of staff in an extremely awkward position. They agreed that a cross-Channel operation against occupied France would eventually have to be launched if Germany was to be vanquished. But they believed it would be a catastrophic error to undertake such an operation before the Germans were rendered incapable of putting up strong resistance. Their personal memory of the slaughter that wiped out a good part of a generation of British young men in France during the First World War was compounded by the bitter experience of their expeditionary force that had been driven into the sea at Dunkirk just two years before.

They considered the American plan for an early cross-Channel invasion to be wishful rather than practical, based on bravado rather than cool analysis. The Americans did not seem to appreciate how formidable the German enemy was or the extremely dire straits in which the British found themselves, badly thrashed by the enemy and their resources severely stretched. "With the situation prevailing at the time," Chief of the Imperial General Staff Brooke acidly noted, "it was not possible to take Marshall's 'castles in the air' too seriously. . . . We were hanging on by our eyelids."

Nevertheless, the British felt they could not offend the Americans. They were worried about domestic pressure in the United States for the Americans to concentrate first on the Japanese and avenge the losses already suffered, and still being sustained, in the Pacific. To reject the American plan for an early invasion of France out of hand, as the British would have liked to have done, might have resulted in the United States turning its back on Europe for the time being, with incalculable consequences.

The British therefore concealed their scorn for the American strategy. Marshall and Hopkins were informed that they agreed with it in principle. The U.S. Chief of Staff believed the British would have to be watched closely to make certain they didn't change their minds, but he and Hopkins returned to Washington convinced that preparations could begin to implement the War Department's plan for an invasion of German-occupied Europe across the English Channel. Eisenhower hoped "that— at long last . . . we are all definitely committed to one concept of fighting! If we can agree on major purposes and objectives, our efforts will begin to fall in line and we won't just be thrashing around in the dark."

As the weeks passed, however, it became apparent that little was being done to translate the agreement on strategy into action. Part of the problem was thought to be inadequate liaison with the British. Marshall dispatched Eisenhower to London toward the end of May to see what could be done about it. Soon after arriving in the British capital, he confirmed "an uneasy feeling" that the senior American officer in England, General James E. Chaney, was being less effective than he should have been in getting things moving. The attitude of the senior British officers with whom Eisenhower conferred was also disappointing. They were anxious enough to see a buildup of American troops and equipment in Britain. But they demonstrated little enthusiasm for the agreed-upon early invasion of France. Eisenhower was left with a sense of frustration. "It is necessary to get a punch behind the job," he moaned. "We must get going!"

Eisenhower's report on the situation was received with consternation by Marshall. He felt he had been misled during his own visit to London two months earlier, as in fact he had been. He wanted someone in Britain upon whom he could rely. Eisenhower told him that the officer chosen had to have Marshall's fullest confidence should be capable of exercising wide-ranging authority competently and be able to adapt easily to any changes in strategy that might be made. He recommended the much-respected Major General Joseph McNarney.

Marshall decided, however, that Eisenhower himself fitted the job specifications and should be sent to London as Chaney's replacement and to build up the American presence there. He probably had such a decision in mind when he dispatched Eisenhower to England on his reconnaissance mission. He had been tested once more and had not been found wanting. Marshall had heard that Churchill and Admiral Louis Mountbatten, chief of the British Combined Operations Staff, had been impressed with Eisenhower and that both felt he was a man with whom they could work.

In the six months since he had arrived in Washington, Eisenhower had taken on an enormous range of responsibilities. As Chief of Operations, he had dealt with military and related developments around the world, in the Pacific, China, and the Middle East, in Africa and South America, in Europe and in the United States itself. He had concerned himself with the accelerated enlargement of the army, with the production of landing craft, warplanes, tanks, and guns, and with doling out the limited available equipment to U.S. forces in the various theaters of operations. He had arranged for the promotion of officers to positions where they were needed and the removal of others deemed not up to their jobs. He had drafted messages to President Roosevelt and letters for him relating to army matters.

In all of this he had performed competently and effectively. Remarkably, he appeared to have made no enemies in the process, with the exception of MacArthur, who was offended by his former subordinate being placed in a position to exercise power over him. It had been "a tough, intensive grind," but Eisenhower had grown enormously in the job. He was still little known beyond army and Washington official circles, but now he was crossing the Atlantic to be transformed into a figure of historic proportions.

He was pleased and flattered to have risen so quickly and to have capped that rise with being entrusted with U.S. forces in the European Theater of Operations. To Mamie he crowed, "I'm going to command the whole shebang."

Eisenhower had already met Montgomery, though only

briefly. He had heard of his reputation as a potential high-flyer, and while on his visit to England he had gone to meet him and size him up. Montgomery received him with little courtesy, showing up late for the meeting and offering a stiff, grudging handshake. He told him, "I'm sorry I'm late, but I really shouldn't have come at all. I'll make it brief." He then proceeded with an analysis of field maneuvers he was then supervising. As he listened Eisenhower lit a cigarette, but was brusquely informed by Montgomery that he did not permit smoking. Eisenhower stubbed out the cigarette but felt humiliated by the manner in which he had been spoken to. He wrote in his diary that he found Montgomery "a decisive type who appears to be extremely energetic and professionally able." But, according to his driver, on the way back to London he "was furious—really steaming mad" and referred to Montgomery as "that son of a bitch." It would not be the last time he would entertain such sentiments about Montgomery.

CHAPTER 6
Whirlwind in Southern England

By late autumn of 1941, more than a year after the evacuation of the British Expeditionary Force from Dunkirk, it was no longer likely that the Germans would attempt to invade Britain. But it was still considered a possibility—not during the coming winter months, when sea and weather conditions would rule out such an operation, but the following spring.

Montgomery was to deal with that contingency. In December, he succeeded General Auchinleck, to whom he had acted so disdainfully, as commander-in-chief in southern England. Auchinleck was sent to assume command of British forces in the Middle East, which were taking a beating at the hands of General Erwin Rommel and his Afrika Korps.

The effect of Montgomery's taking charge in the region was electrifying. General Horrocks said that, "a distinctly peace-time atmosphere" had prevailed earlier despite the war having gone on for so long and Britain having mostly reverses to show for it. But once Montgomery had taken charge, "It was as though atomic bombs were exploding all over this rural corner of Britain."

For Montgomery, preparing men for battle physically and mentally had become more than mere procedure. It had become aspects of an ideology, one of his own devising. His primary task in his new post was to defend southeast England against the Germans if they attempted to invade. But he told his officers they had to understand that a defensive mentality was their worst enemy. Attack was the key to his doctrine; it was the only form of defense that made sense to him in the overall picture. The training of his officers had to focus on the proper organization of command, deployment of forces, preliminary reconnaissance, digestion of intelligence, and preparation for the use of air cover—all for the purpose of bracing to go over to the attack.

Many of Montgomery's officers were required to radically adjust their thinking and procedures, and to do so quickly. Some who were comparatively senior in rank felt humiliated at being obliged to attend lectures to relearn subjects to which they had already devoted their entire adult lives. No allowances were made for them. If Montgomery believed an officer did not meet his standards he told him so to his face, regardless of his rank or previous record and often in the presence of others. He would say, "I am sorry. But you are of no use to me. None whatever." And he would send him packing. There would be no appeal. For fear of arousing Montgomery's contempt and ire, some, never before having been under such intense and relentless pressure from above, felt it prudent to consult Montgomery's staff officers to determine if they were doing anything that might displease him.

Montgomery now had a wider audience for his showmanship. His lectures to his officers were greatly theatrical. After a major training exercise, the officers would be gathered in a large auditorium on whose stage were posted large working maps of the area in which the exercise had taken place for him to use in dissecting how it had been handled. Called to attention, the audience members would snap up from their seats and Montgomery, in battle dress, would cross to center stage from the wings and stiffly call out, "Sit down, gentlemen." He would then say, "Thirty seconds for coughing—then no more

coughing at all." Remarkably, as officers have recalled, there
was none until Montgomery had finished with them, though
that must be an exaggeration because his lectures sometimes
lasted two hours or longer. Officers risked being exposed to a
withering glare from him if they coughed when he was talking
even at other times.

Smoking was also prohibited at Montgomery's lectures, and
officers soon learned it was dangerous to light up in his presence. He was not against smoking on principle. Later in the
war, when he went to visit his troops he would regularly have
aides carry along cartons of cigarettes for him to distribute to
the men. But he wanted no distractions while he spoke. His
ban was also an exercise in discipline and authority.

Learning new catechisms for the theory and practice of combat was not the only adjustment officers serving under Montgomery had to make. He subscribed to Rudyard Kipling's
assertion that "Nations have passed away and left no traces . . .
because their peoples were not fit." He decreed that everyone in
his command had to achieve and sustain top physical condition.

He had intitiated intensive physical-fitness programs when
he had commanded V Corps and then XII Corps, and word of
it had spread throughout the army. Nevertheless, the introduc-
tion of such programs when he arrived at Southern Command
came as a shock to its officers. Regardless of rank or physical
condition, they were required to engage in vigorous exercise.
That included all staff officers younger than forty-five. They
had to take part in weekly exercises, carrying rifles and in full
marching order. Some had not indulged in such exertion for
more than a decade. When told that a colonel, a senior administrative officer, might die if required to undertake the program
of exercise that was prescribed, Montgomery said, "Let him
die. Much better to die now rather than in the midst of battle
when it might be awkward to find a replacement."

Ambulances were brought up to deal with emergencies during training. Details of physical inadequacies were to be noted
so that officers in unsuitable condition could be watched and
dealt with. Montgomery insisted that, "Commanders and staff
officers at any level who couldn't stand the strain, or who got

tired, were to be weeded out and replaced—ruthlessly." An officer later recalled that they loathed what they were required to put up with, but it "shook away the cobwebs." It was easy enough to recognize the value of the torture long after it had been endured. But at the time, officers posted to serve under Montgomery groaned and received the commiseration of their friends when their orders came through. One of them later recalled that when he received his orders to report to Montgomery's headquarters, the brigadier delivering them, "shot me a sympathetic look as if he were sentencing me to immediate execution."

Officers serving under Montgomery in England had to contend with special restrictions. He denied them their traditional right to quarter their wives privately nearby so they could be with them when off duty. He said that if ordinary troops could not have their wives near them, neither could their officers. Besides, it would distract the officers from their duties. Protests flooded into the War Office. Montgomery could not have cared less. He made certain that his decree was obeyed, going so far once as to dispatch an officer on a bicycle to interrogate a woman spotted near a base because he thought she might be committing the transgression of cohabiting with her officer husband in his off-duty hours.

Montgomery's officers quickly learned the sanctity of discipline and the harshness of the likely penalties if it was flouted. Observing a captain emerging from the bakery of a small town in Kent during maneuvers, eating a bun despite orders that food was not be taken until afterward, Montgomery demoted him to lieutenant on the spot.

Many protests were made to the War Office about Montgomery's often-objectionable behavior. That didn't worry him. He didn't care if people took exception to his conduct or demands so long as they were unable to obstruct him or otherwise make it difficult for him to do what he knew was right. With Brooke as his admirer and protector, he had no need to be concerned about that—at least not yet.

He was no automaton. There was the occasional exception, when he permitted an individual officer more leeway than oth-

ers, sometimes by whim, sometimes because the man had qualities Montgomery respected more than he objected to his
shortcomings. He was supremely confident in his own infallibil-
ity. His own on-the-spot judgment was more important to him
than the rules. He was always prepared to jump junior officers
in rank if they struck him as the kind of men he needed and
wanted. On his regular visits to the troops, he kept a sharp eye
out for promising candidates.

> Army commanders with many thousands of troops under
> their command [one of his senior subordinates later said]
> tend to become remote God-like characters whom few know
> even by sight, yet in some extraordinary way Monty's influ-
> ence permeated all strata of S.-E. Command and his knowl-
> edge of the personalities under his command was uncanny.
> Often he would ring me in the evening and make the most
> searching inquiries about some young second-lieutenant
> whom he had noticed on training. He would certainly have
> made a first-class talent spotter for any football club. The
> only way I could deal with these inquiries was to have a
> book containing details of every officer in the division handy
> beside the telephone.

As for the ordinary troops under his command, Montgomery
had them driven to the limits of their physical endurance.
Forced marches and night exercises were standard, not only for
the infantry. Perpetual combat-readiness in the English countryside was the rule, with vehicles dispersed and sentries
posted and alert at all time no matter how insignificant the
installations they guarded. Standards of combat-training were
rigorously maintained and lapses were severely punished. But
Montgomery remained little concerned with saluting, polished
blouse buttons, and related incidentals. The men appreciated
that. It made sense, and it gradually helped them accept the
exertions through which they were put.

Generals in the British Army had always been remote crea-
tures, not only of a far more privileged social background than
almost all of those they commanded, but linked to ordinary

soldiers only through long, forbidding chains of command. However, "Monty" went regularly among his troops, visited their encampments, spoke to them, and showed them that they mattered personally to him and that he was interested in doing everything he could to promote their well-being. The men came to appreciate his efforts to make them understand not only how they would be fighting but what they would be fighting for.

The value of these efforts was recognized by senior army figures. Casualty lists were mounting alarmingly, and reports by British liaison officers in the United States indicated that, despite that country's enormous potential, it might be a while before the Americans would be able to contribute significantly to lightening the load the British were carrying in the conflict. Despite Winston Churchill's stirring oratory, military reverses everywhere had spread a mood of despair over Britain. Sir Alexander Cadogan, Undersecretary of State at the Foreign Office, moaned, "Our army is the mockery of the world."

Montgomery responded to the crisis with seemingly misplaced confidence. High-spirited and hard-driving, he continued to conduct himself in a way that others considered peculiar at best and that under other circumstances would have led his army career into a dead end. He never bothered offering explanations or making a fuss to have his way. He merely proceeded without giving a thought to objections and without tolerating even the harmless weaknesses of individuals, including civilian dignitaries, reckless enough to cross his path. Among them was the Archbishop of Canterbury, primate of the Church of England.

The archbishop, a proud and brave man, announced that even if the Germans invaded he would not leave the coastal area. He said that it was unthinkable for him to abandon the magnificent and sacred Canterbury Cathedral. Like Saint Thomas à Becket, he would face the enemy there and let them do their worst. Montgomery thought that was nonsense. He issued orders that if the Germans landed and the archbishop proved obstinate, he was to be removed to safety. He did not do the archbishop the courtesy of discussing the matter with him.

Though he was courteous and considerate when he chose to

be, neither courtesy nor consideration ranked prominently in his table of values. He had a job to do, had firm ideas about how it should be done, and would not be distracted by what he considered trivialities. At one point, after a grueling few weeks, Montgomery instructed an aide to locate a quiet local inn where he could take a break for a few days to think about defense of the region in a more leisurely setting. Unable to find the sort of place that he believed would adequately serve the required purpose, the aide began scouting large private country houses. He believed their owners would be pleased to have the general as a houseguest.

He made the suggestion to a member of the House of Lords who owned an estate in the region. The man replied that he was expecting houseguests in about two weeks' time but he would be delighted to play host to Montgomery for a few days. Montgomery had mixed feelings about that. The accommodations sounded right, but he feared his host would intrude upon his privacy and would want to chatter away at him during meals.

He knew how to resolve that problem. He would take over a wing of the house, bring his own army cook, and eat his meals separately. When informed, his would-be host was understandably upset. It was not customary for his guests to make demands. But it was war, and he understood there were times when a general had to be alone to relax and think. Since it would only be for a few days, he would accept the ungracious terms imposed on his hospitality.

When the aide reported back to Montgomery, proud of himself for having sorted out a delicate problem, he found that the general had other ideas. "From what you tell me," he said, "it is a lovely place . . . has nice gardens and everything . . . maybe we will stay three or four weeks. Yes, we will—we will be staying for a month. Go back and tell him I have changed my mind and that we are going to bring along a couple of servants as well."

The owner of the estate was outraged. He said he would not be treated like that in his own home and withdrew the invitation. When the aide reported back, Montgomery took a look at a map of the area and decided it was a restricted zone. "Kick him out at once," he ordered. "We can't have him in the way of an invasion." The man was ejected from his country home and Montgomery moved in, handing it over to the army for the duration of the war when he was through with it.

The British Combined Operations Staff was a unique organization. Among its personnel it had achieved something that had always proved absurdly elusive in the American military structure—amicable cooperation between Britain's three armed services. The British had known from the beginning that an invasion of the European continent would be required before the Germans could finally be defeated. For months the Combined Operations Staff, under the command of Admiral Mountbatten, had been examining possibilities for a limited raid on the coast of northwest France to test German defenses there. Only through such an exercise could prospects for an Allied invasion of France begin to be evaluated.

Dieppe was chosen as the target for the raid. It was a port city and the Allies would need control of a major port on the English Channel through which to establish a line of supply when the invasion ultimately took place. It was also well within range of support aircraft flying from British bases. As army commander in southern England, Montgomery was closely involved in planning the Dieppe raid. He was subsequently criticized not for the role he played in it, but for trying to downplay the extent of his involvement.

The raid was to take place July 4, 1942, but inclement weather forced a delay. Then indications that the Germans were aware a raid was imminent forced its postponement. The attack plan was revised but Montgomery had developed doubts about it and urged that it be abandoned for security reasons. It was not. The raid, launched on August 19, was a fiasco. Of 5,000 troops involved, almost all of them Canadian, more than 3,300 became casualties.

By then Montgomery was out of the picture, in a different job in a different place. But in his memoirs he sought to absolve himself from any responsibility for the rout at Dieppe. He as-

serted that he would never have agreed to the changes made
in the original raid plan, which eliminated a preliminary aerial
bombardment in order to maintain surprise as well as substi-
tuted commandos for paratroopers. He implied that the raid
failed because of those changes. That may or may not be true.
But the fact was that the changes were made while Montgomery
was still involved in planning the operation. There is no evidence that he objected to them at the time. Indeed, one history
of the Combined Operations Staff has him chairing the meeting
at which the disputed changes were made.

His denial of any responsibility was groundless. It was also
small-minded. By the time he tried to dissociate himself from
any blame in the affair, he had already achieved fame and glory
and was honored as one of the greatest commanders in British
history. Though he participated in the original planning, he
was by no means in charge of it. None of the others involved
sought to shift responsibility onto someone else. No one openly
criticized Montgomery for the Dieppe failure. But he was obsessed with the need to be right even when he was wrong and
with shifting blame to others when he himself shared it.

It is possible that he did not realize he was fabricating about
his role in the planning of the Dieppe operation. Later in the
war he was often to say things that he believed were accurate
and that others knew were not. To Brooke, who repeatedly
sought to shield Montgomery from the consequences of his
objectionable actions, he sometimes confessed that he was capable of errors. But genuine contrition was not his style. He
was convinced that all his equations always added up properly,
and if they didn't then someone else must have messed them
about.

CHAPTER 7
Eisenhower Emerges from Obscurity

On June 25, 1942, the War Department in Washington formally announced the establishment of a European Theater of Operations for the armed forces of the United States. It announced further that Dwight Eisenhower, the fifty-two-year-old major general who was in charge of its Operations Division, had been named commanding officer in the European Theater, with his headquarters in London. Some newspapers still got his name wrong.

Eisenhower had flown the previous day to the British capital, where he issued a statement declaring that the United States and Britain were moving swiftly to merge their "military and economic strength" to defeat the enemy. Few people in London, or in the United States for that matter, had ever heard of the man who would soon undertake one of the most difficult tasks in military history—forging and leading an operational wartime military alliance based on mutual consent between two nations that had important differing interests as well as notably different national characteristics.

Word spread quickly through the British military establishment and in the London press that Eisenhower was held in sufficiently high esteem at the War Department to be given his prestigious assignment over more than 300 other generals who outranked him. *The New York Times* reported that he was "considered generally to be one of the most brilliant among the younger crop of distinguished Army officers." Eisenhower himself thought his appointment was temporary. He believed General Marshall would arrive in Britain before long to assume command of American forces in the European Theater. He thought that would be appropriate in view of the enormity of the task of laying the groundwork for the destruction of the Third Reich.

The day after Eisenhower's arrival in London, he met with the staff he had inherited from his predecessor in London. It consisted of the same officers whose performance had failed to impress him on his visit the month before and among whom he still found, upon his arrival, a "lack of confidence and some indecision." He didn't single out anyone for blame and was "quite certain that this staff and all commanders now realize we have a unique problem to solve." He expected them to bring enthusiasm, optimism, and diligence to their jobs. What was more, they were to abandon their practice of bucking everything back to the War Department in Washington. He made clear that "no alibis or excuses will be acceptable."

What concerned the Commanding General most [his official diarist wrote] was the cultivation of determined enthusiasm and optimism in every member of his staff and every subordinate commander. He refused to tolerate pessimism or defeatism and urged anyone who could not rise above the recognized obstacles to ask for instant release from this theater.

Eisenhower's first home in London was a suite at Claridge's on Brook Street, the British capital's finest hotel. It was within a few minutes' walking distance of his office in Grosvenor Square, which American correspondents would later come to call "Eisenhowerplatz." Colonel Ernest "Tex" Lee, a former salesman from Texas, ran his office for him. Sergeant Mickey

McKeogh, a former New York City hotel bellhop, was his personal orderly. He arranged for Kay Summersby, the British Motor Transport Corps volunteer who had chauffered for him when he had visited London the previous month, to be assigned as his driver again. She would play a more significant role in his life during the following three years.

Closely in attendance was the recently commissioned U.S. Navy Commander Harry Butcher, a close friend whom he'd had assigned to him as his naval attaché and who shared his hotel suite. Butcher knew little about warships or the navy, but Eisenhower found him useful and comforting to have around as confidant, sounding board, personal assistant, public relations agent, and keeper of his diary.

A former journalist and CBS executive, Butcher persuaded Eisenhower to nurture agreeable, informal relations with the press and to remain accessible to correspondents. Naturally affable, Eisenhower, suddenly a figure of great public interest, readily accepted that advice. Butcher was permitted to feed the press wholesome human-interest stories about Eisenhower's family and modest origins. Newspapers dug up and published photographs that helped fill in the background of this suddenly prominent general—of the Texas railway hovel in which he had been born, of Abilene, where his youthful adventures had been played out, of him and his brothers as youngsters, of him and Mamie as a young couple.

Eisenhower accepted that it was important to have the press on his side and agreed to meet often with correspondents. At the first of the many press conferences he held in London, he had no trouble charming the attending journalists with his easy manner and intelligence, and they remained charmed throughout the war. He was always good copy. He provided what would later come to be called sound bites about Allied unity and inevitable victory to lend spice to the stories the correspondents filed, though Edward R. Murrow of CBS at first confessed in a broadcast, "I don't know whether Eisenhower is a good general or not." *The New York Times* reported at his first London press conference that he "talked informally with British reporters and American correspondents, giving an excellent demonstration of the art of being jovially outspoken without saying much of anything."

While blaming security requirements for his not offering much of significance, he took to answering the questions of correspondents with an apparent fulsomeness and folksiness not common among senior military men. There was nothing pompous or affected about him. He didn't pretend to know more than he did. He didn't pretend to say more than he could. Guided by Butcher, he got to know several of the correspondents well and called them by their first names during press conferences, a flattering, unprecedented intimacy among the British at the time. He was, in short, a regular guy. The image established was of a decent, modest, but authoritative figure who, through intelligence and application, had risen from a humble background to high rank and important military assignment.

In today's more sophisticated public-relations climate, it would be said that Eisenhower was manipulating the press by his chumminess and accessibility. That charge would not be far from the mark. Butcher made him even more popular with correspondents by treating the problems they encountered—censorship, for example—with great seriousness, having Eisenhower take steps to help them out when circumstances permitted. It was thus judged that the general did not hide any more than necessary behind a blanket of secrecy. The *Chicago Daily News* declared, "Correspondents with experience in Paris, London, and Washington from the outset of the war claim they have never seen such an absence of red tape."

There would later be times when they would find him considerably less than forthcoming. While he believed the American public had a right to be told what was happening, and the British public had to have confidence in their American ally, this was war and he considered the press a weapon to be used in it.

Eisenhower did not stay long at Claridge's. The hotel sometimes served as the London base for royalty and other visiting dignitaries from around the world, and it proved too rich for his blood. Not till after the war did this man from the wrong side of the tracks in Abilene come to feel comfortable in the kind of luxurious surroundings the millionaire friends he came to acquire helped provide for him.

He was much flattered when invited to enjoy the subdued comfort of Churchill's country residence at Chequers in Buckinghamshire or the elegance of Mountbatten's Broadlands estate in Hampshire, despite the snootiness of some of the servants he encountered in the latter establishment. But he found his suite at Claridge's, where the walls of his sitting room were painted gold, too much like "a goddamned fancy funeral parlor," and where the bedroom color scheme struck him as "Whorehouse pink." In addition, he was told that the hotel was less likely to withstand the effects of bombing than the somewhat less plush Dorchester Hotel overlooking Hyde Park, to which he moved.

But the Dorchester was not much to his liking either. Butcher soon found a small home in a rural setting not too far away from London that could serve Eisenhower as a retreat. Telegraph Cottage, situated on a ten-acre wooded tract, with two golf courses nearby, was outside the town of Kingston, less than an hour west of Grosvenor Square. Butcher went there with him and, in addition to Mickey McKeogh, he took on two black soldiers—John Moaney and John Hunt—to be servants, to clean, cook, serve, and generally keep the cottage functioning tidily and efficiently.

Eisenhower was able to flee there on some nights and most weekends to escape the artificial atmosphere of hotel life and the social demands to which he was exposed during the week by virtue of being the most important American in London. At the cottage, he would play bridge with members of his staff and visitors. He would sometimes toss a football around with Butcher, Lee, and General Mark Clark, who had been appointed commander of U.S. ground forces in England. A badminton net was erected and put to use. Tin cans were saved for pistol-shooting practice. And there were excursions to the nearby golf courses.

As he had in Washington, Eisenhower put in long hours at

his offices in Grosvenor Square. He needed relaxation when he
could get away. Aside from the pressure of work, his shoulder
was bothering him. He received novocaine injections for neuritis at the London Clinic and was treated by an osteopath. He
declined to have army doctors examine him for fear they would
make him go through a full checkup that would consume more
time than he was willing to spare. He had trouble sleeping and
Butcher would sometimes find him looking out of the window
of his Dorchester Hotel suite in the middle of the night.

His eating habits did nothing to contribute to his well-being.
Considering a lunch break an unnecessary luxury, he often
made a meal of candy bars at his desk. He did what he could
to shun boiled cabbage and brussels sprouts, the fragrance of
which seeped through his Grosvenor Square headquarters from
its kitchens, where the cooks relied heavily on limited British
food supplies. He believed this was going to be "the fartingest
war in history."

Soon after his arrival in England, Eisenhower was promoted
to lieutenant general, a rank sufficiently high for the British
military to take him seriously, though General Brooke did not
consider him important enough to schedule an early meeting
with him. Comparatively limited forces were as yet at his disposal. Despite the War Department's ambitious strategy, hardly
more than 50,000 American troops had so far arrived in the
United Kingdom. Soon after he had established his presence in
London, he set about making arrangements to speed up the
cross-Atlantic flow. That presented problems of a special kind.

The potential for friction between the newly arrived American
soldiers and their British hosts was great. The people of Britain
were enduring food and fuel shortages. Practically everything
else was in short supply as well. Their cities were pockmarked
with the effects of German air raids. Many people had lost kin
or friends in the fighting or at sea. Many others feared for the
safety of sons, husbands, and fathers in far-off combat zones.

American servicemen had difficulty appreciating what the
British had gone through and were still experiencing. For most
of them, being in Britain was an adventure. By British standards, they were exorbitantly paid, often offensively self-

assured, and snappily attired. Young British women were greatly attracted to them. In addition to the glamour of these cocky Yanks, they were loaded with cigarettes, chocolate, coffee, and other desirable goods that were otherwise hard to come by in Britain. They had those things in such profusion that, without a second thought, even the lowliest among them could give or even throw away items that were greatly desired by their British hosts.

Reeling from defeat in battle and fearful because of Soviet setbacks, most Britons were relieved by the presence of the Americans. However, resentment at their comparative wealth and privileges was widespread. Nor was it much appreciated when Americans boasted of how they had come to save Britain from losing the war.

Not happy to be away from home, the Americans found much to ridicule or criticize in the British environment, including driving on the left side of the road, a generally disagreeable climate, and how incomprehensible the language they shared with their hosts often seemed to be. Their blunt comments on such things often aroused hard feelings among their hosts. It was not the way guests were expected to behave. Entertaining the troops, singer Al Jolson drew a huge laugh with his suggestion about unchilled British beer: "Why don't they put it back in the horse?"

English-language radio propaganda broadcasts transmitted by the Germans attempted to intensify the resentments among the British about this supposedly friendly invasion from across the Atlantic. They claimed that American soldiers were raping British women, murdering British men, and generally lording it over the British. Eisenhower was aware of the dangers.

Not only were British forces playing a crucial and so far pre-eminent role in the struggle against the common enemy, but the British provided the base from which the campaign to win the war was to be launched. Not only was it regrettable that the American presence in great numbers among them caused resentment, but it could damage the joint war effort. Eisenhower knew that to be effective the military alliance between the two countries had to be based on genuine friendship and mutual respect as well as a common interest in victory. What was more, these feelings had to extend right down through the ranks.

He issued instructions that American troops were to be prepared for their exposure to Britain and the ways of its people before they set foot in the country. On troopships crossing the ocean, the men were given orientation lectures about how the British, on their comparatively little island nation and with their limited resources, had been steadfastly fighting off the might of the Germans for so long and how they had been heroically alone in that struggle for most of the time. The importance of Allied cooperation was explained, as was the need for American troops to recognize they were to be guests in a foreign land.

Lectures and programs to generate understanding and sympathy for the British continued after the men arrived on British shores and were dispersed to their various bases. Tours of cities that had been badly hit during the German aerial blitz were organized to show the men what their hosts had sustained in their defense of freedom. The army's popular *Stars and Stripes* newspaper was harnessed to strengthen British-American relations. It regularly ran accounts of aspects of British life likely to appeal to Americans, of the longstanding friendship between the two countries, and of British gallantry in the face of a ruthless enemy.

To set an example for his troops, Eisenhower himself engaged in a campaign of conspicuous friendship with prominent British figures. It was, of course, more than just show. There was a war to run. He met regularly with General Sir Bernard Paget, commander of the British Home Forces, Air Vice Marshal Sir Sholto Douglas of the RAF, and Admiral Sir Bertram Ramsay to discuss war developments and review plans for future operations. He also met often with Churchill though, still a little giddy at operating at such heights, he felt awkward knowing that the prime minister regularly reviewed strategy in personal communications with President Roosevelt and probably knew things about top-level American thinking to which he himself was not privy. A man of regular habits, he did not take well to Churchill's late-night dinners and talk sessions that almost invariably went on into the early-morning hours.

On a personal as well as a professional level, Eisenhower got along well with the British. He made no pretense of being anything but a grown-up Kansas farmboy, far from home. Indeed he boasted of it, though he had been away from Abilene, both physically and in spirit, for a long time and, strictly speaking, had never been a farmboy.

In establishing himself in his new job, he had to cope with his comparative inexperience. Unlike senior British officers with whom he dealt, he had never had a combat command. He had spent almost all of his army career in staff and administrative jobs or in one war college or another. Now his limited experience was compounded by the unprecedented nature of his assignment: commanding U.S. troops in a foreign country as part of an alliance whose ground rules had not been completely spelled out.

He also knew there were important matters he did not understand as well as he should have. He was anxious about "Such things as the proper location and scope of authority of Chiefs of Services in a theater of operations; the division of functions and responsibilities between the Commanding General, S.O.S. [Services of Supply] and the commanders of troops in training; the fixing of responsibilities for the establishment of special schools, disciplinary barracks, and like installations." He wrote to his old mentor, General Fox Connor, "I cannot tell you how much I would appreciate, at this moment, an opportunity for an hour's discussion with you on problems that constantly beset me."

Though it was not apparent, the fact was that though Eisenhower strove to exude confidence, he was often anxious and troubled. Some, like Admiral Sir Andrew Cunningham, who would come to admire him greatly, observed "he was not very sure of himself." But he generally managed to conceal his worries, displaying the organizational skills, candor, and modesty that charmed the British as they had charmed his U.S. Army superiors over the years. They were relieved to have a man in their midst dedicated to mutual respect. It might have been otherwise. The job Eisenhower had might have been given to one of the officers they had encountered at the Arcadia conference in Washington six months earlier, who had made little effort to conceal their low regard for the British.

The arrival of U.S. troops and equipment in Britain was accelerated as Eisenhower brought his administrative skills to bear on the situation. At the same time, training programs were intensified to prepare for the Operation Sledgehammer assault on France to take place in the fall of 1942, within the next four months, if the Soviets appeared to be in danger of being forced out of the war, as well as for the major invasion across the English Channel tentatively scheduled for April 1943. Those target dates for action were, of course, not public knowledge and, as the summer slipped away into autumn, public relations became more of a problem. People began asking questions.

Eisenhower's can-do approach to his job helped foster the belief that a major Allied offensive in Europe was imminent. But though ever-greater numbers of American troops were arriving in Britain, and the Allied bombing campaign against Germany was stepped up, there was nothing to indicate to the press or the public that the great assault on Hitler's Fortress Europe was actually about to happen.

Some correspondents were questioning whether they were being bamboozled by slick public relations. Was it possible that when Eisenhower told them he could not reveal to them what was being done, it was because there was not much of significance he could have told them even if security had not been a factor? German armies were pushing the Soviets further and further back. Rommel's Afrika Korps was within striking distance of the Suez Canal and the oil riches of the Middle East. Stories were pouring out of Europe of the horrors of the Nazi occupation. Shortly after Eisenhower arrived in London, the BBC reported that the German occupation authorities in Paris had decreed that all male relatives of wanted Frenchmen who failed to surrender to them would be executed, and stories were beginning to circulate about the fate of Jews at the hands of the Nazis.

When correspondents closely scrutinized what Eisenhower was telling them at his friendly press conferences about ambitious Allied intentions, some concluded that he was offering them not much more than a few drinks, a boyish smile, and anodyne assurances that British-American cooperation was the rock on which victory over Hitler would be built. They did not know, and neither did Eisenhower, that during his first weeks in London Allied strategy and his role in it were being fundamentally transformed.

On his earlier visit to London, Eisenhower had observed that the British were showing discouragingly little enthusiasm for the early invasion of France to which they had agreed in principle. In fact, they remained horrified by the idea. They could not be persuaded that an assault on Hitler's Atlantic Wall would be anything less than a bloody debacle if it was mounted before the the Germans had been substantially weakened through attrition elsewhere.

That was no longer a secret within the Allied High Command. A few days before Eisenhower had flown to London to assume command of U.S. forces in the European Theater of Operations, Churchill had informed Roosevelt in Washington that none of his chiefs of staff favored an early cross-Channel invasion despite the fact that the Americans had been led to believe such an operation had British backing. The prime minister had told the president that, if nothing else, the shortage of suitable landing craft made an early invasion of France a recipe for disaster.

However, Churchill agreed—indeed, strongly argued—that the Allies had to go on the offensive without delay. Instead of France, he proposed that an invasion of French North Africa be given renewed consideration. Plans for such an operation had been made the previous January during the Arcadia conference in Washington, but had then been put on hold. Churchill now told Roosevelt that, in contrast to an early invasion of France, which was bound to be extremely costly in casualties and might fail, an operation against North Africa would provide a comparatively easy Allied victory.

Roosevelt was intrigued. But the American military establishment was enraged by this turnaround. It was a critical moment in the British-American military alliance that was still in the process of being consolidated. U.S. Secretary of War Stimson bitterly accused Churchill of promoting "half-baked" ideas reminiscent of the British military fiasco at Gallipoli in World War I that Churchill, then First Lord of the Admiralty, had also promoted. General Marshall and Admiral King proposed that in view of Britain's revised strategic approach the United States should abandon the defeat-Hitler-first policy. If that happened, the British would continue to shoulder most of the burden of coping with the Germans for the time being while the American armed forces switched their priority to beating Japan.

Most Americans favored such a course. Despite widespread sympathy and admiration for the British, it was the Japanese, not the Germans, who had launched an unprovoked attack on the United States. It was the Japanese, not the Germans, who had forced thousands of captured American soldiers along a horrific death march in Bataan in the Philippines. Though the Japanese advance in the Pacific now seemed to have been halted, it was Japan, not Germany, that had presumed to pose a threat to Hawaii, the Panama Canal, and Alaska and whose battleships had even lobbed a few shells into California from not far offshore. Opinion was strong in America that Japan, not Germany, was the primary enemy and should be dealt with before U.S. forces moved on to deal with Hitler.

But Roosevelt had no intention of being swayed by such sentiment. He remained convinced that Germany, whose might had crushed the once-proud French and whose armies were practically at the gates of Moscow, was the far more dangerous adversary. The president had already instructed the War Department that American troops had to be in combat in the European Theater before the end of 1942. Only in that way could Washington's propaganda machine, with the aid of news correspondents at the front, get Americans to concentrate on the war against Germany.

Once London's determined objections to an early invasion of France were made clear, Roosevelt sent Marshall and Harry Hopkins back to England in July 1942 to sort out Allied strategy with the British. Marshall had not intended for Operation Sledgehammer to be launched in the autumn unless the Soviets genuinely appeared to be on the brink of collapse. But to prevent his hopes for a war-winning full-scale invasion of France the following spring from being sidetracked, he now felt obliged to promote an updated plan for Sledgehammer, with greater detail than he had presented to the British before. Eisenhower was instructed to produce such a plan.

He worked eighteen hours a day at his Grosvenor Square headquarters to get it ready. But he made no effort to conceal his view that trying to crack German coastal defenses and establishing a secure beachhead in France before greater Allied resources were available would be a dangerous gamble. However, he felt the gamble was necessary to convince the Soviets not to seek an armistice that would permit Hitler to redeploy against the Western Allies the massive armed forces he had committed to the defeat of the Soviet Union.

Soviet dictator Joseph Stalin had vigorously complained that his country's allies were doing little to ease the punishment the Germans were inflicting on his people or to relieve the pressure his forces were under. Concern about Russian intentions would strongly influence Eisenhower's strategic thinking right through the conflict.

Russia [he told Marshall] is the great question mark of the war. . . . Defeat of the Russian armies would compel a complete reorientation of Allied strategy. It would practically eliminate all opportunity of defeating Germany by direct action, and would throw the Allies permanently on the defensive throughout Europe. . . . The bleakness of this picture needs no emphasizing.

But the British had more confidence in continued Soviet resistance to the Germans and still wanted no part of Sledgehammer, not even in the updated version Eisenhower had labored to produce. They maintained that if it was launched only to keep the Russians in the war, the limited resources available for the operation meant it would not be substantial enough to draw a single German division away from the Russian Front. And in the unlikely event that a beachhead could be established in France in the autumn, what was to happen then? To the British, the Americans seemed to have no idea. Brooke was alarmed and infuriated by what he took to be the shallowness of American strategic thinking. They seemed to him to be unable to distinguish between what was desirable and what was possible.

American troops had not yet arrived in Britain in sufficient numbers to mount a major operation. That meant Sledgehammer, if it went ahead within the next four months, would be executed by the few British divisions being held in reserve or under training at home. Neither Churchill nor his War Cabinet nor Brooke was prepared to contemplate losing them in what they considered a self-defeating, misconceived gesture. Faced with unshakable British opposition to Sledgehammer, the Americans had no alternative but to agree that the operation should be shelved.

The U.S. War Department was greatly displeased. Marshall had no doubt that it meant rejection of the frontal-assault strategy the Americans had devised to deal with the German war machine and bring the war to a rapid, victorious conclusion. That was the strategy for which Marshall had mistakenly believed he had received British endorsement. Eisenhower was equally dismayed by the decision. He thought it would have seriously damaging consequences for the Allies. It made nonsense of his plans for quickly coming to grips with the Germans in Europe. "I hardly know where to start the day," he said, feeling he was right back where he was when America entered the war in December the previous year and he had been summoned to Washington.

Eisenhower later said that he came to believe that the decision to defer the early cross-Channel invasion was correct. But at the time, in July 1942, he complained "we might have taken Cherbourg this fall with a fair chance of holding it," to begin to roll back the German occupation of Europe had the cautious British not had their way. He said the day it was decided not to attempt to seize an early foothold in France was perhaps "the blackest day in history."

Pressed by Roosevelt to find a suitable alternative for the action he demanded in the European Theater, Marshall grudgingly concluded that an invasion of French North Africa—code-named Operation Torch—would be the "least harmful diversion." In Operation Torch, the Allies would invade and capture French Algeria, Morocco, and Tunisia. Churchill had scored a victory over the American generals. The Western Allies would follow the strategy the British preferred of closing and tightening the ring around Hitler before launching a major direct assault on his European Fortress.

The British agreed that the Torch commander should be an American. The invading forces would be mostly supplied by the United States. And French forces in North Africa, whose leadership was strongly anti-British, were less likely to put up strong resistance if they were led to believe that Torch was almost exclusively a U.S. operation. It was thought in London that Marshall himself would take command. He was highly respected by the British despite their sharp strategic differences. But the U.S. Army Chief of Staff considered it more important for him to remain in Washington at that stage, to continue to galvanize America's war effort. Before leaving London to return to Washington, he chose Eisenhower to command Torch, though it was rumored that he himself would take charge of the operation once it was ready for launching later in the year.

But that was unlikely. Marshall considered Operation Torch no more than a sideshow, a needless North African distraction. He believed the "vicissitudes of war"—possibly developments in Russia—might still lead the Allies to opt for an early invasion of France instead. That would be the operation he hoped to command, with Eisenhower as his deputy. In the meantime he wanted someone he could trust in charge on the spot in London for the moment when, he hoped, circumstances would force an Allied strategic reversal and permit the U.S. War Department to finally have its way.

Eisenhower thought along the same lines. After all, details of the American frontal-assault strategy that had just been blocked by the British had been formulated by him when he had been Chief of Operations in Washington earlier in the year. He accepted that while the invasion of French North Africa had emerged as the agreed-upon operation, Sledgehammer and plans for larger-scale invasion of France should be kept on hold, ready to be activated if circumstances permitted.

But that proved a vain bid to cling to a might-have-been. Roosevelt, not wanting the waters muddied, quickly made it unmistakably clear that Operation Torch was unqualifiedly on the Allied agenda, to the exclusion of any other imminent offensive operation involving American troops. An invasion of occupied France was, for the moment, out of the question.

Eisenhower understood and accepted. In the idiom of his football days, he had been passed the ball and he would run with it, confining his complaints and concerns to his intimates. He was gratified when the British assigned the experienced General Alexander, whom he admired, to serve under him, commanding the British component in Torch. He regretted when Alexander was then almost immediately withdrawn and assigned elsewhere. But he was replaced by Montgomery who, though known to be eccentric and abrasive, was reputed to be an energetic and imaginative tactician as well as a much-respected stickler on training. But Montgomery was also soon removed from the operation to be reassigned, and Eisenhower, his logistical and training problems already beginning to accumulate, believed he had reason to wonder how serious the British really were about the North Africa operation they had promoted so assiduously over the objections of the Americans.

CHAPTER 8
Africa Beckons Montgomery

In August 1942, Montgomery, then still British Army commander in southern England, was invited by General Paget, the British Home Forces commander, to join him on a visit to Scotland to observe a major training exercise in progress there. Soon after he arrived in Scotland, he was instructed to return to London immediately. He was to assume command of the British First Army, which was to take part with the Americans in the invasion and conquest of French North Africa to be launched in the fall.

Montgomery was informed that the War Office was dissatisfied with the way Operation Torch was developing. Time was passing and, though Eisenhower was its commander, no one seemed to know what was going on. The Combined Chiefs of Staff Committee of the two countries had not yet even issued a directive for Torch outlining its objective. Without such a directive, there could be no idea of what forces would be committed and how they would proceed with their mission. "The whole thing" did not sound good to him; "a big invasion in North Africa in three month's time, and no plan yet." He believed his first task in his new assignment would be to press

Eisenhower to devise a satisfactory, comprehensive plan for organizing and implementing the operation.

Montgomery had previously had little to do with Americans. He had met the man he was to serve under only briefly and wondered how he would get on with him. Not till later would he be given a chance to find out. He had barely returned to London before he received word that his orders had been changed. Instead of participating in Operation Torch, he was to fly immediately to Cairo to take command of the Eighth Army in the Egyptian desert.

A seesaw struggle had been going on in the North African desert for two years. It had originally been started by the Italians, who had entered the war against Britain as Germany's ally in June 1940. That was just after the British Expeditionary Force had been driven out of Europe at Dunkirk and a few days before France capitulated to Hitler. With the Western democracies either crushed or reeling from defeat, Italian dictator Benito Mussolini believed he could construct a new Roman Empire without exposing himself or his forces to great risk. While the British were bracing themselves for a German invasion of their homeland, Mussolini ordered Marshal Rodolfo Graziani, the commander of his forces in the Italian colony of Libya, to seize the British protectorate of Egypt.

Though the forces at Graziani's disposal were far greater than those of General Sir Archibald Wavell, the British commander in the Middle East, an Italian attack in September 1940 was quickly beaten back by the British defenders, who went on to push the Italians far back across the sands of northern Libya. They might have achieved a conclusive victory had Churchill not diverted some of Wavell's divisions to Greece in a hopeless attempt to block a German advance there.

In February 1941 the Germans came to the aid of the floundering Italians. General Erwin Rommel, once head of Hitler's personal military security guard, arrived in Libya with his Afrika Korps to take command of Axis operations in North Africa. Officially, Rommel came under Italian command. In fact, he answered to Berlin. Hitler quickly had reason to be pleased with him. Soon after his arrival in North Africa, and even before his forces were up to strength, the man who came to be known as the Desert Fox launched a surprise attack on the British in Libya. Within weeks he had pushed them back almost to the Egyptian border.

To retrieve the situation, Churchill dispatched General Auchinleck, who had been Montgomery's commander in southern England, to replace Wavell as Commander-in-Chief, Middle East. Auchinleck set about rebuilding and restructuring his forces. He brought in fresh divisions to replace some of those that had been clobbered under the withering desert sun by Rommel's newly named German-Italian Panzer Army. General Sir Neil Ritchie was appointed to serve under him, commanding the British Eight Army.

Toward the end of 1941, Ritchie drove Rommel back again across northern Libya. Churchill was visiting Washington for the Arcadia conference at the time, and the Eighth Army's desert success initially helped him promote his disputed proposal for the operation against French North Africa. If the Allies captured Morocco, Algeria, and Tunisia while the British Eighth Army continued to press westward across Libya, Rommel's forces would be trapped and doomed, the entire southern Mediterranean shore would be under Allied control, and Axis mastery of the Mediterranean would be ended.

But British momentum in Libya soon petered out. As the Arcadia conference was drawing to a close in Washington in January 1942, Rommel went on the offensive. In the next few weeks, he drove the Eighth Army back over most of the territory it had regained, convincing some American generals that Churchill, with his grandiose proposals, lived in a world of fantasy. The British were unable to stop the Axis offensive until it had carried Rommel's forces just short of the fortified Libyan port of Tobruk. There the front temporarily stabilized.

But five months later, in June 1942, when Churchill was again in Washington, this time to tell Roosevelt that the U.S. War Department's strategy of an early invasion of France was unacceptable, Rommel resumed his advance. His Panzer Army overran Tobruk and drove on into Egypt. The fall of Tobruk, of which Churchill was informed while conferring with Roosevelt

at the White House, was a humiliation for the prime minister.
He complained bitterly that "seasoned soldiers had laid down
their arms to perhaps one-half their number" and despaired
about what could be done if his troops "won't fight."

The Eighth Army had earlier held out at Tobruk while under
prolonged seige. Its defense had become a symbol of British
vigor, courage, and defiance. Now its fall appeared to be proof
of impotence and lack of will to win. Churchill later said the
fall of Tobruk was the greatest blow he suffered in the war.
Communiqués previously issued in London had boasted of
British successes in the North African desert and the superiority
of British forces there. Now the possibility of disaster loomed
on the only battlefield where British troops had produced impressive, if inconclusive, successes.

No excuse seemed valid, not that the new British Crusader
tank left much to be desired nor that the Eighth Army was short
of armor-piercing shells. Rommel was seen in London as simply
being the better soldier—a tactician and leader of men far superior to any general Britain could send into the field. Churchill
conceded as much when explaining to Parliament the setbacks
in North Africa: "We have a very daring and skillful opponent
against us." People began to mutter about Auchinleck's apparent incompetence.

The enemy was within a few days' march of Cairo. At the
British embassy and military headquarters in the Egyptian capital, clerks burned classified documents. Throngs of people fled
the city for safety elsewhere. Egypt, gateway to the precious
oilfields of the Middle East, appeared about to fall. If that happened, the Germans would be in a position to advance even
further east, overrun Persia, and link up with the Japanese,
who were advancing westward through Burma.

But that threat was greatly exaggerated. The experience of
relentless defeat had cowed British information services into
failing to point out to the public that Rommel was running out
of steam. Not even the British high command fully appreciated
how costly in men and material the German commander's offensive had been to the Axis. His line of communications was
overextended. He had failed to receive promised reinforce-

ments, his great losses in tanks had not been made good, and he was desperately short of supplies. He was also ill.

Auchinleck left his headquarters in Cairo to assume direct command of the Eighth Army and start to whip it back into shape. He forced Rommel to halt his forward momentum just short of the Egyptian town of El Alamein, where the line once more stabilized. However, that achievement, and the fear that it was temporary, failed to satisfy a craving in London for a dramatic victory to dispel growing war weariness and despondency at home. Questions were asked in Parliament and by ordinary people about what was wrong with the army command. British morale was not helped by the announcement from Berlin, reported in the London press, that Rommel, the conqueror, the hammer of the British, had been made a field marshal.

But the situation was being transformed. Under Auchinleck's direct command, the Eighth Army skirmished with Rommel's forces and gradually geared up to launch a major offensive. Longing desperately for a decisive reversal of fortunes, Churchill pressed Auchinleck not to delay launching that attack. But the general wasn't ready. The Eighth Army was made up of British divisions and divisions from other countries of the British Empire, Australia, New Zealand, South Africa, and India. Command problems had to be sorted out. Morale problems had to be addressed for troops who had for so long been required to fight with inferior equipment. The army was still being reequipped and reinforced. Auchinleck informed the War Office at the end of July that ". . . in present circumstances renewal of efforts to break enemy front or turn his southern flank not feasible owing to lack of resources and effective consolidation of his positions by enemy. Opportunity for resumption of offensive operations unlikely to arise before middle September."

Churchill was not willing to wait. He angered Brooke by insisting on the offensive "before Auchinleck can possibly get ready." Churchill's impatience was a reaction to the problems with which he himself had to deal. Not long before, he had been forced to defend himself for the second time that year

against a parliamentary motion of censure over his direction of
the war. The motion had been defeated, but confidence in the
prime minister's leadership continued to erode. He felt "a load
of calamity on my shoulders." As leader of the British people,
he was held responsible by many for the failure of the British
armed forces to produce a convincing victory over the enemy
aside from the defeat of the Luftwaffe by the RAF in the Battle
of Britain two years before.

Diplomatic as well as political pressure on him was intense.
The Soviets were making momentous efforts in their struggle
against the German invaders, but they continued to sustain
horrific losses. Stalin, whom Churchill had just visited in Moscow, was demanding evidence of greater combat commitment
by the Western Allies. The Americans, whose generals felt they
had been steamrolled by Britain into agreeing to the invasion
of French North Africa, had to be given grounds for greater
faith in British battlefield achievement. In addition, Churchill,
failing to appreciate to what extent Rommel's forces were already much weakened, was obsessed with the seeming invinci-
bility of the German desert commander. "Rommel, Rommel,
Rommel, Rommel, Rommel," he moaned. "What else matters
but beating him?"

On a visit to Cairo he was brought up to date on the situation
and realized that comparative strengths in the desert meant
that the enemy was certain to be decisively beaten once battle
there was joined. Advisers assured him that Auchinleck was
bringing the situation under control. But exasperated by the
general's refusal to attack before he was ready, Churchill insisted on a shakeup in the British Middle East command. "I
must emphasize," he said, "the need of a new start and vehe-
ment action to animate the whole of this vast but baffled and
somewhat unhinged organization."

General Alexander, removed from the Operation Torch role
to which he had just been assigned, was brought in to take over
as Commander-in-Chief, Middle East. General William Gott
was chosen to serve under him as commander of the Eighth
Army. However, Gott was almost immediately killed in an enemy air attack and Montgomery, also removed from his new

posting to Torch, was ordered to Egypt to take his place. Victory in the desert had for the moment become Britain's top priority.

Montgomery was delighted with the assignment. Commanding an army in the field was what his life had been directed toward. So many of his lectures and writings had dealt with the specific challenges involved. It was for this role that he had honed his command skills ever since his time in India. He was pleased to be serving under Alexander, who had been a student of his at Staff College. He was certain he could control him. And he looked forward to matching wits with Rommel, whom the British military establishment had come to fear was unbeatable. He was confident "of being able to handle any job successfully if I was allowed to put into practice the ideas and methods that had become my military creed."

Churchill later recounted a story told about what Montgomery had to say about his prospects in the desert as he was being driven, in the company of General Ismay, to the airport for his flight to Cairo.

Montgomery [Churchill wrote] spoke of the trials and hazards of a soldier's career. He gave his whole life to his profession, and lived long years of study and self-restraint. Presently fortune smiled, there came a gleam of success, he gained advancement, opportunity presented itself, he had a great command. He won a victory, he became world-famous, his name was on every lip. Then the luck changed. At one stroke all his life's work flashed away, perhaps through no fault of his own, and he was flung into the endless catalogue of military failures. "But," expostulated Ismay, "you ought not to take it so badly as all that. A very fine army is gathering in the Middle East. It may well be that you are not going to disaster." "What!" cried Montgomery, sitting up in the car. "What do you mean? I was talking about Rommel!"

Montgomery later denied he had said any such thing. But the tale indicated the sort of reputation he was to acquire. Hopeful now that the tide was turning in Africa and in his personal political fortunes, Churchill instructed the Ministry of Information in London to brief British newspaper publishers and editors on the importance of what was about to happen.

Montgomery left England for Cairo by way of Gibraltar on August 10, 1942. He did not take personal leave of his young son. He considered himself too busy for that. Instead, he asked the headmaster of the preparatory school that David attended to look after the boy until he returned, and departed for Egypt before receiving a reply. As for his own mother living in Northern Ireland, she appeared not even to be in his thoughts when he set out to take on a task that had wrecked the careers of two other generals.

CHAPTER 9
Forging Operation Torch

Eisenhower had been in the American army for almost thirty years before he was officially awarded, on August 6, 1942, his first combat assignment. Operation Torch, which he was to organize and command, was to be the largest amphibious military operation ever undertaken. His instructions, when they finally were delivered a week later, were even more ambitious. He was to secure "complete control of North Africa from the Atlantic to the Red Sea." Through sea and air action against Axis installations in the Mediterranean, he was also to facilitate Allied operations against the enemy on the continent of Europe.

That he was awed by his assignment is not surprising. He was required to completely overhaul his thinking and planning. He had previously been proceeding on the assumption that he was to prepare American troops in Britain for an invasion of France just a few miles away across a narrow strip of water. Now he was given only a few weeks to get ready for a massive British-American operation somewhere very far away. "Our target," he said, "was no longer a restricted front where we knew accurately terrain, facilities, and people as they affected military operation, but the rim of a continent where no major military campaign had been conducted for centuries. . . . A beachhead could be held in Normandy and expanded, however slowly; a beachhead on the African coast might be impossible even to maintain." It was all still very much a mystery.

> Ordinarily, [Eisenhower later wrote] a commander is given, along with a general objective, a definite allocation of force upon which to construct his strategical plan, supported by detailed tactical, organizational, and logistical programs. In this case the situation was vague, the amount of resources unknown, the final object indeterminate, and the only firm factor in the whole business our instruction to attack. . . . It was a nerve-racking state of uncertainty in which we had to work and plan.

In his new role, he was answerable to the British-American Combined Chiefs of Staff that had been set up in Washington at the beginning of the year. Themselves answerable to the president of the United States and the British Cabinet, the Combined Chiefs had the job of planning global strategy, coordinating operations against the Axis powers, and arranging for the appropriate distribution and provision of forces and material resources to the various commands of the Western Allies around the world.

Eisenhower, the experienced staff officer, recognized that great difficulties would have to be overcome in establishing an effective combined American-British command when basic procedures of the two countries' military organizations, and even their terminologies, differed, sometimes greatly. To deal with that problem, his Allied Forces Headquarters (AFHQ) was to be manned by a balanced American-British staff. Thus an Englishman was named as Eisenhower's senior intelligence officer, with an American as his deputy. His Chief of Operations was an American with an Englishman as his deputy. Other personnel in those departments were balanced as evenly as possible between Americans and Britons who had to learn to penetrate the mysteries of each other's slang and accents.

A similar division in G-1 (personnel) and G-4 (logistics), where distinctive national practices were too deeply ingrained for a successful merger, would have been counterproductive. Those sections were permitted to have parallel American and British staffs at AFHQ. Nevertheless, Eisenhower sought to create a staff as fully integrated as possible, one in which national differences would be played down so that American and British officers could work closely together in pursuit of their common objective. Policy differences and cultural divergences were impossible to eradicate completely, as was resulting friction. But they were to a considerable extent submerged for the common greater good. Under Eisenhower's direction, AFHQ became a prototype for the Supreme Allied Headquarters that Eisenhower was to head for the invasion of France and the conquest of Nazi Germany two years later.

As his chief of staff at AFHQ Eisenhower chose Major-General Walter Bedell Smith, a cantankerous but highly efficient military manager, and asked for him to be dispatched to AFHQ immediately. However, Marshall, still hoping that "the vicissitudes of war" might force the abandonment of Operation Torch, refused to let Smith leave Washington for London until September.

Aside from the intimidating dimensions of his first combat assignment, Eisenhower felt somewhat disoriented being in London, commanding an Allied team while striving not to indulge a natural national bias. He found it a strain attempting to shed his purely American perspective. He wrote to a friend, "It is so easy to lose contact with the War Department . . . that frequently I am overcome by a 'lost' feeling, and have a desperate desire to jump on a fast plane and come over for a twentyfour hour visit." To his wife in Washington he wrote, "I cannot tell you how much I miss you. . . . I constantly find myself wondering 'Why isn't Mamie here?' "

Through regular communication, often involving lengthy letters, he was careful to remain in close contact and, he hoped, communion with Marshall, though Brooke, the prickly British chief of staff with whom his relations were confined almost exclusively to essentials, was officially as much his superior as Marshall and was right there in London with him.

He had no illusions about Torch. He was well aware of how formidable the operation's organizational problems were and, though it was to be a combined American and British endeavor, he realized that his former colleagues at the War Department's War Plans Division still considered it a huge mistake, politically inspired rather than militarily advisable.

He knew there was much to be said against dispatching half-trained troops across thousands of miles of waters infested with packs of German submarines to storm ashore on coasts in regions for which intelligence data was either sparse or unreliable. It had to be assumed that the invaders would meet resistance from the armed forces of Vichy France, whose leaders were actively collaborating with the Germans and had an army of some 150,000 men garrisoned in North Africa. Air cover, which was to be provided for the operation by aircraft carriers, would be at best minimal.

> From General Ike's standpoint [diarist Butcher observed] we are undertaking an operation of a quite desperate nature which depends only in minor degree upon professional preparation or on the wisdom of military decisions. . . . The unfavorable potentialities are vast. [Eisenhower] feels we are sailing a dangerous political sea . . . in which military skill and ability can do little in charting a safe course.

Important differences between the American and British chiefs of staff over how Torch was to be implemented compounded Eisenhower's anxiety. A debate by transatlantic cable quickly developed over how the resources being put at his disposal for the operation should be deployed. Enough shipping and naval escort vessels would be available for landings only at two locations on the North African coast.

The British wanted both those landings to be on the Mediterranean shore of Algeria, as close to Tunisia as possible, without excessively exposing the operation to enemy aerial attack from German bases on nearby Sicily. They also pressed for fixing an early date for the operation to be launched. They said delay had to be avoided if Tunisia was to be taken before the winter rains started and before the Germans, expected to rush in forces to meet the Allied challenge, were able to establish effective defensive positions there.

However, the Americans were less interested in the Mediterranean, an area that had historically been of particular British concern. They were more worried than the British that fascist Spain, though still neutral, might enter the war on the Axis side and permit the Germans to block the Gibraltar Strait. Spanish dictator Generalissimo Francisco Franco owed Hitler a debt of gratitude for German assistance during the Spanish Civil War in which he had triumphed a mere three years earlier, and Berlin was pressing him to pay up.

If the Gibraltar Strait was sealed by the enemy after Operation Torch had been launched, the lifeline of the Allied invaders would be severed and the invading troops would be stranded on the North African coast. The Americans insisted that Casablanca, on French Morocco's Atlantic shore, which was not exposed to such a threat, should be one of the two target sites in the operation. General Thomas Handy, Eisenhower's successor as Chief of Operations at the War Department in Washington, said, "[W]e didn't know what the hell was going to happen inside [the Mediterranean] and we wanted some way to get out."

A choice had to be made between the American and British views. When they had pressed for an early cross-Channel invasion, the Americans had urged that bold, risky decisions be made. But now, with the War Department still displaying little enthusiasm for Operation Torch, it was the British who strongly urged that risks be taken to achieve the desired objective.

Eisenhower sided with the British in that argument. He agreed with them that if Tunisia was to be taken quickly the Allies had to concentrate on going ashore as far east in the Mediterranean as possible. That would mean no Atlantic-coast landing at Casablanca, at least not at first. He feared that if the War Department's view prevailed, the conquest of Tunisia and the successful completion of his mission would be jeopardized.

He was pained by the differences over strategy that had arisen between himself and his former colleagues at the Operations

Division. As it was, some at the War Department were beginning to wonder whether, in going to London and becoming a supranational commander, Eisenhower was being excessively influenced by British views.

The dispute over landing sites raged for a month. On September 6, 1942, a month after Eisenhower had been appointed Torch commander, Roosevelt and Churchill reached a compromise solution. Additional resources would be found so there could be three landing areas in French North Africa instead of two. There would be two Mediterranean landings sites—at the politically important French North African city of Algiers, which the War Department had initially opposed in favor of Casablanca, and the major Algerian port of Oran. In addition, Casablanca would after all be included in the operation. But landings further east, which the British and Eisenhower believed important to assure a speedy victory, remained excluded. And the date for the launching of Torch was fixed as November 8, 1942, a month later than the British urged. The War Department insisted that the extra time was needed to gather the resources and prepare the troops for the first major American combat involvement in the expanded European Theater of Operations.

This first major combined Allied offensive in the war had to be ready for launching practically from scratch in a mere three months. Organizational and logistical problems were formidable. More than 500 naval, transport, supply, and support vessels would take part, and 110,000 troops, mostly American, would be put ashore in the opening phase. Three distinct task forces had to be created and supplied, two in Britain, one in the United States.

The ones that were to target Algiers and Oran would gather and sail from British ports. In addition to the American troops who would be ferried to battle, huge amounts of supplies and equipment for them would have to shipped across the Atlantic to be unloaded in Britain and distributed to the appropriate units, and then be loaded again on the designated vessels that would transport them to the North African shore.

To Eisenhower's despair, the first shipment of supplies for

the operation arrived in England from the United States without a single crate or box properly labeled. It was a sign of what was to follow. Material shipped across the Atlantic kept going astray. Some of it was unwittingly stored in warehouses after having been delivered to the wrong British ports. A remarkable amount was lost to pilferage after arrival.

Emergency signals kept being sent for replacements. At one point General Clark, the deputy Torch commander, warned that unless the U.S. 1st Division, which was training in England for the invasion, received its long-overdue equipment, "those men will be going in virtually with their bare hands." (Later it would be discovered that all the signals equipment for the Algiers assault was carried to North Africa on only one ship, the unloading of which was a shambles and whose loss would have been disastrous for the whole operation.)

Similar problems were suffered by the Casablanca task force that was to leave from Virginia and cross the Atlantic, heading directly for the beaches of Morocco. Supplies and equipment for it were to be gathered at and near the Norfolk naval installation. As in England, much of it was lost en route there or in dock storage, control over which was quickly overwhelmed by the sheer dimensions of the operation.

Most of the troops assigned to Torch, like their officers, had never been in combat before. Most had been drafted into the army only months before. They had to be trained not only for this huge amphibious operation, for which there had been no significant precedent, but even in the use of their weapons. The coxswains who were to handle the landing craft, taking the men and their equipment ashore, were also inexperienced and untrained, though too few landing craft were available for practice runs. There were doubts whether the shortfall would be made good in time for the invasion.

Ike personally torn [Butcher noted in his diary] between desire to go ahead to do the job with the tools available and the necessity of stating his military belief that the assignment is ultra-risky without the ships and planes and other equipment which they seem blandly to expect him to have but which actually have not been made available. . . . [A]s the British with their genius for understatement might say, the prospect for success is somewhat less than consoling.

A spate of security breaches, including lost classified documents and indiscreet comments by officers and others, led Eisenhower to order "drastic measures" to prevent the enemy from learning or inferring what was going to happen. If the Germans discovered what the Allies were planning, they might compel their collaborators in the Vichy French government to order determined armed resistance to the Torch invasion. Or they might preempt the operation by acting first to seize French North Africa. And even after Allied beachheads had been secured in Algeria and Morocco, troops would have to dart quickly overland across mountainous terrain to seize Tunisia before enemy forces could pour in from Sicily, a mere one hundred miles away, to block their advance and turn the operation into a protracted battle of attrition.

Eisenhower thought the odds favored successful landings. But he told Marshall he believed that the subsequent Tunisia phase of the operation had a less than a 50 percent chance of succeeding. That was not a comforting prognostication for the man commanding it to live with. Butcher observed, "[I]f the expedition flops, Ike's name will be *mud*." He was, however, determined not to allow anyone else, and particularly not his staff, to share his doubts. He believed "the tougher the prospects, the more necessary it is that superior commanders allow no indication of doubt or criticism to discourage the efforts or dampen the morale of subordinates and of troop units."

Organizing Torch was only part of Eisenhower's job. He was also still the senior United States officer and most prominent American in Europe. Various duties and obligations came with that role. He wrote to his son John at West Point about "the dozens of things that happen here daily."

[T]his business of warfare is no longer just a question of getting out and teaching the soldiers how to shoot or how to crawl up a ravine or to dig a fox-hole—it is partly politics, partly public-speaking, partly essay-writing, partly social contact, on to all of which is tacked the business of training and disciplining an Army. All in all, there's never a dull moment—but there are many in which a fellow wishes he could just get into a hammock under a nice shade tree and read a few wild west magazines!

The strain on him was unrelenting. He rarely slept more than five hours a night and often had trouble sleeping even that long. He smoked three packs of cigarettes a day and drank countless cups of coffee. For the most part, he held his fiery temper under control but that often required great effort. The pressures mounted as he tied together the various strands of the operation. He attended an endless succession of staff meetings and high-level conferences and drew up countless reports to Marshall and to the Combined Chiefs of Staff. He tried to keep fully informed of the progress of troop training and of the acquisition of an adequate number of the landing craft and other vessels essential to the operation.

Rivalry among the American services reared its divisive head. Arrangements had to be made for shipping and for warship escorts, both in short supply and badly wanted in the Pacific and for the Atlantic run. At Eisenhower's request, U.S. Navy officers were assigned to London to help overcome the resulting complications. But they served notice that, "We are here only to listen." Eisenhower had to go over their heads to get U.S. Navy cooperation. It was time-consuming and exasperating.

Military politics also foiled his attempt to have a single commander serving under him for air operations, as would be consistent with his unity-of-command philosophy. He had to accept both an American deputy, Major General James Doolittle, to head the Western Air Command in Torch, and Air Vice Marshal William Welsh to head its Eastern Air Command.

In theory, air cover was essential for any successful amphibious operation. But there was much anxiety at AFHQ about whether enough would be available and whether aircraft at the disposal of the Vichy French, though obsolescent, would threaten the success of the invasion. Questions were also raised about the advisability of dispatching American paratroopers from bases in England to seize airfields in Algeria. Even the Germans, the only ones who had so far resorted to airborne ground attacks, had not attempted such long-range operations.

His resources fully stretched, Eisenhower agonized over finding forces to hold in reserve for coping with emergencies such as an obstructive intercession by neutral Spain. There was also the question of how to deal with the Vichy-dominated civil administration of French North Africa and the population there once the invasion had taken place, so that the Allied forces would not have to worry about lack of cooperation or hindrance from them as they went about consolidating and extending their positions.

The only important pro-Allied French movement was led by Charles de Gaulle, whose anti-Vichy Free French movement had been sponsored and was supported by the British. De Gaulle suspected that an Allied invasion of North Africa was being planned. But despite his angry mutterings, he was not brought in on the operation. Nor was he consulted or even informed about it. Aside from Allied suspicions that his movement had been infiltrated by Axis agents, the Gaullists had little support in North Africa and the general himself was detested by the Vichy French. His participation in Torch was thought likely to guarantee armed resistance to the invasion when that might conceivably be avoided. Besides, Roosevelt considered the Free French general a would-be dictator and wanted the Allies to have as little to do with him as possible, a matter that would later present Eisenhower with additional difficulties.

The Torch commander thus had to concern himself with a variety of major problems and scores of lesser ones. His task was not made easier when an ulcer attack incapacitated Bedell Smith, his chief of staff, for a time soon after he finally arrived from Washington to ease his load.

Eisenhower was disappointed by the continuing refusal of the War Department to look more favorably on the operation he was struggling to patch together. He had been a creature of the U.S. Army all his adult life and now felt uncomfortably cut loose from it. General Handy arrived in London from Washington to review Torch plans for the War Department's Operations Division and concluded that, despite Eisenhower's efforts and his pleas for more ships, landing craft, and equipment, many of the resources already earmarked for Torch could better be employed elsewhere in America's war effort.

Eisenhower's relations with the British were also sometimes troubling. They liked him personally but felt anxious about an inexperienced general being in charge of an important undertaking in which British forces were to participate and whose outcome might influence the character of the Allied military alliance. Eisenhower reacted angrily when they tried to bypass his central command of the operation. After Generals Alexander and Montgomery had been assigned and then quickly withdrawn from Torch and sent to the Middle East, General Kenneth Anderson was named to command the British First Army. It was to land at Algiers after the city had been taken and then race into Tunisia before the Germans got there. Anderson was instructed by the War Office that though Eisenhower was his commander, he could appeal to the British High Command before obeying any order from him that he believed might imperil British forces. Eisenhower was having none of that. He did not intend to have anyone serving under him authorized to treat him as if he did not exist. He conceded that it was right for Anderson to be authorized to make such an appeal, but only after informing him and stating his reasons. The British grudgingly acquiesced.

"I live a hectic day by day existence that leaves me thankful that I'm tough," Eisenhower wrote to his brother Earl. Only his closest confidants and aides knew that his stomach was frequently as tight as a knot and that he was often "impatient, tired and nervous." He was losing weight and the neuritis in his shoulder kept troubling him. He missed Mamie and having at least the framework of a homelife to fall back upon at the end of each long, exhausting day.

How intimate his relations with Kay Summersby, his driver, became may never be known. She was a thirty-one-year-old Anglicized Irish woman, a volunteer in the British Motor Transport Corps. Eisenhower had from the start found her both a competent chauffeur and an agreeable companion. But he was not a philanderer by nature. From his letters, both to Mamie and to others, it was apparent that he loved and missed his wife. He worried about her being lonely back in Washington. When he received a message from a friend quoting her as saying all was well, he anxiously wrote his son asking if that meant something had previously not been well.

But there is no doubt that he found the presence of his attractive driver a comfort during this trying period and that they shared a close relationship. Other members of his unofficial family in London, and the generals with whom he conferred or socialized, were aware that he and Kay grew to be far closer than a general and a very junior member of his personal staff normally were. A correspondent thought it unusual when he saw the general plant a kiss on the face of his driver. A friend of Kay noted later that "she took his mind off the war." In a book she wrote long after the war, Kay said that she loved Eisenhower and intimated that their relationship went well past the friendship stage.

As Eisenhower went about molding Operation Torch, an American diplomat in French North Africa was actively pursuing a line of clandestine activity designed to make the job of the invading troops much easier. Robert Murphy, former counselor at the U.S. embassy in Vichy, was in Algiers as the State Department's representative, ostensibly overseeing implementation of a trade agreement. He had been assigned by Washington and by Roosevelt himself "to win over as many of the French military and political leaders as he could, to ensure there would be little or no resistance when the Allied landing occurred."

Murphy had been dealing for months with a group French officers and civilian dissidents in Algeria and Morocco who intended to launch a pro-Allied coup to coincide with the invasion. They hoped to establish a new regime in French North Africa, to be headed by sixty-three-year-old General Henri Giraud, who had been captured by the Germans early in the war. Giraud had escaped from a German fortress prison and had since been living in Vichy France. In contrast to the Vichy leadership, he was known to be staunchly anti-German. It was hoped he would be able to provide the French with the spirit, pride, and moral underpinning of which they had been deprived by the rapid collapse of their army in the war and the emergence of the fascist Vichy regime. Giraud's pro-Allied conspiratorial confederates in Algiers assured Murphy that he would be warmly received as their leader not only by the French in Algiers, Morocco, and Tunisia but also afterward, when the Allied liberation of mainland France finally was launched.

Visiting London in September, Murphy suggested to Eisenhower that the pro-Allied conspiracy in North Africa was so far advanced that the prospects were excellent that the invading troops would meet little resistance. Murphy was by then steeped in the byzantine machinations of French politics into which Eisenhower would himself soon stumble. As he spelled out details of the various factions and interests involved, he observed that Eisenhower, who preferred things uncomplicated and straightforward, "listened with a kind of horrified intentness. . . . The general seemed to sense that this first campaign would present him with problems running the entire geopolitical gamut—as it certainly did." Instead of the clear run onto the beaches of French North Africa that Murphy suggested might be possible, he saw complications and confusions awaiting him. Nevertheless, he would welcome any effective assistance Giraud and his co-conspirators in North Africa could offer.

As the date for the invasion approached, Eisenhower's worries grew. He feared that there were still insufficient resources at his disposal, that his inexperienced troops would face strong French resistance, that the Spanish would let the Germans close the Strait of Gibraltar after the task forces had sailed into the Mediterranean, that German land-based aerial superiority in the region would inflict great punishment on the invading forces, that his first-ever combat command would be marked by disaster, and that the confidence Roosevelt, Churchill, and Marshall had in him would prove to have been totally unwarranted. It did his neuritis no good.

Neither did a visit he made to the west coast of Scotland, where men of the U.S. 1st Division were practicing amphibious landings under the cover of darkness immediately prior to their departure for North Africa. They simulated storming ashore, seizing coastal batteries of the kind they might be exposed to in North Africa, and establishing control in the coastal region. It was evident from the fumblings of the troops that they needed far more training. He feared they would be "sitting ducks if they don't sharpen up." In his diary, Butcher recorded that, "Ike felt pretty low on the return trip" and that it contributed to his "state of jitters."

In cabling a report on his visit to Marshall, Eisenhower, trying to conceal the extent of his concern, said the exercises he observed were "both encouraging and discouraging." He allowed that, "Most of [the troops] did not know exactly what was expected of them. . . . We are short on experience and trained leadership below battalion commander, and it is beyond the capacity of any Division Commander or any Colonel to cure these difficulties hurriedly."

Word Eisenhower received from the United States of preparations there for the task force that was to sail directly to Casablanca from Virginia did little to reassure him. Highly trained marines initially assigned to participate in the operation were reassigned to the Pacific, which was of greater interest to the War Department than this Mediterranean "sideshow," and replaced by newly recruited army troops. Though embarkation day for the transatlantic journey into combat on the North African shore was fast approaching, training exercises in Chesapeake Bay on the Maryland coast often ranged between farce and muddle. In one incident, troops storming an island in the bay after a difficult transfer from a troopship to landing craft were distracted from their assigned task by a refrigerated ice-cream wagon that was waiting for them on the shore. Training for the troops was to continue aboard ship en route across the Atlantic to the beaches they were to storm.

Problems also arose in the senior command for the Casablanca component of the operation. Eisenhower's old friend, the pugnacious General Patton, who was to command the Casablanca

Task Force, was being so obstreperous that senior U.S. Navy personnel with whom he and his staff had to work urged that he be replaced. Eisenhower remained loyal to Patton, whom he believed was one of the most forceful field commanders in the army, and the row blew over.

"As you can well imagine," he wrote Marshall shortly before the invasion convoys were launched, "there have been times during the past few weeks when it has been a trifle difficult to keep up, in front of everybody, a proper attitude of confidence and optimism." Nevertheless, he maintained that he was satisfied with how arrangements for the operation had been falling into place.

During the last week of October, the participating troop transports, warships, and supply vessels set sail from ports in Britain and from Virginia to form up in convoys for the voyage to their Algerian and Moroccan destinations. As Eisenhower prepared to leave London for the British Crown Colony of Gibraltar, where his forward command post for the operation had been established, he was staggered by a panicky message from Robert Murphy in the Algerian capital urging that the operation be delayed for two weeks to firm up French support and minimize resistance to the invaders—an impossibility, with the convoys already en route to their destinations. It did nothing to reassure the Torch commander that such support would actually be forthcoming.

On November 5, after being agonizingly delayed for two days by weather conditions, Eisenhower flew to Gibraltar from Hurn Airdrome near Bournemouth in southern England. It was a journey through fog and rain, wave-hopping so low because of the weather that the pilot of the Flying Fortress in which he traveled had to gain altitude to get into landing traffic at the end of the journey. The small airport at Gibraltar was so congested, and aerial crosscurrents were so strong, that Eisenhower's plane had to circle for an hour and a half before being able to touch down on the only small patch of ground in Western Europe still under Allied control. The Torch task forces were by then well under way and the hastily plotted invasion he commanded was a mere three days off.

By the time Montgomery arrived in Cairo in August 1942, his eccentricities were already legendary in the British Army's officer corps. The fifty-four-year-old general was said to be a bully and a tyrant, capable of penalizing or even dismissing an officer from his job for even minor transgressions, such as being a few minutes late for a conference.* But officers in dread of their new commander were quickly won over by his dynamism and by signs that under his command everything in the battle-weary Eighth Army was going to change for the better.

Montgomery's assumption of command of the army, like Eisenhower's designation as Operation Torch's commanding general, marked the major turning point in his career. His new assignment would soon put him and his ideas to the test in the crucible of combat and lift him from the public obscurity in

*Five decades later, while researching an account of the Dunkirk evacuation, I encountered the son of a man who had been commander of an elite British regiment in the war. An officer himself, he told me that until the day his father died he had despised Montgomery with a passion for the way he had treated officers of whom he disapproved.

which he had so far been confined. But his arrival in Cairo to take on his new job, and reap the glory that would come from it, was marked by a display of gratuitous boorishness.

Having had little time in London to consider how to deal with Rommel before flying out, he gave the matter careful thought on his flight to Egypt. Among the conclusions he reached was that the Eighth Army needed an armored corps that could be used as the vanguard for the offensive operation he intended to launch. On arriving he was pleased to learn that Major General John Harding, who had been a student of his at Staff College, was serving at General Headquarters in Cairo. He immediately contacted Harding and, without consulting Auchinleck, who was still Commander-in-Chief, Middle East, he asked him to draw up a report on how such an armored corps might be formed. It might perhaps be based around the 300 Sherman tanks being shipped from America as a substantive gesture made by Roosevelt to Churchill when word had been received of the fall of Tobruk to the Germans.

Harding was embarrassed by Montgomery's approach. He was still under Auchinleck's command. Officially, Montgomery had not yet arrived, and he was not to assume command of the Eighth Army for another three days. Few people even knew that he was already in Cairo. Until Montgomery contacted him, Harding hadn't known either. But, as requested, within a few hours he presented Montgomery with a rough idea of how an armored corps could be patched together. It was like being back at Staff College, having to live up to the requirements of this stimulating, uncompromising tutor. Auchinleck was told nothing about it.

Early the next morning, Montgomery, still not officially in charge of the Eighth Army, drove out to the fringe of the desert to meet with General de Guingand, who had served under him briefly before, of whom he thought well, and who was now also serving on Auchinleck's staff. Montgomery wanted a concise picture of the situation at the front. De Guingand told him that the Eighth Army defense line was holding but morale was low and a renewed attack by Rommel was expected.

Montgomery then proceeded to Eighth Army headquarters

to assess the situation there. Major General W. H. Ramsden, formerly commander of XXX Corps, had shortly before been appointed acting Army commander. Questioning Ramsden, Montgomery held to an the opinion he had earlier formed that he was not worthy of so senior a position. Accordingly, he announced he was taking immediate command of the Eighth Army, though he had no authority yet to do so, and ordered Ramsden to resume his earlier role at XXX Corps. It was likely to happen in two days anyway, so Ramsden sheepishly departed.

Montgomery then informed Auchinleck's headquarters in Cairo that he had replaced him. It was an act of conspicuous insolence, treating the man who was still Middle East commander as if he didn't matter, even though for Montgomery to wait a few days while he continued to explore the situation would have made no difference.

When he had served under Auchinleck in England the previous year, he had concluded that this distinguished and otherwise respected officer was incompetent. But whatever Montgomery thought of him, there was no excuse for treating him with such undisguised scorn. Realizing he could only humiliate himself further by objecting, Auchinleck chose to back quietly out and continued his preparations to depart from Cairo. Montgomery was impishly delighted to be "issuing orders to an Army which someone else reckoned he commanded!"

He later maintained that it had been essential for him to move quickly and decisively to restore the Eighth Army's fighting spirit and confidence. He also said he had to act because Auchinleck had made plans to give further ground to the enemy, imperiling the British position in the Middle East. That was not true. The enemy forces in the desert were by now far inferior in manpower and equipment to those of the British. The Eighth Army was not yet ready to go on the offensive but Auchinleck's preparations, both to repel the assault Rommel was known to be preparing and then to have the Eighth Army go on the attack, were well in hand. His plans included the possibility of tactical withdrawal but that was because they covered all contingencies, however remote.

Montgomery later maintained that, as far as he knew, Auchinleck had no plans for offensive action against Rommel. It may be true that he had no knowledge of them, but only because he dismissed his predecessor's plans and ideas as worthless without examining them. He had never believed that any plan handed on to him by a predecessor was of any value. He could not accept that anyone could teach him anything about the laws of combat. He refused to be briefed on what Auchinleck had been planning. No one could tell him how to fight a battle, and certainly not a man who was being relieved because he had been deemed inadequate.

De Guingand later revealed that when he first met with Montgomery in Egypt and mentioned existing plans, Montgomery's response had been, "Burn the lot. From now onwards there is only one plan: the troops will be ordered to stay where they are, fight where they are and, if necessary, die where they are." De Guingand said, "To the best of my knowledge he never examined any plans or appreciations that existed at the time."

Whatever criticism could be made of Montgomery's treatment of Auchinleck, the vigor with which he set about revitalizing an army that was in need of fresh leadership could not be doubted. Changes that Auchinleck had prescribed for the Eighth Army were still in the process of being instituted. The troops had been told about changes before, had found them wanting, and were yet to be convinced Auchinleck's ones would be different. Many had been in North Africa for as long as two years, had chased back and forth across the desert, and had begun to feel that theirs was a neglected army, of little interest to the brass hats in London. They had been demoralized by the desert, the heat, and the realization that their equipment was often inferior to that of the enemy. Sluggishness and cynicism were rampant. Montgomery considered dealing with that his immediate challenge.

Taking charge, he proceeded with a personal assessment of the line. Having conferred and dispatched Ramsden back to the command of XXX Corps on the Eighth Army's northern flank, he went on to headquarters of XIII Corps, guarding the southern flank, to meet and confer with its acting commanding general, New Zealander Sir Bernard Freyberg, whom he found to be more to his liking.

Returning to his own headquarters, he met with his staff to make certain its members understood him and his way of doing things. "You do not know me," he told them. "I do not know you. But we have got to work together; therefore we must understand each other and we must have confidence in each other." He went on to say that he did not like the general atmosphere he had found in the Eighth Army, an absence of confidence, a readiness to retreat. "Here we will stand and fight," he said. "There will be no further withdrawal. . . . If we can't stay here alive, then let us stay here dead. . . . [But] the great point to remember is that we are going to finish with this chap Rommel once and for all. . . . We will hit him a crack and finish with him."

We all felt [De Guingand said] that a cool and refreshing breeze had come to relieve the oppressive and stagnant atmosphere. The effect of the address was electric—it was terrific! And we all went to bed that night with a new hope in our hearts, and a great confidence in the future of our Army.

Montgomery did not tolerate lazy adherence to past procedures. A new atmosphere of activity and purpose was created. It included his distinctive, personal way of doing things.

He followed the same routine day in and day out [one of his staff officers later recalled]. He would wake a little before seven each morning, listen to the news on the radio, have a cup of tea in bed, then lie awake for possibly an hour thinking over his plans for the day. This was the period when most of his plans were thought out. He would also make his personal plans for the day, whom he wished to see, where he would drive to on the front, and so on. He would get dressed and be finished with his breakfast by eight o'clock. Between then and nine he would, as he said, finish his work for the day. He would issue a few orders to his ADC, have the duty

officer send out a few signals after reading through the latest
situation report, then send for a liaison officer . . . and outline
where he wanted the L.O. to go that day and what information he wished him to secure covering the day's operations.
Having completed this, Monty would then get into his waiting car, to go motoring all over the front. . . . He would
never permit himself to be tied down with papers nor allow
his daily tour to be given up for office work.

That was something of an exaggeration. The pressure of
events often tied him down far longer with "office work," and
during actual combat he was in regular communication with
his staff and corps commanders. But he was able to maintain
his preferred work habits and work schedule under the most
extraordinary circumstances.

The first morning of his command in Egypt, he bawled out
the young officer who woke him after dawn with a situation
report of the kind Auchinleck had received at that time each
day. He blisteringly told him that he did not want to know
about routine patrol actions and other comparative trivia at that
or any other time. It did not interest him. If anything was going
wrong, his chief of staff would tell him. Otherwise he would
assume everything was as it should be. He would devote himself to the essentials of battle planning. His staff would deal
with everything else. His views on what should and should not
be brought to his attention, and when, were unequivocal.

The wise commander [he wrote] will see very few papers or
letters; he will refuse to sit up late at night conducting the
business of his army; he will be well advised to withdraw to
his tent or caravan after dinner at night and have time for
quiet thought and reflection. It is vital that he should keep
mentally fresh.

Despite his dynamism in dealing with problems, Montgomery generally operated in an atmosphere of incongruous seren-
ity. There was little bustle at Eighth Army headquarters, no
whizzing about of officers and couriers, no raising of voices.

Hubbub was taboo. A monastic calm was maintained, and any officer who violated it was certain soon to change his ways or be sent packing.

Their new commander was at first a mystery to Montgomery's desert troops. He wanted them not to think of him as a remote figure little troubled by their concerns. He was prepared to play the showman. Indeed, he relished the role. Soon after arriving in the desert, he adopted the dashing bush hat of his Australian troops so that the men would easily recognize him on his desert visits and know that he was among them. But he soon realized that the big hat looked silly atop his small face and replaced it with the smaller, dramatic-looking black beret of his armored troops. He liked the dashing image the beret lent him. Though some other generals thought it pretentious, it remained his trademark for the rest of the war.

This small, skinny, fox-faced, squeaky-voiced general went among the troops like no general ever had before, telling them personally that everything was going to be different. And this time it seemed to be different already. Suddenly there was a tremendous amount of activity among them. Regimental, battalion, and company officers, who had been afflicted by the same desert torpor as their men, were suddenly scooting all over the place (though not at Eighth Army headquarters, where calm remained the keynote). Everyone seemed inspired by Montgomery with a new sense of purpose, direction, and importance. His intelligence officer, Brigadier Edgar Williams, said, "One was impressed by his sheer competence, his economy, his clarity, above all by his decisiveness."

At his insistence, newly arrived reinforcements were sent forward at once, as were new tanks and guns. Programs of intensified training were introduced, even for the most seasoned of the troops. The excessively large contingent of officers leading comfortable lives back at headquarters in Cairo—the "Gaberdine swine," the desert troops called them—was sharply thinned. Rumors of a shake-up in the upper echelons of the Eighth Army proved accurate. Montgomery soon began shedding officers he deemed inadequate. One man was "quite useless." Another was "a menace."

Eisenhower would later stress that it was important for a commander to cut out the deadwood among his senior officers, no matter how painful it might be to get rid of old friends. Montgomery suffered no such anguish. He had few old friends, or new friends for that matter, and would never permit an officer he thought incompetent to become even an acquaintance. He was trimming what he considered deadwood for the purpose of combat efficiency, but he was also genuinely unconcerned about whose feelings might be hurt. And he refused to tolerate "bellyaching."

> By this [he later wrote] I meant that type of indiscipline which arises when commanders are active in putting forward unsound reasons for not doing what they are told to do. In the Eighth Army orders had generally been queried by subordinates right down the line; each thought he knew better than his superiors and often it needed firm action to get things done. I was determined to stop this state of affairs at once. Orders no longer formed "the base for discussion," but for action.

To prove that he meant what he said about not even contemplating a possible withdrawal in the face of a German offensive, he ordered that most transport be sent to the rear. Ammunition and other supplies were to be stored at forward areas. All concerned, officers and troops, had to know there would be no giving ground to the enemy; if Egypt and the Middle East needed defending, it would be at the front, not back at the delta or the cities to the rear. But he made it clear that he was determined that they would in any case not need defending because the Eighth Army would be going on the attack after absorbing the attack Rommel was brewing. It was the fearsome German hero who would soon have to worry about retreating.

> [T]here had grown up a Rommel myth [General Horrocks said]. He was regarded by our troops as sort of a ubiquitous and invincible figure. Nobody realized better than Monty that almost the first and most important thing which he had

to do was to replace this feeling with a Montgomery fable. And this he set about doing in characteristic fashion. Very soon the soldiers were discussing this strange, new commander who wore curious hats and, while buzzing about all over the place, constantly stopped and spoke to them. What was even more surprising, he seemed to know what he was talking about. Apart from his immediate staff, the Monty impact started from the bottom upwards; the troops accepted him long before he became, as he ultimately did, popular with their officers.

Everything about Montgomery was different. He developed a unique, highly efficient, highly personal intelligence network. Instead of relying exclusively on conventional military-intelligence procedures, he formed a team of special liaison officers, captains and majors in their twenties and early thirties who served as his eyes and ears. They circulated in his command, keeping him closely informed about what was happening within it far more accurately than normal signals could. That would prove to be of particular importance during battle, when confusion was rampant.

Those liaison officers were intelligent, articulate, and courageous young men. In the course of the war, they saw much fighting and some were killed. Montgomery selected each one personally and called them his "gallant band of knights." He enjoyed their company enormously, far more than he did anyone else's, certainly more than he did the company of his contemporaries. One of his young officers later wrote admiringly of his "gift of listening without interruption to subordinate and very junior officers." His knights held Montgomery in great esteem.

Each morning he would assign them their tasks, sometimes dangerous ones. They would report back each evening, unless their assignments required more time to complete. Sometimes it would be only a matter of confirming the positions and apparent strengths of particular units on the line. Sometimes it was to discover why, as Montgomery put it, certain troops "aren't fighting properly," for which he invariably held their officers responsible.

Under that penetrating gaze [one of this liaison officers later wrote] one learnt to say what one had to, neither more nor less, and never to waffle nor flannel. . . . Quite quickly he imbued in me the confidence necessary to do the job more or less properly—he was par excellence a teacher—and I was greatly helped by increasingly frequent invitations to dine in his mess where, emboldened by the copious draughts of wine always available [though Montgomery did not drink], I suppose I acquired something of the status of one of his licensed jesters.

Montgomery's band of elite young liaison officers were the only ones whose teasing and playfulness he tolerated, and not always only in the mess. Indeed, it was one of his great pleasures. Churchill, who later observed their operations while present during Montgomery's crossing of the Rhine, was much impressed by them and by the dangers to which they were exposed.

For nearly two hours [the prime minister wrote] a succession of young officers, of about the rank of major, presented themselves [to Montgomery]. Each had come back from a different sector of the front. They were the direct personal representatives of the Commander-in-Chief, and could go anywhere and see anything and ask any questions they liked of any commander, whether at the divisional headquarters or with the forward troops. As in turn they made their reports and were searchingly questioned by their chief the whole story of the day's battle was unfolded. This gave Monty a complete account of what had happened by highly competent men whom he knew well and whose eyes he trusted. It afforded an invaluable cross-check to the reports from all the various headquarters and from the commanders, all of which had already been sifted and weighed by General De Guingand, his Chief of Staff, and were known to Montgomery. By this process he was able to form a more vivid, direct, and sometimes more accurate picture. The officers ran great risks, and of the seven or eight to whom I listened on this and succeeding nights two were killed in the next few weeks.

Inevitably, suggestions have been made that Montgomery's uncommonly close relations with his young liaison officers, and with some young boys later in his life, was a sign of repressed homosexuality. There is no evidence that this was true. When he became a member of the House of Lords, he angrily opposed reducing legal restrictions on homosexual acts between adults and called homosexuality "the most abominable bestiality that any human being can take part in." The relation between him and his young liaison officers was as between a Boy Scout leader and his small clique of favorite scouts.

A Swiss boy he later befriended, showering him with affectionate letters and visits in a way that might raise eyebrows, said those with whom he established such intimacy "had to . . . admire him without fail, but before the age when they start to question things and develop their own opinions. When this happened, they were gently phased out and eventually replaced."

Alexander had taken over from Auchinleck as Commander-in-Chief, Middle East, though unlike Montgomery not before the appointed time. And unlike his newly acquired, strong-willed subordinate, Alexander was the very model of a British gentleman, urbane, unruffled, and at peace with himself and with other generals. He assured Montgomery that he would have his full support. He required only that the task to which the Eighth Army commander had been assigned—leading the troops to victory over Rommel—be carried out. During the entire campaign in the deserts of Egypt and Libya, Alexander strove to see that Montgomery's wishes were complied with.

De Guingand was often in attendance when Alexander called on Montgomery in the desert before the battle of Alamein. "Monty," he later recalled, "would rattle out his requests—

troops, commanders, equipment, whatever it might be. His Commander-in-Chief took short notes, and with the greatest rapidity these requirements became accomplished facts."

For Montgomery, it was an ideal relationship. He later said, "I couldn't have had a better C-in-C Middle East, because he only gave me one order: 'You go into the desert and beat Rommel,' and then he left me completely alone. He was nice, I was not nice, I was nasty." Montgomery would have bridled (and later did) at having to serve under a man who presumed to think he knew better than he did about preparing for and engaging in combat, or who interfered in any way with his army. He considered Alexander "a grand chap." But of the man he had once urged be put in command of the British last stand at Dunkirk, he said, "his great asset is his charm, and if he lost that he would go right under as he does not really know much about the business."

Taking command, Montgomery proceeded along the lines he had long espoused. He meticulously defined the limits of his objective, carefully examined the resources at his disposal and those believed to be at the disposal of the enemy, and drew up his plans. That done, he instructed his staff to implement them, filling in the details.*

Montgomery insisted on better liaison with the Royal Air Force than had previously existed. Senior RAF officers on the spot claimed that the efficiency of the air arm depended on it being maintained as an independent branch. Montgomery did not object but wanted the RAF and the Eighth Army to work more closely together. He moved Eighth Army headquarters to Burg el Arab, near the sea, to be near the RAF command. When Auchinleck had taken direct command of the Eighth Army while remaining Commander-in-Chief, Middle East, he had located his forward headquarters in the desert to be near the front line. Montgomery thought that was a silly gesture. Combat commanders needed to think and not be troubled by any problems that might result from being too close to the enemy.

---

*Montgomery's advice to his students had been, "Get yourself a first class Chief of Staff, work him and keep him until he goes mad—then get another one."

Offended by even the appearance of disorder, Montgomery had been dismayed by his first sight of the army's desert headquarters. Officers and men slept on the sand at night. Flies were everywhere. Staff work appeared to him to be haphazard. All that was made to change. Proper quarters were set up in a neatly arranged tent community. Army clerks living in comfort in Cairo were called forward with their typewriters to facilitate forward staff work.

Aside from their superiority in numbers, equipment, air power, and fuel supply, the British had a unique advantage in the imminent clash between Montgomery and Rommel. Through Ultra, the remarkably successful system that had been devised for intercepting German military communications, Eighth Army headquarters was fed a stream of intelligence data on the enemy's plan of attack, including the date it would be launched.

Though pleased to know so much about what Rommel was up to, Montgomery was not completely happy about the Ultra arrangement. He did not like the fact that Churchill also had access to the information it provided, and therefore was in a position to believe he could advise him on how to fight his battles. Nevertheless, because of Ultra intercepts, he knew when and how, prodded by the fantasies of Hitler and Mussolini, Rommel, with inferior firepower, was planning the offensive designed to break through the British line and take Alexandria before advancing on Cairo and the Suez Canal.

As with most of Montgomery's operations, the defense he prepared had a textbook simplicity. Rommel would be blocked from making a frontal assault—which wasn't the German commander's style or intention anyway—by a strong line held by the Eighth Army's Australian, South African, Indian, and New Zealand divisions. He would attempt to break through by means of a wide inland sweep to cut off those divisions but would be foiled by running into the armor Montgomery would position along a desert ridge to block his way. Strongly supported by the RAF, the Eighth Army would fight a static battle, letting the Panzer Army batter itself into defeat. "As a commander in battle," one of his officers said, "[Montgomery] had an uncanny knack of reducing a problem to its simplest proportions, of concentrating on the essentials and cutting out the frills and furbelows."

Under other circumstances, the adroit Rommel might have offered him a greater challenge. But the German commander's poor health undoubtedly colored his handling of the situation. His doctor diagnosed chronic stomach problems, intestinal catarrh, nasal diphtheria, and circulation trouble. He was also suffering a bout of severe depression. His senior subordinates were greatly worried about him, so much so that his chief of staff, Lieutenant General Alfred Gause, advised Berlin that he was "not in a fit condition to command the forthcoming offensive."

Of even greater significance, Rommel's weak supply situation was turning critical. Hounded by the RAF and the Royal Navy, few of the ships meant to supply him from across the Mediterranean were getting through. As Montgomery knew through the Ultra intercepts, and could plan accordingly, a sustained advance by his panzers depended on his quickly capturing British oil stores.

Montgomery's preparations for his first encounter with the enemy were masterful. "The whole plan for the battle was thoroughly explained to us," said General Howard Kippenberger, commanding the 5th New Zealand Brigade, "and I liked it more than that for any action I had taken part in. More pleasing even than the plan itself was the ready, balanced feeling we all had; and that feeling undoubtedly came down from Army Headquarters. . . . All our preparatory moves were made unhurriedly and in plenty of time, and we were completely ready when the blow fell."

Rommel launched his attack just after midnight on August 31, 1942. In mounting his expected inland sweep around the British line, his forces drove into minefields far deeper and more intricate than he had expected and sustained heavy casualties. Among them were two of his key officers—General Walter Nehring, commander of the Afrika Korps, who was wounded, and General Georg von Bismarck, commander of the 21st Panzer Division, who was killed.

The Axis troops were still struggling through the minefields at daylight when the RAF began subjecting them to heavy bombing and strafing. When they continued to push forward despite their losses, they ran into the newly arrived 44th Division, dug in with four hundred tanks and a bevy of antitank guns to retain control of Alam Halfa ridge, which blocked Rommel from achieving his encircling maneuver. With barely enough fuel to keep his own tanks in action another day, the German commander called off his attack and withdrew.

In disorderly retreat, his forces were vulnerable. The bulk of them were exposed to capture or destruction. Montgomery could have closed a trap around most of them and gone in pursuit of those who evaded that encirclement. But such a follow-up didn't fit into his calculations. It was contrary to his principles of combat to undertake an operation that was not planned and prepared. To do so would allow for the possibility of defeat. Rommel was known for his surprises, especially for provoking a tank assault, drawing his own panzers back behind a screen of antitank guns, using them to dispose of the attacking armor, and then, his position considerably strengthened in comparison, going on the offensive himself. Montgomery knew his own resources were far greater than those at Rommel's disposal. He felt he could afford to bide his time.

Auchinleck probably would also have won at Alam Halfa. Indeed, his staff had predicted that Rommel's attack would be made very much along the lines that it was. But the new Eighth Army commander, fresh to combat in contrast to his weary predecessor, exercised more tightly calculated control of the battle than British forces in the desert had previously enjoyed. All his responsible officers knew exactly what their troops were supposed to do. Every aspect of the battle fell into place precisely as he had foretold and planned for. Rommel was permitted to execute none of his customary surprises. The German commander later admitted that he had "placed particular reliance on the slow reaction of the British command, for experience had shown us that it always took them some time to reach decisions and put them into effect."

Though not conclusive, the British victory in repelling Rommel's assault at Alam Halfa and administering an unqualified beating to the Axis forces was an enormous morale booster for the Eighth Army. Montgomery had told his troops the enemy would be battered, humbled, and driven back, and it had happened.

Affection for the general surged through the ranks. He continued his regular visits to the troops to explain to them what had happened and to tell them of the major offensive he was planning that would destroy Rommel and the Afrika Korps. They cheered him wherever he went.

Churchill was delighted with the news from the desert. It appeared to him that he finally had a general who was able to cut Rommel down to size. As with Auchinleck, the prime minister wanted it done quickly. He pressed Alexander to order Montgomery to seize upon the moment and employ his superior forces to go over to the offensive without delay. It would take a heavy toll of German forces and would tie down others that might otherwise be committed to challenging Operation Torch when Eisenhower invaded French North Africa in a few weeks' time. Once that had taken place, what little remained of Rommel's army could be methodically annihilated. The Allies would command the Mediterranean's North African shore. The soft underbelly of Nazi-occupied Europe would be exposed.

Montgomery refused to be rushed. He told Alexander that the Eighth Army was not yet ready to launch a proper offensive. Like Auchinleck, he felt his troops needed more intensive training. Reinforcements and newly arrived equipment had to be integrated into the line. The American Sherman tanks that were being sent were still en route. He warned that if the offensive took place before he was ready, it would probably be repelled, but if it was launched when he decided it should be, total triumph would be assured.

There was another factor in his reluctance to be pushed. He did not want to mount an offensive that would merely force Rommel into the kind of tactical withdrawal the German commander had executed in the past. He wanted him to have time to build up positions so that he would stand and fight at the end of a long, vulnerable line of communications. In that way, the Germans could be decisively trounced rather than just driven back. The defensive line Rommel was constructing, stretching north-south from the desert to El Alamein on Egypt's Mediterranean shore, was just the place for that.

Montgomery had confidently planned the battle he wished to fight at Alamein even before the clash at Alam Halfa. When Churchill and Brooke had visited Egypt before that encounter he had confidently spelled it out for them.

> He knew [Brooke wrote in his diary] that Rommel was expected to attack by a certain date. He showed us the alternatives open to Rommel and the measures he was taking to meet those eventualities. He said he considered the first alternative the most likely one, namely, a penetration of his southern front with a turn northwards into the centre of his position. He explained how he would break up this attack with his artillery, and would reserve his armour to finish off the attack after the artillery had rough-handled it. His armour would then drive Rommel back to his present front and no further. He would then continue with his preparations for his own offensive which were already started. He would attack on the northern part of his front. It would mean hard fighting and would take him some seven days to break through, and he would then launch his Armoured Corps.

Both Churchill and Brooke had been impressed with and encouraged by Montgomery's complete command of the situation and high spirits. But now Churchill was as anxious for the Eighth Army commander to launch the Alamein offensive without further delay as he had been with Auchinleck. He told Brooke the delay "would result in Rommel fortifying a belt twenty miles deep by forty miles broad; that we should never get through owing to a series of Maginot defenses."

Not only did the prime minister consider himself as good a tactician as any of his generals, but his political problems at home were far from resolved. There was still much dissatisfaction in Parliament over his direction of the war effort. One of the leading figures in the wartime coalition government, the Labourite Sir Stafford Cripps, who was serving as Leader of the House of Commons, was threatening to resign over it. The prime minister urgently needed a desert victory to shore up his authority. One government minister observed, "The Prime Minister must win his battle in the desert or get out." And the Americans and Soviets were still to be convinced the British could fight and win.

Churchill continued to press for the desert offensive to be launched in September 1942. Montgomery would not be budged. He had been given a job to do. He knew how he wanted to do it and he would not risk defeat by being rushed, not even by the prime minister. He said if Churchill insisted on the attack taking place before he was ready, someone else would have to be found to do it. Alexander continued to back him up. Though an enraged Churchill might have replaced Montgomery with a general who would do what he wanted, the Eighth Army commander knew he had little to worry about. He realized his "stock was rather high" after his Alam Halfa victory.

He was right. Churchill had relieved both Wavell and Auchinleck, but he could no longer convincingly hold his generals responsible for shortcomings on the desert battlefield. He certainly could not fire the commander who could win a battle, the man who had been responsible for the greatest surge in home-front morale since the beginning of the war. Auchinleck had been replaced because he refused to launch his offensive against Rommel until September. Montgomery told Churchill he planned to wait till the end of October and there was nothing the prime minister could do about it.

CHAPTER 11
El Alamein

Despite being hounded by Churchill to delay no longer before going into battle against the most highly regarded field commander the war had yet produced and to emerge with the desert victory that had eluded his predecessors, Montgomery remained imperturbable. No relaxation was permitted in his officers' and men's preparations for the great offensive he was planning. But the Eighth Army commander continued to go to bed early each night and to sleep undisturbed in the caravan that had been made into eminently livable private quarters for him. A second caravan nearby served as his tactical headquarters.

He showed not the slightest sign of being under pressure. A photograph of Rommel he had affixed to the wall of his operations caravan testified to how little his notorious adversary frightened him. "Of course I knew nothing of the desert," he said after the war. "But that did not matter. What you have to know is war, and then it doesn't matter where it takes place, in deserts, in swamps, or anywhere."

That was a shameless oversimplification. The crucial fact was that the Eighth Army was so much stronger than Rommel's

Panzer Army that unless it was led to commit absurd blunders, it could not possibly be defeated. Montgomery had 164,000 men under his command compared to 100,000 for Rommel—50,000 German and 50,000 more poorly equipped and less highly motivated Italian. He had more than 1,300 tanks (including the newly arrived, formidable American Shermans) to field against the enemy's 500, of which about half were obsolete models. He had almost 2,300 field, antitank, and other guns; Rommel had some 1,300. He was supported by more than 500 attack aircraft; the Germans had 350. He was receiving intercepts of the enemy's communications. Rommel enjoyed no such luxury.

While Montgomery's forces were well-supplied, the Panzer Army's logistical situation was still precarious. One out of every three ships bringing it supplies and equipment across the Mediterranean was sunk by the RAF during the buildup to Montgomery's offensive. Not a single oil tanker got through. A report to Berlin on October 19, 1942, four days before battle was joined, said enough fuel was available for the panzers and other vehicles for only eleven days of normal operations in the desert and enough ammunition for only nine days of fighting. Food and water were also in short supply, and the level of incapacitating sickness among the troops was high and rising.

Nevertheless, it was not going to be a walkover for the British. Knowing Montgomery's offensive was inevitable after his failure to break through at Alam Halfa, Rommel had used the time allowed him after his withdrawal from the Alam Halfa clash to establish a line of deep, continuous defenses across the desert. It ran from the Qattara Depression in the south, a region impenetrable to tanks, to the sea just west of El Alamein. To win, the Eighth Army would have to cross an area that had been turned into a massive minefield—half a million mines had been planted—and only then be able to attempt to break through the enemy positions. Montgomery would have to outwit a man who had repeatedly demonstrated his skills at desert warfare.

Conventional tactics would have had Montgomery lunge at what appeared to be the weakest point in Rommel's line—on its southern flank—thrust through there, and then sweep north to the sea to cut off the main body of defenders. Montgomery sought to fool enemy intelligence into believing that was how he intended to proceed. His plan of deception included the construction of a facade of an army base opposite Rommel's positions in the south, complete with cardboard tanks and guns, five miles of fake railway tracks, and a dummy pipeline.

Guns, tanks, and vehicles were camouflaged everywhere along the line and, so as not to alert the enemy, slit trenches were dug for infantry well before the offensive was to be launched. Troops rehearsed the roles they were due to play once battle was joined, with a strong emphasis on night training.

Montgomery had at first contemplated launching simultaneous assaults on the southern and northern sectors of the line, but he later came to believe that this might present problems. Despite the Eighth Army's superior strength, he was not convinced his forces were yet well enough trained to succeed in so ambitious an undertaking. So while diversionary probes were to be made in the south to tie down the Axis forces deployed there, and to break through if resistance collapsed, the main attack would be in the north, where the infantry was to lead the assault, clearing paths in the minefields for the tanks to thunder through.

X Corps commander General Herbert Lumsden expressed doubts about the plan and particularly about the danger that his tanks would become stranded in the minefield. Some division commanders shared that concern. But Montgomery would not be deterred by such "bellyaching." He was convinced he had figured out the essentials of the forthcoming battle and that victory was certain. To rousing cheers, he personally conveyed that confidence to Eighth Army officers down to the rank of lieutenant colonel in conferences he addressed in the days before the attack was launched. The message he issued to his troops on the eve of the offensive also brimmed with certainty and purpose.

1. When I assumed command of the Eighth Army I said that the mandate was to destroy ROMMEL and his Army, and that it would be done as soon as we were ready.

2. We are ready NOW.

The battle which is now about to begin will be one of the decisive battles of history. It will be the turning point of the war. The eyes of the whole world will be on us, watching anxiously which way the battle will swing. We can give their answer at once. "It will swing our way."

3. We have first-class equipment; good tanks; good anti-tank guns; plenty of artillery and plenty of ammunition; and we are backed up by the finest air striking force in the world.

All that is necessary is that each one of us, every officer and man, should enter this battle with the determination to see it through—to fight and to kill—and finally, to win.

Montgomery's preparations were so thorough and so methodically concealed that October 23, 1942, "passed just like any other day on the Alamein front—until the evening." The assault was launched at 9:40 P.M. exactly on that day. More than a thousand guns shattered the silence of the Egyptian desert with one of the most massive artillery barrages in history (through which Montgomery claimed to have slept), targeting enemy artillery batteries beyond the minefields. The barrage lasted exactly fifteen minutes. An eerie five-minute pause followed, and then the guns opened up again, this time to take out forward enemy positions as sappers moved out to deal with the landmines, marking with white tape and lamps the lanes they cleared for infantry to surge through. The attacking troops were spared a more intensive artillery barrage in their assembly areas because, though the battle was only just being joined, German artillery units were already being ordered to conserve shells.

Montgomery's forces made very limited progress during the night. The problems presented by the minefields were not easily surmounted. To a greater extent than he had foreseen, the barrier of mines was absorbing the initial attack, as Rommel had intended it should. By daylight, British tanks were still caught making their way through the lanes the sappers had cleared. Traffic jams had built up behind them. German artillery, given definable targets, and recovering from both the ef-

fects of Montgomery's initial barrage and from damage done to
German communications by the RAF, began taking a heavy toll
of British troops and armor.

Just then, the Axis troops suffered an unexpected, severe
blow. Their defensive tactics had been devised by Rommel.
But though he sought to conceal outward signs of his physical
infirmities, they had increasingly been getting the better of him.
He had gone to Austria for treatment and rest in September,
leaving General Georg Stumme, one of his panzer experts, in
command.

On the morning of October 24, Stumme set off by open car
to examine the situation at the front personally. He did not
appreciate how far forward British patrols had advanced during
the night until his car ran into machine-gun fire. An officer
riding with him was killed instantly. The driver responded
reflexively, wheeled the vehicle quickly around, and bolted to
the rear, not stopping or slowing down until he had reached
the safety of the German forward command post again. There
he found that Stumme was missing. The general had apparently
fallen out of the car when he had swerved to avoid the gunfire.
His body was later found in the desert. He had been been
suffering from high blood pressure and had died of a heart
attack.

General Wilhelm Ritter von Thoma, another panzer veteran,
assumed command of the Axis forces. But the challenge he now
faced was beyond him. Hitler instructed Rommel to return to
North Africa forthwith. He arrived the following day, October
25. What he found was discouraging. His tank losses were very
heavy—almost half had been destroyed—and, unlike Montgomery, who had lost even more tanks, he could not afford the
luxury of keeping many in reserve.

The defense line he had established was holding. But there
was to be no immediate end to the British onslaught, leaving
even the reduced amount of armor still at his disposal of limited
value because enough fuel was available for only three more
days of fighting at most. Their tankers failing to run the British
gauntlet at sea, the Germans had been flying some fuel in from
Crete. But British bombers had stepped up their attacks on their

main landing field, virtually eliminating that option. Rommel's forces continued to come under heavy artillery bombardment and RAF attack. The German commander wrote to his wife, "The enemy's superiority is terrific and our resources are very small. Whether I would survive a defeat is in God's hands."

Meantime, Montgomery's X Corps was in trouble. It was sustaining heavy tank losses, and General Lumsden, its commander, said that to continue along the lines the battle had begun on was courting disaster. Montgomery disdainfully dismissed that warning. He later wrote, "The 10th Corps commander was not displaying the drive and determination so necessary when things begin to go wrong and there was a general lack of eagerness in the armoured divisions of the corps. . . . [D]etermined leadership was lacking." He summoned Lumsden and told him he had to drive his division commanders harder. If there was "any more hanging back," he warned, they would be replaced by "more energetic personalities."

Montgomery insisted, "Determined leadership [in battle] is vital; and nowhere is this more important than in the higher ranks."

> Other things being equal [he said] the battle will be a contest between opposing wills. Generals who become depressed when things are not going well, and who lack the drive to get things done, and the moral courage and resolution to see their plan through to the end, are useless in battle. They are, in fact, worse than useless—they are a menace—since any lack of moral courage, or any sign of wavering or hesitation, has very quick repercussions down below.

But it was unfair to accuse Lumsden, whom he would soon relieve of his command, and his tank commanders of lacking determined leadership. A slaughter was in progress and the break in the enemy line Montgomery had forecast did not appear in prospect. However, Montgomery would not permit a change in his plan. He had said that victories had often been needlessly forfeited because commanders had flinched when their forces were confronted with enemy resistance that would have been overcome had they persevered. He himself would not be shaken in his resolve. He insisted, "The tanks *will* go through."

But the battle was deteriorating into a high-casualty slugfest. By October 26, three days after the British offensive was launched, it appeared that it was being forced to a standstill and that the victory Montgomery had forecast might prove to be beyond him. Though unwilling (even long afterward) to admit that his original plan had not produced the desired results, he effectively conceded it hadn't by making important alterations to it.

He withdrew the 7th Armored Division from the fruitless feint to which it had been assigned in the south to concentrate his forces even more strongly in the north. But despite their weakening strength, Rommel's forces thwarted this new drive. Montgomery thereupon made even greater revisions in his attack plan. That required withdrawing the necessary forces from the line to regroup for a renewed offensive.

Days were passing with no sign of his promised breakthrough. London was concerned both by the Eighth Army's heavy casualties and by Montgomery's apparent failure to follow up what he had led the War Office to believe was his initial success. Indeed, he was withdrawing divisions from the line when it appeared from afar that they should be employed in consolidating the few advantages already achieved. And he was offering neither explanations nor much else in the way of hard information.

That did not mean he did not appreciate the seriousness of his situation. His initial plan had not succeeded, nor had the alteration he had made to it, nor the further alteration. It had taken almost four days to reach positions he had confidently predicted would be taken within the first few hours of his offensive. He was failing to make good his promises despite being given plenty of time to prepare and having vastly superior forces at his disposal, including the kind of aerial cover that would have had Auchinleck weeping with joy. The gloss was slipping from his reputation as an achiever. Questions were being asked about him back at Middle East Command head-quarters in Cairo, at the War Office in London, and at 10 Downing Street.

The prime minister feared Montgomery was repeating the experience of the British generals who had previously been sent against Rommel—a promising start, but ending either badly or inconclusively. Had his success at Alam Halfa been only a flash in the pan? Even Brooke, his friend, admirer, and advocate, appeared to be having doubts about him. As he indicated in his diary, the Chief of the Imperial General Staff did not take kindly to having to answer for him to Churchill.

What [Churchill asked him] was *my* Monty doing now, allowing the battle to peter out. (Monty was always my Monty when he was out of favour.) He had done nothing now for the last three days, and now he was withdrawing troops from the front. Why had he told us that he would be through in seven days if all he intended to do was fight a half-hearted battle? Had we not a single general who could even win one single battle?

At a meeting Churchill called of his chiefs of staff to discuss the situation, Brooke defended Montgomery, saying he was confident he was preparing to administer a powerful blow against Rommel. Nevertheless, he had doubts about what was transpiring in the desert and paced up and down in his office, suffering "from a desperate feeling of loneliness." He was afraid that he might have been wrong about his protégé, "and that Monty was beat." The alarming casualty reports from the desert aroused the perpetually lurking British fear of a slaughter of World War One dimensions.

Alexander's chief of staff, General R. L. McCreery, accompanied by Richard Casey, the British Minister of State for the Middle East, journeyed from Cairo to see Montgomery on the morning of October 29, six days into the offensive, to find out exactly what the situation was and why no greater progress was being made. Air Marshal Lord Tedder, RAF commander-in-chief in the Middle East, showed up too. He was upset because, despite expectations, the Eighth Army was not advancing fast enough to capture airfields the Royal Air Force badly wanted to use.

Montgomery resented those intrusions but concealed his irritation and exuded confidence. He insisted that he was adhering to his master plan. He was not—then or later—capable of admitting that he was doing what a good tactician was supposed to do: altering his plan significantly when it was not working out as intended. Historian Basil Liddell Hart has observed that his inability to concede as much "has tended to obscure and diminish the credit due him for his adaptability and versatility."

He would not countenance any suggestion that he was not in complete control of the situation at all times. Nor was he prepared to allow those he considered outsiders to insinuate themselves into his affairs any more than he was compelled to. He sought to convince his visitors that the situation was not as bad as some reports said and that it was about to improve dramatically. With so much already committed to the battle, they could only hope he was right.

But now his confidence proved well grounded. A new offensive operation against the enemy line begun on November 2 ran into trouble, costing the British another 200 tanks, but Rommel was virtually at the end of his capacity to resist. His Afrika Korps was down to thirty tanks while the British still had 600. Montgomery was finally able to make a significant dent in the Axis line by plunging into the center where he knew from Ultra intercepts that the defenses were weakest.

Rommel realized that further attempts to prevent a breakthrough would be futile and could result in the destruction of what remained of his army. In a letter to his wife, he groaned about "Air raid after air raid after air raid!" However, Hitler refused to sanction a withdrawal.

It is with trusting confidence in your leadership and the courage of the German-Italian troops under your command [he told Rommel] that the German people and I are following the heroic struggle in Egypt. In the situation in which you find yourself there can be no other thought but to stand fast, yield not a yard of ground and throw every gun and every man into the battle. . . . Your enemy, despite his superiority, must also be at the end of his strength. It would not be the first time in history that a strong will has triumphed over the bigger battalions. As to your troops, you can show them no other road than that to victory or death.

Hitler's bravado had no meaning in the Egyptian desert. Many of Rommel's troops sought an option other than the victory or death that Hitler had demanded of them and surrendered. Among those taken prisoner was General von Thoma, who had reverted to command of the decimated Afrika Korps.

Thoma was Montgomery's guest at dinner that night. Photographs in London newspapers of them together caused a row in the House of Commons, where parliamentarians asked why a British general was socializing with a Nazi.* As far as Montgomery was concerned, it was a professional matter—simply soldier-to-soldier. He wanted to talk about how the battle had been fought. Eisenhower thought of the war as a crusade against evil, but Montgomery, despite his Christian upbringing, was not greatly interested in such matters. His deity was the "Lord Mighty in Battle" who "will go forth with our armies and His special providence will assist our battle."

Churchill defused anger in the House of Commons over the Thoma affair by suggesting that socializing with Montgomery, who did not permit others to smoke in his presence, was addicted to giving lectures, and always went to bed early, was hardly a great pleasure. "Poor von Thoma," he said. "I too have dined with Montgomery."

On November 4, as Eisenhower waited impatiently in England for the clouds to clear so that he might fly to his Operation Torch advance command post at Gibraltar, Hitler finally was persuaded that Rommel had to be permitted to pull back in Egypt to prevent what was left of his forces from being totally wiped out. It was a historic moment. It set the seal on the British

---

*In contrast to Montgomery, toward the end of the war Eisenhower refused even to shake hands with a German general who had surrendered, declaring, "I won't shake hands with a Nazi."

Army's first major victory in the war, and one that was won against Germany's most highly regarded general.

From Cairo, Alexander reported to Churchill that the "Eighth Army has inflicted a severe defeat on the enemy's German and Italian forces under Rommel's command in Egypt. The enemy's front has broken, and British armoured formations in strength have passed through and are operating in the enemy's rear areas. Such portions of the enemy's forces as can get away are in full retreat." The British had paid dearly for their victory at Alamein. Their casualties had amounted to more than 13,000 killed and wounded and they had lost 600 tanks. But there was still more work to do. Montgomery told reporters at his desert headquarters, "I have defeated the enemy. I am now about to smack him."

The news of the desert victory was received with exaltation throughout Britain. People congratulated one another in the streets. Newspaper banner headlines told of "GREAT NEWS" from the desert, and even a newsreader on the normally no-nonsense BBC allowed himself to report "some cracking good news coming in." No one could doubt any longer that Hitler's threatened invasion of Britain was no more than one of the German dictator's pipe dreams and that his ultimate defeat was inevitable. All of Britain was ecstatic finally to have a general worthy of the nation's past military glory. Churchill cabled Alexander, congratulating him on the victory in the desert and praising his "brilliant lieutenant."

Hitler's permission for Rommel to pull back had come too late—or, rather, it might have. The Eighth Army needed to regroup and be resupplied. Its troops had to be rested. But Montgomery still had a powerful fighting machine at his disposal. It still had overwhelmingly superior aerial cover and had built up forward momentum.

In contrast, the Panzer Army had been shattered, had suffered far more damaging losses, and was in a state of confusion between standing fast and pulling back. It could have been overrun, finished off, or corralled by the Eighth Army over the next few days with comparatively little additional effort. It was at Montgomery's mercy. According to a message the British commander issued to his troops, he fully appreciated how strong his position was.

> The enemy has just reached the breaking point and he is trying to get his Army away. The Royal Air Force is taking heavy toll of his columns moving west on the main coast road. The enemy is in our power and he is just about to crack. I call on all troops to keep up the pressure and not relax for one moment. We have the chance of putting the whole Panzer Army in the bag and we will do so.

However, Montgomery chose not to seize that opportunity. As the outcome of the battle for Alamein became evident, some of Montgomery's senior subordinates urged that preparations be made for a concentrated follow-up. To their consternation, the idea was not given serious consideration. Major General Francis Tuker, commander of an Indian division, regretted that "there was no pursuit. Ponderously, crawling through those congested corridors [on the battlefield], heavy tanks and heavy infantry went forward with no burning sense of urgency."

From Montgomery's reluctance to follow up his Alam Halfa victory, Rommel had drawn conclusions of his own about the British commander. He was "quite satisfied that Montgomery would never take the risk of following up boldly and overrunning us, as he could have done without any danger to himself."

Montgomery would later maintain that no more vigorous follow-up was possible than the one that took place because of heavy rains that made the desert impassable for his tanks. But the rains did not begin until Montgomery had already permitted the Axis forces to begin their improbable escape and, in any case, also affected Rommel's forces. He suggested also that no extensive follow-up was possible because he had already exhausted most of his resources in the battle for Alamein. But that was not true. It was Rommel whose resources were virtually exhausted. His tanks were outnumbered twenty to one. He was down to thirty-five antitank guns and sixty-five field guns.

Intelligence intercepts had told of how badly the Axis forces had been pummeled and of the German commander's desperate but futile pleadings for reinforcements and supplies. However, Montgomery would not risk pouncing quickly forward to finish Rommel off. Hot pursuit would have been action too unstructured for his liking, too exposed to the unexpected. He had great respect for Rommel's legendary resourcefulness. When he was ready he would pursue the enemy, overtake him, and deal with him in a carefully calculated fashion. The man who was later to be dubbed Viscount Montgomery of Alamein was not willing to risk frittering away his triumph in the desert sands. As had happened after his Alam Halfa victory, nothing would induce him to engage in offensive action unless he was satisfied that he had sufficient resources and the conditions were absolutely right to rule out the risk of failure. One of his generals said, "We never went into battle unless we had enough of everything."

In this case, there was more than enough. The battered Panzer Army limped across the desert of northern Libya with the Eighth Army inexorably in pursuit, though not in a great hurry. It was a guardedly measured chase, with skirmishes and mostly minor clashes along the route, thirty-five miles west to El Daba, another thirty miles to Fuka, sixty miles farther to Mersa Matrûh, then another eighty miles to Sidi Barrâni. There Rommel, his armor and ranks further depleted, still managed effective rearguard delaying tactics as he withdrew still further toward Tunisia without being overly pressed.

Montgomery declined to delay capturing the prestige prize of Benghazi, which could easily have been bypassed by the British to be picked off later. Had he done so, he would have been able to close in more quickly on the fleeing enemy. He explained to his troops, "[W]e have intervals where we sit still and do nothing, and you may wonder why. The reason is that part of my military teaching is that I am not going to have out here in North Africa any failures." Rommel understood him perfectly.

"The British commander," he said, showed himself "to be over-cautious. He risked nothing in any way doubtful and bold solutions were completely foreign to him."

Montgomery displayed great flair. His army's advance across the desert took on the aura of a triumphal procession, celebrated in exultant communiqués and his boastful pronouncements to the press. But in his victory at Alamein, he had displayed perseverance in what had turned into a battle of attrition rather than tactical genius. Rommel said he showed "lack of resolute decision" in allowing his armored formations "to attack separately, instead of throwing in the 900 or so tanks, which [the British] could safely have committed on the northern front, in order to gain a quick decision with the minimum of effort and casualties." Montgomery won at Alamein because his much greater resources permitted him to keep feeding tanks and troops into the bloody fray while Rommel's forces were steadily worn down to near-exhaustion.

General Marshall considered the victory at Alamein to have been "blown up out of proportion to its importance," but he underrated its significance both strategically and symbolically. It signaled the imminent elimination of Axis control of the southern shore of the Mediterranean. And it provided the British people, the British government, and the British Ministry of Information, all of whom had been so attuned to disappointment and despair, with a desperately needed triumph and a soldier hero to idolize. The fact that Montgomery was eccentric and a showman made that even easier to do. Politically and socially prominent parliamentarian and historian Harold Nicolson said, "Never has there been such a careful creation of a legend."

On November 11, Montgomery was awarded formal recognition of his desert victory. He was knighted and promoted to full general. It was a moment of true glory for him. He had trounced the notorious Rommel. He had routed the mighty Afrika Korps. Yet he probably could have avoided the need for a battle at Alamein by seizing the opportunity to finish off Rommel after repelling his Alam Halfa assault. And his han-

dling of the battle was pointedly questioned by some of his
subordinate commanders.* But most of his officers and all of
his men were in awe of a general who still appeared among
them to tell them personally what was going on, who assured
them that he would guide them to victory, and who had demonstrated that he could do so. He was a soldier's general. They
had taken him to their hearts.

Harold Nicolson wrote in his diary, "There is a certain anxiety
in London regarding the boastfulness of Montgomery's com-
muniques." It was not quite the way British generals were
expected to behave. But Churchill was elated. Montgomery's
triumph over Rommel was his own as well. After Alamein, the
prime minister's critics in Parliament and the press were largely
silenced. Churchill was not completely accurate when he later
gushed, "Before Alamein we never had a victory; after Alamein
we never had a defeat." But it reflected the great sense of relief
and rejoicing in Britain generated by what had transpired in
the desert.

---

*He also aroused criticism with his instruction that the award of the Africa Star medal
be made only to men who had served in the Eighth Army after he had taken command
of it, thus denying it to some who had fought Rommel to a standstill under Auchinleck
before his arrival in Egypt.

CHAPTER 12
Torch Under Way

Eisenhower was unaware of the extent of Montgomery's victory at Alamein until he reached his command post at Gibraltar on November 5, three days before Operation Torch's landings on the coast of French North Africa were to be made. He was greatly encouraged by the news. He had already received intelligence reports that Rommel was pleading with the German general staff to save his Panzer Army from total annihilation. "Seems to be coming true," Butcher noted in the diary, "and the truer the better."

With Rommel routed, one of Eisenhower's main concerns appeared to be eliminated. The Germans having suffered so serious a defeat, it was virtually certain, regardless of the debt Franco owed Hitler, that Spain would not enter the war on the side of the Axis powers or permit the Germans to interfere with Torch's line of communications through the Strait of Gibraltar. Similarly, Vichy France's military commanders in Algeria and Morocco were likely to be impressed by the British triumph in the desert and inclined to offer at most token resistance to the Allied invaders.

The news from the desert went some way toward dispelling

the gloom in which Eisenhower now found himself operating. Gibraltar had small commercial and residential districts, an airfield, and a harbor. But it is little more than a rocky outcropping bulging out from Spain into the Mediterranean. The airfield was separated from Spanish territory, where German agents were known to be based despite Spain's neutrality, by nothing more than a barbed-wire fence. Eisenhower was to stay as a guest of the governor of Gibraltar in comfortable quarters at Government House, which had once been a convent. But offices had been prepared for him in dimly lit tunnels a quarter of a mile below the rocky surface, safe from possible air attack. Eisenhower later described it as "the most dismal setting we occupied during the war." One of his officers said at the time, "If I stay underground here much longer, I am going to grow hair on my back like a mole."

The eternal darkness of the tunnels [Eisenhower wrote] was here and there partially pierced by feeble electric bulbs. Damp, cold air in block-long passages was heavy with a stagnation that did not noticeably respond to the clattering efforts of electric fans. Through the arched ceilings came a constant drip, drip, drip of surface water that faithfully but drearily ticked off the seconds of the interminable, almost unendurable, wait which always occurs between completion of a military plan and the moment action begins.

Eisenhower proudly told correspondents, "Never in my wildest dreams in my West Point days did I think that I—an American general—would ever command the British fortress of Gibraltar." Churchill cabled him that he felt "the Rock of Gibraltar is safe in your hands." But whatever satisfaction the Torch commander derived from that trust was tempered by his persisting anxiety over the safety of the attack convoys crossing U-boat infested waters, as well as about the operation's overall chances of success. Nor was he comforted by the realization that so much fuel was stored in the Gibraltar tunnels that he and his staff could be consumed in an inferno if it was accidentally set ablaze.

As always, he sought to convey an impression of complete confidence and told only his closest intimates—in this case, Butcher—of his worries. So far there had been no reported losses among the Torch convoys heading to their North African destinations, though one of them sailing from Britain was reported being shadowed. There was no telling how extensive that shadowing might be or when a full-scale U-boat attack might be launched. Despite Montgomery's victory at Alamein, there was as yet no indication of how the French fleet based at Oran and Casablanca, or the French army in North Africa, would respond to the invasion. If they proved hostile, the invaders could find themselves in serious trouble.

To the extent possible without violating security requirements, conditions on the Moroccan coast had been closely monitored. It was believed that the usually turbulent Atlantic surf in the area could interfere seriously with the operation. Landing difficulties alone might require the full attention of General Patton, commander of the Casablanca Task Force, even if strong French resistance developed ashore. It might even prove necessary to divert that convoy to an alternative landing point with incalculable resulting confusion.

A residual Spanish threat also remained. While reluctant to tangle with the Allies, Spain might seize the opportunity to increase the size of its thin strip of Spanish Morocco by seizing some of the neighboring French Morocco, which was much larger. A clash between the French and Spanish would greatly complicate matters for the Allies.

Eisenhower had decided to send his deputy, General Clark, to Algiers as soon as possible after the beachheads had been secured to open Allied headquarters there and begin negotiating with the senior French officers in North Africa for the purpose of detaching them from their oaths of loyalty to Vichy and winning them over to the Allied side. He regretted that he himself would not be able to go until adequate communications facilities were established in the Algerian capital so that he could keep in touch with London and Washington. Maintaining such contact, he said, was "of vital importance . . . since it is entirely possible that a situation may arise demanding almost instant communication between this headquarters and Combined Chiefs of Staff." He was dismayed to find that "our radios constantly functioned poorly, sometimes not at all." Though he was the operation's commanding general, Eisenhower's old staff-officer mentality did not permit him yet to be completely confident in that role. In contrast to Montgomery, he dreaded the prospect of being out of touch with his superiors.

Since he could now only wait for news from the African shore, his principal preoccupations were trying to keep track of what was happening and working out how to best employ the services of General Giraud, who was understood ready to promote the Allied cause. The plan was to spirit Giraud out of Vichy France and transport him to Algeria, where his presence would galvanize support for the Torch invaders. Last-minute confusion arose as to the timing and method of getting the general out of France to perform the service required of him. But he was finally ferried by dinghy, submarine, and seaplane to Gibraltar, arriving there just hours before the landings were to be made across the Mediterranean.

Upon his arrival, Giraud was immediately summoned into conference with Eisenhower, to whom he declared himself ready to assume command of the entire Allied operation. Eisenhower was astonished but the French general was not being completely presumptuous. Through intermediaries he had been led to believe that since Torch was to take place on French territory in Africa, he would be put in charge of it. Reluctant to alienate this haughty figure, whose major achievement so far in the war was to have been captured by the enemy, the State Department's Robert Murphy had been reluctant to disabuse the intermediaries of that idea during negotiations over the previous weeks. But it wasn't at all what Eisenhower had in mind, nor what it what he had prepared for.

I wanted him to proceed to Africa [Eisenhower said] as soon as we could guarantee his safety, and there take over command of such French forces as would voluntarily rally to him. Above all things, we were anxious to have him on our side because of the constant fear at the back of our minds of becoming engaged in a prolonged and serious battle against Frenchmen, not only to our own sorrow and loss, but to the deteriment of our campaign against the German.

The most that Giraud would be offered was to be the senior French military and civil figure in North Africa while Allied Forces Headquarters, under Eisenhower's command, continued with its mission of clearing the enemy from the region. Not only did Eisenhower find Giraud's demand to take command of Torch unreasonable, but he had no authority to agree to it. He was himself subordinate to the Combined Chiefs of Staff. The idea that someone could step in and take overall charge of an intricate, carefully prepared assault within hours of it being launched was preposterous. However, Giraud would not be budged from his refusal to take orders about operations on French territory from a man whom he had expected to be his subordinate. To do so, he said, would besmirch his honor and the honor of France.

As ships of the huge attack armada positioned themselves off the landing beaches—remarkably, only one had been torpedoed en route—and as troops prepared to clamber from their transports down cargo nets into the landing craft that would carry them ashore, Eisenhower became locked in dispute with Giraud.

It was a new, unsettling experience for him. He had been persuaded that Giraud would prove to be an extremely useful instrument for the Allies in helping to turn Torch into a quick and painless success. His two political advisers—H. Freeman Matthews of the State Department and William Mack of the Foreign Office—believed Giraud could mean the difference between failure and success for Torch. They now suggested that Eisenhower put Giraud in nominal command of Torch while retaining actual control himself. But Eisenhower felt his honor, and that of the United States, were on the line too and he refused to agree to such a subterfuge.

Instead, this straight-talking Kansan found himself confronted by a stubborn old man of aristocratic bearing who insisted that his dignity was at stake and who spoke of himself grandiloquently in the third person. "General Giraud," he said, "cannot accept a subordinate position in this command; his countrymen would not understand and his honor as a soldier would be tarnished."

As H-hour approached, Eisenhower realized that the Allies would, for the moment at least, have to do without whatever support Giraud might be able to provide. Indeed, the French general announced that he would only "be a spectator in this affair." He was found quarters and retired to them. Eisenhower was left disgusted that the elaborate clandestine work that had gone into preparing a friendly welcome for his troops from the French when they went ashore in North Africa appeared to have been been a waste of time, effort and, hope. As he waited for word on how the landings were proceeding, he once again found sleep elusive.

Having been disappointed by Giraud, Eisenhower was fortunate not to receive detailed reports from his three invasion task forces during that night. The landing phase of the operation was laced with blunders, confusion, and misfortune. Despite the enormity of the operation and the rapidity with which Eisenhower had been required to organize it, everything had been meticulously planned, and the sea crossings had been remarkably uneventful. Troop commanders had been well briefed on their specific objectives and roles. But in the dark, some of the troop transports positioned themselves off the wrong beaches at some of the landing sites. Snarls and delays resulted. The inexperience of the landing-craft coxswains was greatly in evidence. Many of the landing craft broached to in rough surf and others were swamped. Troops found their movement much restricted by the sixty-pound-plus packs on their backs and some drowned because of them after being unloaded by error in water over their heads.

At Oran, a bid by two Royal Navy cutters carrying an American assault force to seize the harbor proved suicidal. It was subjected to fusillades from shore batteries and the guns of a French destroyer, fired point-blank. The first Allied airborne troop operation in the war, designed to seize airfields south of

Oran, proved a farce. Most of the thirty-nine troop-carrying C-47s involved lost their way en route from Cornwall. None reached their planned destination and only nine even reached Algeria. Where troops were landed on the wrong beaches, officers commandeered whatever vehicles they could find—in several cases they had been put ashore far from the men who were supposed to use them—and raced up and down trying to piece together their units before they could proceed with their missions ashore.

However, French resistance proved mostly minimal during the landings. The targeted beaches on both the Atlantic and Mediterranean shores were secured with far fewer casualties than had been anticipated—1,800 (including 500 dead) rather than the expected 18,000. More casualties resulted from accidents than from combat. By mid-morning of the first day of the operation it was apparent that despite the mishaps and confusions, the first major combined operation in the war had been successfully launched.

Patton saw luck or "the direct intervention of the Lord" as responsible. The compiler of a subsequent United States Navy analysis of the assault phase of Operation Torch also saw much for which to be thankful to Providence. He reported, "Secrecy in advance, and concealment, or evasion in movement succeeded beyond all justifiable hope. The weather was far more favorable than could possibly have been hoped for. Shore resistance . . . was much weaker and more disorganized than anyone had a right to expect. . . . Resistance at sea, particularly by enemy submarines, was weaker and slower in developing than could have been expected. . . . I must say seriously and emphatically that I do not believe that under identical conditions of organization and training, this feature of the operation could be repeated as successfully once in ten tries." In other words, Eisenhower had been immensely lucky in his first combat operation.

As news circulated that the operation had been launched and the landings had been successful, cheers rang out in cities and towns across America. In Britain, church bells were rung for the first time since the start of the war. The path to victory over

Hitler appeared to have finally been opened, and Eisenhower had begun his march to fame and acclaim, though it would prove long and troubled. At least the newspapers were no longer spelling his name wrong.

Ironically, the pro-Allied coup in Algiers that Robert Murphy had helped organize had also been a success that night, but not for long. By two o'clock in the morning, pro-Allied French conspirators had seized control of the city from the Vichy authorities. Of even greater significance, Admiral François Darlan was visiting Algiers at the time and had been placed under house arrest by the insurrectionists.

Darlan, one of the main French collaborators with the Germans, was commander-in-chief of Vichy France's armed forces. He had the authority to halt all resistance to the Allied invaders and even to bring French forces in Tunisia over to the Allied side before the Germans could take up positions there. Murphy, who had hurried to the villa in the outskirts of Algiers where Darlan was being held under house arrest by the conspirators, had pressed him to do so. However, because of the confusion in the landings, American troops had not yet reached the city and Murphy was unable to convince Darlan that an unstoppable American invasion of North Africa was really taking place. By the time the troops finally did arrive several hours later that morning, the pro-Vichy authorities in the Algerian capital had reasserted themselves, dispersed the insurrectionists, and freed Darlan. By then the admiral had realized that something important was taking place but he did not know exactly what and decided to weigh his options before making any commitment.

In the meantime, reports that the invasion forces were achieving most of their initial objectives had reached Gibraltar. Refreshed after a night's sleep, Giraud realized that he was in danger of being marginalized by developments and agreed to assist with Torch under the terms he had turned down the night before. Exasperating as the French general had been, Eisenhower decided it was better to have his belated support than none at all.

Though the beach landings had been successful, French North Africa was still far from being under Allied control. Algiers had been taken, later than expected but without difficulty. However, strong resistance had developed around Oran and Casablanca and no Allied troops had yet penetrated into Tunisia to the east, where the terrain and the proximity of German air bases on Sicily were likely to make things difficult. Anything that might assist the achievement of a speedy victory was to be welcomed. Having been led to believe that Giraud would quickly gain the loyalty of the French armed forces in North Africa, Eisenhower made arrangements for him to fly to Algeria the next day to get on with that task while Murphy in Algiers was still vainly trying to enlist Darlan's cooperation. It was the kind of double-dealing that Eisenhower found abominable.

I've promised Giraud to make him the big shot [Eisenhower told Bedell Smith in London] while I've got to use every kind of cajolery, bribe, threat and all else to get Darlan's active cooperation. All of these Frogs have a single thought— "ME." It isn't this operation that's wearing me down—it's the petty intrigue and the necessity of dealing with little, selfish, conceited worms that call themselves men. Oh well— by the time this thing is over I'll probably be as crooked as any of them. Giraud, in his first conference with me, even made a point of his rank. Can you beat it?

When Giraud arrived in Algiers on November 9, the day after the landings, he announced that he had assumed leadership in French North Africa. He directed the French forces to cease fighting the Allied invaders and to come to their assistance. To Eisenhower's renewed frustration, it had no effect whatever. The French military leaders in North Africa felt bound by the oaths of allegiance they had sworn to Marshal Philippe Pétain, the Vichy head of state. None was prepared to follow Giraud's lead. None was even willing to meet with him. Some made it plain that they considered him a traitor to France for collaborating with foreign invaders of French territory.

Instead of Eisenhower's problems with the French being resolved, a row was brewing that was to lead him into uncharted and murky areas beyond his experience. It would also distract

him at a crucial moment from his main role as commanding
general of the forces assigned the job of clearing the Axis powers from the southern rim of the Mediterranean.

With Oran and Casablanca still holding out against the Allied
invaders and Tunisia still to be taken, Robert Murphy in Algiers
was continuing to press Darlan to order French forces to cease
fire. He was having no success. The admiral claimed not to be
able to act without orders from Vichy, and such orders had not
been forthcoming. Darlan was also dismissive of Giraud, flatly
refusing to have anything to do with him. As planned, but now
with added incentive, Eisenhower dispatched General Clark
from Gibraltar to the Algerian capital on November 9, the same
day Giraud went there, to try to sort matters out.

For the next two days, Clark, brash and tough-talking, more
given to threats than persuasion, tried to swing Darlan and the
French generals over to the Allied cause. He too made little
headway. On November 11, in desperation, Eisenhower briefly
abandoned his Gibraltar command post and communications
hub to hop over to Algiers to try to resolve matters himself. He
arrived to find that Clark's efforts had just managed to get
Darlan to issue the requested ceasefire. In the process, Clark
had effectively recognized Darlan, the collaborator with the
enemy, as the titular leader of French North Africa and other
French overseas territories. Relieved to have a ceasefire, Eisenhower approved the arrangement, thereby taking full responsibility for it.

The row over what became known as the Darlan deal was
one of the most painful episodes in Eisenhower's career. He
had failed to recognize the full political dimensions of reaching
an agreement with a man who had been closely identified with
the Nazis. He felt that the matter had to be handled expeditiously and that if he had referred it back to Washington and
London, valuable time would be wasted at the cost of much
blood and bitterness and the loss of an opportunity to quickly
absorb French forces into the Allied operation. He believed he
was acting as a commanding general was right to act.

But outrage erupted in the United States and Britain as soon as word spread that a deal had been made with a man who, until recently, had been de facto leader of the quasi-fascist Vichy French rump state and who was still considered a protégé of Marshal Pétain, the prime Vichy collaborator with the Germans. For many officials in Washington and London, Eisenhower's willingness to come to terms with Darlan quickly overshadowed the fact that the first stage of Operation Torch had been successfully completed under his command. Algiers, and Oran and Casablanca as well by then, were in Allied hands. That probably meant all of Algeria and Morocco were too. In addition, the Germans had lost their chance to step up naval operations from bases in French West Africa, from where their menace to Allied Atlantic shipping might have been increased. Those bases probably would soon be closed to them altogether.

However, questions were asked about whether accepting Darlan as a partner in the struggle against fascist oppression was the shabby level to which the war had now deteriorated. Was it no longer a crusade for freedom and justice? Had it become just another squabble for power? If agreements could be reached with men like that, did that mean understandings would be reached with other despicable figures, perhaps even with Hitler? And why did the arrangements that had been made exclude Frenchmen who had been firmly committed to the Allied cause?

Howls of protest were sounded in Congress and in Parliament. U.S. Secretary of the Treasury Henry Morgenthau considered resigning from Roosevelt's cabinet because of Eisenhower's acceptance of Darlan. British Foreign Secretary Anthony Eden was furious. Churchill informed Roosevelt that the reaction in Britain was angry and bitter. He said he was convinced the arrangement with the admiral "can only be a temporary expedient justifiable solely by the stress of battle. We must not overlook the serious political injury which may be done to our cause." London newspapers called the Darlan deal "revolting" and "disgusting." Questions were asked about what authority Eisenhower had been given to make decisions of such consequence, and whether he was really qualified for the responsible position with which he had been entrusted.

Eisenhower was mortified by the reaction. Never before had he been publicly vilified and charged with incompetence. He was particularly dismayed by suggestions that he himself might be less than fully committed ideologically to the struggle against fascism. It wasn't true. He certainly considered the war to be more than merely a struggle between nations. He personally and passionately abominated the Nazis and the Japanese. He detested them for the grief and destruction they had unleashed upon the world and was horrified by their treatment of the people they subjugated. He wrote his brother Edgar, "I have developed such a violent hatred of the Axis and all that it stands for, I sincerely hope the drubbing we give them will keep that crowd from wanting another war for the next two hundred years."

He understood the concern he aroused by coming to terms with Darlan. Butcher noted that, "Darlan has been billed by propaganda and publicity for two years as a pro-Nazi, and for the public to swallow him as a patriotic and earnest Frenchman is a bit difficult." But Eisenhower could not comprehend the depth of fury that the deal with him provoked. Didn't people realize that war often meant that hard decisions had to be made? Hadn't Churchill, who despised Darlan, said it would be right to "kiss Darlan's stern" if that would win over the French fleet, anchored within the grasp of the Germans in Toulon harbor?

Eisenhower was seeking even more from him. He had embarked on a difficult and complex military enterprise. It was his job to complete it successfully as quickly as possible with as few casualties as possible. He believed the arrangement with Darlan undeniably served that purpose. He told Bedell Smith, "I am simply trying to get a complete and firm military grip on North Africa, which I was sent down here to do. . . . Once the population looks to us as their benefactors, I can tell all the turncoats and crooks to go to hell."

He explained to Washington and London that existing sentiment in French North Africa did not even remotely resemble prior calculations. He said the vision some might have had of the French military there rallying to the Allied cause once the Torch landings had succeeded was wide of the mark.

Foremost [he informed the Combined Chiefs of Staff] is the fact that the name of Marshal Pétain is something to conjure with here. Everyone from the highest to lowest attempts to create the impression that he lives and acts under the shadow of the Marshal's figure. The civil governors, military leaders and naval commanders will agree on only one man as having an obvious right to assume the Marshal's mantle in North Africa. That man is Darlan.

Eisenhower warned that if the Darlan deal was repudiated, hope of securing organized cooperation from the French would be lost at great cost to the Allies in additional troops who would be needed to mount a military occupation of the region. It would also lead to stagnation in operations. He said French armed forces would resist the Allies passively and, in some places, actively, and that hopes of gaining quick control in Tunisia as well as of the French fleet in Toulon would be lost.

Despite believing that Eisenhower had mismanaged a delicate situation, Roosevelt and Churchill came to his aid. Fearing that his position, and therefore that of the Allies, was being undermined by the uproar, they publicly approved the Darlan deal, stressing that it was a temporary arrangement. Roosevelt told a news conference that the agreement with Darlan was a necessary expedient and implied that Darlan, a useful encumbrance, would be shed as soon as circumstances permitted. Darlan complained that he felt like a lemon who would be cast aside when he had been squeezed dry.

The furor refused to die down, and not only over Eisenhower's accepting Darlan as an ally. Correspondents reported that Nazi-like Vichy laws and regulations, notably those discriminating against Jews, remained on the books in French North Africa and continued to be enforced. Eisenhower was persuaded by Robert Murphy that to rescind anti-Semitic legislation introduced by the Vichy regime would enrage the eleven million Muslims in French North Africa. He wrote Mamie, "Many things done here that look queer are just to keep the Arabs from blazing up in revolt." He was advised also that for local political reasons, release was being delayed for several thousand imprisoned European refugees who had sought safety from the Nazis in North Africa "until the military situation was further advanced."

American and British correspondents were astonished to find that a pro-Nazi French militia was still intact and continued to harass pro-Allied French figures in North Africa. Pro-Vichy censors were still censoring French North African newspapers. It was suggested that Darlan remained in secret contact with Pétain. Eisenhower was repeatedly required to explain to Washington what exactly was going on.

Churchill complained to Roosevelt that, "Fascist organizations continue their activities and vicitimize our former French sympathizers. . . . There have been cases of French soldiers being punished for desertion because they tried to support the Allied forces during the landings. . . . If we were to suffer serious setbacks in Tunisia, the Axis may be relied upon to exploit the situation to the full and there is no knowing what difficulties we may then encounter even at the hands of those French men who now appear to be cooperating with us."

That complaint was forwarded to Eisenhower by the White House. It was an extremely trying time for him. He had not been trained to tread a path through a diplomatic maze or deal with complex political and civil affairs. He did not fully grasp what was going on, or its significance. The difficulties he had previously encountered in his army career had been clear-cut and precise. He had always employed his intelligence, decisiveness, and candor rather than guile in coping with them. Now his strong sense of responsibility for his actions was being sorely tested. He was baffled by how his action was misunderstood and how little credit he was given for his worthy motives.

He protested that he was "idealistic as hell" and could not understand "why these long haired, starry-eyed guys keep gunning for me."

I have been called a Fascist and almost a Hitlerite [he complained to his son John]—actually I have one earnest conviction in this war. It is that no other war in history has so definitely lined up the forces of arbitrary oppression and dictatorship against those of human rights and individual liberty. My single passion is to do my full duty in helping to smash the disciples of Hitler. It is, therefore, sometimes rather annoying to see a telegraphic report that some brainless columnist attempts to place me on the other side of the fence.

To Mamie he wrote about "vexatious problems, each requiring hours of dictating, writing, scratching the head and plenty of profanity. War, politics, economics, food, munitions, jealousies, and repeat the list ad infinitum—then you have some idea of the jumble still going through my poor old head!" However, Marshall knew there would was worse to come. "He may think he has had troubles so far . . . ," the chief of staff said, "but he will have so many before the war is over that Darlan will be nothing."

When adequate communications facilities had been established in mid-November, Eisenhower had left Gibraltar to set up his Allied Forces Headquarters in the Algerian capital. Its offices were at the St. George Hotel, a venerable establishment that had been commandeered for military use for the duration.

His main concern—or what should have been his main concern—was the progress of the British First Army as it advanced into Tunisia, commanded by General Anderson, who had replaced Montgomery in Operation Torch when Montgomery had been dispatched instead to Egypt to fight Rommel. Anderson's troops made their initial landing at Algiers the day after Torch was launched. With subsequent reinforcement by sea, they quickly advanced to within fifteen miles of Tunis before running into strong resistance from German troops hastily flown to Tunisia to block their advance. To add to Eisenhower's vexation over the Darlan row, his hope of speedily overrunning the last of the three French North African territories was about to be thwarted.

The two separate contests for North Africa—between the forces clashing in the mountainous terrain of Tunisia and those in the deserts to the east—were about to merge. Acknowledging the hopelessness of his struggle against Montgomery's much stronger and better-supplied Eighth Army, Rommel wanted to pull back as rapidly as possible to Tunisia to link up with the newly arrived Axis forces there. He was under orders from Berlin and Rome not to give ground easily, but he knew he had no option but to withdraw. On November 13, Tobruk, the scene of the Eighth Army's disgrace five months earlier, was retaken by Montgomery, adding to his laurels.

But his advance continued to be cautious. Some chroniclers later held some of his corps and division commanders responsible for the failure of the Eighth Army to complete the destruction of Rommel's army and for not advancing more speedily to close the trap around all the remaining Axis forces in North Africa. But Montgomery had made it clear to his generals that, except in very special circumstances, he was calling the shots. Any initiative that they might have shown, and that might have accelerated the Eighth Army's advance, had been and still was being muted by their understanding that they were not to presume they had better ideas about combat than he did. "I kept a firm hand on the battle," he later said, "in order to ensure that the master plan was not 'mucked about'."

Nevertheless, some of his officers did try to spur him on to a hastier pursuit across the desert. When General Gatehouse, commander of the 10th Armoured Division, reported after the capture of Mersa Matrûh that he was ready and able to dash ahead to cut off the retreating Axis forces, Montgomery let him know that "no mad rush" forward was to be undertaken. He still refused to risk a reverse.

It had been thought that Montgomery's desert victories would work to the advantage of the American and British forces that had landed in Algeria and Morocco. But the reverse was proving to be true. Supplies and fuel desperately needed by Rommel were diverted to bolster Axis forces fighting in Tunisia while his much depleted Panzer Army continued to go begging.

Montgomery's sins in this campaign were those of omission. Some of his successes were sparked by flashes of brilliance. The Eighth Army proceeded relentlessly in a measured pursuit across the desert. Under Montgomery's precise direction, each of Rommel's stop lines was outflanked and overrun. When a gale disrupted the port at Benghazi, which Montgomery had earmarked as a key supply link for his advance, his insistence on logistical control every step of the way set the stage for a rapidly organized and meticulously maintained overland motorized supply line from the port of Tobruk. At every stage, he demonstrated better understanding of the employment of aerial support for his ground forces than any British commander had previously done.

His performance throughout was an exemplary display of tightly controlled soldiering. Indeed, Montgomery offered to write a textbook about it so that other Allied generals might benefit from understanding how he planned and executed the campaign. His steady advance was noted with acclaim in the British press. The BBC crowed that he was about to close his pincers around Rommel. His troops were exhilarated by their succession of comparatively easy victories and their uninterrupted forward momentum. They had the demon Rommel on the run and they reveled in the chase.

Desert Victory, a pioneering documentary about the Eighth Army's triumphs over the enemy, produced by the army's film unit, was about to be released in Britain, America, and other Allied nations to the greater glory of Montgomery and his gallant band of warriors. Wherever it was shown, people sat transfixed and reassured. But the fact remained that Rommel, despite being humbled and able to provide comparatively little cover for the withdrawal of his troops, was permitted to slip back toward Tunisia with a battered but still estimable fighting force. He was much relieved that Montgomery showed himself to be "overcautious."

The British commander [he said] risked nothing in any way doubtful and bold solutions were completely foreign to him. So our motorized forces would have to keep up an appearance of constant activity, in order to induce ever greater caution in the British and make them even slower. I was quite satisfied that Montgomery would never take the risk of following up boldly and overruning us, as he could have done without any danger to himself. Indeed, such a course would have cost him far fewer losses.

It would be interesting to speculate about how the Tunisian campaign (and Montgomery's career) might have developed if the Eighth Army commander had not been removed from Operation Torch to go to Egypt to fight Rommel. General Anderson, his replacement in the French North Africa operation, was in an unenviable position in Tunisia. The British First Army he commanded was initially an army in name only, consisting of little more than a single division and a smattering of other units. It had little air support. Nevertheless, he had been expected to thrust through Tunisia's forbidding mountain landscape to seize the port cities of Tunis and Bizerte before the Germans were able to establish themselves in the region.

Unlike Montgomery, Anderson, a mild-mannered man, was in no position to refuse to be rushed until he could be certain of victory. Upon landing in November, his job was to take Tunisia before the onset of winter weather ruled out the rapid success of his mission. It was a difficult assignment, but not impossible. In his place another general might have avoided the mistake of deploying his limited forces on a wide front while enemy defenses, not yet strongly established, were still vulnerable. A quick, concentrated push by all the forces at his disposal might have succeeded.

For the sake of Allied harmony, Eisenhower was reluctant to complain about Anderson. But he was greatly displeased with him. When his initial attack ground to a halt toward the end of November, two weeks after the Torch landings, Eisenhower instructed him to prepare to launch a new offensive in December.

However, atrocious weather was already setting in. The incessant downpour was torment for the troops making their way through rough terrain. They were perpetually drenched. Their boots were clogged with glutinous mud. Their tanks, trucks, and other vehicles, even the motorcycles of dispatch riders, lost purchase with the ground and bogged down in swamps of mud.

Tunisia was not well provided with good roads. Those that existed had not been meant to carry heavy military traffic and collapsed under the weight of armor. It was now apparant that the British (and Eisenhower) had been justified in fearing that Tunisia might not be rapidly seized unless initial landings by the Allied troops were made farther east than Algiers.

When Eisenhower visited the front just before Christmas and saw for himself how dim the prospects were for breaking through newly established enemy defenses under prevailing weather conditions, he realized he had no option but to cancel the planned offensive. He would have to hold off until the spring, by which time the enemy was likely to be further entrenched.

Though Anderson was the butt of criticism, Eisenhower was burdened with much of the responsibility for what was going wrong. As British Middle East commander-in-chief in Cairo, Alexander might be said to have shared the responsibility for Montgomery's failure to finish Rommel off quickly in Libya. But Montgomery was winning his battles and making relentless, if cautious, progress. In contrast, Eisenhower was commanding general of an operation in Tunisia that had seized up shortly after it had begun.

After the cessation of hostilities at Oran and Casablanca within three days of the Operation Torch invasion, no serious opposition or resistance to the Allies developed in either Algeria or Morocco, nor was any threatening. Nevertheless, Eisenhower, distracted by the Darlan affair and related matters, had been led to believe that the situation at the rear required his close supervision. As a consequence, more of his attention was focused there than should have been at a crucial moment rather than on what was transpiring at the front. Having had no combat experience, he could not fully appreciate what Anderson was and was not doing, nor what he was up against.

Qualms about Eisenhower began to be expressed among the British. Air Marshal Sir Arthur Coningham found him ill at ease. "Political things worried him," Coningham said. "Didn't quite know where he stood." General Sir Ian Jacob, who was deputy military secretary to the War Cabinet, thought,

"Though a man of decisive mind in immediate issues, General Eisenhower is far too easily swayed and diverted to be a great Commander-in-Chief."

> He has [Jacob noted in his diary] certainly had to grapple with a baffling political situation and his downright and honest character has been of great value in that task. Nevertheless his lack of experience of high command, and his naturally exhuberant temperament prevent him from preserving a steady course towards a selected goal. Sudden and frequent changes of plan, often made without the knowledge of those members of the staff who ought to know, increase the general chaos. There is a lack of dignity about the HQ, an air of aimless bustle, a constant chattering of hangers-on and visitors, and at the same time an amateur flavour which makes one wonder how anything ever gets done.

Brooke complained, "Eisenhower seemed to be unable to grasp urgency of pushing on to Tunis. It was a moment when bold and resolute action might have gathered great prizes. . . . It must be remembered that [he] had never even commanded a battalion in action when he found himself commanding a group of Armies in North Africa. No wonder he was at a loss as to what to do."

Churchill wanted to be told why the Allied advance in Tunisia had bogged down. His questions to Roosevelt and to Eisenhower himself implied a suggestion that perhaps the wrong man was in charge of the campaign. In Washington, strategists at the War Department felt confirmed in their view that the entire effort in French North Africa was misconceived. The American press, as well as the British, was also growing disenchanted with the campaign and how it was being run. Eisenhower, "like a caged tiger, snarling and clawing to get things done," found the corps of Allied correspondents who had converged on Algiers far less congenial that the reporters with whom he had exchanged banter in London. They were expected to file daily reports to their radio stations and newspapers but had little to which they could devote their energies except speculation. The *Daily Oklahoman* was not alone in suggesting that "Mud is a silly alibi" for the "failure of the Allied forces to deliver a knockout blow." Closely monitoring developments, Butcher believed, "The boss's neck is in the noose. If anything more goes wrong, he's had it."

The criticism to which Eisenhower had been subjected over the Darlan deal had been directed at his political and diplomatic shortcomings and not his military qualifications. Now, for the first time in his army career, Eisenhower was getting to know what it meant to have questions asked about his competence as a soldier.

His old friend, General Omar Bradley, said the setback in Tunisia "eroded Ike's confidence and temporarily dampened his inborn optimism and cheerfulness." He was afflicted with a virtually permanent cold that he termed "walking pneumonia" and that further undermined his morale. He was heard to mutter that anyone who wanted his job could have it.

All the while he had to cope with the ongoing consequences of having accepted Darlan as the senior administrative figure in French North Africa, a man with whom he had to work. He felt pressed to continue devoting much of his time to answering the complaints that arrived in a seemingly ceaseless stream from London and Washington, as well as from visiting dignitaries who badgered him about the vestigial remnants of Vichy rule in a region supposedly liberated from fascism by the forces of freedom and justice. Angered by press accounts of his failure to deal properly with the situation, Eisenhower imposed censorship on political developments in his command. That served only to compound feelings that he was incapable of extracting himself from a quagmire into which he had led himself. It aroused criticism in the United States and the censorship had to be lifted, exposing him to more criticism of how he was handling the political dimension of his job.

He wrote Marshall, "Sometimes I think I live ten years each week, of which at least nine are absorbed in political and economic matters." Marshall told him he was making a huge mistake. He admonished him to "delegate your international diplomatic problems to your subordinates and give your complete attention to the battle in Tunisia."

On Christmas Eve, while Eisenhower was returning from a visit to the front, he was informed that his main political problem had been resolved. A young anti-fascist monarchist, twenty-year-old Fernand Bonnier de la Chappelle, tricked his way into the Summer Palace in Algiers, where Darlan had his office, and shot the admiral. Darlan died in the hospital a few hours later.

Eisenhower expressed appropriate regrets over the "sudden tragic" passing of a man who had cast so long a shadow over his own reputation. But though he mistakenly expected new problems to arise in French North Africa as a result of the assassination, he was relieved to be able to shift the focus of his attention from the shabbier side of French politics. As had originally been agreed in Gibraltar, General Giraud, who had been acting as military commander of the French forces in North Africa, took over as civil governor as well. Political squabbling among the French would henceforth continue to plague Eisenhower, as would vestiges of Vichyite fascism in North Africa. But he finally felt able to concentrate primarily on defeating the enemy in the field.

Important matters that had been neglected finally rose to the top of his agenda. They included unraveling a command structure that he had permitted to grow confused and inadequate, tightening lines of military communications, reinforcing frontline units, dispatching more heavy equipment to the front, and making better use of the French troops in North Africa that had rallied to the Allied cause.

It was not yet enough to dispel doubts about whether he was the right man for the job. The state of the campaign was reviewed at a summit conference held in Casablanca. Roosevelt and Churchill met there in January 1943, as did the American and British chiefs of staff, to consider Allied strategy for the next phase of the war. Marshall feared that the British would seize upon disappointment over the Tunisia campaign to seek to oust Eisenhower from his position as Allied commanding general and replace him with one of their own more experienced officers. Aside from the continuing questions about his command skills, British troops were now doing most of the fighting. The British were therefore in a strong position to propose that a new commanding general be chosen, perhaps Alexander, under whose command Montgomery had thrashed the fearsome Rommel.

Brooke had no doubt that Eisenhower "had neither the tactical or strategical experience required" for the task with which he had been entrusted. But the British chief of staff recognized the dangers to the alliance of humiliating and offending the Americans by insisting on replacing Eisenhower. Domestic pressures were still being applied in the United States for America to drop the agreed-upon defeat-Germany-first policy and to concentrate instead on beating Japan in the Pacific. Besides, despite Eisenhower's shortcomings, the British were impressed with the way he had created and was running the American-British Allied Forces Headquarters. Whatever AFHQ's shortcomings, it was a truly impressive display of organizational and executive skills in a job that could easily have bogged down in a morass of inefficiency, conflicting views, and clashing personalities.

To Marshall's relief, Brooke therefore refrained from proposing that Eisenhower be relieved of his command. Instead, he suggested that Alexander be appointed Eisenhower's deputy, commanding Allied ground troops in North Africa. At the same time, Air Marshal Lord Tedder would become Eisenhower's deputy in charge of air operations, while Admiral Sir Andrew Cunningham would remain Eisenhower's deputy in charge of naval operations.

Eisenhower would thus remain commanding general, but he would have three experienced British deputies to run the campaign on a day-to-day basis. Brooke noted in his diary, "We were pushing Eisenhower up into the stratosphere and rarefied atmosphere of a Supreme Commander, where he would be free to devote his time to the political and inter-allied problems, whilst we inserted under him one of our own commanders

[Alexander] to deal with the military situations and to restore the necessary drive and co-ordination which had been so seriously lacking."

Eisenhower admired and respected all three of his deputies, with whom he got along well. He modestly expressed surprise that he, rather than the experienced Alexander, was Supreme Commander in North Africa. But he was deeply offended when it seemed that, as Brooke had intended, kicking him upstairs was only a prelude to shifting him out of the way. When the Combined Chiefs of Staff followed up appointing his deputies by issuing British-inspired directives on how they were to function, he responded with fury. He did not intend to become a figurehead while others ran the campaign for him.

"It is my responsibility," he insisted, "to organize to win battles." He did not intend to permit his subordinates to turn him into a figurehead, no matter how much he respected and liked them. He may not have been able to boast of much field-command experience, but he'd been in the army long enough to recognize the wilier aspects of military politics when confronted with them.

To bolster his confidence after the difficult time he'd had, Marshall recommended to Roosevelt that Eisenhower be promoted. He was still only a lieutenant general and was out-ranked by some of the Allied officers he commanded. Marshall suggested that the president recommend to Congress that he be given his fourth star. Roosevelt refused to do so, saying he first had to show better results in his North Africa mission.

Eisenhower was continuing to work long hours to achieve that end. He wrote Mamie that he felt under great strain. Marshall grew worried that he might "overwork himself." He instructed Butcher to try to keep him out of his office as much as possible; Butcher was to get a masseur to rub him down every evening before dinner, make him take a daily nap, get him to go horseback riding or find some other form of exercise, "and do things that relax his mind and body, so he can have a fresh point of view while meeting ever-pressing decisions."

It was during this trying period that he and Kay Summersby grew particularly close. He needed her distracting and flattering

company. He had arranged for her to join him in Algiers to
continue serving as his driver part of the time and also to act
as a personal secretary. Once more, rumors circulated that they
were lovers. The anger he displayed when soldiers whistled at
her in his presence seemed to demonstrate his claim to her
affections. They went horseback riding together. He introduced
her to generals and other dignitaries who visited his headquarters, almost as if showing her off. She sometimes drove him on
visits to frontline command posts though at the time it was
considered improper to take a woman into a combat zone.

Rumors about them made their way back to Washington,
where press photographs of him often showed Kay near him
or in the background. Hurt, humiliated, and bitter, Mamie demanded an explanation from her husband. He wrote her
strongly denying there was any other woman in his life. "You
must realize," he told her, "that in such a confused life as we
lead here all sorts of stories, gossip, lies and etc can get started
without the slightest foundation in fact." Nervous and anxious
by nature, Mamie was not reassured.

Under the arrangements that had been made at the Casablanca summit conference, Montgomery came under Eisenhower's command. However, he was shielded from the
commanding general by Alexander, who, as Eisenhower's deputy in command of ground forces, remained Montgomery's
immediate superior. Alexander continued to permit Montgomery to operate on a long, loose, barely perceptible leash. Eisenhower, busy enough otherwise and greatly respecting his new
deputy, saw no reason to question that arrangement. His
buildup of forces, equipment, and supplies seemed to indicate
that the North Africa situation would head toward a satisfactory, if belated, climax once winter was over.

Montgomery's carefully paced pursuit of Rommel through
northern Libya was continuing. His uncontested capture of
Tripoli on January 23, 1943, was another triumph. That city, a
glittering outpost in the desert and the most important administrative center of Italy's collapsed African empire, had been the
elusive object of Eighth Army offensives over a period of almost

three years. Now Montgomery had taken it for his king, his
nation, and his people, an achievement, he said, that was probably without parallel in history. It was, after all, the first major
enemy city captured by the Allies in the war. Montgomery
entered it just behind his forward troops to receive its surrender
from an Italian official and have a sandwich lunch on the sea-
front.

The Eighth Army had traversed 1,400 miles of desert since
the victory at Alamein. No longer would it have to rely on a
supply line extending across the sands to Benghazi, Tobruk,
and even further back. However, before abandoning the city,
Rommel had ordered its port facilities wrecked and its harbor
blocked. The damage was thorough. Montgomery would have
to wait while it was repaired and cleared and his supplies could
flow through to him by sea route.

He issued orders that his troops were not to risk growing soft
during that time by indulging overly much in the comforts and
pleasures Tripoli had to offer after their long trek from Alamein.
To retain their toughness and efficiency, they would camp out
in the desert as they had done for months. But Montgomery
recognized that they needed and deserved time off. When off
duty they were permitted to visit clubs for officers and other
ranks that were set up in the city for their entertainment and
diversion. Many preferred to visit Tripoli's brothels, at whose
entrances they lined up in orderly queues. Nevertheless, a
tough training schedule was set and enforced. Montgomery
himself passed up a chance to establish his quarters and command post at the magnificent governor's palace, choosing the
desert for himself as well, four miles from the city. There was
still work for him to do.

While clearing operations on the port were undertaken, he
organized a program of lectures to which senior officers of the
Western Allies were invited. He felt it was important for them
to understand from his experiences in the desert how battles
should be fought. Only one American general—Patton—chose
to attend. Patton, who did not make much of an impression on
Montgomery at the time, was impressed by him. He found him

to be "very alert, wonderfully conceited, and the best soldier—
or so it seems—I have met in this war."

Word was coming through at the time of the historic Soviet
victory at Stalingrad. British and American troops in Tunisia
were bracing to crush Axis resistance there as soon as the winter
rains stopped. And now Montgomery, who had been scoring
one success after another, had added Tripoli to his triumphs.
Churchill was ecstatic. The tide had unquestionably turned.

On February 3, 1943, the prime minister, who had visited
Cairo and Ankara after the Casablanca summit conference, flew
to Tripoli to congratulate Montgomery in person and take the
salute at a stirring parade of his "bronzed warriors," who were
barely rested after having made their long way across the North
African desert. It was Britain's first victory parade in the war.
Brooke, who was with Churchill, "saw several tears on his face"
and shed some himself. "The depth of [my] feelings," Brooke
said, "can only be gauged in relation to the utter darkness of
those early days of calamity, when no single ray of hope could
pierce the depth of gloom."

In an emotional address, Churchill paraphrased Shakespeare
to tell Montgomery's troops, "After the war when a man is
asked what he did it will be quite sufficient for him to say, 'I
marched and fought with the Desert Army.' " To the Eighth
Army headquarters staff, the prime minister said, "Your feats
will gleam and glow and will be the source of song and story
long after those gathered here have passed away."

An official British historian later observed, "Since the battle
of El Alamein, the purely fighting side of the 8th Army had
travelled far rather than fought much." But no one doubted
that Montgomery had molded it into a phalanx of heroes.

In contrast to the jubilation over Montgomery's achievements
in Egypt and Libya, the Allied situation in Tunisia remained
far from encouraging. British First Army commander General
Kenneth Anderson and General Lloyd Fredendall, commander
of the American II Corps, who was supposed to be under Anderson's command, had little mutual regard and were barely

communicating with each other. Most senior French officers whose troops had been brought into the line were Anglophobic and refused to permit French soldiers to serve under British command.

To avoid confusion or worse, Eisenhower permitted the forces of the three different Allied fighting elements to be assigned separate sectors of the line during what had been expected to be the winter lull. The First Army held the north, French forces were in the center, and II Corps was in the south. But the Allies were permitted no respite. The Germans had supremacy in the air in Tunisia and used it to advantage. Unlike forward Allied airstrips and even the airfields back in Algeria, where aircraft sank in the mud, the air bases the Germans controlled closer to the front had all-weather, hard surface runways.

In mid-January the Axis forces, under General Hans-Jürgen von Arnim, launched a small but vigorous assault on the center of the line. The poorly equipped and outnumbered French were driven back. British and American units had to be rushed in to support them to prevent a major enemy breakthrough. The ambitious preparations being made for a renewed Allied advance to wind up the battle for Tunisia were thus unhinged.

Rommel was also causing Eisenhower trouble. Relieved of pressure from Montgomery, who was resupplying and regrouping his forces at Tripoli, what was left of his Panzer Army also regrouped and fell back from Libya into Tunisia. The German commander's intention was to break through the Allied line and drive north to capture the supplies he badly needed. He would then push the Allies back into Algeria before wheeling about to face Montgomery when he resumed his westward advance.

The British and Americans were being out-generaled in Tunisia. Despite the stream of supplies and equipment now flowing to them, the First Army's Anderson and II Corps's Fredendall were no match for either Rommel or Arnim. In the north, Anderson's troops failed to gain forward momentum. At Sidi bou Zid in the center, American troops engaged in their first significant clash with Axis forces in the war and were sent reeling back.

That incident was followed five days later by the battle for

Kasserine Pass, where the Americans again were dislodged. They were forced to retreat helter-skelter in an encounter that reflected badly on their fighting abilities and might have proved disastrous if a hastily patched together defense, primarily by British units, had not blocked Rommel's steamroller and if the Axis forces had not run low on supplies. Not wasting effort on lost causes, Rommel turned about from Kasserine and headed back to the French-built fortifications of the Mareth Line, on the Tunisian-Libyan border, to meet Montgomery.

The British commander had earlier declined to act on a request from Alexander to accelerate his advance. But with his troops resupplied and rested, he now crossed into Tunisia to close the vise on the Axis forces in North Africa. When asked by Alexander how the Americans could help when he broke through at the Mareth Line, he dismissively replied, "The American troops must open the road, lift all the mines and mend all demolitions: in fact get the road ready for me to use. . . . I do *not* want the Americans getting in the way."

Averse to having to fight a defensive action, certainly not one he would not be able to maintain for long, Rommel chose not to dig in to wait for Montgomery behind the Mareth Line, which in any case was not a formidable barrier. He prepared to vault forward to catch the advancing Eighth Army by surprise. But Montgomery, assisted by the Ultra intercepts of German military communications, was not caught off guard. "Rommel attacked me at dawn," he wrote to Brooke. "It was very foolish of him. I have five hundred 6-pdr. anti-tank guns dug in on the ground. I have four hundred tanks, and I have good infantry holding strong pivots, and a great weight of artillery. It is an absolute gift, and the man must be mad."

Easily repulsed, Rommel was now out of favor in Berlin. Hitler was furious that his cherished Afrika Korps had been humbled and thrashed. His health having deteriorated again, Rommel was ordered home. More than a year would pass before he and Montgomery would again match wits and forces.

As Eisenhower's new deputy in charge of ground operations, Alexander was in an awkward position. In the Egyptian and

Libyan deserts Montgomery had largely relieved him of concern about the quality and capabilities of the troops fighting under his overall command. But now he didn't at all like what he saw. He had been spoiled by Montgomery's string of successes. He had seen no need to intercede in any significant way in the Eighth Army commander's conduct of the desert campaign. But dealing with the Allied forces in Tunisia who now came under his orders placed him in a different situation.

He reported to Brooke, "General situation is far from satisfactory. British, American and French units are all mixed up on the front. . . . There is no policy and no plan of campaign. . . . This is the result of no firm direction or centralised control from above. . . . We have quite definitely lost the initiative."

Provided with little effective air cover, Anderson's First Army was still struggling to overcome frustrating terrain and weather difficulties, as well as strong enemy action. It was making little progress. Anderson's troops were achieving nothing like Montgomery's seasoned, highly trained, highly motivated and triumphant desert fighters.

Alexander told Brooke, "Am doubtful Anderson is big enough for job. . . ." though "General Eisenhower could not be more helpful. . . ." He was being excessively charitable to the commanding general, whose primary responsibility should have been to closely oversee the campaign, make certain it had a workable plan, and that its shortcomings were being redressed.

However, Alexander was less than charitable in judging the American troops who had come under his command. He was appalled by how they had been routed at Sidi bou Zid and Kasserine. He told Brooke that in addition to being untrained, the Americans "lack the will to fight." If these were the best soldiers the Americans could provide, he dreaded what others still to be shipped across the Atlantic from the United States— the great numbers who would be needed to win the war— would be like.

Part of the problem, and one that Eisenhower had been reluctant to face, was Fredendall. Aside from his dislike of the British and his consequent inability to get along with Anderson, the II

Corps commander was held in contempt by many of his own and other American officers, including his division commanders. He was scorned and ridiculed for having his engineers, who could have been better employed, blast a bombproof command post for him out of rock well back from the front.

Alexander recommended that he be relieved of his command. So did Bedell Smith. Reluctantly, Eisenhower finally did so, replacing him with Patton, who had been based in Morocco ever since the landings, enjoying the hospitality there of the Sultan of Morocco and General Auguste Nogue, the French resident general, a Vichyite whose initial refusal to cooperate with the Allies had been responsible for most of the American casualties in the Torch landings.

Without assigning blame to any individual, Eisenhower sent long letters and reports to Marshall and to the Combined Chiefs of Staff explaining what had gone wrong in Tunisia and what was being done to put things right. Marshall responded by assuring him of his continued full support. But the chief of staff chastised him for bothering to make excessive explanations when he had other things to do. "I am disturbed," he wrote him, "that you feel under the necessity in such a trying situation to give so much personal time to us."

Patton's new job as II Corps commander was to restore the fighting spirit and redeem the reputation of the American troops in North Africa. He intensified training programs and imposed harsh discipline. He undertook tough inspection tours of the corps' positions and training areas. Under his stern command, it began to look battleworthy. Nevertheless, Alexander continued to relegate the Americans to secondary tasks on the battlefront and aroused some bitterness in the process.

In World War II, war correspondents played a far more important role than they had in any previous conflict. There were many more of them, they had greater access than ever before to both military commanders and the actual battlefield, and they benefitted from far better communications. When unsubstantiated reports circulated among correspondents that the British had been slower than they might have been in coming to the aid of the Americans in the Kasserine Pass incident, Eisenhower held headline-hunting correspondents responsible. He blamed "a certain type of reporter" who he believed was prepared "to start a quarrel among friends . . . merely so he can get a story to write about." He ordered that military censors watch out for such troublemaking rumormongers.

But he was even more upset by newspaper accounts of the subsidiary role American troops were being made to play in North Africa by his British deputy. Washington instructed him to do something about it. Marshall warned him that press reports of how American troops were being sidelined by the British were causing much concern in the United States. He said the prestige of American forces was at stake.

There was talk at the War Department and among some high-ranking American officers in North Africa that Eisenhower had gone British in his attitudes, as demonstrated by the way his three British deputies were said to have taken over the running of the war from him. Bradley found it galling "that all U.S. personnel were under strictest orders from Ike not to criticize the British in any way. Why didn't Ike impose the same muzzle on the British? . . . [It] contributed to our growing paranoia that Ike was so pro-British he didn't much care what happened to II Corps."

Eisenhower was inclined to let Alexander get on with his job without interference from above. It was the way he believed the command structure should function. However, under the pressure of criticism he felt obliged to warn him that greater and better use had to be made of American troops in the battle for Tunisia. Bits and pieces of II Corps could not be shoved into the line here and there where they were unlikely to cause much damage. He said the American divisions had to be kept "together as a powerful Corps, even if the logistics of the situation should make the arrangement seem somewhat unwise or risky."

He said the much-maligned II Corps had to be assigned its own sector of battle to demonstrate its capabilities (and redeem its reputation). Otherwise, American troops, who would be providing most of the fighting manpower in the war, would not get the combat experience they needed. What was more, Allied unity would be affected. He told Alexander that if the Americans felt "we have not played a substantial part they will be even more intent upon prosecution of the war against the Japs and commensurately less interested in the grand strategy of beating Hitler first and Japan second."

German propaganda was attempting to picture the British and Americans as "at each other's throats." Though a great exaggeration, this was not without a basis in fact. British commanders were often openly dismissive of the Americans' fighting abilities and the competence of their officers. General Ernest Harmon was enraged when General Anderson cursorily dismissed his battle plans as "just a childish fantasy." Other American officers also reacted bitterly to British disdain. Eisenhower and Tedder felt it necessary to intervene to defuse a heated conflict between Patton and Air Marshal Sir Arthur Coningham over whether lack of air support by the British had been responsible for an American setback on the ground.

At one point, Eisenhower was so upset by the friction and backbiting between American and British officers that he drafted a message to Washington suggesting that he be replaced because, he said, it was apparent that he was unable to adequately control his field commanders. But he was persuaded the situation was not as bad as he thought and he refrained from sending the message.

However, Alexander realized he had to heed the commanding general's warning about the need to use American troops more prominently. He grudgingly assigned II Corps its own sector, responsible for the left of the line, in northern Tunisia. This required a major redeployment. But over a mere two days, more than 100,000 U.S. troops shifted behind British lines to take up their new positions and prepare to show what they could do. To Alexander's surprise and gratification, and to Eisenhower's relief and delight, the Americans went on to play an impressive role in the windup to the Tunisia campaign. They justified Bradley's observation: "In Africa, we learned to crawl, to walk—then run."

The outcome of the struggle for North Africa was now only

a matter of weeks. As the weather improved and the ground grew firm again, Allied forward ground forces were massively resupplied with heavy equipment while Axis commanders, denied such largesse, grew concerned even about whether their infantry had enough ammunition. The Allies soon won mastery of the skies over the battle areas, and the Royal Navy had control of the Mediterranean. Montgomery broke through the enemy's fallback position at the Mareth Line and was advancing to help close the trap on the Axis forces in Tunisia.

He had previously only briefly met Eisenhower, his new commander-in-chief. That was back in England. Now Eisenhower paid a visit to his forward command post. He emerged with mixed feelings about the Eighth Army commander.

Montgomery is of different caliber from some of the outstanding British leaders you have met [he wrote Marshall]. He is unquestionably able, but very conceited. For your most secret and confidential information, I will give you my opinion which is that he is so proud of his successes to date that he will never willingly make a single move until he is absolutely certain of success—in other words, until he has concentrated enough resources so that anybody could practically guarantee the outcome. . . . Unquestionably he is an able tactician and organizer and, provided only that Alexander will never let him forget for one second who is the boss, he should deliver in good style.

Eisenhower did not make much of an impression on Montgomery during his visit to him. "I liked Eisenhower," he told Alexander. "But I could not stand him about the place for long; his high-pitched accent, and loud talking, would drive me mad. I should say he was good probably on the political line; but he obviously knows nothing whatever about fighting."

In the closing stage of the Tunisia campaign, the British First Army and the American II Corps advanced on the key cities of Tunis and Bizerte. There was still much determined enemy resistance to overcome, but the Axis forces in Tunisia were locked in a closing vise and the end was sufficiently in sight for preparations to be made for the next campaign, the invasion of Sicily.

Enfidaville on the coast was the Eighth Army's gateway to northern Tunisia, where the final battles for North Africa would be fought. The mountains and the sea allowed for only a narrow passage through enemy positions there. Horrocks, who had taken command of the Eighth Army's X Corps, questioned the wisdom of trying to break through. He told Montgomery he had no doubt they would be able to do it; he added, however, that he doubted whether there would be "very much left of the Eighth Army" afterward. But Montgomery would not be dissuaded from meeting the challenge. He very much wanted to participate in the final victory in Tunisia.

As Horrocks had forecast, the attack at Enfidaville resulted in heavy Eighth Army casualties. This was unnecessary. With Anderson's First Army and II Corps, now under Bradley, moving into position to bring the Tunisia campaign to an end, the enemy had no escape route. That the Enfidaville attack took place, in violation of Montgomery's aversion to taking risks, might be explained by fatigue. Though he had held up very well physically during the long desert campaign, he was tired. As he pointed out to Brooke in April, "The pace has been a real cracker since I came out in August last, and I have not had one single day off." He was also preoccupied with planning the Sicily invasion, for which he had been chosen to play a major role. Nevertheless, he had made it plain that he was determined that the Eighth Army should be in on "the final Dunkirk" in North Africa for an enemy who was about to be given the options of surrender, extermination, or being driven into the sea.

When he finally accepted that he could not break through at Enfidaville, he ordered the attempt broken off and shifted two divisions and a Guards brigade to the First Army front to assist in the final defeat of the Axis forces while the Eighth Army mounted a holding operation at Enfidaville. Troops of Anderson's reinforced First Army went on to capture Tunis on May 8, 1943, six months after the Operation Torch landings, while II Corps took Bizerte that same day.

Remaining Axis troops in North Africa were cut off on the Cape Bon peninsula with little chance of escape. Admiral Cunningham issued orders that the Royal Navy patrolling the Mediterranean "Sink, burn, destroy. Let nothing pass." More than a quarter of a million German and Italian troops were taken prisoner. It was a greater loss to the Axis than the German debacle at Stalingrad. Eisenhower's mission of ending Axis control of the North African coast of the Mediterranean had taken longer than had been hoped, but was now successfully completed.

In Britain, adulation for Montgomery, hyped by the Ministry of Information, whose officials recognized a charismatic morale-booster when one appeared so prominently on the scene, reached new heights. An eminent artist painted a portrait of him "for the nation" and he was not reluctant to let people know about it. Further glowing accounts of his exploits appeared in newspapers, though they did not require the prompting of the Ministry's propagandists. Correspondents in North Africa found that his achievements, triumphalism, and eccentricities made great copy, and he made the most of it. "It is a strange experience to find oneself famous," he said, "and it would be ridiculous to deny that it was rather fun."

All of that served to fuel his unrestrained egocentrism. Without justification, he took credit for devising the tactics for winding up the campaign in Tunisia. Even in his moments of glory he could act with astonishingly childish pettiness, as the Americans had discovered to their annoyance. Montgomery had made a bet with Bedell Smith that if the Eighth Army entered Sfax in southern Tunisia by April 15, a Flying Fortress would be put at his personal disposal for the rest of the war. Eisenhower's chief of staff did not consider it a serious wager; it had been made jocularly, and there was no suggestion that Montgomery would have to forfeit something if he lost the bet. Yet when his troops entered Sfax at the designated time, he cabled Smith, "Please send Fortress."

At first amazed that Montgomery was serious, Smith tried to joke him out of it but was informed that a bet was a bet, not to be welched on. Smith felt obliged to inform Eisenhower. When Brooke heard of it, he sharply chastised Montgomery. But Eisenhower, though "boiling over with internal anger," wanted nothing to ruffle British-American relations and had the bomber and an American crew delivered. Montgomery kept it until well into the Sicily campaign that followed, when he accepted that it was too big to land at most airfields. Eisenhower then had it exchanged for a smaller Dakota aircraft.

Montgomery made a brief visit to England at the end of the Tunisia campaign. His presence there was supposed to be a military secret. He gave explicit instructions that even members of his family were not to be informed he was back and he did not try to see them. But Londoners were not kept from knowing that their warrior hero was among them. He made no great effort to remain out of sight. His photograph had been prominently displayed in the press for days and just about everyone had seen the *Desert Victory* film of his victory over Rommel. When he got back home, he was cheered wherever he appeared in public. His presence was calculatedly conspicuous. He moved about in his full desert uniform, including his famous beret. Crowds gathered to cheer him and wish him well. People congregated outside Claridge's Hotel, where he was staying, in hope of catching sight of him when he came and went.

Less than a year earlier his existence had been known to only very few individuals outside the army. Now, to his unabashed delight, he was a celebrity throughout the land and in America too, where because of press reports and newsreel film he was more popular than Eisenhower, who, in contrast, was making a genuine effort to stay out of the limelight. Women wrote letters proposing marriage to Montgomery. Countless others wrote to praise and thank him, including an Atlanta Sunday school teacher whose letter was signed by all her pupils, who, she said, "pray for you every night."

He was received at Buckingham Palace, where the king formally awarded him his knighthood, and he called in at 10 Downing Street for a chat with Churchill. However, he was pained while in London not to be invited to a thanksgiving service at St. Paul's Cathedral commemorating the end of the war in North Africa. It made him realize that "if I were pretty popular with a lot of people, I was not too popular on some circles."

That was an understatement. Some officers who had been humiliated by him, or who had friends who had been, loathed him. Some were offended by his boastfulness and publicity-seeking. Some people feared that Montgomery might try to use his immense popularity to enter politics. A story circulated about Churchill telling the king, "I'm worried about Monty. I think he's after my job," and the king replying, "Thank God! I thought he was after mine."

But for people in Britain generally, the eccentricities of the Eighth Army's commander were accepted as part of the makeup of a remarkable soldier whose combat achievements had restored British confidence. They made him more interesting and, to many, even more endearing. To them, he was a lovable character as well as the man who had demonstrated that the British were not irredeemable losers. London sophisticates may have quipped that Montgomery was "In defeat, unbeatable; in victory, unbearable." Some discreet mutterings were made at the War Office that the credit he was given for the desert victory was overdone. Some politicians were wary of what they considered an overly popular military figure. But such quibbles made no impact on the general public. Nor did they make any impact on the general himself.

CHAPTER 13
Omens

As the victorious commanding general in North Africa, Eisenhower had become the most important military figure of the Western Allies. Messages of congratulations for him flooded into Allied Forces Headquarters in Algiers from Roosevelt, Churchill, Stalin, leaders of the other members of the fledgling United Nations, and from a multitude of prominent and ordinary Americans and Britons. Newspaper editorials and magazine articles paid lavish tribute to him. King George awarded him the Knight Grand Cross of the Order of the Bath.

He had grown in stature and, though still not given to airs of grandeur, he had developed a sharper sense of his own importance. The trappings and practices of the high office, authority, and responsibility he held had made that inevitable. He had survived the baptism of frustrations and anguish of his first months in North Africa and had emerged far more confident in his command abilities and prerogatives.

Only fifteen months had passed since he had been summoned to Washington from Texas to sit behind a planning desk. But the pace of change to which he had been exposed had been extraordinary, and was still in progress. He had been promoted to the rank of full general in February 1943—ironically, just before the Kasserine Pass reverse—and now outranked and was authorized to command scores of officers who only months before had been senior to him.

He was still accountable to the Combined Chiefs of Staff. Furthermore, he was first and foremost an American general who could be recalled by Washington and replaced at any time. He was, however, a more independent figure than before. He had organized and overseen the most significant Allied military campaign in the war so far. He had commanded the forces of a multinational military alliance. He had reason to be pleased with himself.

Nevertheless, the completion of his North Africa assignment did not greatly gratify him. Its windup had been anticlimactic. Butcher noted that the victory left him "utterly cold." It had taken too long to achieve and had involved too many mistakes. The struggle for Tunisia had had a dramatic effect on his thoughts and feelings. He was greatly moved by what the troops under his command had endured. Unlike Montgomery, who had fought and commanded troops in the First World War, he had come to grasp far more clearly than ever before what it meant for men to go into combat and die—and for himself to be responsible for them. He had seen how quickly a carefully devised plan, and even a successful operation, could be turned into a bloody rout. Through it all, he had endured the unexpected exasperations and frustrations of what seemed like petty politics that should have had nothing to do with a soldier's task.

And he was not yet free of the political squabbling with and among the French that had tormented him ever since the invasion. He had been able to concentrate more closely on the struggle for Tunisia after the assassination of Darlan, but as the campaign had ground on, he still had been unable to distance himself as much as he would have liked from the maze of French politics. The White House and the State Department made clear that, as senior American on the spot, he had special responsibilities and was expected to fulfill them.

Once Darlan had left the scene, General Giraud emerged as the senior French figure leading the pro-Allied forces and the pro-Allied government in North Africa. But with the backing of the British, General de Gaulle insisted that his own Free French movement was the proper repository of French sovereignty. His claim was difficult to challenge. While Giraud was relatively new upon the political scene, the Gaullists had been actively engaged on the Allied side since the fall of France three years earlier. They were increasingly representative of the burgeoning resistance movement operating within France. An effort to establish a modus vivendi between De Gaulle and Giraud had been made at the Casablanca summit conference in January, but it had failed to produce any substantive agreement between them.

In contrast to the colorless Giraud, laudatory press coverage had made the charismatic De Gaulle popular with the public in the United States and particularly in Britain, where his Free French movement had been officially nurtured and promoted. However, he was out of favor with the American government. Roosevelt considered De Gaulle a self-appointed would-be Napoleon, a dictator in waiting. The State Department preferred to back Giraud until France was liberated and the French people could choose for themselves. But as Allied-sponsored civil governor of French North Africa, Giraud was less than satisfactory. Despite Darlan's departure, pro-Vichy figures who had collaborated with the Germans continued to hold positions of influence and authority, and oppressive Vichyite legislation was still on the books.

Eisenhower, still based in Algiers, had been instructed by Washington to cold-shoulder the Gaullists. That became more difficult to do after the victory in Tunisia. The time for the liberation of mainland France from the Germans appeared to be fast approaching, and the rival French political forces were jockeying in earnest for positions of leadership. Algiers, the most important French city in Allied hands, and one to which De Gaulle had shifted the headquarters of his movement from London, was the natural arena for that struggle.

At first it seemed that camaraderie and reason would prevail in view of the struggle ahead to free France from German occupation. De Gaulle and Giraud agreed on the formation of the French Committee of National Liberation (FCNL), in effect a provisional French government-in-exile, with the two rival generals serving as co-presidents.

Eisenhower believed that this would limit De Gaulle's ambitions and assertiveness and ultimately marginalize him. But he found, as some already had and others would later, that the Free French leader was too shrewd and stubborn to be outmaneuvered. He sought to marginalize Giraud instead by removing him from command of the French armed forces in exile and taking command for himself through the FCNL. When he appeared to be succeeding, Roosevelt reacted angrily. The president crisply told Eisenhower to inform De Gaulle that, "we will not tolerate control of the French Army by any agency which is not subject to the Allied Supreme Commander's direction." The president furthermore told him confidentially that the United States might soon cut off all dealings with De Gaulle.

Having previously been advised to distance himself personally from international diplomatic problems and to concentrate on the military aspects of his command, Eisenhower found himself thrust back into the labyrinth of French politics when a major military concern—the projected invasion of Sicily—deserved his close attention. He was not at all pleased that Roosevelt, bypassing Marshall and the Combined Chiefs of Staff, had begun issuing him instructions directly. Though he could do nothing about it, it complicated his role as primarily the Allied rather than American commander. He also feared that if, as instructed, he tried to muffle De Gaulle, who remained the symbol of French resistance to the Nazis and who was regularly depicted in American and British newspapers as a gallant hero, he would be forced to relive the agony of the Darlan episode when his own character and competence had come under criticism.

What was more, he had growing doubts about whether the forceful De Gaulle could be kept under control. In fact, as was soon demonstrated, he could not. At an Algiers meeting arranged in June 1943, a month after victory in Tunisia, for him and Giraud to patch up their differences, the Free French leader announced stiffly that he was there in his capacity as president of the French government. No one presumed to challenge this proud, lordly figure or his blatant presumption. When Eisenhower deferentially suggested to him that Giraud remain in charge of the French Army, De Gaulle in effect told him it was none of his business. Rumors circulated that a pro–De Gaulle putsch in the French Army was in the works. Contrary to Allied orders, Free French troops who had fought with the Eighth Army against Rommel appeared in Algiers, which was after all the most Frenchified large city in North Africa. Security was tightened around Eisenhower and Allied Forces Headquarters there and he toyed with the idea of carrying a sidearm.

Soon afterward, however, De Gaulle appeared to accept a FCNL agreement on a division of military responsibility between himself and Giraud. A relieved Eisenhower misread the situation. He told Marshall, "I am quite sure that DeGaulle is losing ground." In fact, the Free French leader was jockeying into a position to jettison Giraud altogether from any role in the French leadership, an objective he achieved not long afterward. He established himself unchallenged as sole leader of France in exile and would prove an exasperatingly relentless irritant to Eisenhower as the war went on.

Within days of the launching of Operation Torch the previous November, Churchill had informed Roosevelt that, though the U.S. War Department was still pressing for an early invasion of France across the English Channel, the British were in no hurry to mount such an operation.

The paramount task before us [the prime minister had told the president] is, first, to conquer the African shore of the Mediterranean . . . and secondly, using bases on the African shore . . . to strike at the under-belly of the Axis in effective strength in the shortest time.

Marshall believed such a strategy would prolong the war.*
But Eisenhower had changed his mind about favoring an early
invasion of France over operations in the Mediterranean. Unlike
the British High Command, he did not favor a Mediterranean
strategy on principle. But he had come to agree with the British
that it would be a mistake not to exploit the new situation that
had been created in the region by virtue of the triumph in North
Africa. Marshall reluctantly conceded that this made sense.
Large combat-trained Allied armies and great stores of military
hardware had been assembled in North Africa. It was logical to
employ them in the area rather than shift them back to England
for the invasion of France.

To the despair of the War Department's strategists, the decision to move forward from final victory in Tunisia to Operation
Husky, the invasion of Sicily, followed naturally. It also made
sense for Eisenhower to serve as the operation's commanding
general and for him still to be closely assisted by his British
ground, air, and naval deputies.

Once more Eisenhower regretted that he and his former colleagues in Washington differed on how the enemy could best
be defeated. He feared that their resentment of the British, and
perhaps of himself as well for appearing to favor their views
over those at the War Department, would intensify. He wrote
of his concern to General Handy, his successor as Chief of
Operations.

I am not so incredibly naive that I do not realize that Britishers
instinctively approach every military problem from the viewpoint of the Empire, just as we approach them from the
viewpoint of American interests. But one of the constant
sources of danger to us in this war is the temptation to regard
as our first enemy the partner that must work with us in
defeating the real enemy. . . . I am not British and I am not
ambidextrous in attitude. But . . . I am not going to let national prejudice or any of its related evils prevent me from

*Like Marshall, Montgomery favored an early cross-Channel invasion of France. He
had told Brooke there should be a distraction in southern Europe to tie down enemy
forces but that then, "suddenly . . . we nip across the Channel."

getting the best out of the means that you fellows struggle so hard to make available to us.

Operation Torch had been launched in November 1942 with the biggest amphibious operation ever until then undertaken. Operation Husky, in July 1943, was to be even bigger. Planning for it had begun at Eisenhower's headquarters in Algiers soon after it had been decided at the Casablanca summit conference in January that Sicily would be the next invasion target. Since it was going to happen, Marshall had suggested to Eisenhower at the time that Sicily should be invaded as soon as victory in Tunisia had been achieved, while the Germans were still stunned by their defeat and had not yet had the opportunity to reinforce the island. But Eisenhower and his deputies had been thrown off balance by the strength of Axis resistance in Tunisia before the windup there. As a result, detailed planning for Husky had proceeded in spasmodic and inconclusive fashion until closer attention could be devoted to it.

As the most celebrated general in the North Africa fighting, Montgomery might have been considered the natural choice for ground-forces commander in the Sicily campaign. He himself had no doubt that he was and informed Alexander, "It is clear that coordination, direction and control should be undertaken by one Army commander." He left no doubt whom he had in mind. Alexander was prepared to agree.

But for Montgomery to run the Sicily campaign was politically impossible. The Americans would not tolerate it. Aside from the fact that his conceit and abrasiveness had already rubbed some of them the wrong way, the United States was now ready to provide most of the manpower and equipment in the struggle for Europe and, in the closing weeks of the Tunisia campaign, American generals had redeemed their earlier reputation for ineptitude. None had as yet had the extensive command experience Montgomery had. Nevertheless, it was understood that in Sicily American forces would have to be afforded at least equal prominence as the British. Accordingly, command there had to be divided. Montgomery would lead one task force, consisting of his Eighth Army; Patton, who had done much to whip II Corps into shape in Tunisia, would lead another, composed of the newly formed American Seventh Army.

Montgomery was not pleased with the arrangement. He was afraid that Eisenhower might have ideas of his own about how to mount the operation and might interfere with his planning. He was unchanged in his view of the American as essentially a political figure rather than a military commander. He was, however, content to continue serving directly under Alexander. He hoped the Allied ground forces commander had absorbed enough from him when he had been his student to continue shielding him from any meddling by Eisenhower or his headquarters staff. The easygoing Alexander was indeed intimidated by the assertiveness of the Eighth Army commander.

Even if protected by Alexander from American interference, Montgomery was required to make a difficult adjustment. He and the army he had transformed into a famous, highly motivated, triumphant band of brothers would now have to share the limelight with others. In contrast to his North Africa engagements, he would not be the sole leader, sole planner, sole decider, sole judge in the operation on which he was embarking. He never would be again. There would be limits beyond which even a docile Alexander would be able to guarantee he could have his way. Brooke worried about whether he would be able to reconcile himself to this new set of circumstances.

> Montgomery . . . requires a lot of educating to make him see the whole situation and the war as a whole outside the Eighth Army orbit. A difficult mixture to handle, brilliant commander in action and trainer of men, but liable to commit untold errors, due to lack of tact, lack of appreciation of other people's outlook. It is most distressing that the Americans do not like him, and it will always be a difficult matter to have him fighting in close proximity to them. He wants guiding and watching continually and I do not think Alex is sufficiently strong with him.

Whatever qualms Eisenhower might have had about Montgomery's excessive caution as a combat commander were overridden by his gratification at having so seasoned a fighting general serving under him in the first Allied assault on the home ground of the Axis powers.

General Montgomery is a very able, dynamic type of army commander [Eisenhower observed]. I personally think that the only thing he needs is a strong immediate commander. He loves the limelight but in seeking it, it is possible that he does so only because of the effect upon his own soldiers, who are certainly devoted to him. I have great confidence in him as a combat commander. He is intelligent, a good talker, and has a flare for showmanship. Like all other senior British officers, he has been most loyal—personally and officially—and has shown no disposition whatsoever to overstep the bounds imposed by Allied unity of command.

Though Montgomery was no longer in much of a position to overstep those bounds, he was critical of the way Eisenhower was organizing the Sicily invasion. He had neglected to set up a central planning base for Husky. Ground, air, and naval forces were not working together as closely as they should have to coordinate their roles in the operation. Eisenhower and Alexander were based in Algiers, Cunningham's naval headquarters were in Malta, while Tedder and his air staff operated out of Tunis. Montgomery thought it was "like an orchestra trying to play without a conductor." Bradley, who was to command a corps under Patton in the Sicily campaign, also regretted that there was "little guidance from the top—no one man exerting a firm hand."

The fact remained that despite Eisenhower's determination "to organize to win battles," the other pressing tasks that went with his job continued to distract him. It fell to his three geographically separated British deputies to oversee preparations for the Sicilian campaign. They reported to him at frequent meetings. But administrative and political concerns, especially dealing with De Gaulle, took most of the Supreme Commander's time and occupied most of his thoughts at the time.

He became impatient and grouchy. His mood was not helped

by advice from Marshall, who wanted the Mediterranean activity of the Allies to be concluded as quickly as possible so the Allies could finally get around to preparing to mount their war-ending frontal assault on occupied Europe. Marshall warned Eisenhower not to permit himself to be overly controlled by his planners who, he said, were unlikely to be sufficiently daring.

But having seen the face of war close up, Eisenhower was himself now less inclined to be bold than he had been earlier, and displayed signs of backtracking. The Germans were believed to have placed two divisions in Sicily to reinforce the Italian forces garrisoned there. Eisenhower somberly told the Combined Chiefs of Staff, "[I]f substantial German ground troops should be placed in the region prior to the attack, the chances for success become practically nil and the project [Husky] should be abandoned."

The suggestion that Eisenhower thought the Sicily operation might be too risky to mount infuriated Churchill, who reacted caustically.

> If the presence of two German divisions is held to be decisive against any operation of any offensive or amphibious character open to the million men now in North Africa, it is difficult to see how the war can be carried on. Months of preparation, sea power and air power in abundance, and yet two German divisions are sufficient to knock it all on the head. I do not think we can rest content with such doctrines. . . . It is perfectly clear that the operations must either be entrusted to someone who believes in them, or abandoned.

Churchill condemned "pusillanimous and defeatist doctrines, from whoever they come" as well as the "absence of one directing mind and commanding will power." The British Chiefs of Staff complained to Washington about Eisenhower's apparent lack of resolution. The U.S. Joint Chiefs forwarded those complaints to Algiers, indicating concern of their own. Eisenhower responded with assurances that he had no thought but to carry out his orders to the best of his ability, which was hardly an inspiring response.

As he agonized about Sicily, he fell into a pattern of waking around four in the morning to "begin wrestling with his problems. Sometimes," Butcher observed, "he manages to put himself back to sleep, but rarely." Eisenhower wrote to Mamie, "In my youthful days I used to read about commanders of armies and envied them what I supposed to be a great freedom of action and decision. What a notion! The demands upon me that must be met make me a slave rather than a master."

Initial plans drawn up for the invasion of Sicily proposed two primary landing areas. Montgomery's Eighth Army would go ashore at the southeast corner of the island; Patton's Seventh Army would target the region around Palermo on the northwest corner. Alexander made some minor changes to the plan and forwarded it to Eisenhower, who raised no objections. However, Montgomery called it totally unsound. He told Alexander it "breaks every commonsense rule of practical battle-fighting. . . . It has no hope of success and should be completely recast."

His attitude riled Admiral Cunningham. At one point, Cunningham wrote to the First Sea Lord in London, "I am afraid Montgomery is a bit of a nuisance; he seems to think that all he has to do is to say what is to be done and everyone will dance to the tune of his piping. Alexander appears quite unable to keep him in order."

Realizing he had more than Alexander to contend with if he was to have his way, Montgomery tried to injected a tone of reasonableness and modesty into his arguments.

I know well that I am regarded by many people as being a tiresome person. I think this is very probably true. I try hard not to be tiresome; but I have seen so many mistakes made in this war, and so many disasters happen, that I am desperately anxious to try to see that we have no more; and this often means being very tiresome.

To Alexander, Montgomery was less diplomatic. "There is some pretty woolly thinking going on—tactically and administratively," he told him. "I have no intention of doing some of the things [the planners] suggest." He proposed that instead of being dispersed the attacking forces should be tightly concentrated in the Syracusa region, where his forces were to go ashore. Instead of targeting Palermo at the other end of the island, the Americans would land near him and act in support of his forces. He would quickly fight his way up the eastern coast of Sicily and take Messina, at the point closest to the Italian mainland. He would thus trap the German as well as Italian forces on the island before they could escape.

Ex post-facto analysis, and the way the campaign actually turned out, indicate that a Palermo landing probably would have produced quicker and more satisfactory results. But there was much sense to Montgomery's proposal. This was to be the first major Allied assault on Europe; fierce enemy resistance was to be expected. If the attacking forces were dispersed too thinly, they might soon be in trouble wherever they went ashore. A concentrated attack appeared to stand a far greater chance of quick success.

However, implied in this proposed revision to the plans was continuing lack of trust in the battle-worthiness of the Americans. Montgomery had barely concealed his belief that their role in the operation should be largely confined to drawing off enemy defenders so his troops could spurt quickly up the coast to Messina. He and his Eighth Army were to continue along their paths of glory. Their own pride also at stake, the Americans were not happy about that.

They were joined by some British commanders in questioning Montgomery's ideas. Tedder, who had previously begun to doubt the perspicacity of the Eighth Army commander and had been offended by his manner, expressed objections to the new plan because it would leave too many airfields he wished the Allies to capture in enemy hands for too long. And Admiral Cunningham was worried that failure to seize those airfields quickly might endanger the huge convoys that were to be involved in the operation. Nor did Montgomery's declaration, "I am prepared to carry the war into Sicily with the Eighth Army but must really ask to be allowed to make my own Army plan," sit well with the others involved in the planning. But he stood his ground, and, with Alexander's backing, the revisions he proposed received Eisenhower's cautious blessing.

The final plan had emerged in a haphazard fashion. Central control of planning remained glaringly missing. Bradley groaned that, "Seldom in war has a major operation been undertaken in such a fog of indecision, confusion and conflicting plans."

Eisenhower remained sensitive to claims that it was his British deputies and not himself who were running his command. He was irked by visiting American VIPs who suggested as much and by press reports that did the same. He trusted Alexander, Tedder, and Cunningham. Though regretting that he was often otherwise engaged and unable to give Operation Husky anything like his full attention, he was gratified to have such experienced deputies handling the day-to-day developments. However, he felt obliged to assert himself in the lead-up to the Sicily invasion.

All three of his deputies objected strenuously to his decision to preface the invasion by capturing the small island of Pantelleria, strategically positioned in the Mediterranean halfway between Tunisia and Sicily. The island, fortified by Mussolini years before, contained an airfield and a naval base, both of which could threaten the forces taking part in the invasion, and both of which, in Allied hands, could prove useful. But Pantelleria's cliff-lined shores boasted no beach on which troops could storm ashore. The only access to the island was its heavily fortified port. The interior was a mountainous maze, easy to defend.

Alexander protested that to send troops to seize the island would result in great numbers of casualties and damage prospects for success in Sicily. Cunningham and Tedder agreed with him. But stung by suggestions that he was not being daring enough and that he was not really in charge, Eisenhower would not be deterred. He believed that after a preliminary bombing and naval shelling, enemy forces on Pantelleria would surrender. Aside from the value of controlling the island, it would be a test of the effect of concentrated bombardment in

an amphibious operation that was to be employed in the invasion of Sicily. Cunningham and Tedder gave ground and agreed
it would be worth the effort. Alexander did not, but the attack
was scheduled to go ahead on June 11, 1943, a month before
Operation Husky was to be launched.

Suffering an attack of jitters at the thought that Alexander
might be right, Eisenhower sought to make certain the risk
would be minimal. For more than a week prior to the attack,
he had Pantelleria pounded from the skies. Seven million tons
of bombs were dropped on the small rock island, more than
had been dropped on Axis forces during the entire Tunisia
campaign. That more than did the trick. The Italian garrison
surrendered en masse even before the British troops assigned
to take the island landed. Not a single Allied casualty was
suffered. The neighboring islets of Lampedusa, Lampione, and
Linosa—heavily bombed too—were also taken without difficulty.

Operation Husky would not enjoy such easy success. A force
of 350,000 enemy troops, 60,000 of them German, were deployed on Sicily. There were doubts about whether the Italians
would put up much of a fight, but the Germans certainly would,
and the initial landings were expected to meet strong resistance.
In addition, weather conditions could prove a critical factor in
so large a seaborne endeavor and much of the territory that
would have to be seized after beachheads were successfully
seized was even more mountainous than the rough terrain that
had caused great problems in Tunisia.

One hundred and sixty thousand Allied troops were to be
delivered to the beaches of Sicily on July 10, the first day of the
operation, with 350,000 to follow. The initial landings were to be
made before dawn. The men and their equipment and supplies
were transported by an armada of vessels even larger than
had taken part in Operation Torch. Some 2,500 vessels were
participating, included 1,200 warships—8 battleships and 2 aircraft carriers among them.

Eisenhower arrived at Malta, his forward command post for
Husky, on July 8 to receive news that four ships participating
in the operation had already been sunk heading for Sicily, one

of them carrying 900 troops, of whom 200 were lost. The other three vessels had been carrying armor and other heavy equipment. On the morning of July 9, a storm began to gather in the Mediterranean. The sea was turbulent and grew even rougher as the day wore on. By afternoon, winds reached forty miles per hour. They dropped down to twenty-five in the evening, but Eisenhower feared the worst.

Operation Torch's landings had been undertaken in much calmer waters but, even without the epidemic of seasickness that had now afflicted the invading troops, it had been laced with muddle and mishaps. And what was to be done about the men of the 82nd Airborne Division who were in on the invasion and awaiting takeoff from fields in North Africa? It would be suicidal for them to bail out of their aircraft in a gale.

In Washington, Marshall was monitoring the weather. He cabled Eisenhower, asking if he intended to postpone the operation. By then Eisenhower doubted whether he had much choice. If he waited for improved conditions, surprise—to the extent that it still existed—would be irretrievably lost. It was also possible that an order to back off, if issued, would not be received by all vessels taking part in the invasion. Those that proceeded with it in ignorance would, in effect, be sacrificed.

Eisenhower's living quarters during his brief stay in Malta were in the elegant Verdala Palace, the governor's residence. But his war room was reminiscent of his grim office quarters in Gibraltar during Operation Torch—it was deep in a damp, cold tunnel that, despite summer temperatures outside, required the presence of a smelly oil stove for warmth. It was hardly an agreeable place in which to wait for the news that morning would bring. He left to wait out the results at his palatial temporary abode. The road his car took passed windmills with their blades being driven furiously by the elements. He had seen similar sights in tornado-prone Kansas during his boyhood and knew too well what they might mean for the operation. He "wondered if his luck was running out." He wrote to Mamie that men could be driven mad in moments like that.

There was nothing more he could do. For distraction, he sketched out an idea for a book he might like to write after the

war. Feeling glum and resentful about all the nonsense and
pettiness he'd had to put up with, he told Butcher he would
base it on the key people with whom he had dealt. Butcher
warned him that telling the truth about them would not shield
him from being sued for libel. As it turned out, the book Eisenhower finally did write when the war was over subjected no
one with whom he worked to serious criticism.

Remarkably, in view of the size of the invasion force, the
element of surprise was maintained. The torpedoing of the four
vessels had been chance encounters with U-boats. The attack
convoys reached their destinations without otherwise being
seriously challenged. The winds moderated overnight. Though
the weather still caused much trouble for the airborne troops
sent in prior to the coastal assaults, its earlier ferocity lulled the
Italian defenders on the shore into dropping their guard until
the massive predawn naval bombardment alerted them to what
they were up against.

When the landings began, resistance on the the coast was
quickly crushed. Montgomery's troops went ashore as planned
along a seventy-mile stretch of coast between Syracusa and
Ragusa. Patton's landed on a somewhat shorter stretch between
Scoglitti and Licata not far away. The invaders found that the
seasickness from which many of them had suffered had less
impact on the opening battle for Sicily than the war-weariness
of the Italian defenders, who surrendered to them in droves.
Beaches were quickly secured and arrangements were made to
accelerate the unloading of equipment and supplies for the
advance to the north and inland. By nightfall no serious counterattack had developed. A pre-landing bombing raid on Axis
military headquarters at the San Domenico Hotel at Taormina
up the coast had for the moment knocked out defense communications. Eisenhower was relieved and elated. "By golly, we've
done it again," he crowed to correspondents attending him in
Malta.

Fear that the vast array of vessels offshore, unloading more
troops and equipment, would be subjected to attack once the
enemy recovered balance and was able to organize resistance

proved exaggerated. The pre-invasion pounding of enemy airfields on the island—and within striking distance of it on the
Italian mainland—had sharply reduced the enemy's ability to
provide the ground defenders much aerial support.

By the next morning, however, it became apparent that the
conquest of Sicily would be no walkover. Two German divisions
were due to arrive to reinforce the two already there as backup
for the Italian forces on the island. As the U.S. 1st Infantry
Division went about expanding its beachhead at Gela, the Her-
mann Goering Division, sporting new, powerful Tiger tanks,
launched a fierce attack that drove the Americans back within
a thousand yards of the shore. Only a remarkably accurate
bombardment by two U.S. Navy cruisers lying offshore saved
the troops from being driven into the sea.

Montgomery had less difficulty. His troops advanced beyond
their beachhead without delay and took Syracusa by nightfall
of the first day. But his efforts to thrust quickly up Sicily's east
coast to seize Messina and bottle up the enemy on the island
were thwarted by the Germans, who had taken control of the
main route running east of Mount Etna and its foothills.
Blocked, Montgomery requested authorization to alter his plans
and move northward toward Messina along the other main
route in the region, skirting west of Etna. The route he intended
to use had been designated for use by Patton's Seventh Army
in its progress up the island. Indeed, American troops were
about to deploy on it.

Such formalities did not trouble Montgomery. He later told
Patton, "George, let me give you some advice. If you get an
order from Army Group that you don't like, why you just ignore
it. That's what I do." Without consulting anyone, the Eighth
Army commander now instructed General Oliver Leese, his
XXX Corps commander, to proceed along the route that had
been assigned to the Americans. He then contacted Alexander
and asked him to officially transfer it to his use. The Americans
were to guard his flank and rear as he took on the enemy.

It did not seem unreasonable to the British. The Eighth Army,
though blocked along its planned path, was a tried and proven
force while the newly created U.S. Seventh Army was still to

show what it could do. Once more the Americans felt that they were being treated as auxiliaries. "Monty," the enraged Bradley said, "had nominated himself for the starring role on Sicily, leaving us to eat his dust. An entire American army that had fought its way ashore was to be wasted."

The American bitterness appeared to be more than justified. Despite Montgomery's assurances of his imminent breakthrough to the north, the Eighth Army was failing to make much headway. Indeed, it was making less progress than Montgomery was suggesting in his reports that everything was going well. The Germans had dug in strongly near Catania to block his progress. Montgomery was disinclined to press ahead until his artillery was moved up to prepare the way for his tanks and infantry. Field Marshal Albert Kesselring was surprised by the "slowness of the Allied advance."

Patton complained to Alexander that, as in North Africa, U.S. troops were being unfairly confined to a subsidiary role. Realizing that Montgomery's assurances of a speedy victory would not be realized, not wishing to further antagonize the Americans, and seeking to regain the initiative, Alexander gave him permission to make a reconnaissance in force northwestward. That was all Patton needed to press for more and to change the entire focus of the Sicily campaign.

He sent his troops charging northwest and then northeast in strength. In six days he took control of all of the western part of the island and capped his advance by entering Palermo in triumph. Patton's tactics were in striking contrast to those of Montgomery. He drove his men onward regardless of ground conditions or artillery or aerial support and showed little concern for guarding his exposed flank as he concentrated on forward movement, never indulging in Montgomery's penchant for regularly pausing to regroup.

Unlike Montgomery, he was fortunate to meet little resistance. But taking Palermo served no military purpose. Patton's II Corps, under Bradley, was struggling toward Messina through Sicily's mountainous interior and might have made far better headway had Patton not divided his army to scoot off to the west. Kesselring was delighted at how the Allied forces "just marched and captured unimportant terrain."

But now Patton was set on completing the primary objective of the Sicily operation. Having captured Palermo, and having spent a few days there enjoying the luxury of an Italian royal palatial residence, he rushed eastward along the north coast of the island to seize Messina before Montgomery could get there. His path north still blocked by the Germans, the Eighth Army commander realized what was going to happen and that his troops were going to be denied the victory he had forecast. Having previously tried to elbow the Americans out of the limelight, he now suggested that they take Messina, which seemed inevitable at that point, and even that they should venture into the zone assigned to his own troops to complete the task.

The conquest of Sicily was an important milestone for the Allies. Their forces had successfully begun the liberation of Europe. But the victorious military commanders had little to boast about. Eisenhower had hoped Sicily would be taken in no more than two weeks. But instead of a quick sweep of the island once the beachheads had been secured, it had taken more than a month and casualties were higher than expected.

Italian troops had for the most part withdrawn from the fighting as individuals and as units. But a mere 65,000 German soldiers had been able to hold off almost half a million British and American troops long enough to permit almost all of them to escape across the Straits of Messina to Italy and fight on.

If properly exploited, Allied dominance in the air and the sea might have prevented that from happening. Coordination among the services had been remarkably patchy despite all that had been learned in North Africa. What was more, a landing on the toe of the Italian mainland, while German forces in the region were tied down holding Montgomery back near Catania, would have provided the Allies with an easily acquired beachhead there. It would also have denied the Germans the area to which most of their troops were evacuated from Sicily to avoid being trapped on the island.

In addition to friction between the British and American generals during the campaign, command supervision of the ground campaign was inept. Alexander had failed to exercise control when difficulties arose. Montgomery and Patton—the narrowminded military scientist and the hotheaded brawler—had been permitted to run their respective campaigns with minimal reference to each other. Astoundingly, there had been no detailed plan for conquering the island once the beachheads had been secured. Planning for Operation Husky had been undertaken with nothing like the care and thoroughness it deserved. Alexander later explained that it was felt that the follow-up to the invasion would depend on how the Germans deployed their reserves.

As far as the public in the United States and Britain was concerned, the conquest of Sicily had been an unqualified and much-welcomed success. But Eisenhower made no attempt to dodge the blame for what had gone wrong. He later said that he had not sufficiently appreciated the military situation. As in North Africa, his other duties had distracted him from what was happening during the campaign and had kept him from tying it together when it began to unravel.

Whatever criticism could be made of the Allied effort in the conquest of Sicily, Eisenhower was able to derive much satisfaction from the performance of the U.S. troops involved. In Patton's drive on Palermo and his sweep along the island's north shore to Messina, they had demonstrated aggressiveness, confidence, and battle skill. The thrust of Bradley's II Corps up the middle demonstrated that the early fumbling performances in Tunisia had been left behind. No longer could anyone suggest that the Americans be used only in support.

But Eisenhower was vexed by a chorus of criticism that had arisen among the Americans about Montgomery and the unfavorable comparisons that were being drawn between the Eighth Army commander and Patton. He feared backbiting might chip away at the unity of the American-British alliance. At a press conference after the battle for Sicily was over, he was careful to spread credit for the victory evenly. He told correspondents,

"Today the Seventh Army is worthy to fight alongside the Eighth. I can offer no higher praise."

Patton had fulfilled Eisenhower's expectations. Palermo may not have been much of a battle prize and he had gotten to Messina too late to stop the enemy from escaping, but he had demonstrated to all concerned that he was the hard-driving, battle-winning commander Eisenhower always knew he could be. Patton was a dedicated blood-and-guts warrior. While Montgomery believed the practice of war to be a science, Patton viewed it as a test and a challenge. It defined manliness, both for himself and the troops under him. He was fearless and expected his men to be so as well. A report of an outstanding act of courage in combat could bring tears to his eyes. Hearing that he had refused to take cover when under attack while visiting frontline positions, Eisenhower twice instructed him not to expose himself to danger. For Patton, the greatest crime was cowardice. He would not tolerate it, or what he took for it, among the men serving under him. As the Sicily campaign drew toward an end, that presented Eisenhower with a painful dilemma.

Visiting an evacuation hospital, Patton asked a soldier patient with no apparent wounds what was wrong with him. The soldier replied, "It's my nerves. I can't stand the shelling anymore."

It was the wrong thing to say to Patton. He exploded in fury, cursed the soldier, called him a coward, and slapped him across the face with his gloves. The young man was in fact ill with malaria. But even if he hadn't been, Patton had committed a court-martial offense, and he had done so in the presence of doctors, nurses, and other soldiers. A report made its way through channels to Alexander, who chose to do nothing about it. It was, after all, war.

The incident might have been kept secret had a similar one not taken place soon afterward. This time not only did Patton strike a shell-shocked soldier at a field hospital and threaten to have him shot, but he had drawn his pistol and had seemed about to shoot him himself.

When word finally reached Eisenhower about both incidents,

he was dismayed. Patton's temper tantrums had previously raised doubts about his suitability for senior command. But in addition to being Eisenhower's old friend, he was the most aggressive combat general the Allies had. Eisenhower attempted to hush the matter up, not even reporting it to Marshall. He knew that if the public heard what had happened, "they'll be howling for Patton's scalp and that will be the end of Georgie's service in this war. I simply cannot let that happen. Patton is indespensible to the war effort—one of guarantors of our victory."

But he sharply chastised him in a personal message. He told him there could be no excuse for "brutality, abuse of the sick, nor exhibition of uncontrollable temper in front of subordinates." He ordered him to apologize personally to the individuals concerned. But his hopes that the affair would end there were in vain. News of what had happened had leaked out to American war correspondents. A delegation of them went to question Eisenhower about it at his headquarters. Charles Daly of CBS thought Patton had gone temporarily crazy. Quentin Reynolds of *Collier's* magazine said any of 50,000 GIs in Sicily would be pleased to shoot him if they had the chance.

Dismayed at the prospect of such reports being sent home to feature in newspapers and on the radio, Eisenhower told the correspondents that it would amount to a victory for the enemy. He said that Patton's steamrolling drive in Sicily had made the Germans fear him. The enemy knew, as he did, that the general could make an important contribution to the ultimate defeat of Germany. The Germans were finally on the run but would take heart if Patton were publicly disgraced. Impressed by his faith in the general's importance to the war effort and told that Patton had been strongly reprimanded, the correspondents agreed to spike the story.

It did however leak out later in the year, when the syndicated columnist and radio commentator Drew Pearson reported it, provoking much public anger. Eisenhower had already concluded that Patton's value as a battlefield commander was damaged by his impetuosity and indiscretions. He believed he could still play an important role in winning the war, but not yet. He was too much of an embarrassment. To the fury of the hotheaded victor over Montgomery in the race for Messina, when plans were drawn up for the invasion of France, Bradley, whose performance as II Corps commander under Patton in Sicily had drawn much praise, would be chosen instead by Eisenhower to command the American troops taking part.

CHAPTER 14
Impasse in Italy

The decision to follow the conquest of Sicily with further operations in the Mediterranean had been made by the Combined Chiefs of Staff in May, before the Sicilian campaign had been launched. Once more, it had been been decided upon despite Marshall's complaint that such operations would delay the frontal assault across the English Channel needed to win the war.

But as had been the case with the decision on Sicily, the arguments appeared to favor Britain's Mediterranean strategy over the War Department's. It was still logical to employ the massive Allied forces congregated in the region to follow the Sicilian campaign with further pressure to force already tottering Italy out of the war. On the other hand, a cross-Channel invasion, involving vast redeployments from the region, would require months to organize. For the Western Allies to close down their part of the ground war during that time, bringing the momentum they had gathered in the Mediterranean to a halt, would have given the Germans a respite in the west and required the Russians to cope with the consequences.

The Americans were convinced the British were pressing their strategy primarily because of their long-term imperial, strategic, and commercial interests in the Mediterranean. But they felt obliged by the prevailing circumstances to accept that the invasion of France be delayed until the following year.

Eisenhower was to remain commanding general of the Allied forces in the Mediterranean. Churchill, urging an invasion of the Italian mainland, told him he looked forward to having Christmas dinner with him in Rome. The British were content for him to remain in charge so long as Alexander was working closely under him.

When a Sicily campaign had been under consideration, landings on Corsica or Sardinia instead had also been considered— and were preferred by Eisenhower. Either could be taken with a much smaller invasion force, and, being situated further north off the Italian coast, their capture would make it more difficult for the enemy to plan to repel a subsequent invasion of the mainland if one was to be made, as seemed increasingly likely. But Eisenhower was overruled, partly because Marshall clung to a hope that the conquest of Sicily might end Allied adventures in the Mediterranean, while attacking elsewhere was certain to set the stage for further operations in the region (as happened with Sicily anyway). Unable to reach agreement on how to proceed in the area after Sicily, the Combined Chiefs of Staff left it to Eisenhower, as commander-in-chief on the spot, to make the decision.

The instructions he received were hardly specific. He was to plan operations "best calculated to eliminate Italy from the war and to contain the maximum number of German forces." It was a way out of an impasse on strategy without straining the American-British alliance rather than a deliberate expression of confidence in him as commanding general, though in effect it was that as well.

One night months before, shortly after his victory in Tunisia, when Churchill was to pay a visit to his residence in Algiers (and press his case for an invasion of Italy), Eisenhower had been amused when Butcher asked, "Would you ever have thought . . . two years ago that you would be in . . . far-off Africa, the Allied commander of a great and victorious army, sitting in a villa, waiting a late night call from the Prime Minister of His Majesty's government and growling because the PM was fifteen minutes late?" The conquest of Sicily under his direction had taken longer to achieve than had been expected, but it further cemented his position.

The fall of Sicily to the Allies was a disaster for Mussolini. The flamboyant dictator had promised the Italian people a new Roman Empire. Instead he had brought them grief and destruction. Hundreds of thousands of their young men were dead, had been wounded, or taken prisoner of war. The Allies were masters of the Mediterranean that he had promised would be an Italian lake. Italian cities were being bombed. And now Sicily was lost. Allied propaganda told of worse to come. There could be no doubt that Mussolini was doomed both politically and personally.

Italy and fascism were fundamentally incompatible. Ideologically, fascism requires a strict ordering of society. Germans might be attuned to the sort of discipline that is required, but Italians are for the most part a spontaneous, self-willed people for whom discipline goes against the grain. The system of government with which the fascists had burdened them was thoroughly pockmarked with graft, corruption, and inefficiency so glaring that the Italian army in the field, Mussolini's pride, had never been adequately supplied. It now was short even of food rations for the troops.

The flimsy facade of the fascist state was crumbling. Rail traffic in Italy was hopelessly disrupted by Allied bombing. Strikes and food riots broke out in industrial cities in the north. Even prominent fascists were condemning their once-illustrious *Duce* for leading the country to disaster.

A week after the invasion of Sicily, King Victor Emmanuel III dismissed Mussolini as leader of the country and appointed Field Marshal Pietro Badoglio to serve as acting prime minister. Though it was not publicly announced, Badoglio's task was to extricate Italy from the war.

These developments had the makings of a major coup for

the Allies. Eisenhower knew that "Italy wanted frantically to surrender." It was possible it would not only leave the Axis but could be persuaded to join the Allies in fighting to expel German forces from the country. He issued a statement praising the Italians for ridding themselves of their tyrant and made it clear he was ready to come to terms with the new government.

However, the Allied High Command was shaken by a shiver of alarm. Badoglio had been a member of the Italian Fascist Party. Would dealing with the new Italian regime prove a repetition of the Darlan scandal that had aroused such intense recriminations? Would Eisenhower, whose performance in the Darlan deal had been considered clumsy, permit that sort of situation to recur?

A flurry of warnings and instructions descended on him from Roosevelt and Churchill, from Secretary of State Cordell Hull and Foreign Secretary Anthony Eden, and from the Combined Chiefs of Staff. He was to act cautiously. He was not to exceed his authority as military commander. He was to make only regional agreements, suited exclusively to military needs. He was instructed by Washington to remember that the Allies had decreed that nothing less than unconditional surrender of the Axis powers would be acceptable and that something as close as possible to unconditional surrender should be required of the new Italian regime. Eisenhower was not to be lured into making precipitous agreements. He was to clear everything of consequence with higher authority. In short, he was being warned not to make a fool of himself again.

Churchill believed Italy could be turned into a genuine fighting ally and that "the fury of the Italian population" could be turned against the German forces on their soil. Eisenhower was convinced that was a pipe dream and that all the Italian people wanted was to put the war behind them. He also knew that if significant benefits were to be derived from the developments in Italy, the Allies would have to act quickly, before the Germans took steps to firm up their military position in the country. Wearied by the constraints under which he was required to act, he protested to Marshall.

I must respectfully point out that in a theater of war many problems arise where governments expect and demand the commander take action rather than delay while seeking advice and instruction. I do not see how war can be conducted successfully if every act of the Allied Commander in Chief must be referred back to the home government for advance approval.

To cover his back, Badoglio had made a public declaration of Italy's continued allegiance to the German-led Axis. But he dispatched emissaries to seek information on what peace terms his country could receive from the Allies. He was, however, fearful that if Italy attempted to withdraw from the war, German troops already in the country would act as an army of occupation and more of them would be rushed in to turn all of Italy into a battleground.

Indeed, on the day Mussolini fell, Hitler ordered that additional German forces be shifted into Italy from occupation duty in France. The German dictator had no doubt that Italy was about to desert him. He was even about to withdraw two panzer divisions from the Russian front, though they were badly needed there, and dispatch them south to bolster the position of his forces in Italy.

Badoglio was secretly offered assurances that the Allies would be landing in such strength in Italy that the German forces in his country would be rapidly ejected. He was impressed. But when he learned that the Allied troops Eisenhower was able to commit to the invasion would be far fewer than he had been led to believe, he threatened to renounce the agreement. Brigadier General Maxwell Taylor was dispatched on a secret mission to Rome to determine what exactly the situation was there and to press Badoglio to stand fast.

Taylor, who landed from a speedboat on the Italian coast near Gaeta and was whisked to Rome in an Italian ambulance, found the new Italian leader convinced that the Allies would not be able to oust the Germans from Italy quickly enough. He reported back to Eisenhower that his observations and discussions had persuaded him it would be foolhardy to proceed with a plan to drop a division of U.S. paratroopers on Rome for the purpose of buttressing Italian fortitude and helping prevent the Germans from seizing control of the capital and the strategically important surrounding region.

Eisenhower accepted his judgment but was criticized for not proceeding with the operation anyway. Comparatively few German troops were yet in and around Rome, and Italian resistance, already strengthening in the north of the country, might have been galvanized. Bedell Smith regretted not having sent someone to Rome who might have injected the Italians with enough spirit to fight the Germans, perhaps by threatening that they would otherwise be shot when the Allies won anyway. Kesselring later said, "[W]e hourly expected such a landing to be made, with the cooperation of the Italian forces. Such an air landing would undoubtedly have given a great stimulus to the Italian troops and to the civil population that was unfavorably disposed towards us."

But the risk was not taken and the opportunity was missed. Instead, Eisenhower, angry that things appeared to be slipping out of control and determined to end the impasse, resorted to blackmail to force the Italians out of the war. He sent Badoglio a message threatening to reveal details of a draft armistice agreement that had been made with his emissaries. Not only would the Germans then treat Badoglio as a traitor, but he would not be permitted to seek personal safety behind Allied lines. Before Badoglio could respond, Eisenhower ordered an announcement to be made on Radio Algiers that "The Italian government has surrendered its armed forces unconditionally" and that "All Italians who now act to help eject the German aggressor from Italian soil will have the assistance and support of the United Nations."

Badoglio was left with no choice. An hour later, he confirmed the armistice agreement with the Allies on Radio Rome and fled together with the king to find sanctuary with British forces landing at Taranto in the south.

Eisenhower claimed to abominate politics and diplomacy. But he was beginning to be more adept at that aspect of his job, and particularly in sustaining fundamental American-British unity despite a growing conflict of interests and views and the clash of personalities. He wrote to a friend, "I think sometimes that I am a cross between a one-time soldier, a pseudo-statesman, a jack-legged politician and crooked diplomat. I walk a soapy tight-rope in a rain storm with a blazing furnace on one side and a pack of ravenous tigers on the other. . . . In spite of all of this, I must admit that the whole thing is intriguing and interesting and is forever presenting new challenges."

In view of the pressure he was under, his handling of the Badoglio affair probably produced as good a result as was possible under the circumstances. It was appreciated even by some who had been critical of him. Without being conquered, the Italians were being forced out of the war and might even join the Allies. However, it was still apparent that military planning of Allied operations in the Mediterranean had been dogged by muddle. Eisenhower made no effort to pretend otherwise. He privately admitted in particular that it had been a mistake not to have landed on the northeast tip of Sicily to prevent the bulk of the German forces from escaping to fight again, as they would, with great effect, once the Allies came to grips with them on the Italian mainland.

The general public knew nothing of Eisenhower's problems and worries. A *Time* magazine cover story, then in preparation, described him as a master of "tact and diplomacy." He was considered by the American public not simply to be overseeing operations but to be personally directing them, and to be doing so with great skill.

Marshall's messages of advice to Eisenhower—on, for example, being less cautious and relying less on his British deputies—showed that the chief of staff still thought of him as a protégé who continued to need guidance. Marshall reassuringly repeatedly made it clear that he had his confidence and support. But there were limits. He would brook no further delay in preparing for the cross-Channel invasion of France. Operation Overlord was at last scheduled to take place in the spring of 1944, but Marshall suspected that Churchill would attempt to have it delayed still further.

When the Allies agreed that the invasion of Italy would follow the conquest of Sicily and that Eisenhower would be its commanding general, Marshall had issued him a warning. He had told Eisenhower that he would be losing troops and landing craft from the Mediterranean, where the chief of staff hadn't wanted them to be sent in the first place. Now it was payback time. Despite the imminence of the invasion of Italy, Marshall insisted that seven divisions as well as a goodly number of landing craft be shifted to Britain to prepare for Overlord. The British High Command had felt obliged to acquiesce.

Eisenhower was alarmed. He warned that diminishing the forces at his disposal for the Italy campaign would increase the hazards they would face. But the War Department was unshaken in its view that the Mediterranean was a "graveyard" and that the Mediterranean strategy had been a costly mistake. Marshall rejected Eisenhower's protests. He would have to make do with fewer resources than he had been counting on even though the Germans were pouring reinforcements into Italy and it was apparent that the struggle for the country would be no pushover for the Allies.

For Montgomery, the Sicily campaign had been a letdown. Instead of the easy triumph he had forecast, his proud Eighth Army had bogged down and had been obliged to leave the main prize in the campaign to the American generals whose abilities he had previously disdained. He blamed the haphazard way the conquest of Sicily had been planned and executed, ignoring the role he had played in both. He was afraid that the invasion of the Italian mainland would suffer the same fate.

After a number of options had been considered and discarded, two major landing sites were chosen. Montgomery's Eighth Army would go ashore on September 3, 1943, on the southern tip of the Italian peninsula in Operation Baytown. The U.S. Fifth Army, under Clark, would land six days later in the Gulf of Salerno south of Naples in Operation Avalanche.

Churchill thought Eisenhower was being excessively cautious in concentrating the invasion forces so far south. He urged him to make his landings closer to Rome so as to be able to seize the Italian capital before the Germans got there in force. Eisenhower declined to do so, believing he would not be able to provide adequate air support for the troops undertaking such an operation.

He was once more stung by criticism of his caution. He had wanted to act boldly when Mussolini had been deposed the month before. He had believed the event had presented him with an opportunity to win Italy over to the Allied cause. He had been "full of plans and ideas for exploiting the situation." But bureaucratic restraints had prevented him from doing so. He had been required to clear everything of significance with the Combined Chiefs of Staff and the War Department, and sometimes with the White House and Churchill as well. Conflicting opinions, time-consuming discussions, and a lack of urgency had prevented him from seizing promising opportunities.

Nevertheless, he believed a landing on the tip of Italy could be made by the Eighth Army without difficulty immediately after the conquest of Sicily, while the enemy was trying to regroup on the Italian mainland. Despite Patton's and Bradley's irritation with Montgomery, he told Marshall he was confident of his "ability to handle" the British commander. He said Montgomery had decided to "join the family" and that he was "seeking to become a member of the team and not simply the star player."

But Eisenhower did not understand Montgomery and never would. The Eighth Army commander was not prepared to go along with Operation Baytown except on his own terms. Eisenhower was pressing him to proceed hastily, but Montgomery insisted on first making certain of what he considered sufficient artillery, naval, and air support to guarantee not only success in the operation but a position on the mainland from which he could drive north with absolute confidence. By now he had made not allowing himself to be rushed a matter of principle as well as practice.

He was not at all happy with the way planning for the Italy invasion had progressed. No one in charge seemed to understand the fundamental rules of preparation for combat that he had tried so hard to codify for all concerned. He was understandably baffled and exasperated. Neither he nor Clark were informed exactly what was required of them other than that they were to land at their respective Italian beaches, establish bridgeheads, and head north.

Clark, who had not yet experienced actual combat command and was raring to go, appeared to be able to live comfortably with the situation. Montgomery, who even in the best of circumstances was uncomfortable with any plan devised by others, remained sharply critical. One of the great campaigns in history, the liberation of the European continent from German military control, was about to be launched. But it appeared to him that amateurs of limited understanding were in charge. Even simple command procedures had been neglected. Two weeks before he was scheduled to send his troops ashore at the boot of Italy, he complained in anguish to Alexander, "I have been given no clear object for the operation. . . . Request definite instructions."

Alexander responded with a handwritten note that told Montgomery what he already knew. He was to secure a bridgehead on the toe of Italy "to enable our naval forces to operate through the Straits of Messina." When he had forced the enemy to retreat, he was to "follow him up with such force as you can make available, bearing in mind that the greater the extent to which you can engage enemy forces in the southern tip of Italy, the more assistance will you be giving to [Clark in Operation] Avalanche."

He was assigned no specific location, city, or town as the focus of his efforts on the mainland, an absurdity to a man who always insisted that every detail of preplanned offensive or defensive action had to be spelled out in advance. No concerted plan linking the Baytown and Avalanche operations had been formulated. He was leading the first Allied invasion on the mainland of Hitler's Fortress Europe and his orders amounted to a half-page of a generalities.

Montgomery objected to more than just procedures. He doubted whether his Operation Baytown made sense. It seemed to him that, rather than split the attacking force, it would be better to beef up Operation Avalanche at Salerno and thereby cut off whatever enemy troops were deployed in Italy's deep south. If, however, his operation was designed merely as a diversion to tie down German units prior to Clark's landing at Salerno, shouldn't they be roughly synchronized rather than take place almost a week apart? The Germans would be given time to escape northward. He later wrote, "[T]he way the whole party was stage-managed, is past all belief."

He was aware that his own circumstances had changed significantly. He was still an enormously popular figure, instantly recognizable by the troops and the public. But Patton and Bradley had emerged from the conquest of Sicily as much-admired fighting generals with whom he would have to share the limelight. In the future, Alexander, though still ground-forces commander, might be unable to favor him in the field. That could determine how resources—manpower, equipment, air support, everything he needed to guarantee success in combat for the Eighth Army and himself—would be doled out.

He knew the American army and division commanders didn't like or respect him. Patton had been "nearly irrational" in his determination to beat him to Messina. Montgomery realized that something had to be done to ease their antipathy. A few days before the invasion was to be launched, he made an uncharacteristic effort to socialize with them, inviting them to the luxurious villa he had commandeered at Taormina in Sicily as his headquarters and residence. Eisenhower was there, along with Patton and Bradley. Montgomery was relaxed and friendly, though Bradley observed that "his famous conceit stood out even in this company." Eisenhower took the occasion to present him with the American Legion of Merit, and they drove up the coast to Messina to peer across the water to mainland Italy two miles away.

It was an agreeable sight but Eisenhower felt frustrated by Montgomery's refusal to be rushed.

I believe [he said later] there is a picture of Montgomery and me looking across the Strait from Messina. I believed that the Germans would withdraw [from the tip of Italy], that we could make a landing practically unopposed. General Montgomery wished to have everything fully prepared and thought there would be considerable German opposition. Meanwhile there was General Patton moaning—asking that he be allowed to make the crossing. I told General Alexander I believed we could do it in a row-boat. We sat there in Messina from 17 August until 3 September."

In the early hours of September 3, the Eighth Army's XIII Corps crossed the Straits of Messina to the Italian mainland. Prior to its dispatch, bombers, four battleships, and heavy guns planted on heights above the Sicilian shore subjected the area where the British beachhead was to be established to intensive bombardment. Over several days, the guns—600 of them— had been hauled into place over Sicily's poor roads and mountain tracks. That was the way Montgomery insisted it should be.

It was a time-consuming, wasteful, and needless exercise, because German troops had abandoned the region days before. Only two German infantry battalions were still in the area, and they were ten miles back. Italian troops stayed behind when they left but offered no resistance. Mines had not even been planted on the beaches. Once the British had landed, Italian soldiers who had survived the bombardment volunteered to help unload their supplies and equipment. The beachhead was quickly secured without great effort. The only difficulty was dealing with animals that had escaped from a nearby zoo during the bombardment.

This first Allied landing on the European mainland was a great morale-booster but had little military significance. The buildup of German forces farther north in Italy was accelerating, and a hard-fought contest with them for control of the country was still to be faced. But congratulations were in order, and Alexander visited Montgomery to offer them and to inform him of the armistice with the Italians that had just been arranged by Eisenhower. He told Montgomery that the Italian Army was switching sides and was expected to be very helpful to the Allies in the Italian campaign. The Eighth Army commander doubted that very much. He believed that, aside from being desperately war-weary, Italian troops would not be able to cope with the Germans. He was convinced the Italian surrender would make little difference to the job that lay ahead for the Allied armies.

He was already being proved right about that. Though Marshal Badoglio had announced the armistice and had fled to Calabria to seek safety behind British lines, he had neglected to issue orders to the Italian Army to follow suit and switch allegiance as well. The Germans had already begun to disarm the Italians. Many of them wasted no time in disposing of their weapons, slipping into civilian clothes, and heading home.

If Clark expected a warm welcome and support when troops of his U.S. Fifth Army went ashore on beaches at Salerno on September 9, 1943, he was disappointed. For some, the landings were unopposed. But others met determined resistance. The U.S. 36th Division, never before in combat, was subjected to heavy German artillery and aerial attack. The main landings south of Salerno of British divisions attached to Clark's army also ran into trouble. Nevertheless, all the major landing areas appeared to have been secured by nightfall. Combined with Montgomery's landings farther south, it seemed that the Allied Italian campaign was off to an encouraging start. Eisenhower was much pleased and relieved. However, within forty-eight hours Clark was running into trouble.

The Germans had expected the Salerno landings to take place about where they did. Weeks before, Hitler had personally ordered, "In the case of an enemy landing, the area Naples-Salerno must be held." The newly formed German Tenth Army had established its headquarters just south of Salerno. Its commander, General Heinrich von Vietinghoff, had eight divisions at his disposal, including the four that had been able to escape from Sicily before Patton reached Messina. Two of Vietinghoff's divisions had been badly weakened by losses, but his army was still a strong fighting force. Five of his divisions went on the attack, seeking to drive the four divisions Clark had put ashore back into the sea.

Clark panicked. He angered Eisenhower by planning to pull the Fifth Army headquarters he established on land back to a warship offshore. Eisenhower wished he had put Patton in command of the operation. He was also annoyed with Montgomery again. After establishing its bridgehead in the south, the Eighth Army was supposed to rush to Clark's assistance. This meant traversing difficult terrain. But, the Germans having withdrawn most of their forces from the region, Montgomery was meeting no great resistance. Alexander urged him to move quickly. The BBC reported that the Eighth Army, masterfully driven by its famous commander, was dashing up the Italian boot. Butcher had believed, "Monty will move as he has never moved before. He is the potential hero of a grand melodrama and he will be quick to grasp the possibility of adding further luster to his name."

It wasn't happening that way. Unwilling to risk a German surprise counterattack, Montgomery ignored instructions to move rapidly to the aid of Clark's battered forces. He proceeded instead with his customary caution, taking seventeen days to cover 300 miles. Believing there was little to be cautious about, a number of war correspondents accompanying the Eighth Army went on ahead and made contact with Clark's troops more than a day before Montgomery's advance units did. To criticism of what even the German commander called his "very cautious advance," Montgomery maintained, "I just arrived in time to relieve the pressure, and make the Germans pull out."

But by then Clark's situation had eased. Eisenhower had diverted landing craft that had been heading through the Mediterranean for operations in the Far East to reinforce the troops ashore at Salerno. And air and sea power had been hastily concentrated to smash the German counterattack. It was, finally, a demonstration of nimble staff work under Eisenhower's direction in a crisis, and it achieved the desired results.

There now began the arduous climb by the Allied forces up the Italian peninsula, Clark's Fifth Army up the west coast, Montgomery's Eighth along the Adriatic and up the middle where terrain permitted. Foggia, with its precious airfields from which Allied bombers would be able to raid German cities, fell to Montgomery soon afterward, Naples to Clark a few days later. Montgomery maintained a steady advance despite increasingly stubborn German resistance. However, each of his successes led to another enemy defense line a few miles further north. Clark's experience was much the same.

By the end of the year, four months of hard slogging had carried the Allies barely seventy miles beyond Salerno. Eisenhower was dismayed that, "The going in Italy is painfully slow." He foresaw "a long, tedious, and costly campaign to take Rome." It seemed like a replay of the previous winter's difficult struggle in Tunisia. Marshall upbraided him for not being more daring in his effort to reach the Italian capital. Eisenhower was "grieved to think" that Marshall did not give him credit "for cracking the whip." He later wrote, "[I]t wearies me to be thought of as timid, when I've had to do things that were so risky as to be almost crazy."

He was especially bitter about the scolding from Washington because it was Marshall who, in his insistence on preparing for the invasion of France across the English Channel, had taken away some of his landing craft and bombers. Without them Eisenhower would not seriously consider a landing further north in Italy to leapfrog enemy defenses. After the war, General Siegfried Westphal, chief of staff to Field Marshal Kesselring, the commander of German forces in the region, said the Germans were convinced such a landing would have succeeded and would have changed the entire character of the Italian campaign.

If the forces employed in the landing at Salerno [Westphal said] had been used instead at Civitavecchia [on the coast near Rome] the results would have been much more decisive. If this latter operation had been carried out, Rome would have fallen to the Allies' hand within a few days at the most. It was well known that there were only two German divisions in Rome and that no others could have been brought up quickly enough to defend it. In conjunction with the five Italian divisions stationed at Rome, a combined sea and air landing would have taken the Italian capital in seventy-two hours. Quite apart from the political repercussions . . . this would have resulted in cutting off at one blow the supplies of . . . five German divisions.·

Montgomery was scathing in his criticism of the Allied military command for other reasons. He believed the movements of the Fifth and Eighth armies could have been coordinated far more efficiently. He deeply regretted that his ability to make the relevant decisions had been much reduced since his days of glory in the North African desert.

To the irritation of the Americans, the British press, fed embellished reports by the Ministry of Information in London, nevertheless kept Montgomery on the highest of pedestals. The BBC continued to report his progress as if the Eighth Army were galloping forward when, in fact, it remained a struggle for his troops to make any significant headway and he repeatedly halted his advance for the purpose of "winding up his tail."

Even when stalled, Montgomery sought to give the impression that everything on his front was proceeding exactly as planned. It had become his habit, almost a compulsion, to claim a tactical success when there was none. Forced by ground conditions to delay a major offensive planned for late November at the Sangro River line, he declared, "The Germans are . . . in the very condition in which we want them. We will now hit [them] a colossal crack." He did indeed, with strong air and artillery support, and it looked good in the newspapers at home though less was said when the enemy rallied and his drive fizzled out.

He continued his regular morale-boosting visits to the front line. They were especially important now that things were not going well. Whatever concern he had about how the campaign was developing, his sense of self-importance remained intact. He boasted to an acquaintance that, in addition to a personal airplane and no less than five cars at his disposal, he'd had the Royal Navy provide him with a motor launch with a crew of seventeen for him to nip around the coast when he wished to. But Italy was an even greater comedown for him than Sicily. The campaign there was for the most part dreary, unheroic, costly drudgery under very dissagreeable conditions.

As winter closed in, it grew wet and cold. Movement was often across seas of mud. Even in the best of weather, Italian roads could not easily support the advance of the Allied divisions, with their armor and trucks. The Germans had blown up roads and bridges. Supply convoys were sometimes held up for days. Instead of withdrawing to the north as they had been expected to do, the enemy was pouring in reinforcements. Under the restraints imposed by the weather, the landscape, and the shortage of landing craft, Montgomery and Clark were reduced to nibbling their way forward and Rome, expected to have been taken by then, remained tantalizingly out of reach.

In November, Eisenhower had ordered the establishment of a forward command post in Italy for Allied Forces Headquarters. He was upset by how the easy life enjoyed by staff personnel at AFHQ in Algiers contrasted with the cold, rain, mud, and death faced by the men at the front. The move also permitted him from time to time to escape from the streams of VIPs who forced themselves upon his time in Algeria. Such dignitaries were unlikely to trouble him with their presence while fighting was still in progress not far away.

The command post was set up at Caserta just north of Naples. But Eisenhower objected to some of the arrangements made nearby. Some senior officers had commandeered for their private use luxurious villas on the island of Capri in Naples harbor. He angrily announced that "[N]one of those will belong to any general as long as I'm Boss around here," and ordered that they be turned into rest centers for combat troops—"not a playground for the Brass."

Official communiqués and press reports presented a much watered down impression of how difficult and slow the Allied advance in Italy had become. Just as Montgomery and his achievements were making headlines in Britain, Eisenhower was seen across the United States as the guiding hand of the triumph for freedom and democracy the Allies were forging in Europe. Soon after the Salerno beachheads had been secured, an American Legion post in New York City passed a resolution urging him, "by reason of his outstanding 'leadership qualities,' " to run for president. When Eisenhower heard about it, he dismissed it as, "Baloney. Why," he asked, "can't a simple soldier be left alone to carry out his orders?"

Nevertheless, he found himself briefly tapped by the political circus back home. Word spread that the Republican Party, seeking a popular figure to oust Roosevelt from the White House after three terms there, might choose MacArthur, the hero of the Pacific theater, to run against the president in the election campaign the following year. That led to suggestions that if MacArthur was chosen by the Republicans to be their standard bearer, Roosevelt would pick Eisenhower, the American hero of the European theater, to run as his vice-presidential candidate on the Democratic Party ticket. But Eisenhower, who would be elected president as a Republican a decade later, found the idea absurd.

> I can scarcely imagine anyone in the United States [he wrote] less qualified than I for any type of political work. I know only one method of operation—to be honest with others as I am with myself and to demand of everyone around me undivided devotion to the cause of winning the war.

Eisenhower had no doubt that his own role was that of a career soldier, though despite his celebrity status he wasn't confident about where it was leading him. Notwithstanding the acclaim he was receiving, he believed he had a lot to answer for, including the Darlan deal, confusion over the Italian armistice, and the failure of the campaigns in North Africa, Sicily, and now Italy to be concluded more quickly and with fewer casualties. When the success of the Salerno landings had been in doubt, he had gloomily thought that if it ended in diaster, "he would probably be out."

But the Americans had not been thrown into the sea at Salerno, and the press, radio, and newsreels still pictured him as both a military genius and a great guy, though the War Department still considered the war in the Mediterranean to be of secondary importance, merely a prelude to Operation Overlord, which had definitely been scheduled, over British objections, to take place in a few months' time. In view of America's predominant contribution in manpower and hardware, it was understood that an American would be commanding general in the cross-Channel invasion of France. It was believed that Marshall, who had played the central role in organizing the American war effort and who was respected by all, would be appointed. Indeed it was thought that, because he was staying in Washington, he was being saved for that main event.

Roosevelt suggested as much to Eisenhower in November 1943 when he passed through North Africa en route to a meeting with Churchill in Cairo and the general took him on a tour of battlegrounds in Tunisia where American troops had fought. Roosevelt told him that Marshall deserved to be Supreme Commander of Overlord and to have the glory that would go with it. "You and I," he said, "know who was Chief of Staff during the last years of the Civil War, but practically no one else knows. . . . I hate to think that fifty years from now practically nobody will know who George Marshall was."

Harry Hopkins, Roosevelt's confidant, who was with the president on the trip, told Butcher that Marshall definitely would command Overlord, and Admiral Ernest King told Eisenhower that he could expect to take Marshall's place as Army Chief of Staff in Washington when that happened. Marshall himself was confident he would be named to Overlord and had begun contemplating a command structure of his own choosing for the operation.

The prospect of going back home to be planted behind a desk appalled Eisenhower. It would be an elevation in status of the kind he could not have dreamt of a year before, but he hoped he would instead be permitted to stay as commanding general in the Mediterranean while someone else succeeded Marshall as U.S. Chief of Staff.

The strain of the Italian campaign, compounded by the convoluted politics and diplomacy involved and concern about his career, was taking its toll. He felt weary and anxious. He wrote to Mamie, "Nothing has been exactly right and everybody about me is having a tough time. I try to hang on to some

shreds of good disposition, but it does get tough at times." At
a Cairo conference, during which Eisenhower reported to the
Combined Chiefs on the progress in Italy, Marshall was worried
by how tired he looked. He advised him to take a vacation
and let his staff handle the campaign for a little while. Deeply
anxious about the stalemate in the fighting, Eisenhower didn't
want to, but Marshall in effect ordered him to take at least a
few days off. He reluctantly gave in and traveled to Luxor and
Jerusalem to see ancient monuments and religious sites. Kay
Summersby went with him.

Roosevelt in the meantime was having second thoughts about
whom to choose to command Overlord. Marshall had proved
himself an expert in his dealings with Congress. As chairman
of the Joint Chiefs of Staff, the respect his calm firmness of
purpose, authoritativeness, and integrity evoked had brought
a measure of coherence to the confusions of war, as seen from
the corridors of power in Washington. Roosevelt had come to
rely heavily upon him. In addition, to shift him from the role
he played with such competence might produce needless complications in the command structure. Some at the War Department feared that his departure from the influential Combined
Chiefs of Staff to become Overlord's Supreme Commander
would make it more difficult to assert American views on strategy over those of the British.

Nevertheless, the president was reluctant to deny Marshall
the opportunity that was his due to lead the Allied forces to
victory over Hitler. To relieve himself of that burden, the president shrewdly asked Marshall's advice on the appointment.
He hoped that a man of such great dignity would be above
recommending himself for the job and that he would suggest
Eisenhower, the only other likely American candidate. But Marshall declined to let the president off the hook by offering the
selfless advice that was being solicited. He said instead that
he would agree to whomever Roosevelt chose. The president
would have to decide for himself.

Having already just done so, he told Marshall that Eisenhower would be Overlord's Supreme Commander. Roosevelt's
compliment to Marshall—that he didn't feel "he could sleep at

ease if you were out of Washington"—was unlikely to have gratified a man who was immune to flattery and who had just been denied the opportunity to lead the most monumental military campaign in history.

The British regretted that Marshall had not been chosen. Churchill considered him a better general than Eisenhower, more competent, more decisive, and tougher. But the selfless Marshall hastened to assure Eisenhower of his continuing support, and the British, who continued to get along excellently with Eisenhower on a personal level, were careful not to publicize their preference. Some American generals believed he continued to succumb too readily to British influences. But everyone was impressed with how effectively he had fashioned and maintained the American-British military alliance.

With the invasion of France soon to be launched from England, harmony in the alliance was more important than ever. Brooke, one of the few who did not think highly of Marshall and preferred Eisenhower to him, grudgingly conceded that he now had "a certain amount of experience as a commander and was beginning to find his feet." With his tolerance of eccentricities, his candidness, modesty, consideration for others, and infectious grin, he was adept at getting generals who might otherwise want to have nothing to do with one another to work together. Even the hypercritical Montgomery would later acknowledge that.

> I know of no other person who could have welded the Allied forces into such a fine fighting machine in the way he did, and kept a balance among the many conflicting and disturbing elements which threatened at times to wreck the ship.

When Marshall informed him that he would command Operation Overlord, Eisenhower was genuinely surprised. Had Marshall been chosen instead, as was expected, Eisenhower, recalled to the War Department, probably would have fallen back into the obscurity that was the fate of generals who served with distinction but without headlines in Washington and London during the war, planning, organizing, and getting things done on behalf of the generals and troops in the field. Marshall was saved from the obscurity that awaited him by his postwar service as Secretary of State, in which role he devised and implemented the historic Marshall Plan that rescued Western Europe from the threat of Communism and economic and political chaos after Nazi Germany had been crushed.

Eisenhower was touring Fifth Army positions in Italy on Christmas Eve when the public announcement of his appointment to command Overlord was made. Two days later, he issued his farewell to the troops.

> I take my leave of you with feelings of personal regret that are equaled only by my pride in your brilliant accomplishments of the year just passed. All together you comprise a mighty machine which, under your new commander, will continue a completely unified instrument of war to make further inroads into the enemy's defenses and assist in bringing about his final collapse. Until we meet again in the heart of the enemy's Continental stronghold, I send Godspeed and good luck to each of you along with the assurance of my lasting gratitude and admiration.

Eisenhower wanted to get to London as quickly as possible to start work on preparations for Overlord, though he was still tired, disappointed at how little progress had been made in the Italian campaign, and often crotchety. Again Marshall made him take a vacation. He urged him to go home and see Mamie before moving to London. Eisenhower wrote to Mamie, "I miss you terribly. . . . I do hope I can have a visit with you before too long." But he told Marshall he didn't want to go home. He said there was too much still to be done before he left Italy. However, the chief of staff pressed him, warning that the enormous responsibility with which he had been entrusted would put him under even greater strain than he had experienced before.

I am interested in that you are fully prepared to bear the strain and I am not interested in the usual rejoinder that you can take it. It is of vast importance that you be fresh mentally and you certainly will not be if you go straight from one great problem to another. Now come on home and see your wife and trust somebody else for twenty minutes in England.

Marshall told Roosevelt he had brought Eisenhower home "over his strenuous objections." But Eisenhower finally agreed that he probably could do with a rest and a momentary change of pace, and made arrangements to spend some time in Washington before assuming his new command in England. In view of Overlord's enormous support requirements, it was also a good idea to renew personal contact with the movers and shakers at the War Department.

Montgomery was leaving Italy too. On Christmas Eve 1943 he was officially informed that he was being summoned back to England to assume command of the 21st Army Group and prepare it for the invasion of France. He had long been confident that no other general would be chosen to command the British component of Overlord. But he had not been an automatic choice. Eisenhower much preferred Alexander. Brooke said that was because he "was not fond of Monty, and certainly could not handle him."

A number of senior British officers also thought Alexander should have been chosen. Pro- and anti-Montgomery factions had developed in the British military establishment. It was widely agreed he was a difficult man to deal with professionally. Judgment on him was generally divided between those who thought his military skills more than compensated for his abrasiveness and those who thought that he was an excellent training officer, but no more than that.

There were grave doubts about whether American generals would be willing to work with him for long. Many of them made no secret that they believed he was not nearly the master of the battlefield he was cracked up to be. They certainly would not accept the abuse he customarily dished out to those who did not measure up to his standards. Nor were they likely to take well to being lectured by him on the science of war. In contrast, the Americans liked the unpretentious, generally affable Alexander.

Churchill was among those who had doubts about appointing Montgomery to serve under Eisenhower. After Sicily and Italy, he had also come to question whether his exalted reputation was entirely warranted. But Montgomery was still the most celebrated soldier in the British Army, unsurpassed as a morale-booster both for his troops and the British public. That had to be considered an important factor as the strain and cost of the war told increasingly on the home front. Besides, Montgomery had important backers. Brooke had no doubt that he was the finest of the Allied commanders and War Minister P. J. Grigg also believed that he had demonstrated an unrivaled mastery of tactics and logistics. Churchill was won over. Eisenhower later said he had been won over as well.

On December 30, Montgomery said good-bye to the officers and men of his headquarters staff in Italy. It was a suitably dramatic leave-taking for the man who had led the Eighth Army to glory. The ceremony was staged in the partly bomb-damaged opera house of the southern Italian town of Vasto. Though some of the divisions that had been the vanguard of the Eighth Army's triumphs in North Africa had already been detached from it and assigned elsewhere, it was an emotional moment.

Montgomery thanked the men for their support and asked them to provide his successor as Eighth Army commander, General Oliver Leese, who had been one of his corps commanders, with as much support as he had received from them. But he was glad to be leaving Italy where the campaign had been marked by what he considered "a first class administrative muddle" and where more of a damp, cold winter and a tough struggle up the Italian mountain spine lay ahead.

He had already conferred in Algiers with Eisenhower and Bedell Smith on the role he was to play in the invasion of France. He was pleased to learn that they appeared finally to have come to their senses and that he was to be in charge of the opening phase of Overlord, commanding the American troops that were to be involved as well as the British. Not only that—Eisenhower instructed Montgomery to take personal control of Overlord planning until he himself returned to London to take charge.

On December 31, 1943, Montgomery left Italy for England by way of Marrakesh in Morocco, where Churchill was convalescing from pneumonia. The prime minister gave him a copy of a preliminary blueprint for Overlord that had been drawn up by COSSAC (Chief of Staff to the Supreme Allied Commander), the special invasion planning staff in London. Montgomery asked for time to examine it, but the prime minister wanted his immediate reaction. He looked through the plan before going to bed that night and presented Churchill with a concise gut assessment in the morning.

> The initial landing [according to his main observation] is on too narrow a front and is confined to too small an area. By D + 12 a total of 16 divisions have been landed on the same beaches as were used for the initial landings. This would lead to the most appalling confusion on the beaches, and the smooth development of the land battle would be made extremely difficult—if not impossible. Further divisions come pouring in, all over the same beaches. By D + 24 a total of 24 divisions have been landed, all over the same beaches; control of the beaches and so on would be very difficult; the confusion, instead of getting better, would get worse. My first impression is that the present plan is impracticable.

Eisenhower had also seen the plan. He had told Montgomery that he had doubts about it too, for largely the same reasons, and instructed him to "analyze and revise" it. The revision was to be ready for when he arrived in England from Washington. He also sent word to the planners in London that Montgomery was acquainted with his ideas for deployment of ground forces for the invasion. He said, "Please look upon him as my representative in getting forward with these things as rapidly as may be practicable."

Eisenhower returned to Washington a far more important figure than when he had left it eighteen months before. He was now a full general and had the trust and acclaim of the president, Congress, and Americans from sea to shining sea. His visit home included high-level conferences with Roosevelt, Secretary of War Stimson, Marshall and the other chiefs of staff, and other senior figures. He was now one of them. He used the opportunity to impress on them the need to provide him with adequate resources and authority to make Overlord a success. He particularly urged accelerated delivery of landing craft and displayed much concern about the failure to sort out his claim to control Allied air power prior and during the operation.

The time he and Mamie had been apart had complicated their relationship. It had been maintained by loving letters between them during his time away. But he was a different person now. He had been under relentless pressure, made momentous decisions, dealt with world figures, and shouldered enormous burdens. Prior to his return, he had warned her to expect him to be different. "I miss you terribly," he had told her in a letter. But he had added, "I know I am a changed person—no one could be through what I've seen and not be different from what he was at the beginning." Now Mamie saw how true that was. Not only did he look older but, though he had written that he loved her, he was abrupt and impatient. He now had a great, historic purpose in life and she was wounded by the realization that she could not figure greatly in it.

She was still a provincial army wife, very much concerned with trivialities and proprieties. She was aggrieved that other officers returning on home leave brought their wives wonderful gifts from Naples—magnificent leather handbags and beautiful scarfs—while he, in charge of the entire shebang, brought her nothing to compare with those things. It was inconsiderate and humiliating. What could she tell her friends?

Eisenhower protested that unlike many serving under him,

his responsibilities had not allowed him much time to go shopping. There was, of course, more to it than that. He could easily have sent an aide to do his shopping for him. It simply hadn't occurred to him. However, while in Washington, he did not forget to get Roosevelt to sign a photograph of himself for Kay Summersby.

It was commonly known at his headquarters that the relationship between Eisenhower and Kay, who had transferred with him to Italy, had long before gone well past the general-and-his-driver stage. Among her other official tasks was dealing with much of his non-official correspondence, the countless letters he received from ordinary people. But her most important function was still to flatter him by her attractive presence. According to Kay, they were in love.

The most descriptive account of their relationship came from Kay in a book ghostwritten for her years later. Her prose was evidently influenced by romantic novels and television soap operas. She said that in Algiers, where they had grown particularly close, Eisenhower tried desperately to control his feelings about her but was not always able to do so.

> "Goddamnit, can't you tell I'm crazy about you," he barked at me. It was like an explosion. We were suddenly in each other's arms. His kisses absolutely unravelled me. Hungry, strong, demanding. And I responded every bit as passionately. He stopped, took my face between his hands. "Goddamnit," he said. "I love you."

It has been suggested that this account, written for Kay when she was old and sick, was the invention of a woman who had imagined things after the fact for reasons of self-esteem or perhaps to make her memoirs more salable. But there is no doubt that Eisenhower, who went off with her alone when circumstances permitted—in Algeria, during his vacation in the Middle East, and later in the south of France—was very fond of her and permitted her to spend much time in his presence. He introduced her to King George, Roosevelt, Churchill, other

visiting dignitaries, and all his senior generals. Patton said Eisenhower always acted like a show-off when she was present.

It would hardly have been strange if he had fallen in love
with her. He was long isolated from Mamie and family life. She
was an attractive, charming woman who shared his liking for
a number of things, including horseback riding and bridge.
And she was available, on the spot, at his beck and call. There
is no written or spoken suggestion that they consummated their
relationship. She suggests that she was willing but that he
always drew back, saying, "If only things had been different."
However, as proof that their relationship went past the stage
of mere friendship, in her book, *Past Forgetting: My Love Affair
with Dwight D. Eisenhower*, she included a photograph of a note
in his handwriting that she said he had slipped into her hand at
the end of an enjoyable day of sightseeing together in Jerusalem
toward the end of 1943: "Good night—there are lots of things
I could say—you know them. Good night."

Mamie was naturally upset by the persisting rumors about
them. She was hurt and angry when, during his stay in the
capital, Eisenhower sometimes called her Kay by mistake. The
situation wasn't helped by the fact that Mamie, who was rarely
in robust good health, was not feeling well while he was home.
Having nursed a cold for weeks, neither was he. They argued
and at one point he told her he looked forward to getting back
to "my theater where I can do what I want."

His trip to Kansas for a family reunion during his break from
his duties in Europe (without Mamie who, because of a heart
murmur, was advised never to fly) was a great pleasure for him.
Everyone there was impressed by how confident, authoritative,
and important the boy from Abilene had become while still
retaining his warmth, although he did not seem as open as he
had once been. The burdens he had shouldered had changed
him for them as well.

The occasion was tarnished by the decline of his eighty-two-
year-old mother toward senility after his father's death. She
was delighted to see him, crying and laughing at the sight of
him after so long. But she had no idea what he had been up to.

He also visited his son John and some of John's fellow cadets at West Point, where he enjoyed listening to their advice on military matters and was warmed by his memories of his own days there.

When he left Washington for London on January 12, 1944, to begin molding Operation Overlord into shape, Mamie, more wounded than comforted by his visit, told him, "Don't come back until it's over, Ike. I couldn't bear to lose you again."

General Dwight David Eisenhower

U.S. ARMY

Field Marshal Sir Bernard Law Montgomery

Eisenhower and Montgomery, a troubled and mutually
frustrating collaboration

General George C. Marshall, U.S. Army Chief of Staff, was disappointed not to have been named Allied Supreme Commander himself but gave Eisenhower, pictured here with him, his full support.

U.S. ARMY

Montgomery's victory at El Alamein was a great relief to Prime Minister Winston Churchill, who was increasingly held responsible in Parliament for Britain's string of military reverses. The two men are pictured here with Montgomery's puppy, named Rommel.

BRITISH INFORMATION SERVICE

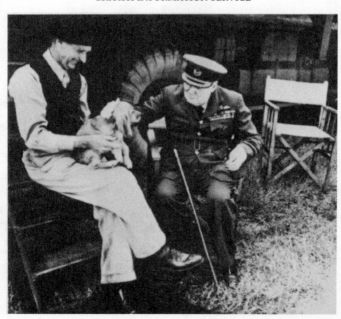

Field Marshal Sir Alan Brooke, Chief of the Imperial General Staff, who provided Montgomery with moral support in his discord with Eisenhower

General Omar Bradley, commander of the U.S. 12th Army Group, whose elevation to equal status with Montgomery aroused much resentment in Britain

A portrait of Field Marshal Earl Alexander of Tunis who, for a time, acted as a buffer between Eisenhower and Montgomery

Field Marshal Erwin Rommel, the most celebrated German general in the war, twice met and twice trounced by Montgomery

General Walter Bedell Smith, Eisenhower's chief of staff, an
increasingly bitter critic of Montgomery

U.S. ARMY

Roosevelt and Churchill with their Combined Chiefs of Staff
and other officers at the Casablanca summit conference

General George S.
Patton, commander of
the U.S. Third Army,
whose rivalry with
Montgomery for battle
honors grew increas-
ingly bitter

Eisenhower escorting the U.S. Chiefs of Staff—Air Force
commander General Henry Arnold, Admiral Ernest King, and
General George Marshall—on a visit to Normandy
shortly after D-Day

General Bradley, Air Chief Marshal Sir Arthur Tedder,
Eisenhower, Montgomery, and General William Simpson

American infantry going ashore at Normandy on D-Day. Some
of the landings at Utah Beach were made with little difficulty,
but those at Omaha Beach were a "nightmare."

Toward war's end, German losses were so great that units were
reinforced by hastily recruited middle-aged men and youths.

Eisenhower sharing a
laugh with a soldier

COURTESY DWIGHT D.
EISENHOWER LIBRARY

Eisenhower decorating
Montgomery, whose popu-
larity among ordinary
Americans was almost as
great as it was among
Britons

COURTESY DWIGHT D.
EISENHOWER LIBRARY

President Eisenhower and Montgomery touring the Civil War battlefield at Gettysburg, Pennsylvania

Personal Message from the Army Commander

TO BE READ OIT TO ALL TROOPS.

Now that the campaign in Africa is finished I want to tell you all, my soldiers, how intensely proud I am of what you have done.

2. Before we began the Battle of Egypt last October I said that together, you and I, we would hit Rommel and his Army "for six" right out of North Africa.

And it has now been done. All those well known enemy Divisions that we have fought, and driven before us over hundreds of miles of African soil from Alamein to Tunis, have now surrendered.

There was no Dunkirk on the beaches of Tunisia; the Royal Navy and the R.A.F. saw to it that the enemy should not get away, and so they were all forced to surrender.

The campaign has ended in a major disaster for the enemy.

3. Your contribution to the complete and final removal of the enemy from Africa has been beyond all praise.

As our Prime Minister said at Tripoli in February last, it will be a great honour to be able to say in years to come:—

"I MARCHED AND FOUGHT WITH THE EIGHTH ARMY."

4. And what of the future? Many of us are probably thinking of our families in the home country, and wondering when we shall be able to see them.

But I would say to you that we can leave to-day only one thought, and that is to see this thing through to the end; and then we will be able to return to our families, honourable men.

5. Therefore let us think of the future in this way.

And what ever it may bring to us, I wish each one of you the very best of luck, and good hunting in the battles that are yet to come and which we will fight together.

6. TOGETHER, YOU AND I, WE WILL SEE THIS THING THROUGH TO THE END.

B. L. Montgomery.

Montgomery's message to his Eighth Army troops after final victory in North Africa

---

I would like to put before you certain aspects of future operations and give you my views:

1. I consider we have now reached a stage where one really powerful and full-blooded thrust toward Berlin is likely to get there and thus end the German war.

2. We have not enough maintenance resources for two full-blooded thrusts.

3. The selected thrust must have all the maintenance resources it needs without any qualifications and any other operations must do the best it can with what is left over.

4. There are only two possible thrusts one via the Ruhr and the other via Metz and the Saar.

5. In my opinion the thrust likely to give the best and quickest results is the northern one via the Ruhr.

6. Time is vital and the decision regarding the selected thrust must be made at once and Paragraph 3 above will then apply.

7. If we attempt a compromise solution and split our maintenance resources so that neither thrust is full-blooded we will prolong the war.

8. I consider the problem viewed as above as very simple and clear-cut.

9. The matter is of such vital importance that I feel sure you will agree that a decision on the above lines is required at once. If you are coming this way perhaps you would look in and discuss it. If so, delighted to see you lunch tomorrow. Do not feel I can leave this battle just at present.

In a personal message to Eisenhower, who had just taken over from Montgomery as Allied ground-forces commander in Europe, the British commander urges him not to pursue a broad-front advance against the enemy.

PERSONAL AND CONFIDENTIAL

Tac. H.Q.,

21 Army Group.

30 November, 1944.

My dear Ike

In order to clear my own mind I would like to confirm the main points that were agreed on during the conversations we had during your stay with me on Tuesday night.

2. We have definitely failed to implement the plan contained in the SHAEF directive of 28 October, as amended on later dates. That directive ordered the main effort to be made in the north, to defeat decisively the enemy west of the RHINE, to gain bridgeheads over the RHINE and the IJSSEL rivers, and to deploy in strength east of the RHINE preparatory to seizing the RUHR.

We have achieved none of this; and we have no hope of doing so.

We have therefore failed; and we have suffered a strategic reverse.

3. We now require a new plan. And this time we must not fail.

The need to get the German war finished early is vital, in view of other factors.

The new plan MUST NOT FAIL.

4. In the new plan we must get away from the doctrine of attacking in so many places that nowhere are we strong enough to get decisive results.

We must concentrate such strength on the main selected thrust that success will be certain.

It is in this respect that we failed badly in the present operations.

Montgomery's low regard for Eisenhower's abilities as a military commander are reflected in the hectoring tone he adopted both in letters (part of one is shown left) and in personal meetings with the supreme commander.

Personal

HEADQUARTERS:
21 ARMY GROUP.

2-12-44

My dear Ike

I have your letter of 1 Dec,
written from Simpson's HQ.

I am disturbed at your last para.
You say

"I beg of you not to continue
to look upon the past performances
of this great fighting force as a
failure &c &c"

I have never done anything of the sort;
and I have never said anything which
could convey that impression.

On our talk, and in my letter to you
of 30 November, I took as a basis

for discussion the SHAEF directive of 28
October; I said we had failed to
carry out the plan contained therein.
When one reads that directive one has
to admit that that is so.

I should be sorry if you thought I
had said, or implied, anything
else.

Yrs. always

Monty.

Letters Montgomery sent to Eisenhower
revealed their inability to communicate
effectively with each other.

Put in my Monty file.   7-6-45

My dear IKE

Now that we have all signed in Berlin I suppose we shall soon begin to run our own affairs.

I would like, before this happens, to say what a privilege and an honor it has been to serve under you. I owe much to your wise guidance and kindly forbearance. I know my own faults very well and I do not suppose I am an easy subordinate; I like to go my own way.

But you have kept me on the rails in difficult and stormy times, and have taught me much.

For all this I am very grateful. And I thank you for all you have done for me.

Your very devoted friend

Monty

Montgomery's expression of gratitude to Eisenhower after the German surrender was in sharp contrast to the sentiments he privately voiced about him during the war in Europe.

THE WHITE HOUSE
WASHINGTON

He said again he would like to get a committee of Tedder,
Gale, Whiteley, Gruenther, Beedle Smith, etc., to cite
chapter and verse to show where Monty had been timid and
uncertain, rather than the bold hero he tries to make himself
out to be.

He also told an interesting fact that I had not known before.
When there was need for a new British Commander at El
Alemein (I cannot remember the name of the man who was being
replaced) a General named Ganss, or something like that,
was ordered to take over. This General was on his way to
Cairo and was killed just shortly before he reached there
-- a bomber got the train he was travelling on. Therefore
Monty was assigned. So it was an accident that Monty got the
command in the first place.

The President went to church, complainingly bitterly that
church services did not start until 11:15 here in Augusta, which
makes his golf game start late.

The official diary of President Eisenhower, kept by his personal secretary, records his tentative idea, years after the war, of gathering generals who served under him in Europe to refute Montgomery's disparagement of his command decisions in Europe.

ARMY & NAVY CLUB,
PALL MALL.
S. W. L.
WHITEHALL 8721-6

8·v·59

My dear Mr President,
I feel I must
write to tell you how distressed I have
been over these recent outbursts By my
old chief. I just don't think he realises
what he writes or says — neither do I
understand the motive. It's a pity he
has no chief of staff at hand, now that
he has retired!
Naturally I still retain an
affection for him — (I don't know whether
that is the right word!); But these attacks
against you of all people tries my loyalty
very hard.
All I can say is that I believe
in his heart of hearts, he is now sorry
for what has happened.

A note to President Eisenhower from Montgomery's wartime chief of staff, General Francis De Guingand, expressing regret at Montgomery's critical remarks about the supreme commander in his memoirs and on television

CHAPTER 15
Prelude to Invasion

As Army Chief of Operations in Washington a year and a half earlier, Eisenhower had drawn up plans for Operation Roundup, an Allied invasion of France from England to take place in the spring of 1943 and bring the war to a rapid, victorious conclusion. Now it was January 1944; Operation Roundup had been renamed Operation Overlord, was scheduled to be launched that coming May, and Eisenhower was returning to London to be its Supreme Commander.

For most of the previous year, the COSSAC, General Frederick Morgan, his American deputy, Brigadier General Ray W. Barker, and their staff had been mapping out the preliminaries for Overlord. Their start had been modest. Morgan had found an unoccupied room at Norfolk House, an office building in London's St. James's Square, a few blocks from Piccadilly Circus, and had laid claim to it. "The equipment," he later wrote, "consisted of desks and chairs we found in the room, and we were lucky enough to find a few sheets of paper and a pencil that someone had dropped on the floor." By the time Eisenhower returned to London, COSSAC (the acronym was used to refer to Morgan's planning group as well as to Morgan himself) had expanded at Norfolk House to become a large, bustling organization.

Overlord would be a far more momentous operation than those that had preceded it, and far more depended on its success. Details for establishing a secure beachhead on the coast of northern France against strong resistance had been closely examined. Feasibility studies had been undertaken. Proposals had been drawn up. A great quantity of relevant data had been gathered.

It was far easier for the staff at the newly established Supreme Headquarters, Allied Expeditionary Force (SHAEF) to move forward from there than it would have been to start from scratch. Eisenhower had doubts about the COSSAC invasion plan when he first saw it but he later paid tribute to Morgan's work. He said, "He had in the months preceding my arrival accomplished a mass of detailed planning, accumulation of data, and gathering of supply that made D Day possible." His praise for COSSAC was reciprocated.

> I had to hand over to General Eisenhower [Morgan wrote] a hideous complexity of problems connected with the articulation of higher command into which there entered not only military but international considerations. . . . But here, at long last, was the man to solve these and, indeed, any other problems, one already well acquainted with all the actors who were to take part in the forthcoming drama and who, moreover, had already led an Anglo-American army to notable victory.

There was little doubt where the landings would have to take place. COSSAC planners had scrutinized the west coast of the European continent from the Netherlands to Spain. The region around Calais was closest to southern England and was therefore an obvious choice. But that area was the most strongly fortified of any along Hitler's Atlantic Wall. As for the region just north of it, close to the German border with Belgium, any advantage derived from surprise, if it could be maintained, would be neutralized by how quickly the Germans would be able to reinforce their defending forces there.

Brittany was too far south for adequate fighter cover to be provided. That left the French coast between Brittany and Pas de Calais. It was there, on the beaches of Normandy, that the Allied troops would go ashore on D-Day.

It would be essential for the invaders to be adequately supplied once they had established themselves in France or they might be driven back into the sea. The Norman port of Cherbourg was not as good for that purpose as Antwerp, farther north in Belgium. COSSAC had long been pondering that problem and had produced plans for what became the Mulberry artificial harbors that were floated across the English Channel to Normandy to keep the troops supplied immediately after D-Day.

Timing for the invasion had also been narrowed down by COSSAC. What was necessary was moonlight sufficient for paratroops to drop with relative safety at night to coincide with a low tide that would permit landing craft to get to the beaches to disgorge their troops, tanks, and trucks. That narrowed the choice of dates down to the beginning of May or two weeks into June. Later than that and the Allies might not have time to gather sufficient momentum on land to crush German resistance before winter conditions came to the aid of the enemy.

British himself, and with a COSSAC staff that was at first mostly British, Morgan had to deal with the qualms of his government and the British military establishment about the agreed-upon spring 1944 timing for the cross-Channel assault. Brooke made no secret that he still had doubts about an invasion of France until the Germans showed greater signs of cracking. Churchill was deeply worried. "When I think of the beaches of Normandy choked with the flower of American and British youth," he said, "and when in my mind's eye, I see the tides running red with their blood, I have my doubts." The prime minister also grumbled about forces he said were lying effectively idle in Britain, training for an operation that was not to take place for several months, when there were other opportunities to be exploited in the Mediterranean region. Morgan came to be considered by many of his compatriots as far too Americanized, as would some other British generals who worked under Eisenhower at SHAEF.

In the meantime, both the U.S. Army Air Corps and the RAF had war-winning plans of their own and no wishes to come under the jurisdiction of others. The U.S. Navy was still more interested in the Pacific, and the Royal Navy was still too fully stretched to devote much attention to future planning. In addition to clashes of interests and attitudes among the services, now that Germany's defeat was not only certain but likely soon to be achieved, divergent national objectives between the Americans and the British were emerging on such matters as dealing with the Russian ally and what to do with Germany once it was conquered, both of which had important bearing on strategic considerations.

Morgan had done what he could to prevent those and other differences from obstructing the development of invasion plans. He pointed out, "The COSSAC staff, containing as it did men and women of six fighting services of two different nations, was bound of its nature to contain all the elements of discord." But like Eisenhower he strove to forge an atmosphere of camaraderie and overriding common purpose. Shortly after COSSAC had begun functioning, an American general making a transatlantic phone call from Washington to an American general at Norfolk House offered his view of what was wrong with the way planning was shaping up and finished by saying, "But for Christ's sake don't tell the British." He was informed that the laughter his warning aroused came from two British generals and one British admiral who had been listening to the conversation.

COSSAC planning had dealt with all sorts of problems. As well as invasion preparations, invasion details, and post-invasion logistics, it had included deception plans, arrangements for civil administration in liberated France, a rapid airborne seizure of Berlin if the German Army and government suddenly collapsed, the military occupation of Germany, and much else. But COSSAC had labored under a fundamental constraint.

The key problems it had sought to address could only be resolved by individuals more senior and more experienced than
Morgan in operational command in the war, and that could only
happen when those individuals finally could extract themselves
from their other campaigns to devote their full attention to
Overlord. Specifically, firm decisions could not be made for the
operation until a Supreme Commander with sufficient authority was appointed. The task for Eisenhower when he took
charge was momentous. He was required to absorb the extensive planning that had already been done, update and revise it
in accordance with his own strategic thinking and the resources
and intelligence available to him, and make the appropriate
decisions.

Before leaving Washington to return to England, in answer
to a question from Roosevelt Eisenhower had told the president
that being Supreme Commander sounded good to him. "It has
a ring of importance," he jocularly told him, "something like
Sultan." He didn't feel like a sultan. He was flattered to have
been chosen and was anxious to get cracking on his new assignment. But he knew he would face great challenges in the weeks
and months ahead and had no doubt that his competence as a
commander-in-chief would once again be sorely tested.

Montgomery had no such concerns as he left command of the
Eighth Army in Italy. He was brimming with confidence when
he arrived back in England on January 2, 1944, to assume command of the British 21st Army Group. Having been instructed
by Eisenhower to take control of Overlord planning in England
while he was in the United States on home leave, he immediately proceeded to do exactly that.

Headquarters for him had been set up at St. Paul's School in
London, where he had been a boy student. The headmaster's
room, which he had never before visited, was chosen for his
office. Letters were sent to him by people living in the area
asking that he locate his headquarters elsewhere. Having endured four years of enemy air raids, they feared that the presence of so famous a figure would attract German bombers.
Montgomery was contemptuous of such requests and even
chose living quarters across the street from St. Paul's.

But he wasted neither time nor energy on peripheral matters. Within hours of his arrival in London, senior COSSAC planners were informed that their presence would be required at St. Paul's for a conference at nine the following morning. At that gathering, they presented the outline of the plan they had drawn up for the assault on the Normandy beaches, the first phase of the invasion, which was code-named Operation Neptune. Montgomery made no pretense of seeing any more value in it than he had when Churchill had asked for his opinion in Morocco.

In crisp teacher-to-student manner, he declared that it could not work, that it was based on too narrow a front. He restated his view that, as planned, the assault would not be powerful enough to establish a secure beachhead. He explored wider options for the invasion, describing the problems each presented with regard to logistics, likely enemy responses, advantages, and drawbacks. He said that his analysis of the essentials showed that the assault force would have to consist of five rather than the three divisions COSSAC had proposed, with two divisions in reserve, and it would have to be put ashore on a much longer expanse of coast.

There would also have to be important alterations in the command structure for the operation. Montgomery said it was too complicated and was likely to be prone to confusion once the assault was launched. The British 21st Army Group and the American First Army, which included the forces that would land on D-Day, would manage their own combat areas under his general direction. Armies that trained separately, had their distinctive military procedures, and even used different kinds of ammunition, would best fight independently, under their own commanders. It would simplify logistical and operational control. The lines of command, communication, and supply would be tidy, as Montgomery always instructed his students that they should be.

Not all of these ideas were exclusively Montgomery's. Eisenhower's gut reaction to the COSSAC plan had also been that the invasion force had to be stronger than three divisions. Churchill felt the same way. Bradley, now commanding the

U.S. First Army, shared many of Montgomery's detailed ideas, as did others. Indeed, COSSAC itself was aware of the limitations of its proposals and had insisted for many months that nothing really could be planned until a Supreme Commander was assigned to the operation and given a reasonably accurate estimate of the resources that would be at his disposal.

But it was Montgomery who presented clear, concise, and comprehensive ideas for the actual invasion that was to take place, stripped to their essentials, presented as firm instructions about how things should and would be done. Some of those to whom he lectured, or who heard that he had appeared to assume command of Overlord, questioned his authority. But he made certain everyone knew that Eisenhower had authorized him to get things moving.

For the COSSAC planners, Montgomery's exposition at St. Paul's was an animating experience. They had been pondering Overlord problems for months. With Allied combat emphasis having focused on the Mediterranean strategy, many had grown fatigued and even doubtful about the chances of success for the invasion. Conscious of the recalcitrance of the British High Command, some had begun to suspect that it might not even be attempted in the foreseeable future. Major General K. G. McLean, one of the senior planners, said, "There were many cold feet on the operation."

No longer. Some COSSAC planners grumbled at how their labors had been curtly discounted by Montgomery, as if they had no value whatsoever, and how they personally had been treated like amateurs. Nevertheless, they were sent away from Montgomery's presentation with a sense that things were finally about to happen and that they had some hard, important work to do in reexamining details and options.

The invasion of France would be by far the most important task Montgomery had ever undertaken, and the 21st Army Group was the highest command he had ever held. That inevitably meant that some of the senior officers who were to serve under him had their own ways of doing things. It also meant that, as usual, some of those ways and some of those individuals would not meet with his approval. He was generally disin-

clined to employ any senior officer who had not once been a
favored student of his or who had not already satisfactorily
served under him. Several officers found themselves relieved
of their commands, replaced by Montgomery men, and shifted
to second-string assignments at the moment of the greatest
opportunity in their military careers. It aroused much bitterness.

Ten days after his return to England, Montgomery summoned the general officers under his command in Overlord to
a meeting at which he made his views clear about the basic
principles of war and the management of battle. His confident
pronouncements served once more to refresh tired minds and
expose those assembled to a dynamic, if bombastic, approach
to problems that had to be solved. But though these were seasoned officers, Montgomery could not keep himself from ad-
dressing them as if they were second lieutenants still wet
behind the ears.

It was more apparent than before that not everyone in the
British military establishment had succumbed to admiration for
him. Some entertained doubts about him because theirs was a
deeply entrenched bureaucracy and his dynamism shook some
of their cobwebs. They reacted strongly to his attempts to alter
long-existing procedures, as in the case of changes in the structure of British Army divisions that had been recommended
earlier for the sake of efficiency. But though those changes were
uncontroversial, the War Office had not yet gotten around to
authorizing them. Learning of it, Montgomery simply instructed that they be made. When word got back to the War
Office, outraged complaints were made to War Minister Grigg.

Grigg shared the objections that such high-handedness
aroused. Montgomery recognized that it was a mistake to make
an enemy out of someone so highly placed, and someone who
had been his admirer. He made arrangements to see the minister, exposed him to the charm of which he was capable when
he chose to be, apologized, and explained that a sense of urgency had made him take precipitous action. Grigg became an
even stronger supporter of him than he had been earlier. If
Montgomery had made a practice of cultivating friends, he

might have emerged from the war with even greater achievements than those with which he is credited. But it was beyond
him. Sometimes he seemed driven to giving gratuitous offense.

On January 13, Montgomery left London to review troops
training in the north of England. Eisenhower was due to arrive
in Britain that night. Though Eisenhower was no stickler for
protocol and did not mind, it was a discourtesy not to be on
hand in the British capital to welcome the Supreme Commander. A week later, Eisenhower met with his senior staff,
Montgomery included, to review some key elements of the
COSSAC invasion plan. At the meeting, the content, clarity,
and conciseness of Montgomery's presentation of his ideas for
Overlord greatly impressed him. However, when Eisenhower's
car, driven by Kay Summersby, had reached Norfolk House
for that meeting, the parking spot reserved for the Supreme
Commander was occupied by the car in which Montgomery
had already arrived. It was another minor impertinence. Eisenhower again didn't give it a second thought, and Kay quickly
sorted the matter out. But Montgomery appeared almost childish in his haste to test the limits in the new relationship that
was being established between himself and Eisenhower.

He raised eyebrows at SHAEF and in Washington a few days
later by announcing publicly that he was taking "command of
the British Army and the American Army of which General
Eisenhower is the Supreme Commander." Such a declaration
was liable to give a misleading impression of the role to which
he had been assigned. It suggested that Eisenhower was a
mere figurehead in Overlord and that the British—in this case
Montgomery—were really running the show. Asked at a press
conference about Montgomery's self-serving, ambigious announcement, Eisenhower urged the assembled correspondents
not to "go off on the end of a limb."

The British general had been tactless and had spoken out
unnecessarily. However, what he said was essentially accurate.
No public disclosure was being made, but the plan was for him
to be the Allied ground-forces commander for the invasion. He
was to remain ground-forces commander until an American
army group was established in France alongside the British

army group, at which time Eisenhower would directly assume
that role himself.

As Overlord's Supreme Commander, Eisenhower was no less
bedeviled by doubts and worries than he had been before, and
not only about the possibility that the operation might fail.
Despite his efforts to conceal his concern, he also feared he
would again ''be the target for those [American] critics who say
the British have cleverly accepted an American as Supreme
Commander but have infiltrated British commanders for land,
sea, and air.'' The continuing glorification of Montgomery in
the British press and the emphasis London newspapers placed
on Eisenhower's managerial rather than military talents fueled
gossip about who was really in charge. The Supreme Commander was wounded by such talk, as a notation in his diary
testified.

> Much discussion has taken place councerning our command
> set-up. . . . Generally speaking the British columnists . . .
> try to show that my contributions in the Mediterranean were
> administrative accomplishments and ''friendliness in weld-
> ing an allied team.'' They dislike to believe that I had any-
> thing particular to do with campaigns. They don't use the
> words ''initiative'' and ''boldness'' in talking of me, but often
> do in speaking of Alex and Monty.

But his exasperation at being damned by the British with faint
praise did not diminish his determination to eliminate, prevent,
or smooth over British-American friction. After a complaint
from the War Office about a problem in communications with
Washington, he told Marshall that when such situations arose
to ''please make it appear, whenever possible, that the mistake
was made by me since I am always in a position to go and make
a personal explanation or apology.''

Much has been written about how harmoniously SHAEF
functioned under Eisenhower's guidance. It was indeed a remarkable display of unity in the pursuit of a common objective.
The Supreme Commander's ability to get along well with every-

one involved remained undiminished, as even the enemy knew. According to a German intelligence report filed a month after Eisenhower returned to England, he was "noted for his great energy, and for his hatred of routine office work. He leaves the initiative to his subordinates whom he manages to inspire to supreme efforts through kind understanding and easy discipline. His strongest point is said to be an ability for adjusting personalities to one another and smoothing over opposite viewpoints."

However, despite accounts that suggested otherwise, the atmosphere at Supreme Allied Headquarters—whose staff grew to number more than 16,000—was less than perfectly harmonious. COSSAC chief General Morgan, who became SHAEF's Deputy Chief of Staff, later said that his "dominant recollection" was "the awkwardness of the British [there]. It seemed that their idea of cooperation was that others should co-operate with them and not vice versa."

On the British side [Morgan wrote] there had been generated a widespread belief that General Eisenhower was little more than a politico-military figurehead, adept, might be, at the resolution of conflict on the higher diplomatic levels, but inexperienced, untried and little to be relied upon in the fields of tactics and strategy. For that matter there was no American who could bear comparison with the veteran British, notably with their popular hero Montgomery. By contrast, on the American side this same General Montgomery was held in no very high esteem. Careful analysis of his comparatively small campaign in North Africa had brought American soldiers to the conclusion that there was no great military virtue in the slogging match at El Alamein followed by the procession to Tunisia when, they estimated, if it had not been for the intervention of American and British Armies from the west, Rommel would have made his orderly withdrawal to Europe in his own good time.

Little of this filtered up to Eisenhower. Though regretting what he did learn of it, as long as the recriminations remained reasonably discreet and did not interfere with the workings of his headquarters he pretended they did not exist. Instead, he enthused about British-American camaraderie and cooperation. To have done otherwise, and to have brought the mutual scoffing fully out into the open, probably would have intensified it, with disagreeable consequences.

Unlike most of the American generals, the Supreme Commander was prepared to accept that Montgomery was responsible for a great and glorious triumph in North Africa. The victor of Alamein was still the most highly acclaimed British war hero and Eisenhower was anxious that all concerned treated him with the respect such status warranted. He certainly intended to treat him that way himself.

However, he could not overcome feeling ill at ease in Brooke's presence. They got along well enough, but the British chief of staff's clipped manner grated on Eisenhower, while Brooke, not the most diplomatic of men, had difficulty concealing the persisting doubts he had about the Supreme Commander despite his efforts to come to terms with him.

> The main impression I gathered [Brooke wrote in his diary] was that Eisenhower was no real director of thought, plans, energy or direction. Just a coordinator, a good mixer, a champion of inter-Allied co-operation, and in those respects few can hold the candle to him. But is that enough?

However, other senior British figures—notably Cunningham, now the First Sea Lord, and Air Marshal Tedder—remained fond of Eisenhower and respected him as a commander. And he was popular with the British as well as the American press and public. He gradually employed that popularity, and the fulsome support of Roosevelt and Marshall, to infuse the role of Supreme Commander with far more substance than had been intended, certainly by the War Office in London, which remained uneasy entrusting command over British forces to a foreigner whose competence it doubted. And there was persisting concern about how Eisenhower and Montgomery would get along now that they were working closely together, without Alexander as a buffer between them.

The plane carrying Eisenhower back to Britain from the United States in mid-January had landed at Prestwick, in Scotland, from where the private train assigned to him carried him to London. The British capital was shrouded in a damp, dense winter fog when the train pulled in to the Primrose Hill station. A car was waiting to take him to the central London townhouse residence that had been made ready for him just off Berkeley Square.

He had not yet been issued his formal Overlord instructions by the Combined Chiefs of Staff. Important differences between the British and Americans were still unresolved. The British continued to object to bolstering Overlord preparations at the expense of the operations in the Mediterranean. But Eisenhower's mission had to be defined in some way or other and a compromise directive for him was finally produced, though not until mid-February. Even then it was a very general description of the Supreme Commander's objective: "You will enter the continent of Europe, and, in conjunction with the other United Nations, undertake operations aimed at the heart of Germany and the destruction of her armed forces." Eisenhower was entrusted with preparing for the invasion, but he knew that Churchill and the British chiefs of staff would be looking over his shoulder and breathing down his neck, as would the War Department in Washington.

He was pleased that Tedder, with whom he had worked well in the Mediterranean, was named Deputy Supreme Commander. And he had brought Bedell Smith from Italy to continue as his chief of staff. Smith soon tangled heatedly with Brooke, who accused him of denuding the Italian campaign of experienced officers to staff SHAEF's upper echelons. It was proof that—directive or no directive—Eisenhower would have to struggle to establish his authority.

A number of fundamental matters had to be sorted out from the beginning. Prime among them was the importance of Over-

lord in the wider scheme of things. Eisenhower had no doubt
that it would be the most important undertaking for the Western Allies in the war and that, together with the Soviet Army's
advance from the east, it was the operation that would lead to
victory over Nazi Germany. If Overlord failed, it would not be
merely a setback for the Allies; it would be an unmitigated
disaster. The Russians might be tempted to pull out of the war
after driving Hitler's armies from Soviet soil, a process that was
well under way. The war with the Germans in the west might
then simply go on and on. As far as Eisenhower was concerned,
everything else in which the Western Allies were engaged in
the European theater had to be peripheral to Overlord.

But that opinion was not unanimously held by the Allied
High Command. Impatient, fidgety, and fearful of Soviet power
in the postwar world, Churchill continued to insist that the
Italian campaign, which he believed could still lead the armies
of the Western Allies into Central Europe, not be downgraded
and that other operations be considered in the Mediterranean.
The U.S. Navy's insistence on fighting its private war in the
Pacific meant Overlord planning had to proceed nervously on
the assumption and hope that an adequate naval task force
would be available for support when the time came. Most troubling for the Supreme Commander was the dispute over who
should control Allied air power based in Britain.

Eisenhower's experience in North Africa, Sicily, and Italy had
taught him the crucial importance of coordinated aerial support
for ground and amphibious operations. But in assuming command of Overlord, he was confronted with the quasi-indepen-
dent roles that were being played by Britain's Bomber
Command, under Air Marshal Sir Arthur Harris, and the U.S.
Strategic Air Forces in Britain, commanded by General Carl
Spaatz. Both had been heavily engaged in raining death and
destruction down on Germany and on strategic targets elsewhere in German-occupied Europe. Neither Harris nor Spaatz
believed Overlord was the great opportunity it was said to be.
Nevertheless, Eisenhower considered it essential to incorporate
control of their bomber operations into his plans for the buildup
to the invasion. Specifically, he wanted to employ them for the

so-called Transportation Plan devised by Churchill's science adviser, Professor Solly Zuckerman.

Zuckerman, described by one of Bradley's aides as a small, mysterious man in an old, unpressed suit, was one of the British scientists who had been recruited from their various laboratories and lecture halls to put their knowledge and occasional brilliance to work on behalf of the war effort. During the latter part of 1943, he had made a close study of the effect of Allied bombing of enemy targets in Sicily and Italy. He had concluded that selective, intensive raids against railway installations over an extended period of time could do the enemy the most damage by paralyzing the rail systems on which it depended to transport men and equipment to areas where they were urgently needed.

It followed from that conclusion that knocking out the railway networks in France and Belgium was the best use to which Allied air power could be put in the weeks before the invading troops were to be sent across the English Channel. If that plan worked, German forces manning Hitler's Atlantic Wall would be quickly starved of supplies and reinforcements when the crunch came.

Eisenhower was persuaded, but the idea was dismissed as hokum by Harris and Spaatz. Aside from insisting that his aircraft were not capable of the kind of pinpoint bombing that was required to make Zuckerman's railway-bombing plan effective, Harris believed Overlord would result in the needless slaughter of Allied troops. He was convinced that the Luftwaffe could be destroyed and Germany could be crushed by permitting his bombers to continue uninterruptedly with their saturation bombing of its cities and strategic installations. Spaatz also considered Overlord unnecessary. He claimed that if he had thirty clear flying days, his bombers would destroy Germany's industrial infrastructure and, in particular, demolish its fuel-production capacity, and that would be the end of the war.

Personality conflicts were involved as well. In the process of making history, Harris was not much taken by the idea of deferring to the upstart American Supreme Commander, who not long before had been a junior desk general. Nor did he think much of Air Marshal Sir Trafford Leigh-Mallory, who was Eisenhower's deputy in charge of air operations and who strongly promoted Zuckerman's railway plan. Harris believed that Leigh-Mallory, who had previously headed Britain's Fighter Command, had no idea how bombers could or should be used. Spaatz was equally dismissive, considering Leigh-Mallory not very bright and disliking him personally. He and Harris recoiled at the idea that they were to surrender to him effective control of their precious bombers, which were doing such a comprehensive job of pulverizing Germany.

Eisenhower found himself in the awkward position of having Allied officers whom he was not empowered to command obstructing the implementation of his plans for a historic operation that he believed had to be given the highest priority. It wasn't only the Bomber Barons, as they came to be called, with whom Eisenhower had to tangle over aerial strategy. Churchill was reluctant to force "Bomber" Harris into subservience to Eisenhower. He said Harris's Bomber Command and the U.S. Strategic Air Forces should certainly coordinate their operations with Eisenhower's headquarters, but that they should be answerable directly to the Combined Chiefs of Staff rather than to the Overlord Supreme Commander. That would mean Eisenhower would be Supreme Commander in name rather than fact.

The prime minister, and, even more strongly, Foreign Secretary Anthony Eden, also objected to the saturation bombing of the French and Belgian railway networks that Eisenhower favored. They were thinking ahead to the postwar political climate, when hatreds resulting from the inevitably heavy civilian casualties would complicate relations between Britain and its cross-Channel neighbors.

But Eisenhower argued that the object of Overlord was liberation of Europe from Nazi rule, and that might not happen if the Germans were able to use Belgian and French railways to reinforce their troops on Hitler's Atlantic Wall when the Allied troops went ashore. He insisted that his control and use of air power was central to plans for the invasion. "I get tired," he wrote to Marshall, "of trying to arrange the blankets smoothly over several prima donnas in the same bed."

In demanding that Spaatz and Harris come under his command, he pressed with greater firmness and determination than he had previously shown when challenging High Command potentates. A few months before he might have backed down in the face of Churchill's strongly expressed objections and the obstinacy of Harris and Spaatz. But he was now well positioned to have his way. He threatened to resign if he was denied it. He knew that short of a catastrophe, he could not be replaced. Aside from the outrage his departure would generate in the United States, the resulting command confusion, at a time when the invasion was imminent, would have been monumental. He was centrally engaged in a host of intricate problems related to Overlord.

The debate carried on over a period of three months. Eventually, both he and the British gave ground, they more than he. He accepted a formula that gave him effective control of tactical-bombing operations when he would need them most, during the crucial weeks prior to D-Day. During that time, British and American bombers would unload tens of thousands of tons of bombs on French and Belgian railway installations, railroads, and bridges. Whether more damage would have been done to the enemy's ability to resist if the Bomber Barons had been permitted to follow their own policies without interruption for the sake of Overlord has been argued ever since. But there is no doubt that sharply restricting the ability of the Germans to move reinforcements and supplies about when the invasion of France was launched greatly assisted the Allied forces in securing their beachhead in Normandy. Eisenhower's ability to more or less win that argument against formidable opposition helped consolidate his authority as Supreme Commander.

But the image he projected as resolute commander was somewhat tarnished by his equivocation over Operation Anvil, the planned invasion of southern France. If Anvil were made to coincide with Overlord, it would force the Germans in France to fight simultaneously on two fronts and hasten the collapse of their defenses. The U.S. chiefs of staff maintained that the operation was important to the success of Overlord; it would tie down German divisions that otherwise might be thrown against the Overlord invaders. It would also liberate ports on the French Mediterranean coast. Cherbourg, the port scheduled for rapid capture on France's Normandy coast, was not large enough to accommodate a massive amount of traffic. But American divisions still to be shipped from the United States, and Free French divisions gathered in North Africa to liberate their homeland, could be quickly fed into Europe through the much larger Marseilles in the south. The involvement of the French divisions would produce much more coordinated support from the French resistance.

Eisenhower had strongly favored Anvil when he took over as Overlord Supreme Commander. But, exposed in London to British arguments, he grew concerned that the continuing difficulties for the Allied forces in the Italian campaign would mean that insufficient resources could be made available for the assault on southern France. He wrote to Marshall that he was beginning to doubt whether Anvil could be launched at the same time as the cross-Channel invasion. The U.S. Chief of Staff agreed that the success of Overlord could not be put in jeopardy by diverting necessary resources from it. He said that the decision on Anvil was Eisenhower's to make, but he believed that the British were critical of the whole Anvil idea because they feared the commitment to the Italian campaign would be downgraded still further if the operation took place. He told Eisenhower he wanted "to be certain that localitis is not developing and that pressure on you has not warped your judgment."

Eisenhower was stung by the suggestion that he was easily persuaded to change his mind. He strongly denied that his decisions were being influenced by the British. "In the various campaigns of this war," he told Marshall, "I have occasionally had to modify slightly my own conceptions of campaign in order to achieve a unity of purpose and effort. . . . [B]ut I assure you that I have never yet failed to give you my own clear personal convictions about every project and plan in prospect."

However, it was becoming increasingly evident that broadening the invasion front in Normandy and enlarging the assault force for the cross-Channel assault required a great many more landing craft than had been previously calculated, as well as additional warships and minesweepers. The British argument that those could be made available only if the Anvil operation was called off was difficult for Eisenhower to counter. However, he came under unrelenting pressure from Washington to stick with Anvil. Roosevelt had him reminded that the Soviets, who had been promised Anvil as well as Overlord, and with whom operational coordination was considered crucial once the invasion of France was under way, would be grievously slighted by its abandonment.

Eisenhower found himself in an extremely difficult situation. Logistical shortfalls led him to favor postponement of Anvil while strategic and tactical considerations suggested that it had to coincide with Overlord after all. At one point, after Eisenhower had shifted from one emphasis to another, Bedell Smith warned him against informing the War Department of his current thinking lest he give the impression back in Washington that he was wishy-washy.

Ultimately, all concerned did come to accept that if resources had to be devoted simultaneously to Anvil and Overlord, prospects for the success of the latter would be undermined. Eisenhower decided "that we are simply striving for the impossible" and that the assault on southern France would have to wait. The British still looked askance on the operation, but now Eisenhower insisted that Anvil would have to be launched as soon as circumstances permitted during the summer, to provide Overlord with assistance, however belated.

One reason why he regretted the delay was the effect on De Gaulle. Committing Free French troops, due to participate in Anvil, to the liberation of France would help appease the contentious Free French leader. He was still being confined to the periphery of Allied action and was outraged not to be permitted to play a significant role in the Overlord invasion of his country, especially since his Free French army was now a well-organized fighting force.

Eisenhower had hoped that many of the problems and per-
plexities of coping with civil aspects of the liberation of France
could be avoided and he could get on with fighting the war if
he could deal with De Gaulle's French Committee of National
Liberation. But Roosevelt and the State Department remained
suspicious of the French general. They recoiled at the idea of
France being liberated only to be handed over to a self-
appointed ruler, and they continued to deny De Gaulle and the
FCNL the recognition they demanded. Roosevelt favored free
elections in France, under Allied supervision, after the war was
won. Eisenhower was instructed to act accordingly in whatever
dealings he had with De Gaulle.

That added to his catalogue of complications. Fearing the
emergence of rival political forces in liberated France, De Gaulle
served notice that he would withhold from the Allies the support of his Free French army, as well as the Gaullist underground resistance movement in France, if he continued to be
frozen out.

Eisenhower had been able to block a Washington-sponsored
open break with the general. He had also been able to extract
from him an agreement that the Free French divisions would
be put under his command in return for an assurance that they
would participate conspicuously in the liberation of Paris and
the rest of their homeland. But that accord was voided by instructions from Washington that he was not to recognize De
Gaulle officially. De Gaulle responded by declaring his Committee of Liberation the provisional government of France, with
himself at its head. He insisted that he and it be treated as such
no matter what Roosevelt thought of him. Trying to keep on
top of Overlord's logistical difficulties, strategic differences, and
other problems, Eisenhower was lumbered with trying to find
a solution to that dilemma as well.

As ground-forces commander for Overlord, Montgomery was
having a wonderful time. In North Africa, Sicily, and Italy, he
had been able to plan the operations of only a single army.
Now, subject to the approval of his fully preoccupied Supreme

Commander, he could decide how three armies—British, Canadian, and American—would invade France and begin the liberation of Nazi-held Europe. He found the challenge and the
opportunity to put his ideas into practice exhilarating. He
thought deep and hard about the challenges involved, gave
lectures to his senior subordinates, and drew up plans.

Spearheading the initial invasion assault, the 1st and 4th divisions of Bradley's U.S. First Army would go ashore at Omaha
and Utah beaches, just east of the Cherbourg peninsula in Normandy. The 50th Division of General Miles Dempsey's British
Second Army would land at Gold Beach east of Omaha. The
3rd Canadian Division, attached to the British I Corps, would
land at Juno Beach, east of Gold. And the British 3rd Division
would land at Sword Beach east of Juno. They would be bol-
stered by troops of other divisions, brigades, specialist combat
units, and naval assault forces. Air support from bombers,
fighters, troop transports, and reconnaissance planes was to be
closely integrated. Three airborne divisions, two American and
one British, were to drop behind enemy lines on the night
preceding the landings.

Once the troops were ashore, the beachheads were to be
speedily joined up to give Montgomery control of a long, uninterrupted stretch of the Normandy coast. The heart of Montgomery's follow-up plan was an imaginative disposition of
forces and objectives. His 21st British Army Group on the left,
consisting of the British Second Army and the Canadian First
Army, would drive quickly inland to seize the key communications center of Caen before nightfall on D-Day and penetrate
enemy defenses. At the same time, the Americans on the right
would direct their efforts toward cutting off the Cotentin Peninsula and seizing the port of Cherbourg before sweeping out
south and west.

Phase lines drawn to illustrate how Montgomery thought the
operation was likely to develop in the days that followed the
landings—by D+17, D+20, D+25, D+35 and D+60—as ever
greater numbers of Allied troops were fed into the battle, thirty
divisions by D+35. According to his presentation, by ninety

days after D-Day, the Allies could be expected to be lined up along the River Seine, ready to regroup and then plunge forward to liberate the rest of German-occupied Western Europe.

Though enjoying himself enormously in outlining his doctrines of combat to arrays of senior officers, American as well as British, and experiencing a great sense of fulfillment, Montgomery remained awkward and uncomfortable dealing with military men who were in a position to judge his ideas, even when they were not being critical. General Bradley, who was his subordinate in the opening phase of the operation, met with him frequently in England. He found Montgomery to be "usually aloof, almost withdrawn, and not readily open to suggestions. . . . He left me," Bradley said, "with the feeling that I was a poor country cousin whom he had to tolerate." Nevertheless, Bradley observed that Montgomery's plan "made a profoundly favorable impression on Eisenhower, Bedell Smith—all of us in fact."

When Montgomery sent Eisenhower a copy of the notes he used in lectures to Overlord officers down to the rank of lieutenant colonel, the Supreme Commander told him that to say he was enthusiastic about his approach "is merely understatement. You have hit exactly the right note and have punched home your points perfectly. . . . [T]here is no doubt in my mind that everything one man can do to make this a success you are doing."

Montgomery made an equally strong impression on the king and Churchill at his St. Paul's headquarters on May 15, 1944, three weeks before D-Day, when, in the presence of Eisenhower, generals who were to command Overlord armies, and senior SHAEF officers, he outlined the difficulties that had to be overcome but confidently ran through a final review of his Overlord plans.

The Supreme Commander had begun with an introductory review of objectives before his air, sea, and ground deputies made their presentations. But the star of that session was undoubtedly Montgomery. Lord Ismay later wrote of how overwhelmed his audience was by his presentation: "Plans and preparations were now complete in every detail. All difficulties had been foreseen and provided against. Nothing had been left to chance. The troops had been intensively trained. Every man knew exactly what he had to do. They were full of ardor and confidence. Their equipment left nothing to be desired. . . . Overlord was in fact a perfectly normal operation of war which was bound to succeed."

While his staff, instructed on essentials, had gotten on with the job of filling in the details of the invasion plan, Montgomery had been devoting his attention to the one key to success his staff could not handle, building the morale of the troops and the British public. He toured the country, calling in at troop training grounds everywhere. When he arrived at a military base, he would go out into the field, climb onto the hood of a car or jeep, and call the men to gather close around him. He wanted them to see that Montgomery, the general who won all his battles, was there with them, cared for their well-being, and would lead them to victory. He visited American troops as well as British, going in among them to ask about their hometowns and about how they were doing.

Bedell Smith paid tribute to his effect on the morale of the soldiers. "Confidence in the high command is absolutely without parallel. Literally dozens of embarking troops talked about General Montgomery with actual hero-worship in every inflection. And unanimously what appealed to them—beyond his friendliness, and genuineness, and lack of pomp—was the story (or, for all I know, the myth) that the General 'visited every one of us outfits going over and told us he was more anxious than any of us to get this thing over and get home.' This left a warm and indelible impression."

Montgomery also visited war factories, dockyards, and rail terminals to assure the people working there that they were as much a part of the war effort as the men he would lead into combat in France. He flattered them by imparting non-classified military information about how the Germans would be defeated. Wherever he went, reporters and press photographers went as well. He became the symbol of victory, rivaling Churchill in popularity.

Some politicians were alarmed by the specter of a Napoleon

rising in their midst, a demagogue whose fame and popularity could tempt him into dangerous domestic pursuits. He displayed no political ambition, but Churchill was suspicious. He muttered, "It would seem to be about time that the circular sent to generals and other high commander about making speeches should be renewed. . . . There seem to have been a lot of speeches and interviews lately."

But the people of Britain needed the pep talk Montgomery offered. Everyone knew the invasion of France was imminent and was anxious about it. The war had been dragging on for five years for them, had claimed hundreds of thousands of casualties, and had caused much grief. Now the big push was about to take place. Would it succeed? Fully stretched, Britain would be unable to supply many more troops for subsequent major offensives if it did not. The Second Army Montgomery was sending to France was the last full army the British could put in the field. And even if the invasion was successful, how many more sons, fathers, and brothers would feature in the casualty lists? What about reports that the Germans were developing a missile that the RAF and antiaircraft gunners would not be able to shoot down? And when would austerity and the blackouts end?

If Montgomery had any worries, he did not exhibit them. This was his first prolonged stay on home ground since becoming a celebrity, and it had a profound effect on him. The loner, the man who went to bed early each night, the general who had offended colleagues in the British Army, the scratchy-voiced social misfit whose preferred attire was a tanker's beret and floppy battle dress, was now sought after socially by prominent London figures. He was becoming one of them, recognized and acclaimed everywhere, and he reveled in his new status.

In contrast to Montgomery, Eisenhower drew no satisfaction from his prominence among his British hosts as senior American in town. He was distressed being required to meet social obligations and attend meetings of little relevance to his mission. He also felt that being headquartered in the British capital was not conducive to his staff's exclusive concentration on the difficult job at hand. Shortly after arriving back in England, he had therefore issued instructions for his headquarters to be moved elsewhere, away from London's distractions.

The plan was for SHAEF to be shifted to Bushey Heath, not far from RAF Fighter Command headquarters in Stanmore, just northwest of London. But the U.S. Corps of Engineers, which was given the job, made a mistake over the name and started building what came to be a veritable self-contained hut and tent town, code-named Widewing, at Bushy Park just southwest of the capital. By the time the error was discovered, "too much earth had been moved to make it economic to back-track."

Preparing for Overlord and related matters consumed virtually all of Eisenhower's waking hours, although, because his sleeping problems persisted, he had more of those hours than most people. A series of security scares did nothing to ease his fear that things could go catastrophically wrong. It seemed grotesque when it was learned that classified Overlord documents had slipped from a poorly sealed envelope in a Chicago post office because a sergeant had mistakenly addressed it to his sister back home. How many more mistakes like that had there been, and was the enemy already aware of when and where Overlord would be launched?

The strain showed on Eisenhower's face and in his more frequent outbursts of bad temper. On March 29 he wrote to Mamie, "All my conferences this morning have been of the irritating type. People had misquoted me, others have enlarged on my instructions, still others have failed to obey orders. So I had a big field day, and ended up by tanning a few hides. I feel positively sadistic—But I undoubtedly got a certain amount of of satisfaction out of the process."

Butcher noted, "Ike looks worn and tired. . . . He looks older now than at any time since I have been with him." He suffered from tinnitus in one ear, eye strain, high blood pressure, and an almost chronic cold. These were all minor complaints. He had a basically strong physical constitution and they did not affect his control of his job. But they were wearying. He wrote to Mamie, "I'm having a flare-up with my insides, accompanied by shooting pains! I think it's just the old trouble, but at times it's worrisome." Bedell Smith was also worn down. He was fed up too, and was "damned well going to get out of the Army after the war."

Eisenhower had managed to have Telegraph Cottage west of London rented for him again and was pleased when he could get away, go there, and escape briefly from his duties and cares. He played some golf and bridge and sketched landscapes, though he had no illusions about the quality of his artistic skills. He went horseback riding at nearby Richmond Park, arrangements being made for him to gain access to it when it was barred to other visitors.

At the cottage he enjoyed the presence of Kay Summersby, who regularly accompanied him there from Widewing along with other staff. In view of the pressure he was under, she was now more than ever a comfort and a pleasure. At his office, he had even taken to having tea with her many afternoons. Nevertheless, he felt guilty about their relationship and about the sour moments he'd had with Mamie during his home leave in Washington. He wrote affectionate letters to his wife to make amends.

But everyone in his entourage knew that he found Kay's company greatly therapeutic. One of his aides once observed that he "blinked at Kay" when someone mentioned Mamie, as if they shared a secret concerning her. Though Kay was a British subject, he arranged for her to be commissioned a lieutenant in the American Women's Army Corps. Rumors continued to circulate about the intimacy of their relationship, but there was still nothing to suggest that they made love, and indeed the fervor of their romance seemed to have toned down somewhat.

Eisenhower's closest professional relationship was with Bedell Smith. As his chief of staff, Smith had far more to do with the day-to-day running of Overlord preparations than Eisenhower himself. But he was a difficult man temperamentally. His stomach ulcers inflamed his fiery temper, to which even Eisenhower was exposed from time to time. Shortly before they had left Italy, they had engaged in a furious argument when Smith declined an invitation to join Eisenhower for dinner one night. Eisenhower, who was himself feeling out of sorts at the time, considered it an act of insubordination and angrily threatened to leave Smith in the Mediterranean when he went on to Overlord in London, to which Smith snarled, "That suits me."

They subsequently exchanged apologies. Eisenhower was fortunate that they were able to adjust to each other's temperaments and moods. Smith was an angrily confident, take-charge figure. Even more than Eisenhower he forged SHAEF, with its vast staff and countless problems, into an efficient administrative machine. He dealt with or otherwise diverted many of the difficulties and pesterings that might have increased the load the Supreme Commander was carrying at a time when virtually all of Britain was an armed camp manned by some three million troops under his command. Tanks, trucks, guns, and an assortment of other equipment and supplies had been and still were being gathered in vast quantities at ports, depots, in towns and villages, and even along roads across the land for the most massive military operation in history.

At a final general-staff preparation conference on May 26, ten days before Overlord was due to be launched, Churchill, who was attending, rose, gripped his lapels firmly, and dramatically announced, "Gentlemen, I am now hardening to this enterprise." Eisenhower said at that moment he "realized for the first time" that while he had been striving exhaustingly to piece the operation together, the prime minister, with whom he had often conferred about it, "hadn't believed in it" at all "and had had no faith that it would succeed." It was a painful discovery.

CHAPTER 16
Overlord

"I am very uneasy about the whole operation," General Brooke wrote in his diary the evening before Overlord was launched. "At best it will fall so far short of the expectations of the bulk of the people, namely all those who know nothing about its difficulties. At worst, it may well be the most ghastly disaster of the whole war."

British concern was heightened by awareness that Rommel, Montgomery's former adversary, was waiting for the invaders across the English Channel. Despite his defeat in North Africa, the German field marshal retained a mythic reputation for brilliance, shrewdness, and resourcefulness. However, Montgomery, though knowing Rommel would "do his level best to 'Dunkirk' us," was pleased to have the opportunity to match wits with him again.

The previous November, Hitler had sent Rommel to inspect and improve German Atlantic-coast defenses. A dispute had quickly developed between him and Field Marshal Gerd von Rundstedt, the German commander-in-chief in the west, on how best to defend the Atlantic Wall against the invasion from England they knew would soon be coming. Both knew that this wall, as Rundstedt later said, was not as formidable as was widely believed; that it was, in fact, largely "an illusion, conjured up by propaganda—to deceive the German people as well as the Allies."

Rundstedt believed that the Germans were unlikely to prevent the Allies from getting ashore in strength somewhere along the coast between Holland and the Bay of Biscay. He thought it was therefore essential to man it comparatively lightly, keeping strong forces back in mobile reserve, to rush in to drive the invaders back into the sea once their main point of assault was determined, before they could secure a beachhead.

Rommel considered such tactics an unaffordable luxury. His experience of Allied aerial supremacy in North Africa had led him to conclude that the invaders had to be immediately trounced on the beaches wherever they landed before their overwhelming air cover could guarantee that they would be able to stay and expand inland. That meant strong deployment on the coast. Rommel was officially subordinate to Rundstedt, but in the weeks leading up to the invasion the German command in the west was locked in controversy over which policy to follow and who was really making the decisions.

The two field marshals competed for control of the Atlantic defenses, with Hitler intervening sometimes to favor one, sometimes the other. Rundstedt and Rommel were mistakenly convinced the invasion would come at the point of France closest to the coast of southeastern England, around Calais, and deployed the strong German Fifteenth Army there. Hitler accurately believed instead that the landings would be made in Normandy but, uncharacteristically, he permitted his generals to have their way even after D-Day proved him right and them wrong. Persuaded by Allied deception operations to believe the Normandy assault was a large-scale diversion for the real thing to come, the Germans kept their Fifteenth Army poised in the Calais area to repel the invaders for more than two weeks after the invasion was launched 200 miles away down the coast. It spared the Allied forces, Eisenhower, and Montgomery much grief.

* * *

At the end of April 1944, Montgomery had moved his 21st
Army Group headquarters to Portsmouth, on England's south
coast, from where much of the invasion armada would be de-
parting. He ventured forth from there to continue his busy
round of visits to the troops and war-production workers. He
found such activity sufficient reason not to attend a number
of high-level staff conferences held by Eisenhower at SHAEF.
Having devised the basic invasion plans, he was confident that
his hand-picked planning staff could deal with whatever problems had to be resolved. Everything was under control.

When Churchill showed up at Portsmouth and wished to
address members of his 21st Army Group headquarters staff on
troop dispositions, Montgomery forbade him to do so. He told
the prime minister he would "never allow you to harass my
staff at this time and possibly shake their confidence in me."
He had his way. The British leader had led the country during
its darkest hours, but he had become more expendable than
the man who commanded the troops who were about to blast
their way into Hitler's European fortress. He had to defer to
him. Montgomery boasted about the incident in his memoirs.

D-Day was to be in early June. Eisenhower had been forced
by the persisting shortage of landing craft and minesweepers
to delay launching the invasion until then rather than in May,
as had originally been planned. Mockingly, May proved gloriously bright; the waters were calm and the skies clear. It was
ideal invasion weather, while the approach of June was heralded by severely deteriorating conditions, making it necessary
to consider a further delay. The alternative to an early-June
launch was one in mid-June, when the tides and moonlight
would again be favorable. But if weather conditions were still
bad then, the invasion would have to be postponed for several
weeks. With autumn weather closing in soon after to restrict
operations, such a delay was out of the question. Overlord had
to be launched in early June.

During the first days of the month, Eisenhower was faced
with making his most difficult decision of the war. Overlord
was geared to be set in motion. Elements of the forces involved

had already been activated. A delay would be disastrous for morale and probably for security as well. He was also worried about "the effect of delay upon the Russians." The invasion of southern France they had been promised had, to their anger, already been postponed. If they chose to withhold cooperation on coordinating operations after the invasion, it might seriously complicate matters for the Western Allies.

The decision when to invade could not be made at the last minute. Tens of thousands of troops had to be moved to the ports of southern England and loaded onto the vessels that would take them across the English Channel. Airborne troops had to be dispatched in advance.

On June 4, Montgomery told Eisenhower he was ready to proceed with the invasion the following day, as was tentatively planned, regardless of the weather forecast. But the Supreme Commander's chief naval and air force aides objected strongly because Group Captain J. M. Stagg, SHAEF's chief meteorologist, had only gloom to report about the weather. A storm was brewing. The waters of the English Channel were rough, high waves were crashing against the Normandy beaches where the landings were to take place, and the skies had closed in over the Channel and the French coastal region, ruling out essential aerial support. And Eisenhower was convinced that, "Success or failure might easily hinge upon the effectiveness . . . of airborne operations."

Failure on D-Day would be the greatest disaster the Western Allies had suffered in the war. That the U.S. high command considered it a possibility was underlined by a message that Marshall would be arriving in London in a few day's time. He wanted to be on hand in case hasty consultations had to be undertaken by the Combined Chiefs of Staff. He said such consultations might be necessary if "we have a very insecure hold on a beachhead" and a decision had to be made "as to whether to withdraw or to continue the operation."

On the afternoon of June 4, when the pressure on Eisenhower about whether to give Overlord the green light had intensified still further, reports reaching Stagg led the meteorologist to conclude that a break in the weather would develop late on

June 5, and carry on into the following day. That was it. Eisenhower saw no alternative but to seize the moment. At a meeting
called for 4:30 on the morning of June 5, he gave the order for
Overlord to be launched in the early hours of June 6.

As with North Africa, as with Sicily, as with Italy, on the eve
of battle the Supreme Commander, having made his agonizing
decision, was for the moment largely irrelevant. The wheels
were in motion and they would turn inexorably toward victory
or defeat, or perhaps something horribly inconclusive in between. Lacking Montgomery's certainties, Eisenhower feared
that though the landings would succeed, the price to be paid for
them would be horrendous. Denied Montgomery's doctrinal
convictions, he was incapable of pretending to believe otherwise. His stomach tightened like a knot. But whatever he felt
remained concealed within him. Outwardly he was calm, composed, his temper under close control at this critical moment.
But he sat down at his desk and scribbled a few sentences on
a sheet of notepaper in preparation for disaster.

> Our landings in the Cherbourg-Havre area have failed to gain
> a satisfactory foothold and I have withdrawn the troops. My
> decision to attack at this time and place was based on the
> best information available. The troops, the air and the Navy
> did all that Bravery and devotion to duty could do. If any
> blame or fault attaches to the attempt it is mine alone.

He folded the note, stuck it in his wallet, and carried it around
with him.

During the morning, he visited troops of the British 50th
Infantry Division at a Portsmouth pier where they were being
loaded onto a landing craft. At an afternoon press conference,
despite lighting one cigarette after another, he impressed correspondents with his apparent calm and confidence. In the evening, he headed for Newbury to visit men of the 101st Airborne
Division who, along with men of the 82nd Airborne, were to be
dropped over the Cotentin peninsula hours before the coastal
landings were to take place. Leigh-Mallory, commanding Overlord's air component, had vigorously advised against their dis-

patch. He had predicted that four out of five of the paratroopers would be killed or wounded. Eisenhower had ruled against him, but his gamble that Leigh-Mallory's forecast was mistaken did not sit easily on his mind.

The paratroopers were lined up on the airfield with their rifles and their packs. Their faces had been charcoaled for camouflage. Some were already boarding the C-47s that would carry them into combat. No ceremony attended the Supreme Commander's visit. He had his car parked some distance from the troops and walked over to them. Lacking Montgomery's showmanship and dreading what might lie ahead for the men, he offered them no rousing Shakespearean call to battle. He had done that on paper in his Order of the Day for D-Day, a copy of which each of the troops received that night. It told them they were embarking on a "great crusade" to "bring about the destruction of the German war machine, the elimination of Nazi tyranny over the oppressed peoples of Europe, and security for ourselves in a free world. . . . I have full confidence in your courage, devotion to duty, and skill in battle. We will accept nothing less than full victory!"

But, mingling with the men being sent to achieve that victory, he shunned bombast and bluster. He sought to make contact with individual paratroopers, asking them where they were from and about their families and what they intended to do after the war. They cheered him and pressed forward to shake his hand.

Eisenhower then walked with their commander, General Maxwell Taylor, to the C-47 Taylor was to board to lead his men into the fray. At the foot of the plane's ramp he shook Taylor's hand, wished him well, and went back to his car. He then drove to the division's headquarters building, from the top of which he watched the troop transports lumber across the runway, rise into the sky, and roar off toward France. Kay Summersby later wrote that when the last had gone, "General Eisenhower turned, shoulders sagging, the loneliest man in the world."

By then the bombing of German coastal defenses was well in progress, Allied warships were moving into position for their pre-invasion bombardments, and troop transports were preparing to set out from ports along England's south coast. Back in Portsmouth, where his forward command post had been set up, Eisenhower examined incoming dispatches. General Clark had finally taken Rome. Eisenhower sent off telegrams to him and others at AFHQ congratulating them at this belated triumph and telling them that he looked forward to meeting them soon in the heart of Europe. But his thoughts were elsewhere.

It would be hours before first reports would come in from France and the ships offshore. He needed company. He and some of the people closest to him at the moment—Butcher, Kay Summersby, Bedell Smith, Tedder, SHAEF's Chief Administrative Officer General Sir Humphrey Gale and SHAEF Deputy Chief of Operations General Sir John Whitely—sat around drinking coffee. Few words were spoken. Everything now appeared trivial or irrelevant except the invasion, and it was either too late or too early to say anything about that. Butcher finally broke the ice. "To hell with it," he muttered, and went to bed. One by one, the others, including Eisenhower, did as well.

Montgomery felt no need to compose a secret communiqué of defeat to ward off a jinx. Whatever his private eleventh-hour concerns, he radiated assurance that the plans he had devised for the invasion would produce victory. Everything was in place. He had made certain all senior field officers perfectly understood their missions and how to go about successfully completing them. He had sorted out a last-minute hassle over pre-landing bomber support. Intelligence intercepts indicated that the enemy was still being fooled by deception schemes, including dummy landing craft in English ports closest to Pas de Calais, where the enemy's Fifteenth Army waited in vain. Nevertheless, he recognized that German defenses in Normandy were likely to be substantial, German resistance was likely to be fierce, and casualties might be heavy.

His message to the troops offered them his personal assurance of success. "On the eve of this great adventure," he told them, "I send my best wishes to every soldier in the Allied team. To us is given the honor of striking a blow for freedom which will live in history; and in the better days that lie ahead men will speak with pride of our doings. . . . I want every soldier to know that I have complete confidence in the successful outcome of the operations that we are now to begin."

As with Eisenhower, there was nothing more he could do for the moment. Throughout his stay in England during the buildup to Overlord, he had made little effort to see his mother or other members of his family, once even spurning his sister, who had come to see him when he was on one of his tours. She had waited nearby to be allowed to see him but, though informed that she was there, Montgomery chose to ignore her presence. On D-Day eve, however, he did make one concession to the importance of the occasion. He traveled to Hindhead to see the people looking after his son and to make arrangements for David's care if he was unable to see to it in the future. He had made no attempt to see the boy for many weeks and chose not to do so now either, using as an excuse the possibility that his arrival at the boy's school might lead to speculation that D-Day was imminent.

He then returned to his headquarters at Portsmouth and went to bed at his usual early hour. The fact that he was about to face the greatest challenge of his life was not permitted to upset his ordered ways.

Eisenhower managed to get some sleep that night. But when Butcher went to see if he was awake shortly before seven, he was not only already dressed, but his full ashtray testified that he had been awake for some time. Butcher was bringing good news. He was able to report that the airborne troops had not suffered the disaster that Leigh-Mallory had foretold. Only twenty-one of the 850 C-47s carrying the American paratroops had been lost. Only eight of the 400 aircraft ferrying British airborne troops into action had been lost. Further reports coming in told of virtually no enemy air or naval activity. The seas off the landing beaches were choppy but the storm of the previous day had petered out. The skies were partly cloudy, but not enough to interfere with aerial support for the invasion. The planes of the RAF and the U.S. Eighth and Ninth Air Forces had rained death and destruction on enemy coastal positions.

Reaction from the Germans, as confirmed by their communiqués and intercepted messages, confirmed that the Normandy landings had caught them unawares. But few reports were coming through on how the invasion was proceeding. "I have as yet," Eisenhower cabled Marshall in Washington at eight A.M., "no information concerning the actual landings nor of our progress through beach obstacles. Communique will not be issued until we have word that leading ground troops are actually ashore."

He left shortly after eight A.M. for Montgomery's headquarters to see if there was any news there. But the British commander knew little more than he did and made it plain by his attitude that he didn't particularly welcome visits at that moment, not even from the Supreme Commander. He had arranged the battle front with great calculation and conviction and he now had no wish to be disturbed as he waited for word on how the dispositions he had made were working out. His reputation as a combat commander, the meaning of his life, depended on what was happening across the English Channel.

He wrote a note to Brooke, whose unwavering support had made it possible for him to be a central figure in this historic event and the only one to whom he was prepared to reveal that there might be chinks in his confidence.

I would like to thank you for your kindly help and guidance during the past five years. It has not been an easy time—for anyone. My great desire throughout has been to justify your confidence in me and not to let you down and I hope I have been able to do this to your satisfaction. I cross over to France tomorrow night—if all goes well—and may not see you again. So good-bye and good luck.

As the hours passed, it appeared there was no reason yet to be gloomy. The Germans still appeared to have been caught off guard, which in fact was what had happened. The Wehrmacht's meteorologists had also been hard at work and had submitted a report the day before that only clouded skies and rough seas could be expected during the following two weeks. The enemy had therefore relaxed its guard. Despite the enormous, unconcealable Allied buildup in southern England, no German naval patrol had been deployed in the Channel that night. No special alert had been ordered on land.

Many senior German officers were not at their duty stations, having gone to Rennes to participate in war games. Rommel was away from his post too. Taking advantage of the inclement weather, he had driven back to Germany to celebrate his wife's birthday with her. As reports were fed back to Berlin that the invasion was taking place, Hitler was asleep at his aerie in the mountains of Bavaria and his aides chose not to wake him.

At fifteen minutes past midnight on June 6, the first invaders, British glider-borne troops, had landed to seize Pegasus Bridge over the Caen Canal. Less than an hour later, U.S. paratroops dropped over Sainte-Mère-Église forty-five miles away on the Contentin peninsula, others coming down in flooded areas nearby, where a number of them drowned. At 6:30 A.M. the first troops stormed ashore from landing craft. Little resistance was met by the British at Sword and Gold beaches. At Juno, the Canadians ran into stiff fire but overcame it and by nightfall were approaching Caen, which Montgomery had forecast would fall the first day. The U.S. 4th Infantry Division encountered little resistance at Utah Beach and soon was able to link up with the paratroopers who had dropped inland during the night.

But the story was different at Omaha Beach. There the U.S. 1st Infantry Division ran into the German 352nd Division, which had been on maneuvers in the area and primed for battle. The invaders at Omaha came ashore below cliffs from which the German defenders subjected them to barrages so severe that they were in danger of being pushed back into the sea before nightfall. If that happened, Montgomery's plans would be badly upset. The Americans on the right and the British and Canadians on the left would be exposed to a German thrust between them to limit the effectiveness of the long-fronted beachhead Montgomery had counted on securing quickly. The seizure of Cherbourg and its precious port would be, at best, delayed, as would the breakout to the right on which so much was premised.

News of the situation at Omaha—"a nightmare," Bradley called it—alarmed Eisenhower. "I could see," Butcher noted, ". . . he wished he were running the 21st Army Group so he could do something about it himself, but from where he sits, he just can't step in." He could, however, lend help, and sent word for tactical bombers to carry out instrument-guided bombing of the area even if it risked hitting American positions. Together with the almost suicidal courage and determination of a comparative handful of U.S. soldiers and the skill of naval gunners offshore, this helped the invaders establish a firm hold on Omaha before nightfall, though it extended to only a little more than a mile inland. But the lay of the land so favored the defenders that it might well not have happened. Montgomery later told Brooke, "If you saw Omaha beach you would wonder how the Americans ever got ashore."

Though not yet fully informed of how the battle was progressing, the British commander arranged to cross over to France that night to assess the situation on the spot. He told General John Kennedy at the War Office, "If things were not going well . . . he would put them right; if they were going well, he would make them go better."

Montgomery later observed that the afternoon and evening of D-Day had been Overlord's critical moments, when ". . . parts of the lodgement area were not linked up, and we were liable to defeat in detail. The answer to invasion across the sea is a strong counter-attack on the afternoon of D-Day when the invading force has not proper communications and has lost certain cohesion. That was Rommel's chance. It was not taken, and we were given time to recover—thank goodness!"

News of the invasion was received with jubilation by the people of the United States and Britain. Newspapers carried front-page maps of the Normandy coast and announced that it was the beginning of the end of the war. Churches held impromptu religious services. One was scheduled for Madison Square Garden in New York. At a morning press conference, Roosevelt warned against excessive rejoicing. "The war is by no means over. . . . [Y]ou don't just walk to Berlin. The sooner this country realizes that, the better."

On the evening of D-Day, Eisenhower met with Tedder, Leigh-Mallory, and Admiral Sir Bertram Ramsay to assess the day's achievements to the extent that they were known. Things had gone far better than anyone except Montgomery had dared forecast. Despite the initial trouble at Omaha Beach, more than 150,000 Allied troops had been put ashore in Normandy and would not be driven off (though that was not yet accepted as fact). Though casualties figures were not yet in, reports indicated they were considerably lighter than expected. They would turn out to total 8,000 killed, wounded, and missing. Large gaps had been blasted in Hitler's Atantic Wall.

In retrospect, it was apparent that the landing phase of Overlord was a triumph. Nevertheless, Montgomery's ambitious program for D-Day had not been completely fulfilled. In addition to the trouble at Omaha, most disappointing had been the failure to take Caen. That communications center had instead been occupied by the 21st Panzer Division, which had moved quickly to preempt the British advance in the area. Things thus appeared to be both good and bad, and no one dared predict what would happen next.

The destroyer HMS *Faulknor*, carrying Montgomery, reached the French side of the Channel shortly after dawn on June 7. Bradley went aboard from his command ship to report on what was happening at Omaha. Troops of the U.S. V Corps had dug in there but had failed to make much progress or secure much space for the reinforcements and equipment that were to be brought ashore for the linkup with the British troops landed to the east at Gold Beach. If that linkup was not quickly achieved, Rommel, who was hurrying back from Germany, would certainly try to drive a destructive wedge between the separate beachheads.

Montgomery realized the linkup was more pressing than cutting off and taking the Cotentin peninsula and altered his plan accordingly. He wanted the U.S. VII Corps, which had landed against much less resistance at Utah Beach, to expand eastward while the British at Gold Beach were to expand westward. Both would relieve enemy pressure at Omaha so that a fifty-mile-long solid breach in the German coastal defenses could be secured.

Later on D + 1, Eisenhower arrived offshore aboard the British minelayer HMS *Apollo* for a close look at developments. Bradley joined him on the *Apollo* off Omaha and reported that the situation had greatly improved after the first horrendous hours the previous day. But serious problems remained. German artillery fire was obstructing the unloading of supplies both at Omaha and Utah. Not enough artillery, trucks, or even ammunition had yet been brought ashore. Only a fraction of the supplies that were supposed to be off-loaded for the troops at Omaha had in fact been landed. Tanks were desperately needed. Twenty-seven of the thirty-two revolutionary new Duplex-Drive "swimming" tanks had sunk after being debarked from landing craft the previous day. Similar off-loading difficulties were being experienced by the British and Canadians further east.

Pockets of resistance were still holding out at Omaha. Many beach obstacles had not yet been cleared and some beach exits had not been secured. Another problem concerned the paratroopers of the 82nd Airborne, who had dropped without great loss but had not yet been able to regroup and were scattered across the countryside.

Montgomery went aboard the *Apollo* to give Eisenhower a comprehensive report of how the battle was developing. Despite the difficulties that still had to be overcome, and particularly the failure to take Caen as yet, he said that things were generally under control. He was confident enough to order that tactical headquarters be established for him ashore. Members of Eisenhower's party were sorry that the Supreme Commander had not yet also set foot in France. There was little he could do there. But it would have been a headline-grabbing symbolic gesture. However, he wasn't interested in those, and, having conferred with his principal commanders aboard the *Apollo*, he returned to England where, that evening, he received a signal from Montgomery reporting, "General situation very good and am well satisfied with results of today's fighting."

In fact, Montgomery was not satisfied. But aside from his constitutional inability to admit that anything might not be happening the way he planned it, the last thing he wanted was SHAEF to be alarmed by the progress of the operation when the true picture had still to develop. He did not want Eisenhower to start breathing down his neck.

But the Supreme Commander had reason to be concerned. The remaining gap on the coast was still to be closed. Additional forces, particularly heavy equipment, were still coming ashore too slowly—an extremely serious matter in view of the expectation of more bouts of rough weather that would further interrupt the flow. Essential aerial support would also be obstructed by a bad turn in the weather.

Early on the morning of D + 2, Montgomery went ashore to be better placed to deal with the situation. His tactical headquarters had been set up on the grounds of a chateau at the village of Creully. Security was tightened when a frightened German soldier was found hiding under a bench on the chateau grounds. But Montgomery was heartened by the failure of German counterattacks to drive the Allied forces back into the sea at any point. Even in the Omaha area, the Americans were now expanding their beachhead.

By that evening Montgomery felt comfortable enough with the situation to conclude a letter to a friend about how things were turning out with pleasantries about how, "The country here is very nice; green fields; very good crops; plenty of vegetables; cows and cattle; chickens, ducks, etc."

Concerned though he was about getting more men and equipment ashore before the weather broke, the enemy had far greater worries about reinforcements and supplies. The concentrated bombing of French and Belgian railway lines that Eisenhower had insisted upon made nonsense of German contingencies for bolstering defenses in Normandy, as did the continuing attention Allied fighter-bombers paid to any military and goods movements on the roads of northwest France. It was as Rommel had feared and as Eisenhower had planned.

By D + 6, the fifty-mile-long Allied bridgehead was consolidated and the Allied position ashore was beyond danger. That same day Churchill, who had been pestering his commanders to let him set foot in France, went across the Channel with Brooke to visit Montgomery at his chateau-grounds headquarters. As usual, the British commander exuded supreme confidence.

Eisenhower also visited Normandy that morning, going ashore at Omaha, escorting all three U.S. chiefs of staff, Marshall, Admiral King, and General Henry Arnold. Bradley briefed them on the situation. Marshall said he was impressed with how well things were going. Bradley's troops had by then captured the key town of Carentan and were preparing to drive up the Cotentin peninsula to take Cherbourg. Marshall said he thought the Germans would probably be defeated before Christmas. The German commanders, Rundstedt and Rommel, both appeared to share the belief that theirs was a lost cause. They urged Hitler to permit them to go over to the defensive. But the Führer refused to tolerate such defeatist sentiments. He flew to France to instruct them personally to drive the Allied invaders out of France.

They had no hope of accomplishing that task. Though still in its early stages, the Normandy campaign was shaping up in a manageable fashion for the Allies. Montgomery was drawing the worst the enemy could deliver onto his left, where he would absorb it and wear it down, while the Americans not only took Cherbourg but would be able to sweep around for the great Normandy breakout.

Like a scientist who saw his ingenious theory being proved in practice, Montgomery was delighted with himself. He told De Guingand, "[I]t is great fun fighting battles again after five months in England." But Caen was still in German hands, while the Americans were beginning to make a painful discovery about how difficult it was to fight their way through the charming *bocage* terrain of the sector of Normandy they were assigned to clear, where hedges, often six feet high or higher, sometimes interlaced in overhead canopies and rooted in high earthen embankments, flanked seemingly endless, winding country roads.

Eisenhower's son John, just graduated from West Point, had just arrived in London. His temporary presence was a gift from Marshall, who knew how close father and son were and who believed the Supreme Commander's burden would be at least marginally lightened by his presence. Eisenhower described it as "a Godsend. . . . I love to be with him." He had John accompany him on a visit to the British and American sectors in Normandy, took him to meet Churchill, and spent as much time as he could spare with him before John's return to army duty in the United States later in the month.

John described his father as a "little fretful" at being denied the opportunity to command the Normandy campaign. He said he was "like a football player sitting on the bench, anxious to get in the game." At SHAEF, Montgomery's brief reports about how well things were going aroused some irritation because they were not overly detailed. But it was accepted that the commander on the spot, the man who had beaten Rommel, knew what he was doing and had things under control.

CHAPTER 17
Normandy

Anxiously out of things, Eisenhower had returned from the waters off Normandy to the SHAEF tactical head-quarters at Portsmouth on D+1 exhausted from the ordeal that the overture to Overlord had been for him over twenty-two long weeks. To Butcher, he seemed "tired and almost listless." Reports of increasing enemy resistance worried him and he feared that the press was being dangerously premature in its accounts of how the battle was developing. Reporters were advised by him not to "paint a false picture of optimism; indeed the situation is somewhat critical and we are now in the inevitable race for build-up."

As the days passed, the Supreme Commander grew irritated with Montgomery. He felt he was reneging on an assurance that Montgomery would provide him with accurate nightly impressions of how the battle was developing. Reports were coming in from Montgomery's headquarters at Creully but contained little detail, though communication hitches were partly responsible. Caen had not yet fallen. The British advance was being contained by the Germans. It was clear that Montgomery was having to make important alterations to his plans, and Eisenhower felt it was wrong for him not to keep the Supreme Commander better informed about them. When a correspondent complained to Eisenhower that he and his colleagues were being told too little about what was going on in Normandy, he sardonically replied that he had been hoping to get the news from them.

Churchill already knew that it was not Montgomery's habit to concern himself overly much with the anxieties of his superiors. The general had been able to get away with that sort of conduct when he was winning battles in North Africa and when he was protected by Brooke and shielded by Alexander. But now questions were raised about why, despite his insistence that all was going well, the Allied attack was bogging down in the increasingly congested coastal perimeter in Normandy.

When a panzer division thwarted a British effort to break through, Montgomery said he had forced the Germans to squander strategic reserves by plugging holes in their defensive line. He was right about that, but he made it sound as if Rommel had run into a trap he had set. Some observers back at SHAEF saw it only as a setback for the British troops who took heavy casualties in that clash. Even those who accepted Montgomery's interpretation of the encounter began to grow impatient with his assurances that everything was under control when it appeared that the entire campaign might be grinding to a bloody halt.

Montgomery was well aware of the danger of failing to expand the beachhead more quickly. Unless it was deepened, there would be insufficient space to accommodate the additional divisions that were to be landed as well as the enormous amounts of supplies and equipment that needed to be put ashore. Amost 30,000 tons of stores were required to keep the Allied armies in action each day.

Battle-trained German troops, including veteran units shifted from the Russian front and ideologically motivated SS troops, were fighting harder, more daringly, and more effectively than the Allied soldiers, great numbers of whom had never seen combat before. When the British commander received reports that this or that British unit was fighting poorly or was demoralized by heavy casualties, he blamed its officers rather than the troops who, he believed, would do whatever was required of them if properly led.

Whatever his feelings, Montgomery showed no signs of jitteriness. He had no wish to arouse concern back at SHAEF. He had devised the campaign and now he was superintending its execution. He intended to remain exclusively in charge. He did not want anyone looking over his shoulder, asking questions and offering advice. Nevertheless, suspicions were gradually aroused at SHAEF that, having confidently described how the battle for Normandy would be fought, he intended to keep the fact that it was not developing that way a secret by making reassuring but unfounded pronouncements. He told Eisenhower, "You can be sure there will be no stalemate." "Operations . . . proceeding entirely according to plan and will continue without a halt." "I will continue battling on the eastern flank until one of us cracks; it will not be us." None of that seemed to describe what was actually happening in Normandy.

Some of the Americans believed Montgomery was failing to achieve more because his overriding priority was saving British lives. General J. Lawton Collins, commanding the U.S. VII Corps, thought that consideration "was always uppermost in Montgomery's mind." The issue certainly was on the minds of the War Cabinet and the British Chiefs of Staff. A veteran of the First World War, and aware of how thin Britain's manpower resources had become, Montgomery needed no warnings about the danger of a replay of a bloodbath on the western front. His wariness seemed confirmed by a captured German intelligence report claiming, "A successful break-in by the [British] is almost never exploited to pursuit. If our own troops are ready near the front for a local counter-attack the ground is immediately regained."

Montgomery's assurances to Eisenhower that all was well grew ever less convincing. The Supreme Commander could not help wondering whether his ground-forces commander actually knew what he was doing. Was it possible that he had been flummoxed by developments and was reacting with nothing more than the excessive caution for which he was notorious in American circles, and among some of the British generals as well? Morgan, whom Montgomery had humiliated by cursorily dismissing COSSAC's pre-Overlord plans out of hand, attributed his failure to produce the promised capture of Caen to his "incurable defensive-mindedness."

High on the list of those sharing such a concern were air force commanders, both American and British, who had been counting on the capture of the flat plain beyond Caen, where airfields, which Montgomery had called vital for improved tactical support for his troops, could be established. Montgomery had confidently predicted that the territory would quickly be in Allied hands, but it was still out of reach and the air commanders complained bitterly. One of his sharpest critics, Air Marshal Coningham of the 2nd Tactical Air Force, said he and Montgomery "had constant trouble."

An alarming new development in the war was putting Eisenhower under additional pressure to produce results. Allied intelligence had known that the Germans were experimenting with jet-propelled bombs. Aerial reconnaissance had earlier reported that the enemy was constructing mysterious launch sites in the Pas de Calais area. On June 13, a week after D-Day, the first German V-1 rocket exploded in southern England. Almost 7,000 of these "buzz bombs" were to follow during the next two months, including 2,500 that fell on London. Over 6,000 people were killed and 18,000 injured. Thousands of others were made homeless. But the main impact of those rockets was to instill terror. They arrived day and night, heralded a few seconds before impact by a low-pitched buzz that threatened instantaneous death and destruction.

From the first appearance of the German rockets, nerves were frayed in England, tempers were short, and expectations were of worse to come. Butcher recorded that "most people I know are semi-dazed from loss of sleep and have the jitters, which they show when a door bangs or the sounds of motors, from motorcycles to aircraft, are heard." Eisenhower himself reluctantly took to spending his nights in an air raid shelter. Churchill pressed him to give high priority to dealing with the German rockets, and the Supreme Commander felt obliged to divert bombers from tactical operations to attack the launch sites. This had limited effect, which focused attention even more sharply on the failure of Montgomery to live up to his rapid-advance forecasts and seize the area from which the buzz bombs were being launched.

Eisenhower at first declined to press the British commander to make better progress. Butcher observed, "[A]pparently Monty wants to tidy up his 'administrative tail' and get plenty of supplies on hand before he makes a general attack." On June 18, D + 12, he appeared to be ready and presented Eisenhower with a comprehensive report of the situation as he saw it.

1. . . . we have been working on the original directive issued by me in England and we have:

(a) gained a good lodgement area in Normandy.

(b) linked up all our different thrusts to form one whole area, and made the area we hold quite secure.

(c) kept the initiative, forced the enemy to use his reserves to plug holes, and beaten off all his counter-attacks.

(d) replaced our casualties in personnel and tanks, etc. . . .

(e) placed ourselves in a sound position administratively.

2. After the very great intensity of the initial few days we had to slow down the tempo of the operations so as to:

(a) ensure we could meet the enemy counter-attacks without difficulty.

(b) build up our strength behind the original assault divisions.

And while doing this we had to continue our offensive operations in order to get well positioned for the next moves, and also to ensure that we kept the initiative. . . . [W]e are now ready to pass on to other things and to reap the harvest.

He issued fresh instructions to General Dempsey, commander of the British Second Army,* to mount an offensive to

---

*Unlike American army commanders, neither Dempsey nor General Henry Crerar, commander of the Canadian First Army, were permitted much operational leeway. Montgomery maintained close and tight control over them, in sharp contrast to the freedom of action Alexander had permitted him when he had been a mere army commander. Montgomery did not presume to treat Bradley the same way, though at that time the U.S. First Army was also under his command. His instructions to Bradley were framed as advice and suggestions.

seize Caen. At the same time, Bradley was told to proceed with clearing the Cotentin peninsula. Eisenhower was pleased with the indication that his worries might have been baseless and that, after the initial get-started difficulties, the Normandy campaign was about to be lifted out of stalemate. He hinted as discreetly as he could that this time he expected results. "I am in high hopes," he wrote Montgomery, "that once the attack starts it will have a momentum to carry it a long ways."

But that same day a storm gathered over the English Channel. By afternoon, it had reached severe proportions and rarely tapered off during the following three days. Troops earmarked for the new offensive could not get ashore. Neither could supplies. One of the artificial Mulberry harbors was wrecked. Some 800 craft of various sizes capsized or were beached. The bid to take Caen had to be postponed. Eisenhower later moaned, "When I die, they can hold my body for a rainy day and bury me during a thunderstorm for this weather will be the death of me yet."

When the attack was launched in calmer weather four days later, Montgomery signaled SHAEF that it was his intention to make the enemy crack. But the advance gained little ground. Montgomery not only did not answer questions that were again asked about what was going wrong; he declined to acknowledge that they were being raised. He was dismayed that Eisenhower and others seemed to have forgotten the plan he maintained he had set out with absolutely clarity prior to the invasion for all concerned to understand. According to that plan, once ashore and firmly established, he would draw the main enemy forces onto the British sector of the Allied line on his left while Bradley's Americans on his right would secure the Cotentin peninsula before making the breakout through the German line of defense.

Not all of Montgomery's growing band of critics at SHAEF, where some Americans had taken to calling him "Chief Big Wind," remembered it that way. Some were convinced his pre-invasion assurances that he would penetrate "quickly and deeply into enemy territory" meant that he intended a British breakout on his left as well as an American breakout on his right. He later claimed his critics completely misunderstood his plan. He maintained that a "penetration" on his left was meant only to guarantee that the Germans would concentrate their armor against him there and to secure enough ground to eliminate any possible threat to the security of the bridgehead.*

Whatever was actually the case, the doubters had come to think that, apart from having secured the beachhead, little else he was doing was working. No one forgot his promise about how quickly Caen would fall to him (another month would pass before he took it) or his description of how the Allies would advance steadily toward identified phase lines in France that, it seemed, they were unlikely to reach by anything like the dates he had predicted.

In contrast to the reaction of the planners back at SHAEF, Montgomery for the most part retained the confidence of his officers in the field. A War Office visitor to his headquarters observed, "His relations with his staff and his commanders are 'matey,' but it is clear that they have the most terrific respect for him, and there is not the least doubt that he is in absolute control." But some among them could not help wondering what was going on when they were told first one thing and then something completely different. Lord Carver, later to become Chief of the Imperial General Staff but then commanding an armored brigade in Normandy, said, "One was so often being told that the coming battle was the one that was going to break through and that no losses must deter one. Then the whole thing would come to a grinding halt, and instead of being told one had failed, one was told that one had served one's purpose in containing the enemy."

Montgomery's inability to admit he had to think again about anything was to blame for the confusion. He had never been one to parade his ifs, ands, and buts. He had made his campaign forecasts as if explaining simple mathematical equations: he would do this and the result would be that. The certainty

---

*Even his admirer, War Minister Grigg, later said, "Of course Montgomery's original idea was to break out of the bocage country around Caen into the open in the first few days after the landing."

with which he explained things had made it appear that that was all there was to it. Of course, there was much more. He knew that as well as anyone, particularly after his experiences in North Africa, Sicily, and Italy. In his lectures he regularly referred to unforeseen difficulties that might have to be faced. But his presentations always made it seem that if his plans were followed, if the essentials he defined were observed, the difficulties would be overcome. When they were not and he was compelled to make adjustments, his conceit kept him from doing anything but insisting that what was happening was actually what he had planned all along.

That was now happening in Normandy. Eisenhower failed to grasp, and Montgomery was incapable of even trying to tell him, that though a stickler for a tidy battlefield he was doing more than a bit of tidying up. Despite his forecasts, not much ground was being gained by the British and Canadians, whose attacks were repeatedly beaten back by the Germans. At least one senior British officer at SHAEF considered his claim that everything was going as planned "absolute rubbish." But as the days turned into weeks with not much ground changing hands, the enemy, for whom great losses were potentially catastrophic, was being relentlessly worn down, and that was more important. Montgomery had never been interested in minor successes. Whether it was his original intention or not, he was now aiming for a decisive victory that would send the exhausted Germans reeling, rather than merely forcing them to withdraw to new defensive positions a few miles back, as they had in Italy.

Unlike Eisenhower, Brooke found Montgomery's explanation of what he was doing "wonderfully clear and concise." Only to Brooke did he feel able to concede that because Rommel was using his strategic reserve to plug holes in his line, he himself had been obliged to "think again . . . not to get off balance."

Eisenhower meanwhile was plagued by fear that the Allies were getting locked into a "World War 1-type" bloodbath in Normandy. On July 7, with the Allies still confined to their bridgehead a month after D-Day, Eisenhower wrote Montgomery of his concern.

I am familiar with your plan for generally holding firm with
your left, attracting thereto all the enemy armor, while your
right pushes down the peninsula and threatens the rear and
flank of the forces facing the Second British Army. However,
the advance on the right has been slow and laborious, due
not only to the nature of the country and the impossibility of
employing air and artillery with maximum effectiveness, but
to the arrival of [German] reinforcements. . . . It appears to
me that we must use all possible energy in a determined
effort to prevent a stalemate or of facing the necessity of
fighting a major defensive battle with the slight depth we
now have in the bridgehead. . . . I will back you up to the
limit in any effort you may decide upon to prevent a dead-
lock.

Tedder and Bedell Smith thought Eisenhower "lacked the
firmness of will to deal with Monty as he should." They urged
him to stop treating Montgomery with deference, to start issuing him unequivocal orders, and to instruct him forcefully "to
get moving." But Eisenhower still feared that such an approach
to Britain's most famous military hero would exacerbate strains
in the British-American alliance and he refrained from doing
so, though he himself was under intensifying pressure.

More than one of our high-ranking visitors [he later wrote]
began to express the fear that we were stalemated and that
those who had prophesied a gloomy fate for Overlord were
being proved correct. A grave risk that always accompanies
an amphibious undertaking against a continental land mass
was finding itself sealed off in a bridgehead. Adequate elbow
room is a prerequisite to the build-up of troops and supplies
necessary to a decisive, mobile battle. When possibilities of
supply and reinforcement, as well as terrain, favor the defense, there exists the chance that in spite of successful landing the battlefield may thus easily become a draining sore in
the side of the attacker rather than the opening stages of a
destructive campaign against the defender's main forces.

Montgomery's eccentric behavior in dealing with his superiors ruled out the possibility of an easy relationship between him and the Supreme Commander. Eisenhower once said, "Monty is a good man to serve under; a difficult man to serve with; and an impossible man to serve over." But that did not mean it was inevitable that the two of them would have a fundamental difficulty in communicating. Yet that is what happened.

Eisenhower managed to maintain rapport with many men of strong personality and diverse opinions. But Montgomery could not function well in the field as part of a team he did not lead. His egocentric nature made it impossible for him to respond to the complex situation in which he found himself except by insisting that he had not been mistaken about anything. It was not merely a matter of sustaining the morale and retaining the confidence of his officers and troops. In his boyhood he had erected strong emotional defenses and had never taken them down.

To mounting exasperation at SHAEF, where the feeling grew that things might be going catastrophically awry, Montgomery responded, "I am . . . quite happy about the situation," though in fact he wasn't at all happy about it. Taking Caen on D-Day and penetrating still deeper inland was something he could not deny he had confidently promised. It was down on paper. As a general convinced that maintaining the morale of his troops was a top priority, he must have been dismayed by signs of the men's sagging spirits as the battle bogged down and casualty rates climbed. He must have been confounded by the difficulty his and Bradley's troops and armor were having struggling through Normandy's difficult hedgerow landscape to which Overlord planners had given insufficient consideration.

But more than a million troops were now ashore, as were vast quantities of equipment. The weight of German armor was being drawn onto Montgomery's left and held there, setting the stage for the American breakout on the right. The British commander knew the enemy was doomed. Criticism of his performance back at SHAEF did not faze him. But he marveled at being nagged to abandon tactics that, though not working exactly as intended, were serving the desired purpose perhaps even better than he had hoped. He was contemptuous of the failure of others to recognize his achievement.

Bradley's aide, Major Chester Hansen, concluded, "Monty is beginning to believe the Monty legend, that he is a great man in history, fully convincing himself of his godlike role." But the British general failed to convey a godlike impression. At one of his meetings with Bradley, Hansen observed that Montgomery, "moves his face briskly and searchingly about the table as though discovering whether or not you were listening to him."

Though still reluctant to complain overly much about Montgomery, Eisenhower told Churchill that he was unhappy with the way the battle was going. With newspapers beginning to dwell on the lack of progress in Normandy, the prime minister expressed doubts about Montgomery to Brooke at one of his late-night meetings.

[Churchill] began to abuse Monty [Brooke recorded in his dairy] because operations were not going faster, and apparently Eisenhower had said that he was over-cautious. I flared up and asked him if he could not trust his generals for five minutes instead of belittling them. . . . He was furious with me, but I hope it may do some good in the future.

Brooke was especially angry because Churchill was offering "not . . . a single word of approval or gratitude for the excellent work Monty had done." Among the Americans, only Bradley sympathized with Montgomery's difficulties. While believing the ground-forces commander could be mounting stronger attacks, Bradley appreciated the effect of what he was doing in minimizing German "interference with the American army from the east." He had no doubt that it had been Montgomery's intention all along to have his British and Canadian troops "hold firm near Caen, like decoys, drawing the main weight of the German counterattack and blocking them from getting at me."

The Americans had battled against fierce enemy resistance to

link up with the British on their left after the near-disaster at
Omaha. They had struggled through the *bocage* to clear the
Cotentin peninsula. And they had seized the port of Cherbourg
to accelerate the flow of troops and supplies. Bradley knew that
if Montgomery had not tied down the bulk of the German forces
in France, his own troops would have had a far more difficult
time than they did in finally breaking out from the Normandy
beachhead. He could not understand why Eisenhower and Bedell Smith were critical of Montgomery for persisting in doing
what he said he would do.

> They were both intimately acquainted with the Overlord
> ground strategy formulated months before [Bradley later
> wrote]. That called for Monty not to "break out" but to hold
> and draw the Germans to his sector, while I "broke out" in
> my sector and wheeled to the east. We adhered to that basic
> concept throughout the Normandy campaign with no major
> changes in strategy and tactics.

But apparently the Russians shared the doubts others had
about Montgomery in Normandy. Their advancing troops were
reported to have put up a roadsign near Minsk saying 1,924
KILOMETERS TO CAEN.

Eisenhower may not have fully appreciated the extent of the
victory Montgomery was forging in Normandy, but the German
commanders knew well enough what has happening. Hitler
had already denied his generals permission to undertake a strategic withdrawal from Caen, which they knew would soon be
lost and the defense of which was costing them dearly. Rommel
and Rundstedt requested permission to conduct the battle as
they saw fit—in other words, for him to stop interfering. They
wished to prevent their armies from being encircled west of the
River Seine. Instead, they were instructed to confine Allied
forces to the Normandy bridgehead, a task that, they realized,
Allied air power made impossible. Rundstedt, who was replaced by Field Marshal Günther von Kluge as senior German
military commander in the west, had already realized even

more than that. When Field Marshal Wilhelm Keitel, the commander-in-chief of the German Army, asked what should be
done, Rundstedt had replied, "Make peace, you idiots! What
else can you do?"

On July 17, the staff car in which Rommel was traveling was
attacked by an Allied fighter-bomber; Rommel was badly injured and he too had to be replaced. The German Army command was shaken three days later as a result of an abortive
attempt to assassinate Hitler. Several high-echelon officers were
either among those involved in the plot or had known about it
and kept it secret. Countless others fell under suspicion, including the newly appointed commander in the west.

At a time of crisis for the forces over whom he had just
assumed command, Kluge became "very worried." He was
afraid he would be arrested at any moment. That fear was
compounded by the German field marshal's belief that even a
battlefield success would not be taken by Hitler as proof of his
loyalty. Faced with the possibility of execution, he was unable
to give his full attention to the battle. General Günther Blumentritt, chief of staff of the German armies in the west, said that
Kluge, who should have been devoting all his attention to trying to salvage an impossible combat situation, "was looking
back over his shoulder anxiously—towards Hitler's headquarters."

The field marshal was finally driven to commit suicide. That
would be weeks later. By then Rommel had also taken poison,
obliged by Hitler's security services to do so if he wanted to
save his family from Gestapo persecution after he had been
executed. Though the big Allied breakthrough had not yet occurred, the Germans were very precariously placed in Normandy. Since they were forbidden by their Führer to withdraw
anywhere, Montgomery's tactics continued to compel them to
fill holes in their lines here and there rather than concentrating
reserves for a big push that might have unsettled the Allied
position.

In mid-July, with stalemate still at the front and a cloud of
gloom shrouding SHAEF, Bradley inserted a beam of hope with
a plan for an operation to achieve the long-awaited Normandy

breakout. In Operation Cobra, his troops would finally blast out of the hedgerow countryside on a very narrow front in the Saint-Lô area to plunge into Britanny and sweep eastward toward the Seine. The U.S. Third Army under Patton, which had been brought over to Normandy, would be thrown into the battle.

As Allied ground-forces commander, Montgomery fully approved of Cobra and produced a plan of his own to provide support. He would launch an offensive, code-named Goodwood, to coincide with Cobra. "My whole Eastern flank will burst into flames," he told a delighted Eisenhower, giving the impression that he was finally going to blast through the German defenses.

That was not what he had in mind. He intended to mount a strong assault and was prepared to break through if the opportunity presented itself. But he knew he would face determined resistance and, indeed, he forced the Germans to commit virtually all of their reserves to meet his attack, which prevented them from shifting to meet the challenge posed by Bradley's Cobra onslaught.

But his crowing, given generous coverage in the British press, had once more led Eisenhower to expect much more. When he called Goodwood to a halt after achieving modest gains and declared himself satisfied with what it had accomplished, the reaction was predictable. Eisenhower's fury was "blue as indigo," according to Butcher, or "red as a hot coal," according to Bradley. Eisenhower demanded whether "with 7000 tons of bombs dropped in the most elaborate bombing of enemy front-line positions ever accomplished [to support Goodwood], only seven miles were gained—can we afford a thousand tons of bombs per mile?" Even the London *Times*, whose correspondent had been among those who had been offering exaggerated accounts of Montgomery's intentions, and that had prematurely headlined a British forces breakout into "Open Country," chided, "It is always better to do the booming after complete success has been secured."

"As a patriotic Briton," Kay Summersby said, "I shared the universal British respect for General Montgomery's historic success in the desert. . . . But as a SHAEF staff member, as part of the official family, and as secretary-driver to General Eisenhower, I grew to dislike the very name of Montgomery. . . . He gave the Supreme Commander more worry than any other individual in the entire Allied command."

At SHAEF there was talk of recalling Montgomery and appointing someone in his place who would make a more determined effort to crash through German defenses. Suggestions were made that he might be sent off to be governor general of Malta, or somewhere else where empty bombast would do no harm.

If he had been American, Eisenhower probably would have replaced him after Operation Goodwood. Bradley believed Eisenhower "would have sacked Monty there and then" if he thought he could. He certainly was considering it, and at one point felt the need to get an urgent message to Bedell Smith to caution him against even hinting at "the subject we have been discussing." It would have provoked outrage in Britain. Churchill would have had to answer to Parliament for it. Bradley's aide, Chester Hansen, noted in his diary, "[I]t would be folly to criticize Montgomery due to his great prestige position among the British [amongst whom] he occupies an almost professional papal immunity in his position." Though Tedder would have backed the Supreme Commander, Brooke, still believing the Americans were ham-handed amateurs at war, might well have resigned as British Chief of Staff.

Even the American public, which was not aware of doubts circulating about Montgomery's merits, would have been astounded if he were replaced. American correspondents were still reporting on the mystical aura of certainty and high level of morale he inspired in his troops.

[The troops'] confidence [said a battlefield report in *The New York Times*] is inspired by a small, wiry man who to many of them is a legendary figure. When "Monty" retires into the sacrosanct spaces of his private tent to think out and devise with meticulous care his next strategic move, no one dares approach within even loud-speaker distance.

Worried about the effect of criticism of the British general, Eisenhower passed word along that if any critical comment was to be leveled against any senior commander because of the conduct of the campaign, it was to be directed at him as well as Supreme Commander. But Eisenhower's way of dealing with him perplexed Montgomery. At one moment he urged Churchill "to persuade Monty to get on his bicycle and start moving." But a few days later he was informing the British commander, "I am perfectly positive that you are doing exactly the right thing." He would thank Montgomery "for the clear exposition of your ideas which I am bound to say seem to me perfectly sound and practicable," and then urge him to consider changing his tactics. He offered veiled hints that, while he was doing well, he should be doing better. "I cannot tell you," he wrote to him, "how happy I am that the advance has picked up such fine momentum. I know that you will keep hammering as long as you have a single shot in the locker."

A false start, costly in casualties, delayed success for Bradley's Operation Cobra, but the American troops on the right of the Allied line were finally about to leave the hedgerows behind them. With powerful aerial support, they broke out through Coutances and Avranches into open country. The enemy line of containment was shattered. On August 3, Bradley unleashed Patton's Third Army. It quickly pivoted east to turn the German flank.

Having assumed direct tactical command of the German forces, Hitler still refused to permit the withdrawal that might have averted the total disaster that was shaping up for his forces in France. He still believed they could drive the Allied armies back. By the time he finally was persuaded to permit a withdrawal beyond the Seine, forty of his divisions had been been badly mauled, some of them had been effectively wiped out, and his forces in France were in confusion and despair. By holding on the left and breaking out on the right, Montgomery had produced a triumph.

Nevertheless, at SHAEF and among the Americans he was denied the full credit he deserved for that achievement. The contrast between his lack of punch and Bradley's untrumpeted vigor in the breakout from the beachhead was striking. Public criticism of the British commander was beginning to surface in the American press. It was suggested that as general in charge of ground forces, he was letting the Americans take the biggest risks and the heaviest casualties.

A serious rift had opened between the Western Allies that would grow deeper as the months passed. Bradley later said, "It fell to the British to pin down superior enemy forces . . . while we maneuvered into position for the U.S. breakout. . . . [T]he British endured their passive role with patience and forbearing. . . . In setting the stage for our breakout, the British were forced to endure the barbs of critics who shamed them for failing to push out vigorously as the Americans did. The intense rivalry that afterward strained relations between the British and American commands might be said to have sunk its psychological roots into that passive mission of the British on the bridgehead."

Ironically, Montgomery's triumph in Normandy—his greatest achievement—marked the beginning of the most difficult and frustrating period of his entire career.

CHAPTER 18
Generals at War

The defeat of Germany had been inevitable from the moment the United States had been forced into the war three years earlier. Once the breakout from the Normandy beachhead had been achieved and four Allied armies were in forward motion across France, that defeat clearly would not be long delayed. With that in mind, Churchill had begun concentrating with ever greater urgency on postwar prospects. He was profoundly concerned about the threat to Western interests that could be posed by a triumphant Soviet Union.

The Russians were well placed to seize and retain mastery in Eastern and Central Europe by virtue of the territory that was likely to fall to the Red Army in the months ahead, before Germany was finally crushed. Churchill believed that, properly supported, American and British forces in Italy would be able to accelerate their trek up the Italian peninsula despite stubborn enemy resistance, cross the Alps through the Ljubljana Gap, push into Austria, and estabish a presence in parts of the the Balkans before Stalin could take control of the entire region.

But Marshall was more than ever convinced that the Allies were stuck in "a blind alley" in Italy. And Eisenhower was now determined that the launching of Operation Anvil, the disputed invasion of southern France, should no longer be delayed. Three American divisions were being reassigned from the Italian campaign to take part in Anvil. Churchill was furious. He snarled that no one but himself appeared capable of seeing that the Russians were spreading across Europe like a tide.

That fearsome prospect was not the only factor provoking the prime minister's rage and influencing his strategic thinking. Britain's prestige was on the line. Eisenhower was Allied Supreme Commander in Europe. British deputies were working closely under him, but the Americans were making the key decisions. The landing in the south of France, despite strong support from the RAF and Royal Navy, would be primarily an American and French affair. The British, who had uninterruptedly fought the Germans the longest, and part of the time all alone, were being well and truly elbowed from center stage.

Eisenhower should have been shielded from Churchill's anger by a chain of command that went through the Combined Chiefs of Staff. But he was on hand in England and the prime minister never stood on ceremony. Eisenhower became the direct target of the prime minister's harangues against Anvil. Their discussions on the subject were sometimes heated in the weeks following D-Day, when Eisenhower feared the battle for Normandy was getting nowhere. He grew angry when Churchill accused the United States of trying to play the "big strong and dominating partner" in the alliance and of "bullying" the British. That wasn't the way he saw it.

He was unmoved by Churchill's warnings about what the Soviets might get up to after Germany's defeat. So was Roosevelt, who believed the United States could deal amicably with "Uncle Joe" Stalin. The president's primary concern remained bringing the war quickly to an end with the fewest possible casualties. The U.S. Joint Chiefs of Staff were firm in their belief that the Italian campaign had already consumed far too much of the resources that could have been more wisely expended elsewhere against the enemy. Not only was Eisenhower supported by Washington in his determination to mount Anvil; he was now specifically admonished not to succumb to unrelenting British pressure to abandon it.

Concern persisted in the American capital that the Supreme Commander bent too far backward not to antagonize the British. He protested to Marshall that it wasn't true. But the fact remained that he had developed a very special personal relationship with the British. He had become close to several of his senior British subordinates at SHAEF and had gotten to know some members of the British Chiefs of Staff well. Despites persisting doubts about him at the War Office, at this stage theirs was for the most part a relationship marked by mutual respect and admiration.

He was enormously popular among the British people, and he admired them for what they had endured. He was flattered to be received almost as a friend by King George, to be accepted as an honorary member by London's exclusive Athenaeum Club, and to receive countless other honors in London and around the country. Unlike most other American generals, for whom the British experience was almost incidental, Eisenhower was unable to think reflexively in nationalistic, confrontational terms with regard to Britain, even when American and British interests and views diverged.

His insistence on Anvil despite British objections was not based on American preferences but on his views as Allied Supreme Commander. The logic was the same as it had been before. If the Germans had to contend with invaders in the south of France as well as in the Norman countryside, their lines were bound to crack sooner rather than later, and through the great port of Marseilles he would be able to rapidly introduce "between 40 and 50 divisions" from the United States and from French North Africa for the final showdown with the forces of the Third Reich.

Churchill was deeply upset by the failure of his effort to browbeat Eisenhower. He informed him "with considerable emotion" that he might request an audience with the king in order to "lay down the mantle of my high office." His resignation would impose additional strains on the American-British alliance, but Eisenhower stood his ground. He told Churchill that though British views may have justifiably prevailed in many Allied undertakings, that did not mean they were right all the time.

Despite his threat the prime minister did not step down, but he did take his case to Roosevelt. However, the president was no longer as easily influenced by him as he had once been. Eisenhower was pleased to learn that he had told Churchill they both would have to abide by the decisions of the Supreme Commander in military matters. It was not something the prime minister wanted to hear, nor was it something he intended to quietly abide by. He continued to press for Anvil's abandonment. The strong language he at times employed threatened the warm rapport that Eisenhower had established with him. Several times, the Supreme Commander felt called upon to make the firmness of his position absolutely clear, even warning him of the dangers of a rift.

> In two years [he told him] I think we have developed such a fine spirit and machinery in our field direction that no consideration of British versus American interests ever occurs to any of the individuals comprising my staff or serving as one of my principal commanders. I would feel that much of my hard work over the past months had been irretrievably lost if we now should lose faith in the organisms that have given higher direction to our war effort, because such lack of faith would quickly be reflected in our field command.

Churchill knew the dangers but fought his corner as long as he thought there was a chance he might win. He finally accepted that he could not and grudgingly gave his blessing. In the predawn hours of August 15, American paratroops dropped almost completely unopposed near the small inland southern French town of Le Muy. Soon afterward, troops of General Alexander Patch's U.S. Seventh Army began going ashore east of Toulon. They were joined by elements of General Jean de Lattre de Tassigny's French First Army. The Germans had been expecting a possible landing elsewhere in the south, and the meager opposition the invaders met was quickly overwhelmed.

Churchill was on hand, aboard a destroyer offshore, to see the troops land. He cabled Eisenhower, congratulating him on how efficiently and effectively Operation Dragoon, as Anvil had been renamed, had been organized and launched. Eisenhower replied that now that the prime minister had apparently adopted the operation, he was sure it would "grow fat and prosperous" under his watchfulness.

Within two weeks the major ports of Toulon and Marseilles were seized and almost 60,000 prisoners captured. The American and French forces, comprising the newly formed 6th Army Group under U.S. General Jacob Devers, began pushing northward to link up with the troops of Patton's Third Army fanning out from Brittany after the Normandy breakout.

The Anvil controversy had been the most difficult diplomatic-military issue with which Eisenhower had had to deal. Wavering and indecisive at first, bending this way and that, he had subsequently come to a hard-and-fast decision and had stuck to it in the face of Churchill's persistent, forceful, bitter, and sometimes personal challenge. It had been a wearying but ultimately satisfying experience and had earned him additional respect in London, even, grudgingly, from the prime minister. However, he still did not know how to get Montgomery to do what he wanted him to do.

Rarely in war do things happen as expected. None of the Overlord commanders—not Eisenhower, not Montgomery, not Bradley—had believed German resistance south of the Seine would collapse as comprehensively as it did once the Allied forces had broken out of the Normandy bridgehead. It had been assumed that the Germans would gradually fall back to the river, where they would regroup and establish new defensive positions in France from which they would have to be forcibly ejected.

The Allied plan was clear. "Anticipating the Germans would make a textbook retreat to the Seine," Bradley said, "we would draw up our combined ground forces opposite the river. There we would pause for several weeks to rest up and refit our divisions, fully open our supply ports in Cherbourg and Brittany, create logistical lines to our front and stockpile gasoline, ammunition and food. When all was ready we would cross the Seine and strike toward Germany."

But that plan had been overtaken by events. It had been made obsolete by Hitler's refusal to permit his forces to undertake a strategic withdrawal once the Allies had secured their Normandy bridgehead and by Montgomery's steadfastness in drawing the enemy's armor to destruction. The British commander's pre-invasion phase line forecast was for the Allied forces to reach the Seine by ninety days after D-Day. Though that prediction had been much derided over the previous weeks, they had in fact gotten to the river before the end of August—by D+79.

German losses in troops and equipment had been immense. SHAEF reported to the Combined Chiefs of Staff, "The equivalent of 5 Panzer Divisions have been destroyed and a further 6 severely mauled. . . . The equivalent of 20 Infantry Divisions have been eliminated and a further 12 very badly cut up and have suffered severe losses. Included . . . are 3 of the enemy's crack Parachute Divisions. . . . Total enemy casualties amount to over 400,000. . . . The total continues to mount."

Of 2,300 tanks and assault guns, the Germans had been able to bring only about a hundred back across the Seine. The German commander-in-chief in the west had twice been changed and a score of German army, corps, and division commanders had been killed or captured. It appeared that the Allied forces would not after all face stiff resistance as they fought their way to and across the natural barrier of the Seine and sped on toward Germany.

Weeks before, Montgomery had drawn up plans for such a contingency. If the strong German resistance that was expected at the Seine did not materialize, the plan for a pause during which the Allies would regroup and prepare logistically before attempting to cross the river would be dropped. The enemy would not be given "a chance to catch his breath." Instead,

"Every endeavour [would] have to be made to force the crossing without pause."

That had been hypothetical at the time and considered unlikely. But now the point had come to review the situation and for new decisions to be made. The moment had also arrived for planned changes in the Allied command structure to be instituted. Montgomery was to lose out on both.

Once the Normandy bridgehead had been secured and the breakout from it had begun, Eisenhower, while remaining Supreme Commander, was supposed to take over from him as ground-forces commander. Criticism in American newspapers of "British dominance of the command and conduct of the invasion" when the Americans outnumbered the British on the field of battle would alone have been enough to make sticking to the changeover plan inevitable. The Washington *Times-Herald* complained, "It is generally recognized in congressional circles and common gossip in military circles that General Eisenhower is merely a figurehead and the actual command of the invasion is in the hands of the British General Staff."

It was 1944, an election year in the United States, and the direction of the war was the key issue. Eisenhower was once more served notice by Washington that he must not be seen to be overly influenced by Churchill or his British subordinates. Marshall told him, "[T]he Secretary [of War Stimson] and I and apparently all America are strongly of the opinion that the time has come for you to assume direct exercise of command. . . . [T]he reaction here is serious and will be, I am afraid, injected into the debates in Congress."

Montgomery was, of course, disappointed at being relieved of ground-forces command. Aside from his natural desire to remain in charge, he was perplexed by the continuing failure of Eisenhower and others at SHAEF to appreciate, or even understand, how brilliantly he had masterminded the Normandy campaign. He had hoped that, in recognition of that achievement, the plan for him to hand ground-forces command over to the Supreme Commander would not be implemented. He agreed with Brooke that "Ike knows nothing about strategy" and was afraid that the Supreme Commander would make a mess of the great opportunity with which the Allies were now presented.

He also believed that Eisenhower had no idea "of the trouble he was starting" by making command changes when things of great significance could be made to happen if the moment were seized without disruptive changes. He told Brooke that he had explained "very clearly to Eisenhower that the direction and control of the land battle in France is a whole-time job for one man" to which he would be required to "devote his whole and undivided attention."

Montgomery's concern about that was fully justified. The Supreme Commander was still required to devote much close attention and a great deal of his time to a variety of other matters. They included coordinating strategy with the Russians, responding to an assortment of proposals from the British Chiefs of Staff and Churchill personally about possible operations elsewhere in Europe, dealing with De Gaulle, fielding a flood of communications from the U.S. chiefs of staff and the War Department, and badgering Washington for additional troops and equipment to wind up the war in Europe at a time when Congress, which considered Hitler effectively beaten, was already pressing for the conversion of some war-production factories to civilian production. In addition, an endless flow of senior American visitors, including members of Roosevelt's cabinet, passed through London to confer with him on crucial issues—including how Germany was to be dealt with after the defeat of its armies and even demobilization plans for the largest army the United States had ever put in the field.

Eisenhower chose to ignore Montgomery's warning about commanding the ground battle being a full-time assignment, his presumption in lecturing him, and his insinuation that he was not up to the job. He knew the strategy he intended to employ. Once across the Seine, Allied armies would advance both north and south of the Ardennes Forest, "two massive, mutually supporting thrusts" toward the Rhine and the German heartland. That would require day-to-day coordination of what would be two separate campaigns. Eisenhower believed those campaigns would be integrated most efficiently, and with the least confusion, by two separate army groups, both under his command. That was the way things had been tentatively planned before the invasion.

Montgomery would retain command of his 21st Army Group, which would proceed along the northern route. It consisted, as before, of Dempsey's British Second Army and Crerar's Canadian First Army. A new, all-American Army Group—the 12th—would be created for the drive south of the Ardennes toward the middle of Germany. Bradley would be its commander, deploying two armies, the First under General Courtney Hodges, and Patton's Third. The 12th Army Group became officially operational on August 1, 1944 (it was soon to gain another army, the U.S. Ninth, commanded by General William Simpson). Montgomery was to continue as Allied ground-forces commander until September 1, when he was to surrender that position to Eisenhower, a move Brooke thought "likely to add another three to six months to the war."

The handover was handled awkwardly. The attitude of the military authorities toward war reporting was much different from what it was later to become. There was no intention of "doing the enemy a favor" by giving correspondents as much information as they subsequently claimed a right to have. But the news of the command change leaked out and was interpreted by the press in a way that greatly offended the British public.

The groundwork for outrage had already been laid in Britain. Deputy Supreme Commander Tedder had found that "one of the most disturbing features of the campaign [in the British] press . . . had been the uninhibited boosting [in Britain] of the British Army at the expense of the Americans." Although the Americans far outnumbered the British in the field and were doing far more of the fighting, it was understandable for British newspapers to concentrate on the activities and achievements of British troops and far less so on those of the Americans. As a result, the British public had come to think that their soldiers were doing most of the fighting, or at least as much as the Americans. Tedder feared that this had been "sowing the seeds of a grave split between the Allies. . . . [I]f the British public believe all they are being told now," he said, "they will not like being told a very different story by the Americans."

He was right. In mid-August, word spread in London that American newspapers were saying that Bradley, in taking command of an army group in France, was attaining "status equal to Montgomery." It generated much resentment in Britain, where it was seen as a humiliating and unwarranted "demotion" of the British hero. It seemed a shabby way to treat a general who had redeemed the reputation of the British Army in North Africa and whose battlefield achievements in France had been front-page news in the London press for weeks.

Denials from SHAEF that Montgomery had been demoted did not quiet the protests. British newspapers demanded to know what was going on, not only with regard to the command structure but with operations in France generally.

> We feel it our duty [said the London *Daily Mirror*] to demand that General Montgomery be offered an apology. . . . Throughout the war much confusion has been caused by the issue of untrue statements and ill-advised "directives." . . . [S]omething is seriously wrong; something which cannot but have an adverse effect on the harmony of Anglo-American cooperation in the field. In general the handling of war news has been amateurish, inconsistent and confusing. One day official optimism runs high; the next, someone cautiously "plays it down." It is time efficiency was established in this vital matter.

Such impatience had long been brewing. The treatment of Montgomery brought it to a boil. Eisenhower sought to defuse British anger by telling a London press conference that anyone who thought Montgomery had been demoted misunderstood what was happening. He said that the British commander was a "great and personal friend" for whom he had great admiration. He called him "one of the great soldiers of this or any other war." He urged people to understand that the command change had been planned well before D-Day and that it was not a reflection on Montgomery's considerable skills.

But going public did not remove doubts among the British about the quality of American military leadership. People asked questions about why Eisenhower remained Supreme Commander when they were led by their newsreel films, their newspapers, and War Office communiqués to believe that Montgomery was one of the most oustanding military figures of modern times, as even Eisenhower himself had felt obliged to concede. Nor were hurt feelings soothed by the satisfaction expressed in the American press that the U.S. armies in France were finally coming under direct American command, which they effectively had been all along despite having been formally under Montgomery's orders.

The changes that were now taking place were of far greater significance than SHAEF tried to pretend, and the reasons went much deeper than adherence to an earlier planning decision. American preponderance over the British in the field was already recognized as a historic and irreversible changing of the guard. The Americans welcomed it with smug confidence; the British acknowledged it with regret and not a little bitterness. The Americans, barely feeling the strain, had twelve million men in uniform. The British, stretched practically to the limit, had less than half that number.

The Americans now had four armies in the field in France, including the Seventh Army that was thrusting north after having landed in the south. More U.S. divisions were en route across the Atlantic. The British were hard-pressed to keep their single Second Army up to strength. Montgomery was believed by the Americans to be "so conscious of Britain's ebbing manpower" that he hesitated to engage in an operation in which "a division may be lost" because it was practically impossible for the British to replace it. "When it is lost, it's done and finished."

The American breakout from the Normandy beachhead that had been blueprinted by Montgomery marked the moment that Britain conspicuously passed the baton of superpowerdom over to the United States. Under the circumstances now prevailing, it was a delusion to expect the Americans to permit a British general to remain in charge of the campaign in France.

But Montgomery was not one to graciously accept being re-

lieved of a command he believed it was essential for him to
retain, and certainly not when he was to hand it over to a
general he thought incapable of exploiting the great opportunity he had created. The Germans had been so thoroughly
routed in Normandy that they were in disarray. Montgomery
was convinced that only a general with his grasp of the equations of battle could provide the follow-up with the planning
and close supervision that was required. What had earlier been
planned as a measured advance against the enemy could be
turned into hot pursuit.

The British commander had never liked Eisenhower's plan
for a divided advance on Germany north and south of the
Ardennes. After the rout of the Germans in Normandy, he
considered it idiocy. "We have now reached the stage where
one really powerful and full blooded thrust towards Berlin is
likely to get there and thus end the German war." Instead of a
divided advance against the routed German forces, he called
for a concentrated northeastward thrust of "a great mass of
Allied armies"—his own and Bradley's. Such a surge would
clear the French coast as far as Belgium, establish forward air
bases, and then push on across the Rhine into the Ruhr district,
Germany's industrial hub.

It was a striking vision. Forty Allied divisions would form a
solid phalanx that would thunder unstoppably forward before
the enemy could recover balance and reestablish a stable defense line. Powerful armored and mobile columns would bypass enemy centers of resistance. Those would be mopped up
by infantry following on. The momentum would carry the Allied forces into the heart of Germany. The war could be over
before Christmas. It was a fascinating, imaginative proposal,
and one that set the stage for a British-American dispute on
strategy that would arouse much bitterness in the following
months.

Montgomery, the military scientist, had produced what he
was convinced any general with even half a brain could see
was an imaginative and eminently workable plan. There were
problems with it that he made no effort to point out. The terrain
that would have to be traversed by his mass of Allied divisions

was laced with canals and river tributaries. It might therefore prove unsuitable in places for rapid armored advance. What was more, the forces involved might be diminished during their advance by the need to protect their flanks against threats posed by bypassed enemy positions. By the time they were in a position for the proposed thrust into Germany to destroy the Third Reich, they might be too weakened to deal with the divisions Hitler might have desperately assembled to prevent that from happening.

But those arguments were not necessarily overwhelming. The Germans were for the moment in sufficient disorder for a daring surge against them to have made significant headway, taking the port of Antwerp, a target of highest priority for supplying the Allied armies on the continent, and overrunning the launch sites for Hitler's buzz bombs, which were continuing to bring death and terror to southeastern England.

Nor were even greater successes beyond the realm of possibility. General Günther Blumentritt was "absolutely convinced" that the war could have been over within four months, "that there would have been a saving of Allied lives . . . had Montgomery's plan been carried out" while the German front was completely disorganized by the rout in Normandy.

In addition to military and personal reasons for promoting his plan, Montgomery had pressing national interests to consider. He had graduated to a position beyond that of mere general. He was Britain's major protagonist in the field. He now had duties well beyond the call of battle. His country, staggering under the impact of war costs, was on the brink of bankruptcy. He was obliged to weigh the implications in his calculations.

The British economy and man-power situation [he wrote] demanded victory in 1944: no later. Also, the war was bearing hardly on the mass of the people in Britain; it must be brought to a close quickly. Our 'must' was different from the American must; a difference in urgency, as well as a difference in doctrine. This the American generals did not understand; the war had never been brought to their home country.

Montgomery was convinced that unless the thrust he proposed was given the highest priority, any chance of ending the
war before year's end would be forfeited and Britain's already
desperate situation intensify.

However, in urging his plan on Eisenhower, he had lost contact with the reality of his own status. He was behaving as if
he still had the full confidence of the Supreme Commander. He
knew Eisenhower planned a broad-front advance across France
and into Germany in accordance with strategy that had been
carefully worked out. But he had made little effort to bring
Eisenhower in line with his thinking, or even to see him, while
he had developed his plan. He sprang it on him full-blown, in
effect peremptorily informing him that he was wrong and didn't
really understand the situation. It had never been his style to
consult if he could avoid it. He could not accept that consultations, even with generals he considered inadequate, were
sometimes essential if only as a matter of courtesy. He also
could not assimilate the fact that, even after he had been proved
right in Normandy, others believed he had been wrong and
was unreliable.

It might be said that he sometimes said things he knew were
less than true for reasons of troop morale or to prevent outside
interference with his operations as they matured. But he was
often too closed up within himself to make a realistic reading
of situations or the reaction of others. When he outlined his
daring plan to Bradley, he received the impression that it had
drawn his "complete agreement." But Bradley, who was reluctant to argue with a man given to lecturing him as if he were
just out of West Point, believed the basic assumption of Montgomery's plan was not just mistaken; it was "downright crazy."
He said, "We would be putting all our money on a horse that
looked good in the paddock but had a tough time getting out
of the starting gate and had never shown well on a fast track."
Bedell Smith thought the proposal was "the most fantastic bit
of balderdash ever proposed by a competent general." Eisenhower told Marshal, "Examination of this scheme exposes it as
a fantastic idea." Morgan observed cynically, "Montgomery,
principally celebrated hitherto for cautious deliberation, con-

ceived the notion that, were he to be accorded every priority to the detriment of the [Americans], he could, in the shortest order, overwhelm the enemy, drive on to Berlin and bring the war to a speedy end."

Too many people at SHAEF felt they had been misled by Montgomery when he had impressed them with his pre-invasion explanation of how tidily the Normandy campaign would be wrapped up. They were not prepared to be bamboozled by him again, nor did they believe he was serious when he suggested that he was willing to serve under Bradley if necessary in the ambitious operation he proposed. The British chiefs of staff would never have permitted it.

Persisting with a fetish of requiring his superiors to visit him rather than the other way around, Montgomery sent De Guingand, his much-liked and respected chief of staff, to convince Eisenhower of the wisdom of his plan. When De Guingand was unable to do so, Montgomery tried it himself. He asked the Supreme Commander to come to his tactical headquarters in France to discuss strategy. Eisenhower had Bedell Smith fly over from England with him to take part in the discussion. But Montgomery, aware that Smith now was undisguisedly critical of his judgment, insisted that he not participate in the discussion, which offended both the Supreme Commander and his influential chief of staff. "What makes me so Goddamn mad," Smith growled, "is that Monty won't talk in the presence of anyone else. He gets Ike into a corner alone."

Montgomery did nothing to make up for this self-defeating act of discourtesy by lecturing Eisenhower on how a Supreme Commander should remain above the battle, supervising from on high but not interfering while "Someone must run the land battle for him." Eisenhower did not have to be told whom he thought that "someone" should be.

Aside from everything else, it was the wrong time to suggest that American ground forces come once more under his command. The battle for Normandy behind them, Bradley, and particularly Patton serving under him, had ideas of their own for a rapid advance toward Germany, and they appeared to have done more to put them into practice. The irrepressible

Patton, with dazzled news correspondents in tow, was plunging through the foundering enemy, seizing and creating opportunities. Headlines, particularly those in American newspapers, trumpeted his successes. He bragged that his army was advancing faster and farther than any in history.

The contrast with Montgomery's earlier tardiness in cracking through at Caen was glaring. Patton was meeting nothing like the resistance with which the British and Canadians had been forced to cope. He did not have to halt to regroup, a practice that Patton said "seemed to be the chief form of amusement in the British armies." Anxious to advance where Montgomery's forces had been fought to a standstill, he had pleaded with Bradley for permission to do so and "drive the British back into the sea for another Dunkirk."

If the deployment of forces had been different at the time— with the Americans positioned where Mongomery's troops were, and Patton ready to blaze northward through the routed German forces—it is possible the proposal for a concentrated drive to the north might have swayed Eisenhower. But the idea of a British general now taking command of the bulk of American forces in France was a non-starter. Eisenhower, under pressure from Washington, told him that he was obliged to take American public opinion into account. Montgomery replied, "Give people victory and they won't care who won it."

Eisenhower was faced with a conundrum. Though the Germans had been sent scrambling back, he was not as convinced as Montgomery that they were incapable of regrouping sufficiently to resist a concentrated Allied thrust. Nevertheless, at that stage the Allies—with their lines of communications stretching back to Cherbourg and the Normandy beaches— were logistically incapable of long sustaining the plan he preferred for mounting major offensives both north and south of the Ardennes.

Weighing the various factors, he produced a compromise. While not giving Montgomery all he wanted for the concentrated drive he proposed, he agreed to grant him "operational coordination" in the north. His northern thrust would have the support of Bradley's U.S. First Army. Indeed, Bradley was instructed that his "principal offensive mission" was to offer Montgomery that support. At the same time, however, as commander of the newly established U.S. 12th Army Group Bradley was to continue cleaning up the Brittany peninsula and to prepare to advance across the middle of France toward Metz and the German border.

That meant Montgomery would get priority in the allocation of supplies, but not nearly as great as he wanted. "[S]o we got ready," the frustrated British commander told Brooke, "to cross the Seine and go our different ways. . . . The trouble was we had no fundamental plan which treated our theatre as an entity."

Many of the Americans were also unhappy with Eisenhower's compromise. They were displeased that Montgomery had been able to extract as much as he had from the Supreme Commander. Some of Patton's officers were heard muttering, "Eisenhower is the best general the British have." Bradley was especially angry. He had to scrap the offensive plans he had drawn up for the divisions he was now instructed to commit to the support of the British drive. He was vexed for personal reasons as well. The war was coming to an end and he did not wish to be made to play a lesser role in the windup. He saw Eisenhower's compromise decision as having the effect of downgrading him from the equal status with Montgomery he had just attained. Though normally of a balanced temperament, and not usually caught up in the anxieties of military politics, he was becoming enraged by Montgomery's self-exaltation. He believed "Monty's plan sprung from his megolomania. He would not cease in his efforts to gain personal command of all the land forces and reap all the personal glory for our victory."

The war in Europe had taken a decisive turn by the late summer of 1944. The Germans were in full retreat across Eastern Europe. Finland, which had been allied to the Germans, had signed an armistice with the Russians. Hitler's forces had been pulled out of Greece. After consolidating their Operation Dragoon beachhead on the Riviera, the U.S. Seventh Army and French First Army were driving north into the Rhône valley.

The German military command was badly shaken by the ongoing arrests of officers believed to have been implicated in the plot to assassinate Hitler.

It was recalled that the First World War had come to an unexpectedly rapid conclusion in 1918 when the resistance of the German armies and the government in Berlin had suddenly collapsed. Was that about to happen again? Rumors were rife in the United States and Britain. People talked about it and prayed. Newspapers speculated about when it would happen. Eisenhower was subjected to repeated questioning about how many weeks or months it would take to wind things up in Europe. At press conferences, he repeatedly warned against excessive optimism.

The liberation of Paris fueled expectations. But it also added to Eisenhower's problems. Churchill later quipped that the heaviest cross he'd had to bear in the war had been the Cross of Lorraine, the symbol of Charles de Gaulle's Free French movement. But Churchill's dealings with De Gaulle were more straightforward than Eisenhower's.

The Free French leader remained offended by the refusal of the Allies to formally recognize his FCNL, as well as by the Allied issuance of special French currency for the liberation of his country. To defuse his anger and retain the cooperation of the Free French army, Eisenhower made friendly gestures to him. He accepted General Pierre Koenig, De Gaulle's chief military aide, as a senior Allied officer of equal rank with army group commanders Bradley and Montgomery. He helped persuade Washington to seek better relations with the Free French leader and to invite him to the American capital for consultations with Roosevelt.

De Gaulle was pleased finally to receive formal diplomatic recognition from the Americans, but not pleased enough to let things rest there. He announced in mid-August, as the German rout in Normandy gathered pace, that he was shifting his headquarters from Algiers to the French mainland to reestablish a sovereign government of France there. That presented a problem because, as Supreme Commander, Eisenhower was in charge of areas of the country liberated from German military occupation. He had not been authorized to transfer authority to anyone else.

That matter might have been tactfully sidestepped for the moment but for the question of the liberation of Paris. Toward the end of August, elements of Bradley's First and Third Armies were near enough to the French capital to take it. Its liberation would be a historic, joyous event. But militarily it would be inconvenient and costly. If the Germans decided to fight to hold the city, casualties both military and civilian could be heavy and destruction extensive. What was more, vast amounts of supplies and the appropriate transport would have to be diverted to feed two million Parisians. It was tactically advisable to bypass the city.

As a soldier, De Gaulle agreed. But as would-be leader of liberated France he could not accept it. Underground resistance fighters within the city were not prepared to wait. They had already disregarded instructions from the Free French command not to rise up yet against the German occupation forces. If they were able to seize control of the city, De Gaulle knew he might face a powerful political challenge from the Communists, who had a strong presence in the resistance movement.

When Eisenhower informed him that he had decided to bypass Paris, De Gaulle replied that if the Americans did not take the city, Free French troops attached to the U.S. First Army would be ordered to do so. The threat angered Eisenhower. He was Supreme Commander of all Allied troops in Europe, including the Free French. But De Gaulle was prepared to order them to act contrary to his instructions and there was nothing he could do but submit. He fabricated a military excuse for sending the U.S. Fourth Division and a British contingent, accompanied by French troops under General Jacques Leclerc, to liberate the French capital. De Gaulle was there to take the cheers of the ecstatic crowds when they entered the city on August 25.

Eisenhower asked Bradley to join him in celebrating the event with a visit two days later. He invited Montgomery to come along also, but Montgomery said he was too busy. It was plain to him that by succumbing to De Gaulle and diverting forces to take Paris when the Germans still could be decisively routed in the north, Eisenhower had again demonstrated his tragic limitations as Supreme Commander.

General Siegfried Westphal, who was about to become German chief of staff on the western front, shared the British commander's belief that the Allied forces could have gainfully employed much more aggressive tactics.

The overall situation in the West [Westphal observed] was serious in the extreme [for the Germans]. . . . A heavy defeat anywhere along the front, which was so full of gaps that it did not deserve this name, might lead to a catastrophe, if the enemy were to exploit his opportunity skillfully. A particular source of danger was that not a single bridge over the Rhine had been prepared for demolition, an omission which took weeks to repair. . . . Until the middle of October, the enemy could have broken through at any point he liked with ease, and would then have been able to cross the Rhine and thrust deep into Germany almost unhindered.

As was soon to be demonstrated to Montgomery's detriment, that assessment was not completely accurate.

On September 1, 1944, it was announced that Montgomery had been made a field marshal in recognition of his "outstanding service in the memorable and possibly decisive battle" that he had "personally conducted in France." The promotion was widely acclaimed in Britain. It had been a long time since ordinary Britons had taken one of their generals so warmly and proudly to their hearts. However, political considerations were very much involved. The promotion was meant to compensate for the downgrading of Britain's most popular war hero on the day that Eisenhower took over from him as Allied ground-forces commander.

To mark that occasion, the Supreme Commander moved his headquarters to France, near the village of Granville at the base of the Cotentin peninsula. It was some 400 miles from the front lines and had poor communications with forward command posts. Montgomery said it was suitable for a Supreme Commander but useless for a ground-forces commander who was supposed to keep his finger on the pulse of his armies.

By shifting his headquarters to France, Eisenhower contributed to the ever-growing impression that the war was heading toward a rapid conclusion. He again tried to dampen down premature optimism, though he told Marshall he agreed that "signs of victory appear in the air."

Montgomery had wasted no time in exploiting the partial support Eisenhower had given him for his thrust northeast toward the German heartland. Seeking to make do with fewer divisions than he had requested, take advantage of the German rout, and dispel his reputation for excessive caution, he issued instructions to his commanders that "any tendency to be 'sticky' or cautious must be stamped on ruthlessly. . . . The proper tactics now are for strong armoured and mobile columns to by-pass enemy centres of resistance and to push boldly ahead creating alarm and despondency in enemy rear areas."

Disappointed by the performance of some of his command-ers, he summoned Horrocks, who had been badly wounded in North Africa, out of recuperation in England to lead XXX Corps of the British Second Army and sent him racing northward to spearhead the drive against the splintered German forces. On September 3, Brussels was liberated. The following day, Ant-werp fell.

But to Montgomery's dismay, Bradley had by then been able to extract from Eisenhower permission to let Patton's Third Army thunder eastward south of the Ardennes. Patton had already been doing that with dazzling success. He had been blasting his way through enemy resistance in central France and driving on toward Metz and southern Germany, though without formal authorization or the allocation of enough sup-plies. They were still not coming through in quantities sufficient to permit all the Allied armies to engage the enemy as aggres-sively as their commanders would have liked. Patton had made good his shortfall by capturing German oil stores and through trickery (spiriting away fuel meant for the First Army). But he needed still more to sustain his momentum. Now he had some, courtesy of the Supreme Commander, who had no wish to slow his old friend down when he was doing so well. But it cut into the priority in transport, equipment, and supplies that Montgomery understood he had been given.

The British chiefs of staff complained, but Eisenhower believed they were merely pressing Montgomery's single-thrust idea, which he had already rejected. It was now clear that the fundamental divergence on strategy between the British and Americans could not be papered over. Eisenhower regretted that the Allies "cannot hang together so effectively in prosperity as they can in adversity," but he intended to exercise the command with which he had been entrusted in accordance with his own ideas.

Seeing the chance to bring the war to a rapid conclusion slipping away, Montgomery again tried to press home his argument for a high-priority, single, concentrated offensive.

> [W]e have now reached the stage [he told Eisenhower] where one really powerful and full-blooded thrust towards Berlin is likely to get there and thus end the German war. . . . We have not enough maintenance resources for two full-blooded thrusts. . . . If we attempt a compromise solution and split our maintenance resources so that neither thrust is full-blooded we will prolong the war.

But with "Blood-and-Guts" Patton permitted to go his own way, and to receive extra logistical support from the limited stocks available, it was explicitly confirmed that control of Allied strategy had been irretrievably wrenched from Montgomery's (and Britain's) grasp.

Convinced that Eisenhower was "completely out of touch with the land battle," the British commander requested a meeting with him to argue his case in person. Eisenhower invited him to his headquarters near Granville. But Montgomery, claiming to be too busy, pressed him to come to him instead at his tactical headquarters at newly liberated Brussels. It was not a clever way to go about influencing the Supreme Commander. Eisenhower was suffering at the time from an injured leg. A few days earlier, the small plane in which he had been traveling had made an emergency landing on a Normandy beach and he had badly wrenched his knee while helping to push it along the sand. The injury was still painful. Nevertheless, he flew to Brussels on September 10 to confer with Montgomery. In view

of Eisenhower's difficulty in getting around, they met aboard
his aircraft.

In another of his displays of effrontery, the field marshal
said that Eisenhower's chief administrative officer, General Sir
Humphrey Gale, should not be present during their discussion
but that his own, General Sir Miles Graham, should. Not wishing to make a fuss over it, Eisenhower agreed, and then had
his strategy subjected to criticism so severe that it bordered on
ridicule. Montgomery's intelligence chief, Brigadier Bill Williams, believed, "Patience and tolerance made Monty overstep
himself. At first he just made his point. The fact that Ike let him
go on made Monty overstep." Eisenhower was finally moved
to warn the field marshal, "Steady, Monty! You can't speak to
me like that. I'm your boss."

Montgomery muttered an apology and then, with his usual
clarity of presentation, proceeded to impress the Supreme Commander with details of a daring new plan. He offered the prospect of a major leap forward against the enemy, one that, if
successful, would certainly bring the war to a rapid conclusion.
He proposed that three airborne divisions—two American and
one British—seize bridges across waterways in the Netherlands
to open a corridor through which the British Second Army
would plunge to turn the flank of the enemy's Siegfried Line
and storm on into Germany.

Bradley had his doubts about the plan but considered it "one
of the most imaginative of the war. . . . Had the pious teetotal-
ling Montgomery wobbled into SHAEF with a hangover," he
said, "I could not have been more astonished than I was by the
daring adventure he proposed."

The plan presented Eisenhower with another Montgomery
dilemma. It was no more than the British commander's single-
thrust proposal with an added twist. But it seemed to offer an
opportunity to seize a bridgehead across the Rhine at Arnhem,
a foothold opening the door to the German heartland. However, Eisenhower did not have enough faith in its prospects
to abandon his strategy of having his armies advance more
cautiously on a broader front. It was worth risking, but he
didn't intend to provide the field marshal with everything he

wanted in terms of support and supplies for this ambitious undertaking. That would have meant halting the American advances everywhere else, which he thought would be "crazy."

He instructed Headquarters, Communication Zone, responsible for logistics (and now comfortably ensconced in Paris, to the Supreme Commander's considerable irritation*), that its "first priority . . . is the maintenance of the United States units in forward areas and the provision there of the necessary reserve supplies as will allow continuity of attack when major offensives into Germany can be undertaken."

But the Supreme Commander gave Montgomery authorization to proceed with a modified plan. The field marshal jumped at the chance. Driven by frustration to prove the correctness of his vision and to refute the accusation that he was habitually overcautious, he acted in a way contrary to his basic principles. He relaxed his insistence on meticulous preparations, logistical certainties, and thorough assessment of intelligence to guarantee success.

Operation Market Garden was timed to be launched in mid-September. The paratroopers spearheading the operation were given a mere six days to prepare for an extremely hazardous undertaking that required considerable knowledge of the terrain. Aircraft availability was not reliably confirmed, and on the appointed day not enough proved to be available to deliver the airborne troops to their targets simultaneously. Allied intelligence mistakenly reported that Arnhem was defended by concentrated German antiaircraft defenses, so little was done in the way of preparatory bombing. To avoid antiaircraft fire, the British airborne division landed almost ten miles from its targets and had to undertake a forced march to reach them. An intelligence report that elements of two German divisions were regrouping near Arnhem was ignored.

Market Garden was doomed to failure before it began. Several

---

*By the time Eisenhower learned how COM Z had appropriated the hotels and other quarters the Germans had vacated in the French capital, and how its personnel was living in luxury in sharp contrast to the troops in the field, it was deemed too late to do anything about it without wasting additional resources and complicating supply procedures.

members of Montgomery's staff had grave doubts about it. But they were conditioned not to challenge Montgomery's view of things. De Guingand might have done so, but he was away sick. General Dempsey did advise the field marshal to drop the operation, but to no avail. Two days before it was to be launched, Bedell Smith was sent by Eisenhower to tell Montgomery that intelligence reports told of the two German divisions refitting in the Arnhem area. But Montgomery refused to be deterred and, having authorized him to proceed, Eisenhower did not feel he could now instruct him not to do so, even though the head of his intelligence staff predicted a defeat. Patton bitterly noted in his diary, "Monty does what he pleases and Ike says 'yes, sir.' "

The operation was a disaster for the Allies. The British 1st Airborne Division was virtually wiped out trying unsuccessfully to take the bridge over the Rhine at Arnhem, and the U.S. 82nd and 101st Airborne Divisions also sustained heavy casualties. Had Market Garden succeeded and opened a door into Germany, Eisenhower would have been obliged to reconsider his thinking about Montgomery's concentrated-thrust ideas. He later suggested that he had been prepared to do so. But nothing fails like failure, and the shambles that the operation turned out to be confirmed the Supreme Commander's belief that Montgomery was not the general he was cracked up to be. He was angry with himself for having permitted him to proceed with Market Garden. "What this action proved," Eisenhower later said, "was that the idea of 'one full blooded thrust' to Berlin was silly."

Montgomery granted that some of his calculations for the operation were wrong. The evidence was overwhelming. But even long after the war he refused to accept that his basic plan had been a mistake. In his memoirs he maintained that if Market Garden had been properly backed by Eisenhower, and given the air power, troops, and administrative support it deserved, it would have succeeded. Nevertheless, one of his chief aides said the failure Arnhem did not make him despondent.

He was as cocky as ever. In his mind it was essential to pretend it was not a major defeat in order to keep up morale and deceive the enemy. He found no difficulty in doing precisely that because of his peacock vanity. His reaction was: 'It is no good pining—as a good soldier I must get on with the next move.' This fitted both his moods, eg one, that as the best general in the world he must plan his next operation, and two, his peacock vanity, which would not let him admit defeat.

Market Garden was more than a botched operation. It suddenly brought the Allied commanders down to earth. Thoughts of a speedy victory over Hitler were dashed by the realization that the Allies had missed the boat, that the enemy had managed to recover from the Normandy rout and was no longer in disarray. Brooke was bitter over what he considered Eisenhower's failure to grasp the fleeting chance to end the war quickly by concentrating the Allied assault as Montgomery had proposed rather than attempting to advance on a thin, broad front. However, Montgomery had by then committed another monumental error that made prolongation of the conflict inevitable.

Horrocks had taken Antwerp for him at the beginning of September. But the field marshal had neglected to make certain that the fifty-mile-long coastal approaches to that city's giant port were cleared of German troops. Control of those approaches was essential if the port was to be opened to Allied shipping. If supplies did not flood in through Antwerp, they would still have to be convoyed up by truck from Cherbourg and the French Channel-coast beaches. A "deep thrust in strength into Germany" could not be adequately supported that way. Hitler had ordered his forces to defend the Antwerp sea approaches to the death, and they were given time to dig in to do so. It was a serious blunder not to have dealt with that situation while the Germans were still in confusion and when Montgomery's momentum might have done the trick with little difficulty. Brooke agreed it was a grievous mistake.

Without the use of the port of Antwerp, the progress of the Allied armies had been noticeably thinning even before the

Market Garden setback. A million gallons of fuel were required each day to keep Allied aircraft, armor, and vehicles in motion. In addition to vast quantities of other supplies for the troops, enormous amounts were needed for the liberated populations of Paris, Brussels, and other cities. Without Antwerp, far less than required was being delivered, and even that had to be transported hundreds of miles after being off-loaded to the south.

As Supreme Commander, Eisenhower was even more to blame than Montgomery for not having appreciated what was at stake and for failing to require that the appropriate action be taken. Instead of pressing the field marshal to deal urgently with opening the large Belgian port for Allied use, he had authorized him to "defer the clearing out of the Antwerp approaches" when he had given Montgomery permission to proceed with Market Garden. Now that the Arnhem operation had failed, Montgomery was belatedly informed in no uncertain terms by Eisenhower that he was no longer to delay opening Antwerp's port.

But the field marshal still appeared not to have gotten that message. SHAEF Deputy Chief of Staff Morgan was summoned to the office of his boss, Bedell Smith, one day, and he found Smith "white with passion at his desk whereon lay a telephone receiver from which came tones of voice that I recognized."

"Look, boy," said Bedell, "that's your bloody Marshal on the other other end of that. I can't talk to him any more. Now you go on!" . . . I listened to all the arguments for rushing on to Berlin and against stopping to open up the port of Antwerp as he had been ordered. Seizing a momentary pause I told the Field Marshal, as instructed, that unless he immediately undertook the Antwerp operation, he would receive no more supplies along the tenuous lines still running right back to Cherbourg and the Norman beaches. All priority would be given to the Army Groups of Center and Right.

It is, of course, impossible to say whether Germany could have been crushed in short order after the Normandy breakout.

But that could only have happened if Eisenhower had kept a tighter control of the campaign. In particular, he would have had to make certain that Montgomery quickly cleared the enemy from the Antwerp approaches so that the port facilities could be used to fuel a rapid advance into the German heartland.

Not for another five weeks would Montgomery's Canadians finally perform that task, and not until another three weeks had passed, after mines and wreckage had been cleared, would the first Allied supply ships be able to enter the port. By then, the onset of turbulent weather over the North Sea would sharply limit its use. Whatever possibility there would have been for a rapid Allied northern drive into Germany had been forfeited.

As a soldier, Montgomery prided himself in never having disobeyed a direct command. But that was a petty conceit. At his level there were discussions, and exchanges of cables and letters if thought necessary, at the conclusion of which the senior commander issued his instructions and expected them to be acted upon. Eisenhower never felt the need to tell his generals that those instructions were not a subject for further examination.

> In both the U.S. and British armies [an official U.S. Army historian observed] it was understood that proposed plans might be debated and various viewpoints developed. General Eisenhower encouraged this type of discussion and often invited criticism of his plans. It is possible, however, that he added to his own command problems by failing to make clear to Field Marshal Montgomery where the "discussion" stage had ended and the "execution" stage had begun. . . . Perhaps the Supreme Commander, accustomed to more ready compliance from his U.S. army group commanders, delayed too long in issuing positive directions to Montgomery. Perhaps, anxious to give a full voice to the British allies, he was more tolerant of strong dissent from the field marshal than he should have been. Whatever the reason, some of his SHAEF advisers thought him overslow in . . . closing debate on the question of command.

Bradley's aide, Major Hansen, complained in his diary, "Ike apparently unable to say 'go to hell' [to Montgomery] for diplomatic reasons." The British commander remained undaunted by Eisenhower's refusal to see things his way. He continued to press his views, to badger him with his insistence that it was "not possible" for all the Allied armies to move toward and into Germany simultaneously. He was unrelenting in his demands for all necessary support and supplies for the concentrated offensive he advocated. Confidential moral support from War Minister Grigg, who shared Montgomery's scorn for Eisenhower's military skills, and from Brooke helped sustain him in his campaign to change the Supreme Commander's mind and persuade him that a broad-front strategy was no strategy at all but merely a scattering of buckshot in the hope of hitting something.

However, as the progress of the Allied armies slowed, the Supreme Commander grew ever more convinced that he was right and Montgomery was wrong. As demonstrated at Arnhem, the German Army appeared to be sufficiently recovered from its Normandy rout to be capable of inflicting serious punishment on the Allied forces. Despite its losses in France and despite the army purge that had followed the attempted assassination of Hitler, it had regrouped. With much shorter supply lines than the Allies enjoyed, it was braced to resist the invasion of the German homeland. For Eisenhower, that testified to the wisdom of his broad-front advance. It would bring Allied might to bear clear across the front so that the revived but depleted enemy would nowhere find respite or an opportunity to counterattack.

On September 20, while success for Market Garden was still a possibility, SHAEF headquarters was moved to the Trianon Palace at Versailles. Two days later, when the operation's failure at Arnhem was evident, Eisenhower met with his senior generals for a previously planned strategy review. SHAEF's shift to the outskirts of Paris was symbolic. It was time to sort out differences among the generals and establish a coherent plan for finally crushing the German Army. Bradley, Patton, and Hodges attended the conference. Montgomery chose not to. He sent his chief of staff De Guingand in his place.

Conditioned to expect such conduct from Montgomery, Eisenhower reacted to this snub with equanimity. He was probably relieved not be exposed once more to the field marshal's nagging, though he wrote to him, "I regard it as a great pity that all of us cannot keep in close touch with each other because I find, without exception, when all of us can get together and look the various features of our problems squarely in the face, the answers usually become obvious."

Despite Montgomery's absence, Eisenhower told his assembled generals, "The envelopment of the Ruhr from the north by 21st Army Group, supported by 1st Army" remained "the main effort of the present phase of operations." With Patton encountering increasingly effective resistance with his advance south of the Ardennes Forest, Montgomery's northern drive into Germany still seemed to offer the greatest possibilities and opportunities.

Delighted, De Guingand cabled Montgomery that Eisenhower supported "your plan 100 per cent." It may have sounded like that to him, but he had misunderstood. Eisenhower was not giving Montgomery control of Bradley's First Army, only its support. Montgomery had been given his chance at Arnhem and it had been bungled. He was now to be kept on a much tighter leash.

The misunderstanding was soon cleared up. But Montgomery was outraged by the way Eisenhower, always seeking to keep friction to a minimum, insisted that whatever their differences, the two of them were agreed on essentials. The field marshal considered that a blatant insult and could not refrain from issuing a rebuttal.

I cannot agree [he wrote to Eisenhower] that our concepts are the same and I am sure you would wish me to be quite frank and open in the matter. . . . I have always said stop the right [Patton] and go on with the left but the right has been allowed to go on so far that it has outstripped its maintenance and we have lost flexibility. . . . [Y]ou will have to put every single thing into the left hook and stop everything else. It is my opinion that if this is not done you will not get the Ruhr.

Each passing day made him more convinced that Eisenhower was "completely out of touch with what is going on" and "does not really know anything about the business of fighting the Germans." He conceded that the Allied forces were killing and capturing a lot of the enemy but maintained that "Ike's policy was only skin deep and anyone could deflect it." From the reports he received, he concluded that the Americans "did not know how to combine artillery with infantry, put all divisions in the line and had no supports to leap-frog and make headway, that they were everywhere too weak to break through."

He went over Eisenhower's head to complain about him during a visit to his headquarters by Marshall on October 8. He told the U.S. Army Chief of Staff there was "a lack of grip and operational direction and control was lacking. Our operations had, in fact, become ragged and disjointed, and we had now got ourselves into a real mess."

Marshall was the wrong man to say that to. He had not been greatly impressed by Montgomery's achievements in North Africa or Normandy and he believed Eisenhower had given him too much leeway. He later recalled that it had been "very hard for me to restrain myself because I didn't think there was any logic in what he said but overwhelming egotism."

Montgomery already had an enemy in Bedell Smith, but that did not prevent him from sending Eisenhower's chief of staff a letter of complaint meant to be shown to the Supreme Commander. He told him, "The present organization for command within the Allied forces in Western Europe is not satisfactory." He suggested that Eisenhower's performance might have been suitable for the requirements of political life but was inadequate for fighting a war. He urged that a different single ground commander be named for the campaign to take the Ruhr and sweep on to Berlin.

Tested beyond its limits, Eisenhower's temper finally gave way and he threatened a complete break between himself and the British commander. Rebuking him sharply for the first time, he openly questioned his achievements in France and his understanding of what was happening there. He wrote to him that he misunderstood the "real issue now at hand." The real issue, he said, was the British commander's continuing failure to clear the approaches to the port of Antwerp, a matter that was in no way colored by questions of who commanded what in the wider campaign. He said Montgomery now had a lot to do to clear those approaches so that the port could finally be used by the Allies, and to clean up the area his forces had already overrun. He intended, therefore, to give Bradley the task Montgomery had previously been assigned of seizing the Ruhr, with Montgomery acting in support. Eisenhower told the field marshal that if he found command arrangements unsatisfactory, "We have an issue that must be settled soon in the interests of future efficiency."

I am quite well aware [he told him] of the powers and limitations of an Allied Command, and if you, as the senior Commander in this Theater of one of the great Allies, feel that my conceptions and directives are such as to endanger the success of operations, it is our duty to refer the matter to higher authority for any action they may choose to take, however drastic.

Montgomery realized it was not an idle threat and backed off. He knew that bringing in "higher authority" to resolve his differences with Eisenhower might undermine his position irreparably. If it came to a showdown at the Combined Chiefs of Staff, the Americans would win. He accepted, for the moment at least, that he could press the Supreme Commander no further. He responded quickly to Eisenhower's challenge by, in effect, apologizing. He assured him, "You will hear *no* more on the subject of command from me."

I have given you my views and you have given your answer. That ends the matter and I and all of us here [at 21st Army

Group headquarters] will weigh in 100% to do what you want and we will pull it through without a doubt.

He signed the message, "Your devoted and loyal subordinate, Monty." Which must have elicited wry smiles at SHAEF.

By mid-autumn of 1944, with the approaches to the port of Antwerp still to be cleared and supplies still being trucked up from Cherbourg, it was becoming apparent that hopes had been dashed for an end to the war before the year was out and that Allied war-winning momentum would not be regained until the following spring. Not until then could the massive Allied preponderance in manpower, armor, and air power be expected to prove effective. Eisenhower later wrote that there was much to be said at the time for going over to a defensive posture in the ground war "in order to conserve all our strength for building up the logistic system and to avoid the suffering of a winter campaign. . . . [But] we were certain that by continuing an unremitting offensive we would, in spite of hardship and privation, gain additional advantages over the enemy. Specifically we were convinced that this policy would result in shortening the war and therefore in the saving of thousands of Allied lives."

The Supreme Commander also had to consider the effect that going on the defensive for the winter would have on Allied unity. The British remained unhappy with how things had been developing, and the French under De Gaulle were behaving with increasing defiance of Eisenhower. The Soviets were complaining that the Western Allies still were not doing as much as they could to defeat the common enemy. Not only would a lull in the fighting give the Germans a chance to strengthen their defenses but it might undermine the Supreme Commander's authority.

However, the aim of shortening the conflict by remaining on the attack was not to be fulfilled. Over the next months, the Allies were forced into a war of attrition. It was the kind of combat the British in particular, through their gruesome experiences in the First World War, most feared. Once more, they, and their American comrades-in-arms, were made to struggle with the enemy for yardage in places, with hundreds of miles still to go. It was a damp, cold, foggy autumn, which restricted aerial support for the troops and presented them with much more than the enemy to contend with. Digging in or trying to advance through swamps of mud was torment. Flu, respiratory illness, and trenchfoot were widespread and debilitating.

Everywhere the Germans offered intensified resistance in defense of their homeland and its approaches. Troops of the U.S. First Army took Aachen, the first German city to fall to the Allies, on October 21, but only after clearing it of its defenders in a ferocious house-to-house struggle, a sign of what might lay ahead. The First and Ninth Armies sustained 35,000 casualties trying to drive the enemy out of the thickly wooded Huertgen Forest east of the city. Patton had covered a lot of ground through the middle of France but, for all his bravado, his further progress was blocked at Metz.

By the middle of November, despite his promise of loyalty, Montgomery had again begun sniping at Eisenhower, "harping," Brooke noted in his diary, "over the system of command . . . and the fact that the war is being prolonged." In view of the high casualty rate and the failure to make greater headway against the enemy, he had reason to do so. Had he been ground-forces commander and achieving such poor results, he certainly would have come under blistering criticism from the War Office in London as well as the Americans.

He wrote to Brooke that the directives the Supreme Commander issued "have no relation to the practical necessities of the battle. . . . If we go drifting along as at present we are merely playing into the enemy's hands and the war will go on indefinitely. . . . [H]e has elected to take direct command of very large-scale operations and he does not know how to do it. . . . I think we are drifting into dangerous waters."

British correspondents were aware of the gloom and grumbling permeating Montgomery's headquarters and High Command in London. British newspapers took up suggestions that perhaps Eisenhower was out of his depth as Supreme Commander. Brooke believed that he had become "entirely detached and [was] taking practically no part in the running of the war." Instead, said the British chief of staff, Eisenhower was spending his time "with his lady chauffeur on the golf links at Rheims," where a forward SHAEF headquarters had been established.

The British chief of staff told Montgomery that nothing could be done about it for the moment and urged him not to issue further challenges to the Supreme Commander. But he believed that something had to be done because disquiet over the pace of the campaign and the alarming casualty levels were having an effect. He said he was "pretty certain" that the disappointing results of operations then in progress would "provide us with sufficient justification for requesting the American Chiefs of Staff to reconsider the present Command organization and the present strategy on the Western Front."

Brooke still did not think it possible to replace Eisenhower with a British general or have him kicked upstairs, as he had been in North Africa, to have a British general run the war for him. But he wondered whether Bradley would be more effective if he took overall command of the ground forces under Eisenhower, with Montgomery and Patton commanding the army groups.

Brooke had taken his complaints about the situation to Churchill. The prime minister conveyed them to Roosevelt, telling the president it was necessary "to place before you the serious and disappointing war situation which faces us. . . . When we contrast [the] realities with the rosy expectations of our people, the question very definitely arises, 'What are we going to do about it?' " He suggested a Combined Chiefs of Staff conference in London "where the whole stormy scene can be calmly and patiently studied."

It had no effect. Roosevelt once more responded with an expression of confidence in Eisenhower. The British were obliged to accept that his secure standing with the president, the War Department, and the American people ruled out the possibility of any change in the command structure that might indicate criticism of Eisenhower's performance. Indeed, the Supreme Commander's elevation to the rank of General of the

Army was at that moment being processed in Washington. He would receive his fifth star, and match Marshall and MacArthur in rank, on December 20. He had earlier forecast the war would be over by then.

Montgomery was thoroughly frustrated by the state of affairs. He didn't think that replacing Eisenhower with Bradley, as Brooke suggested, would make much difference, even if it could be arranged. He believed the problem went further than Eisenhower, that the fault lay with Americans and their "curious idea that every Army Commander must have an equal and fair share of the battle." He remained certain that a single, fully supported, concentrated thrust to Berlin was the only sensible strategy. But he tried to reconcile himself to the task of commanding the drive into Germany north of the Ardennes while Bradley commanded an advance south of it, though even that was more than he was being offered by Eisenhower. Bradley had forces operating north of the forest as well. "Ike seems determined to show that he is a great general in the field," he told Brooke resignedly. "Let him do so and let us all lend a hand to pull him through."

Brooke knew it was easier for the irrepressible Montgomery to suggest such a modus vivendi with the Americans than to live by it. He again warned the field marshal against challenging Eisenhower on strategy. "Without hesitation," he advised him, "a) Not to approach Eisenhower for the present, b) Remain silent now, unless Eisenhower opens the subject." That moment arrived on November 28, when the Supreme Commander visited his headquarters to review developments. Montgomery still had no way of dealing with him without giving offense. Once more he proceeded to lecture him on what he had permitted to go wrong with the campaign and how Allied strategy had to be changed at once.

Eisenhower considered it pointless to enter into a debate with him. He heard him out, but by failing to take issue with him left the self-obsessed Montgomery with the impression that he had finally made his point. One of Montgomery's young aides assigned to look after Eisenhower (the field marshal had retired early, as usual, despite the visit of his superior) found the

Supreme Commander less than pleased by Montgomery's ha-
rangue and warned the field marshal about it. But Montgomery
could not believe that his eminently clear and incisive presentation had not made Eisenhower see the light. "I proved to him,"
he wrote to Brooke, "that we had definitely failed and must
make a new plan. . . . He admitted a grave mistake has been
made and in my opinion is prepared to go almost any length
to succeed next time. Hence his own suggestion I should be in
full operational command north of the Ardennes with Bradley
under me."

It was a total misreading of the Supreme Commander's views.
For one thing, Eisenhower knew that Bradley would not serve
under Montgomery, nor would he want him to. But he had let
the field marshal prattle on instead of making his own position
absolutely clear. Encouraged by this, Montgomery followed the
meeting up with a letter to confirm the main points that he
believed had been agreed upon.

In that letter, he chastised the Supreme Commander for
allowing the strategy of a northeastward surge by his 21st Army
Group, as outlined in a SHAEF directive weeks before, to be
thrown off course through lack of command backing. As a
consequence, he said, the Allies had suffered "a strategic reverse." He said, "We require a new plan. And this time *we must
not fail*. . . . In the new plan we must get away from the doctrine
of attacking in so many places that nowhere are we strong
enough to get decisive results."

Once more he charged that the doctrine of advancing on a
broad front had been shown to mean no single attack was
strong enough to be decisive. Despite his determination to
avoid debating strategy with the Americans in person, in desperation he proposed a conference with Eisenhower and Bradley for the first week in December to consider his proposals and
to spell out Allied objectives for the winter. Their chiefs of staff
would also be permitted to attend, though those chiefs, he said,
"must not speak." That was meant to silence the irascible Bedell
Smith, who no longer made much effort to conceal how little
he thought of Montgomery. The field marshal did not want to

face Smith's taunts as he tried to steer the Supreme Commander toward what he considered a realistic assessment of the possibilities.

The disparagement of Eisenhower seemed more stark on paper than it had during his face-to-face encounter with Montgomery. The Supreme Commander was greatly offended by both the content and tone of the letter. It appeared to be a comprehensive denunciation of everything he had done since taking over as ground-forces commander after the Normandy breakout and made him "hot under the collar."

He responded with a letter of sharp rebuttal, criticizing Montgomery's own performance. He wrote that things would have been better if Allied forces had managed to advance quickly from the Normandy beachhead *as we had hoped*," and implied that, not Montgomery, but "Bradley's brilliant break-through made possible the rapid exploitation by all forces which had cleared France and Belgium and had almost carried us across the Rhine." He told the British commander, "I most definitely appreciate the frankness of your statements . . . but I beg of you not to continue to look upon the past performances of this great fighting force as a failure because we have not achieved all that we could have hoped." He agreed to a conference to review strategy. But he rejected the suggestion that Bedell Smith be barred from speaking at it, curtly informing Montgomery that he would not insult his chief of staff by obliging him to remain mute.

Eisenhower had been so enraged by Montgomery's latest reproach that he had misunderstood the main point of the field marshal's criticism. In a follow-up message, Montgomery asked him to understand that he had not issued a blanket criticism of Eisenhower's command (though he certainly believed one was warranted). He had only maintained that the plan Eisenhower had outlined a month earlier—giving priority to his operations—had not been implemented. He was right about that, and Eisenhower promptly apologized for his misinterpretation. But their relationship had reached a point where a rupture between them seemed imminent.

* * *

The conference on strategy that Montgomery had requested took place at Maastricht on December 7, 1944, the third anniversary of America's entry into the war. Tedder, Bradley, and Bedell Smith—all critics of Montgomery—were present, along with Eisenhower and Montgomery.

Again the field marshal urged a concentration of forces to blast across the Rhine north of the Ruhr and drive quickly on to Berlin. It was very much a restatement of his previously proposed strategy. Patton, advancing through France toward central Germany, and Devers's 6th Army Group coming up from the south, would have to be reined in so that all available resources could be devoted to his thrust. According to Bradley, Montgomery made a poor impression on the others attending the meeting by refusing to accept there was any merit to anyone else's views.

Eisenhower agreed that a thrust along the northern route, as Montgomery wished, remained the strongest option. He would shift command of Bradley's Ninth Army to him for that purpose. The field marshal would have top priority, but Bradley's First and Third Armies and Devers's Seventh Army would not be starved of supplies and would be permitted to continue their aggressive operations.

Neither Bradley nor Montgomery was pleased with the Supreme Commander's decision. "This was a classic Eisenhower compromise," Bradley said, "that left me distinctly unhappy. It tacitly implied that my 12th Army Group offensive had failed," which it partially had. Montgomery felt even worse. His sense of despair was almost complete. "We shall split our resources," he complained once more to Brooke, "and we shall fail." The Maastricht conference seemed to him to vindicate his aversion to debating strategy with those who took exception to his views. He had a distinct sense of being backed into a corner, playing "a lone hand against the three of them," Tedder, Bradley, and Bedell Smith.

They all arrived . . . and went away together [he told Brooke]. It is therefore fairly clear that any points I made which caused Eisenhower to wobble will have been put right by Bradley and Tedder on the three-hour drive back to [Bradley's headquarters at] Luxembourg. . . . I can do no more myself. . . . If we want the war to end within any reasonable period you have to get Eisenhower's hand taken off the land battle. I regret to say that in my opinion he just doesn't know what he is doing.

Five days later, Churchill called Eisenhower to a meeting in London, along with Brooke and other senior figures, in an effort to restore a measure of harmony. Brooke, never the diplomat, used the occasion to criticize Eisenhower unrestrainedly for violating the principle of concentration of forces. The British chief of staff expected that Churchill, who considered himself a military expert, would back him on what he considered this cardinal principle of combat and urge the Supreme Commander to change his ways. To his surprise and disgust, Churchill came strongly to Eisenhower's defense. Brooke was so dismayed that he seriously thought of resigning. Churchill limply told him the following day that he had supported Eisenhower only because he had been a guest, far outnumbered at the meeting by those who disagreed with him.

He asked Brooke to prepare an analysis of the situation to present to the Combined Chiefs of Staff because, though the war was being won, he and his War Cabinet remained greatly troubled. There was no doubt that the British people would be paying for the cost of the war long after the last shot was fired and that each day the conflict continued would add to the price that would have to be met. Britain was close to economic exhaustion.

Having entered the war a world power, Britain was emerging from it much reduced in status. The United States and the Soviet Union would be the great powers in the postwar world. Proof of that had been given at the Teheran summit conference the previous November, when Roosevelt and Stalin had reached strategic decisions for the Allies with which Churchill had disagreed but with which he had been obliged to go along.

However, British pride remained intact, as did British determination not to be reduced to a mere appendage of the Americans in this endgame; otherwise Britain might be confined to a similar role when postwar decisions were made. There was still hope. Much depended on Montgomery not being further downgraded as the war drew toward its conclusion. He remained the British paladin in the field. Important opportunities were still there to be seized: the Rhine was still to be crossed; Hitler's Ruhr lifeline was still to be severed; Berlin was still to be taken. Patton's hell-for-leather drive south of the Ardennes had been stalled, making Montgomery even better placed to achieve all of those, win the war, and redeem his reputation as master of the battlefield—if only Eisenhower would let him.

CHAPTER 20
The Bulge

By mid-December 1944, the Allied commanders believed the war of attrition on the western front had been won. It was thought the strength of the German forces had been sapped in the autumn battles and that their "crust of defenses" was thin, brittle, and vulnerable. It was believed that only the winter now stood in the way of final victory and that once the ground firmed and the skies cleared, the Rhine would be crossed, the last resistance would be crushed, and the Third Reich would be consigned to history.

G-2 at SHAEF would have been happier knowing what was happening to several German divisions that appeared to be in the process of being redeployed and whose whereabouts had become a mystery. Cloud cover had impeded aerial reconnaissance. Whatever deployments the enemy might be making were taking place on German soil, where information of the kind that had been provided by the resistance underground in France and Belgium was no longer available.

Some reports had been received of the Germans strengthening their forces west of the Rhine. The U.S. First Army's chief of intelligence warned, "It is possible that a limited scale [German] offensive will be launched for the purpose of achieving a Christmas morale victory for civilian consumption. Many PWs now speak of the coming attack" just before Christmas. But it was believed the Germans were no longer strong enough to embark on a major counteroffensive.

What was more, the Ardennes, where some enemy activity had been spotted, was difficult terrain. German armor may have plunged through that massive forest region a few years earlier, but that had been when conditions had been more favorable to their success. Now four American divisions held a line between Malmédy and Trier. They were undermanned because of recent losses and stretched thinly. Some were effectively on rest and recuperation, recovering from their ordeal in the Huertgen Forest. But an attempt by the weakened Germans to break through again in the Ardennes was considered so unlikely that it didn't seem to matter.

On December 15, Montgomery informed Eisenhower that he intended to return to England on December 23. He wanted to spend Christmas with his much-neglected son, for whom his concern had seemed to express itself largely in sending small gifts, including pictures of himself, communicating with the people into whose care he had put him (the headmaster of his preparatory school and his wife), and making certain David had no contact with his family, especially his elderly mother, the boy's grandmother, whom from personal experience he considered "a menace with the young."

In his letter to Eisenhower, he included a demand note for five pounds, pointing out that they had made a bet months before on whether the war would be over by Christmas, and the Supreme Commander had lost. It was in jest this time. He was not really pressing for payment, as he had in the case of the Flying Fortress in North Africa two years earlier. But in view of his recent criticism of the Eisenhower, it was tactless. Having come to expect such conduct from Montgomery, the Supreme Commander laughed it off, replying that he still had more than a week to go.

Nothing of a critical nature seemed to be developing on the winter-shrouded front and neither of them had any suspicion

that circumstances would prevent the field marshal from making the trip home. Confidence at Montgomery's headquarters
was total, as a pronouncement it issued demonstrated.

> The enemy is at present fighting a defensive campaign on all
> fronts; his situation is such that he cannot stage major offen-
> sive operations. Furthermore, at all costs he has to prevent
> the war from entering on a mobile phase; he has not the
> transport or the petrol that would be necessary for mobile
> operations, nor could his tanks compete with ours in the
> mobile battle. The enemy is in a bad way; he has had a
> tremendous battering and has lost heavily in men and equip-
> ment.

That was Bradley's view as well. No thought was to be given
to falling back into a defensive posture to ride out the winter
that had already begun setting in. Pressure on the enemy was
to be maintained. In keeping with his broad-front doctrine,
Eisenhower authorized Bradley to prepare to launch offensives
by his First and Third armies on both sides of the Ardennes.
Bradley was warned, however, that Montgomery was planning
an advance in the north and that his own armies would have
to be pulled up short if they did not make rapid and convincing
progress. As it turned out, their efforts were for the moment
not to be tested. Just before dawn on December 16, the Germans
unleashed a powerful ground attack against U.S. positions in
the Ardennes.

It was a bold stroke, devised by Hitler himself against the
advice of his generals. They had told him that they did not have
sufficient remaining forces to make a success of so ambitious
an operation. But he still had fantasies of winning the war.
His panzers would plunge through the forest again, cross the
Meuse River, recapture Antwerp, and drive a wedge between
the American and British armies. Strains between the two allies,
well known to German intelligence, would be aggravated, un-
dermining their alliance. The hard-pressed British might back
out of the war or a major battlefield setback might induce the
Americans to shift their emphasis to the Pacific, leaving the

weaker British to fend for themselves. They might even again be driven into the sea for a "second Dunkirk." The Germans would then be able to shift their forces eastward to cope decisively with the Russians.

One reason why neither Eisenhower nor Montgomery had seriously considered the possibility of a German counteroffensive in the Ardennes was the apparent futility of such an operation. Neither of them could have believed that an experienced tactician would sanction an attack that, in view of the imbalance of forces, was doomed to failure if not immediately then soon afterward. It would be impossible for the Germans to sustain an armored assault against strong forces, especially in difficult terrain, for even a few days without capturing the Allied oil stores they desperately needed for their tanks and trucks. Even then they would not be able to go on very long once the skies cleared and the Allied tactical air forces were able to punish them for their recklessness. Those were thoughts Hitler refused to entertain.

Eisenhower was attending the wedding of his valet, Sergeant McKeogh, at the chapel at SHAEF's Versailles headquarters when word reached him that a major German attack might be developing in the Ardennes. Bradley was there too, having come to Versailles to discuss with the Supreme Commander the offensives his armies were about to launch. Bradley initially believed the German move was a "spoiling attack" meant to disrupt those offensives. It seemed to him unlikely that the Germans would choose the inhospitable Ardennes for their starting point if they intended a desperate last throw against the Allies.

Eisenhower wasn't sure about that, but there was not much he felt he could do until more specific information on what was happening was received. A premature reaction against something that didn't amount to much would needlessly disrupt planned operations. The wedding guests proceeded to a reception that Eisenhower was throwing for the newlyweds, after which the playing cards were broken out for a few rubbers of bridge.

As the night wore on and more detailed reports flowed in, it became apparent that the German action was indeed the opening phase of a major enemy operation in the Ardennes. Tanks of the 6th Panzer Army, under SS General Josef "Sepp" Dietrich, had blasted forward between Saint-Vith and Malmédy in the north. At the same time, General Hasso von Manteufel's 5th Panzer Army was thrusting through the heart of the forest. General Erich Brandenberger's Seventh Army was moving forward in the south, covering the left flank of the attacking forces.

Eisenhower was alarmed. Bradley still maintained it was probably a limited feint by the enemy—aside from his doubts, he feared that if it aroused excessive concern, Montgomery would be handed even more operational priority than Eisenhower had already awarded him. Nevertheless, the Supreme Commander instructed Bradley to cancel his planned offensives and to shift two of his divisions into position to worry the flanks of the German assault. He also summoned Devers and Patton to meet with him, Bradley, and his senior staff officers two days later, by which time the enemy's intentions would be clearer. He informed them that despite some lingering doubts, it appeared that the Germans were bent on more than mischief.

In fact, twenty enemy divisions, including seven armored divisions, had burst through positions thinly held by U.S. First Army units in the Ardennes. What was more, the Germans appeared to have uncommitted reserves with which to expand the bulge they had driven into American lines. Bradley's chief of staff wondered, "Where in hell has this sonuvabitch gotten all his strength?"

The first days of the Battle of the Bulge were some of the worst that American troops experienced in the war. The temperature plunged to below zero, and it snowed. Overcast skies denied the men air support. Units were overwhelmed and cut off. Casualties were heavy. Men panicked. Thousands were captured. Reports of the massacre at Malmédy, where surrounded American troops who had surrendered were machine-gunned, further undermined morale.

The prospect of a major reverse seemed real enough for desperate measures to be taken. The initial success of the German assault led Eisenhower to fear that much worse could be in store. Having previously appealed in vain for additional divisions to be sent from the United States, he had few reserves with which to meet this challenge. He issued instructions that service troops were to prepare to guard strategic bridges. Soldiers who had been imprisoned for crimes, including murder and rape, were offered their freedom if they volunteered to go into the line. Even more radically, Eisenhower issued a circular offering black soldiers—most of whom were assigned to service units—the opportunity to volunteer to serve as infantrymen "without regard to color or race."

Bedell Smith warned him that such a move was contrary to War Department policies and positively dangerous in terms of race relations in the army. Eisenhower, who had no strong feelings about such matters and wasn't looking for extra trouble, backed off. Instead of being integrated into existing units, the 4,500 soldiers who volunteered were formed into platoons that were all-black, except for white officers and noncoms, and that were not committed to the line until later.

Confusion had been quickly sown all along the front, and not only by the strength and success of the German counteroffensive. Under orders from Hitler, English-speaking German soldiers trained to act like Americans—to the extent of being able to open a pack of cigarettes in the casual American macho way—infiltrated American lines in captured American jeeps. Their mission was to sever telephone lines, plant false indicators that roads were mined, shift roadsigns around, and generally cause as many snarls as possible to assist the German attack.

Most were soon caught and executed as spies. But they caused much confusion, primarily by leading their captors to believe that many more of them were loose behind Allied lines. A major effort was made to find these phony Americans. Military Police held roadside interrogations of thousands of GIs, asking them questions it was assumed any American could answer. Things were extremely difficult for British soldiers who happened to be in the area and who might not have known the names of American state capitals, the fine points of American football, or the marital arrangements of Hollywood stars. Even many

Americans were less than fully informed of such esoteric trivia. The resulting turmoil was described by Bradley, who was himself required to prove who he was.

> [A] half-million GIs played cat and mouse with each other each time they met on the road. Neither rank nor credentials nor protests spared the traveler an inquisition at each intersection he passed. Three times I was ordered to prove my identity by cautious GIs. The first time by identifying Springfield as the capital of Illinois (my questioner held out for Chicago); the second time by locating the guard between the center and tackle on the line of scrimmage; the third time by naming the then current spouse of a blond named Betty Grable. Grable stopped me but the sentry did not. Pleased at having stumped me, he nevertheless passed me on.

Rumors spread that SS Obersturmbannführer Otto Skorzeny, who had daringly rescued Mussolini from Italian guerrillas in northern Italy the year before, had himself infiltrated Allied lines for the purpose of assassinating Eisenhower. It was said that Skorzeny and his squad of elite troops had gone undercover to make contact with agents and sympathizers in Paris who would assist them in that mission. Posters with large photographs of Skorzeny were put up at government buildings all over the French capital. It had only recently experienced euphoric liberation, but rumors spread there that the Germans were again seizing the initiative and would soon be returning in force. Personal security for Eisenhower was intensified. Armed guards, some equipped with machine guns, were posted in and around the palace at Versailles. The Supreme Commander's travels away from SHAEF were sharply restricted. When he insisted on traveling, his vehicle was preceded and followed by jeeps flush with armed bodyguards.

The German counteroffensive and the reports that the Allies were sustaining heavy casualties aroused much concern in the United States and Britain. It was evident that the Allies, and particularly their military commanders, had been caught napping, a sentiment that a news blackout ordered by SHAEF did

nothing to discourage. It was rumored that the Germans might
be in the process of undoing months of Allied success and that
final victory in the war, already considered overdue, would be
further delayed.

Eisenhower was careful not to appear downcast. He told his
generals, "The present situation is to be regarded as one of
opportunity for us and not of disaster." He believed that by
emerging from behind its fixed defenses, the enemy "may give
us the chance to turn his great gamble into his worst defeat."
Eisenhower intended not only to snuff out the German counteroffensive but to launch a counter-counteroffensive as soon as
possible to take advantage of the enemy's foolhardiness in undertaking so improbable an operation. Patton had other ideas.
"Hell," he said, "let's have the guts to let the sons of bitches
go all the way to Paris. Then we'll really cut 'em up and chew
'em up."

Eisenhower was amused by the suggestion, but Patton's proposal was not really an option. Instead he instructed the Third
Army commander, who had been preparing to plunge east into
Germany's Saarland, to wheel three divisions about—no easy
task—and go in relief of the 101st Airborne, beleaguered in the
road-junction town of Bastogne, whose capture was essential
to the success of the German attack.

Montgomery was dismayed that the Americans had allowed
themselves to have gotten into such a fix, something that would
never have happened had he been ground-forces commander.
He cabled Brooke, ". . . there is a definite lack of grip and
control and no one has a clear picture as to situation. . . . There
is an atmosphere of great pessimism . . . due, I think, to the
fact that everyone knows something has gone wrong and no
one knows what or why."

He himself had acted immediately to beef up defenses for his
positions in Belgium to prevent the breakthrough the Germans
had in mind there. His almost reflexive professionalism in a
crisis situation was immediately evident, and he was pleased
to be given the opportunity to put it on display. He suggested
to General Whiteley, Eisenhower's British deputy chief of operations, that he be put in operational command of all troops

in the northern sector of the front. Essential communications between Bradley's Luxembourg headquarters south of the Ardennes and Bradley's First and Ninth armies north of the forest were in danger of being severed. He said the consequences could be serious unless the command difficulties were resolved the way he proposed.

Whiteley and General Kenneth Strong, Eisenhower's British intelligence chief, saw the sense in that, though neither of them was a great admirer of the field marshal. They presented their view to Bedell Smith, whose first reaction was to suspect a British conspiracy against Bradley. But Eisenhower had already recognized the appropriateness of Montgomery taking full command in the north to deal with the situation. On second thought, so did Smith.

Bradley was sounded out on the proposed shift. He was suspicious of being upstaged and being left with only Patton's Third Army south of the Ardennes under his command. He told Smith, ". . . if Monty's were an American command, I would agree with you entirely. It would be the logical thing to do." But he warned that the Americans would not appreciate serving under the British commander for an extended period. He was assured that the U.S. First and Ninth armies would be returned to him when the German offensive was crushed.

Eisenhower proceeded with the switch on December 20, informing Montgomery by telephone that the two American armies in the north were to come under his command. He had a bad connection. To Montgomery, it appeared that the Supreme Commander was panicking. To him it sounded as if Eisenhower had finally recognized that he had been wrong all along and was now begging a true professional to help extract him from deep trouble. He told Brooke that Eisenhower had been "very excited and it was difficult to understand what he was talking about; he roared into the telephone, speaking very fast. The only point I really grasped was that 'it seems to me we have now two fronts' and that I was to assume command of the Northern front. . . . He then went on talking wildly about other things."

Montgomery could not have been more wrong about Eisenhower's reaction at that moment. He was under great pressure, but he was acting neither in panic nor confusion. There was no sign of the earlier wavering that had appalled Brooke. To make such a command shift at the height of a crisis was both decisive and daring. Risking the ire of Marshall, whom he did not even inform of his decision until later, and the American press, as well as the gloating of Montgomery's British cheering squad, was a courageous act in view of the backbiting pressures to which he had been subjected for months.

The German counteroffensive wasn't all that was worrying him. The Soviets showed little sign of resuming their steam-roller advance on Germany from the east. They had deliberately stalled their forces on the Vistula River in Poland—for political reasons, as it later turned out, to guarantee the imposition of a Communist postwar government for the country. How long the Soviets intended to stay put there, allowing the Germans a partial respite in the east, could influence whether the Battle of the Bulge, which was shaping up as the largest single battle in the history of the U.S. Army, was only a desperate last fling by Hitler or would be followed by other signs of resurgence by the enemy on the western front.

Eisenhower had to know Soviet intentions so that he could plan how to reshape his strategy after the Ardennes disruption. He pressed Washington for arrangements to be made for a SHAEF representative to go to Moscow to pursue the matter. But though Stalin agreed to receive such an envoy, he neglected to set a date for the visit and there was no telling how that new venture into military diplomacy would work out.

These were especially tense days for the Supreme Commander. He was much gratified by the moral support that came with his new promotion to General of the Army, and with other indications of Marshall's confidence in him.* But he found himself reliving his worst experience so far in the war.

The forces under his command had been on the advance ever since North Africa. There had been setbacks, but not since

---

*During the Battle of the Bulge, Marshall issued instructions at the War Department that the Supreme Commander was not to be badgered with advice that might distract him from getting on with his job as he saw fit.

Rommel's breakthrough at Kasserine Pass had he had to confront an enemy on an offensive rampage. He was anxious about the extent of the German Ardennes salient—fifty miles deep and sixty miles wide—and how long it would take to clean out. He was distressed by the casualty reports and rattled by accounts of the increased level of desertions and of units disintegrating under enemy attack.

He knew there could be no amicable resolution to the Montgomery-Bradley rivalry after the Battle of the Bulge was over, and was annoyed by De Gaulle's insistence that he not authorize withdrawal from any liberated territory in France, regardless of pressing tactical considerations. On top of all of that, the tight personal security that had been imposed on him at Versailles made him feel claustrophobic. "He is a prisoner of our security police," Butcher wrote, "and is thoroughly but helplessly irritated by the restrictions on his moves." No doubt all of those factors contributed to his decision at that time to refuse to commute the death sentence imposed on Private Eddie Slovik, the first American soldier to be executed for desertion since the Civil War. He later would commute the sentences of others charged with similar offenses.

Meanwhile, Montgomery wasted no time in assuming the full command in the north for which, denied overall ground-forces command, he had been pressing so persistently. His small corps of young liaison officers had already reconnoitered the area and provided him with the most accurate picture available of the situation. Within hours of receiving Eisenhower's authorization, he called in at General Hodges's First Army and General Simpson's Ninth Army command posts to see what they were up to and show that he had taken charge. He reported to Brooke that he found morale among the Americans very low. He said both Simpson and Hodges "seemed delighted to have someone to give them firm orders." He considered both American generals "not really very much good."

According to a British officer who was with him, Montgomery stomped into U.S. First Army headquarters "like Christ coming to cleanse the temple." The field marshal's G-2, said Hodges, who "looked as if somebody had punched him in the tummy,

or indeed kicked him in the crotch . . . was mightily relieved
to find a father-figure showing up to sort it all out for him."
Simpson reported to Eisenhower, "I and my Army are operating smoothly and cheerfully under command of the Field
Marshal. The most cordial relations and a very high spirit of
cooperation have been established between him and myself
personally and between our respective Staffs."

If he expected gratitude from the Americans, which he certainly did, he was disappointed, or would have been if he'd
had the ability to comprehend the true feelings of others. Both
Hodges and Simpson were soon offended by Montgomery's
patronizing attitude and lectures. To the consternation of Bradley, the field marshal, who had shortly before assured Eisenhower that no pullback would be necessary, proceeded to give
ground to shorten the line and to shift over to a defensive
mode in exposed positions. Excessive or not, the move was
competent, clearheaded soldiering, guaranteeing that the advance of the Germans, the extent of whose reserves was still
not apparent, would not turn into the Allied catastrophe that
some had earlier feared. Eisenhower had good reason to be
satisfied, and Brooke as well. But the British chief of staff knew
how profoundly personality and national factors were at stake
and hastened to warn Montgomery not to let the command
over the two American armies that he had been given go to his
head.

> Events and enemy actions [he told him] have forced on Eisen-
> hower the setting up of a more satisfactory system of com-
> mand. I feel it is most important that you should not even in
> the slightest degree appear to rub this undoubted fact in to
> anyone at SHAEF or elsewhere. Any remarks you may make
> are bound to come to Eisenhower's ears sooner or later and
> that may make it more difficult to ensure that this new setup
> for Command remains even after the present emergency has
> passed.

But Montgomery could not control himself. On Christmas
Day he invited Bradley north to coordinate tactics with him all

along the front. He began "by lecturing and scolding" his visitor "like a schoolboy." Though he did not blame Eisenhower by name for what had gone wrong in the Ardennes, he made it plain that he believed incompetent generalship was responsible. Bradley listened and said little. Montgomery wrote to Brooke that night that his visitor had "agreed entirely" with everything he had said. "Poor chap; he is such a decent fellow and the whole thing is a bitter pill for him. But he is man enough to admit it and he did."

He was unable to recognize how far from the truth that was. "Monty," Bradley later wrote, "was more arrogant and egotistical than I had ever seen him. . . . Never in my life had I been so enraged and so utterly exasperated. It required every fiber of my strength to restrain myself from an insulting outburst. . . . However, to avoid a potentially crippling breakdown in the Allied command, I kept my counsel."

The situation still appeared precarious at the time. But the skies soon cleared sufficiently for Allied air power to end hope the Germans might have had of turning their attack into anything but a busted gamble. By December 26, when Patton's divisions, completing a remarkable maneuver, relieved beseiged Bastogne, it was clear that the German counteroffensive was doomed. Patton served notice, "The Kraut has stuck his head in the meat grinder and I've got the handle."

As had happened after the breakout from Normandy, Montgomery now failed to grasp that others thought less highly than he did of his role in the Battle of the Bulge. Nor could he appreciate that they were not persuaded that what had happened had vindicated his insistence on a concentrated thrust by him into the heart of Germany rather than a wider advance.

Once again he and Eisenhower had trouble understanding each other. A meeting between them on December 28 left Eisenhower believing that, with the German attack routed, Montgomery would quickly resume the forward march of the forces under his command. However, the field marshal wasn't at all certain he'd be ready to move, as expected, by New Year's Day. At the same time, he was left believing that Eisenhower would permit him to retain full operational control of the two U.S.

armies north of the Ardennes over which he had been given
temporary command.

Prompted by such misapprehensions, and believing himself
to be the hero of the hour, Montgomery forgot Brooke's admonition that he watch his language. Instead he wrote a nagging
and highly critical letter to the Supreme Commander on December 29. In it he listed the errors he said had been made by the
Allied command over the previous three months and warned
him that "we will fail again" if the command structure he proposed was not instituted at once. "[O]ne commander must have
powers to direct and control the operations; you cannot possibly
do it yourself, and so you have to nominate someone else."

Eisenhower was flabbergasted by such arrogant presumption,
which was magnified by Montgomery daring to instruct him
that "it will be necessary for you to be very firm [in assigning
him operational control in the north], and any loosely worded
statement [of the kind the British commander had come to
dread] will be quite useless."

Having just successfully quarterbacked victory in the Battle
of the Bulge, the Supreme Commander was riled by renewed
criticism of him in the British press, combined with paeans of
praise for Montgomery's achievements and brilliance. Bradley
had already stopped listening to BBC news reports because "it
makes me mad." Bradley's aide, Major Hansen, wrote in his
diary of the "slavish hero devotion" of the British press, which
was "careful not to associate the lack of success at Caen with
[Montgomery's] name . . . and the disaster at Arnhem."

Nevertheless, there was still much work for everyone to do
in exploiting the failure of the German counteroffensive. The
U.S. First Army, still under Montgomery's command in the
north, was to launch an offensive coordinated by Bradley to
coincide with an attack by troops of Patton's Third Army. A
few days before its scheduled launch, the British commander
sent De Guingand to SHAEF headquarters to explain his decision to delay the attack. De Guingand was shocked by his
reception and also by the extent to which the relationship between Eisenhower and Montgomery had become strained. He
saw Eisenhower in his office, flanked by Bedell Smith and Ted-

der, both looking somber. A decision had been made to do something about the contentious British commander.

Eisenhower "very quietly started to explain how serious matters were." The Supreme Commander told De Guingand that Montgomery's action had made the position of Bradley, "one of his ablest commanders," intolerable and that he might lose him as a result. He asked De Guingand whether Montgomery "fully realized the effects of the line taken up by the British Press, and how Monty himself had helped to create this crisis by his campaign for a Land Forces Commander and by the indiscreet remarks he had passed." Eisenhower said he was "tired of the whole business" and that "it was impossible for the two of them to carry on working in harness together."

Eisenhower showed De Guingand a cable he had drafted for dispatch to Marshall in his capacity as chairman of the Combined Chiefs of Staff. In it, the Supreme Commander suggested that Alexander be brought in to replace Montgomery. In effect, he was saying that unless Montgomery was removed, he himself would step down.

De Guingand was stunned. He realized that if that message was sent, Montgomery would be made to go home in disgrace. Regardless of continuing British criticism of Eisenhower, with Roosevelt's and Marshall's full support the Supreme Commander was untouchable. It would be a major scandal and would dangerously sour British-American relations, just as Hitler's propagandists had been trying to do.

De Guingand appealed to Eisenhower to delay sending the cable for twenty-four hours so that he might "solve the impasse." He then hastily reported to Montgomery what Eisenhower had said and what he was planning to do. Montgomery was astonished. He was baffled by why his proposals had not been seen to be sensible, if not downright obvious to anyone with any grasp of the science of warfare. Though he would not tolerate "bellyaching" from the generals under his command, he could not understand why Eisenhower was reacting so sharply to being told simple facts. De Guingand later wrote, "It was one of the few times that I saw Montgomery really worried and disturbed, for I believe he was genuinely and completely taken by surprise and found it difficult to grasp what I was saying. . . . I don't think I had ever seen him so deflated. It was as if a cloak of loneliness had descended upon him."

De Guingand told the field marshal it was necessary for him to apologize to Eisenhower. Badly shaken, he realized his career was at stake and that he had no alternative. He cabled Eisenhower his regrets.

> . . . understand you are greatly worried by many considerations in these difficult days. I have given you my frank views because I have felt you like this. I am sure there are many factors which may have a bearing quite beyond anything I realize. Whatever your decision may be you can rely on me one hundred percent to make it work and I know BRAD will do the same.

Montgomery signed the cable, "Your very devoted subordinate." He also informed Eisenhower that he would advance the timing of the offensive in the north, delay of which had so angered the Supreme Commander and Bradley. The apology was accepted without fuss, as was the field marshal's implied promise to mend his ways. This was no time to exacerbate friction in the British-American military alliance. Eisenhower cabled back, "I truly appreciate the understanding attitude [your cable] indicates," adding, it being January 1, 1945, "the earnest hope" that the new year "will be the most successful for you of your entire career."

When Churchill visited Montgomery's headquarters three days later, he was relieved that relations between the two men appeared to have improved. The prime minister cabled Roosevelt that Eisenhower and the field marshal "are very closely knit, and also Bradley and Patton, and it would be disaster which broke up this combination, which has . . . yielded us results beyond the dreams of military avarice."

But if Montgomery appeared reconciled to Eisenhower's leadership, the British press was less so. Reporting on the delayed disclosure of Montgomery's role in the Ardennes battle, the London *Daily Express*, under the headline MONTY'S 'FIRST TEAM'

IN, saw the temporary transfer of the bulk of Bradley's 12th
Army Group to Montgomery as a "move . . . greeted everywhere in the Allied lines with enthusiasm and an immense
return of confidence." The London *Daily Mail* said, "According
to information obtained in reliable political circles, Field Marshal Montgomery took command of all the armies along the
whole northern flank of the German salient several days before
the idea was confirmed in the highest quarters. Apparently the
situation was so desperate that Field Marshal Montgomery,
using his own initiative, threw in all his weight and authority
and asserted his leadership, which was accepted by those
around him."

Butcher observed that British press "rumblings . . . have now
grown to a roar of demand that there be a British deputy commander for all of Ike's ground forces. The implication is clearly
given that General Ike, greatly as he is respected, has undertaken too much of a task himself." To make matters worse,
Montgomery's irrepressible conceit strengthened doubts among
Britons about Eisenhower's command abilities, though this time
his intention had been exactly the opposite.

Despite his criticism of the American generals, which remained confidential except for some leaks to correspondents,
he was afraid that Allied solidarity was being damaged by inac-
curate London press interpretations of how the Battle of the
Bulge was fought. He had told Churchill and others how impressed he had been with the fighting skills and heroism of
the American troops in that clash. With the prime minister's
approval, he called a news conference on January 7 to put an
end to the carping of the British newspapers, to put on record
the high regard with which he held the Americans, and to say
how proud he was to be fighting alongside them.

His remarks to the assembled correspondents included a generous tribute to American troops and to Eisenhower (about
whom he had written confidentially a few days earlier, "As a
commander in charge of land operations, [he] is . . . completely
and absolutely useless"). He told the press conference how
grieved he was that British newspapers had printed uncompli-
mentary articles about the Supreme Commander who, he said,

"bears a great burden" and had a right to expect "our fullest support." But the limelight dazzled him. As his aides looked on in despair, he went on to destroy the effect he had meant to produce by his description of the role he himself had played when "the situation began to deteriorate."

> General Eisenhower placed me in command of the whole Northern front. I employed the whole available power of the British Group of Armies; this power was brought into play very gradually and in such a way that it would not interfere with the American lines of communication. Finally it was put in with a bang, and today British divisions are fighting hard on the right flank of First US Army. You have thus a picture of British troops fighting on both sides of American forces who have suffered a hard blow. This is a fine allied picture. The battle has been most interesting; I think possibly one of the most interesting and tricky battles I have ever handled, with great issues at stake. The first thing to be done was to 'head off' the enemy from the tender spots and vital places. Having done that successfully, the next thing was to 'see him off' . . . and make quite certain that he could not get to the places he wanted. . . . He was therefore 'headed off,' and then 'seen off.' He is now being 'written off.'

What had actually happened was nothing like the impression Montgomery gave at that news conference. He had played an important role in the battle, maintaining coherence among the Allied armies in the north and putting his own reserves into place to block a possible German breakthrough. But he had not saved the Americans from disaster, as he implied he had done. That had been done by the American troops themselves and their lower-rank officers, who paid a heavy price for the failure of their top commanders to anticipate the German offensive. They had stood fast at Bastogne and other strategically vital points to bring the enemy drive to a standstill. And Patton had come to their rescue.

Though the presence of British troops in a defense posture had been important, comparatively few of them had been in a position to be directly engaged in the battle. The British suffered some 500 casualties; the Americans suffered 70,000. Montgomery had not "seen" or "written" anybody off. Indeed, the field marshal's failure to react more aggressively after the German drive had been halted permitted the bulk of the attackers to withdraw unscathed.

Many of the Americans first heard of Montgomery's remarks from a German English-language propaganda radio broadcast mistakenly believed to be a BBC report. It deliberately exaggerated the British commander's boastfulness. Bradley was furious when he learned of it. "After what has happened," he told Eisenhower, "I cannot serve under Montgomery. If he is to be put in command of all ground forces, you must send me home." He said Patton felt the same way and issued a public statement of his own stressing that Montgomery had been given only temporary command of the two American armies and that the German counteroffensive had been stopped in its tracks before that had happened.

Montgomery's tactlessness dashed Eisenhower's hope he'd had of establishing a reasonably satisfactory working relationship among the commanders of his army groups. He understood and sympathized with Bradley's disgust at being portrayed as an incompetent. The suggestion that the American troops who had fought off the German attack had to be rescued by the British also rankled. Eisenhower made his feelings clear to Churchill, who tried to make unambiguous amends in a House of Commons speech with what amounted to a repudiation of Montgomery's press-conference comments.

> I have seen it suggested that the terrific battle which has been proceeding . . . on the American Front is an Anglo-American battle. In fact, however, the United States troops have done almost all the fighting and suffered almost all the losses. . . . The Americans have engaged 30 or 40 men for every one we have engaged and they have lost 60 to 80 men for every one of us. . . . Care must be taken in telling our proud tale not to claim for the British Army an undue share of what is undoubtedly the greatest American battle of the war and

will, I believe, be regarded as an ever famous American victory. . . . The gap was torn open as a gap can always be torn
open in a line a hundred miles long. General Eisenhower at
once gave command to the north of the gap to Field Marshal
Montgomery and to the south of it to General Omar Bradley.
Judging by the result, both these highly skilled commanders
handled very large forces at their disposal in a manner which
. . . may become a model for military students in the future. . . . Let no one lend themselves to the shouting of mischief makers when issues of this momentous consequence
are being successfully decided by the sword.

Montgomery had served the Allied cause well during the
Battle of the Bulge. But his egotism and irrepressible tactlessness did neither himself nor Allied unity any good at a
critical moment when important decisions affecting both him
and it were about to be made. Even in Britain, where his popularity remained undiminished among the populace, some had
begun to think less of him. The military attaché at the American
embassy in London reported back to Washington, "I have the
strong impression that most British officers, including many in
influential posts in the War Office, are much less enthusiastic
over Montgomery than is the British public." And War Minister
Grigg, who had offered him his unwavering support during
the previous difficult months, wanted to know, "Why is it that
whenever I mention the name of Montgomery [in the House of
Commons], there is always a cold hush?" Lord Ismay later
expressed the wish that someone would "muzzle, or better still
chloroform Monty." Ismay said, "I have come to the conclusion
that his love of publicity is a disease, like alcoholism or taking
drugs and that it sends him equally mad."

CHAPTER 21
The Long Winter

Barely had the German counteroffensive in the Ardennes been repelled when the British formally served notice that they wanted Allied command arrangements to be reviewed. Churchill might have felt obliged to offer a tacit apology to Eisenhower for Montgomery's tactlessness, but his chiefs of staff, exasperated with the way the Americans were running the war, wanted to know how the Supreme Commander intended to follow up the Battle of the Bulge to effect the final conquest of Germany. Brooke shared Montgomery's view that, "We have reached a stage . . . where the very highest professional skill is required in the future planning and conduct of the war, and I am afraid it is in the hands of amateurs."

The British conceded that faulty Allied intelligence had assisted the German Ardennes counteroffensive but maintained that it had "succeeded far beyond . . . the advantages gained by surprise." That was a damning commentary on Eisenhower's leadership. Historian Sir Arthur Bryant concisely summed up British concerns.

With their man-power and resources all but exhausted after five years of war and with no possibility of making good further losses, they had staked everything on an early victory in the West and had seen it, as they felt, thrown away by the inexperience of the American High Command. The war . . . had been prolonged into another year and, unless a very different method of conducting it was now to be adopted, seemed likely to continue until, not only their own position, but that of Europe was desperate.

Britain's interests in this part of the world were more distinctly, directly, and historically at stake than those of the United States. Yet not only had Eisenhower made strategic decisions to which the British took exception but, now that victory in Europe was in sight, the balance of interest in the American High Command was shifting decidedly toward winding up the war in the Pacific. The British feared the war in Europe would be permitted to drift through inept direction toward a conclusion that might take even longer to reach and leave them with serious postwar difficulties in addition to those that were already inevitable.

The argument made was the same Montgomery had been trying to impress on Eisenhower for months—that the Allies could not bring the war to a rapid conclusion if the Supreme Commander persisted with his broad-front strategy. The British urged, as Montgomery now did yet again, that the primary effort be put into one major offensive. It should be under a single ground-forces commander, one who would adhere to the instructions issued earlier by the Combined Chiefs of Staff for greater concentration on the northern wing. Little effort was made in London anymore to conceal the belief there that ever since Montgomery had been relieved of overall command of Allied ground forces, it had been amply demonstrated that Eisenhower had too much on his plate to handle that job as competently as was necessary.

Though irked by such criticism, Eisenhower could not be shaken from his belief in the broad-front approach. The Ardennes experience had demonstrated that the Germans were still capable of putting up a punishing fight. He still agreed that the advance north of the Ardennes offered the best opportunities. But he continued to believe that if he weakened his line anywhere, the Germans might once more mount a vigorous breakthrough attempt that would again inflict heavy casualties and delay final victory. SHAEF still had only limited intelligence on what sort of reserves the enemy was managing to patch together east of the Rhine. He therefore decided there would be no crossing of the river to penetrate into the German heartland until its west bank had been effectively cleared of enemy forces along its entire length from the Netherlands to Switzerland.

The British considered it absurd for a commander to limit his options in such a way when opportunities for rapid advance might arise, particularly in Montgomery's sector. They pressed Eisenhower at least to allow for other possibilities, depending on circumstances. The Supreme Commander felt obliged to concede that he would "seize the Rhine crossings in the north immediately this is a feasible operation and without waiting to close the Rhine throughout its length."

He was of two minds about the British. On the one hand, he was "fed up with [Churchill] who was continually telling him what to do . . . and now that the war was almost won he would get on with it in his way." However, he was pained by how the relationship between the Allies had come under such severe strain. He wanted to restore British confidence in SHAEF and his own leadership. He considered an idea being floated in London of having another senior British officer slotted into the Allied command structure to serve immediately under him.

It couldn't be Montgomery. Working more closely with the field marshal than he was already required to was an appalling thought. He certainly would lose Bradley and Patton and possibly Hodges as well if they were made to take orders from him.

But Alexander, who was still commander of ground forces in the Italian campaign, was a credible candidate for the job. He and Alexander respected and liked each other and the other Americans were unlikely to object to him. He contemplated shifting Tedder to another job and bringing Alexander in to replace him as deputy Supreme Commander, with emphasis, as in North Africa, Sicily, and Italy, on ground operations.

Marshall did not like that idea at all. "My feeling is this," he wrote to Eisenhower. "Under no circumstances make any concessions of any kind whatsoever. You not only have our confidence but there would be a terrific resentment in this country following such action. You are doing a fine job and go on and give them hell."

As organizer of America's war effort, Marshall was much more sharply aware of how disproportionate were the contributions of the two countries to defeating the enemy. The United States had more than twice as many men in uniform as Britain, was taking far more of the casualties, and provided most of the supplies and hardware by far. A British officer observed that though his regiment in the north was considered "Super Heavy . . . its equipment was American. . . . The sands were running out. This was [our] last Big Show."

Marshall also did not share the sense of fraternity with the British that Eisenhower had developed through agreeable exposure in London and at SHAEF. He felt they had no grounds for complaint. He believed that, having prevailed with their insistence on the invasion of North Africa and on a Mediterranean strategy instead of an early cross-Channel invasion, they were largely responsible for the war not already being won. He wanted the British-American alliance to remain as firm as possible. But he advised Eisenhower that the Americans should not permit themselves to be led astray on strategy again. He warned him against bending over backward to molify his British critics. He felt so strongly about it that if a British ground-forces commander were appointed under Eisenhower, as Brooke wished, he himself "will not remain as Chief of Staff," which was unthinkable.*

After the implied rebuke Montgomery had received from Churchill for his unfortunate press-conference remarks about the Battle of the Bulge, the field marshal was much restrained in his public utterances. To Bradley's disgust, he was permitted

---

*Marshall was not simply being hostile to the British. He was desperately trying to prevent a toning-down of support in Congress for the American effort in Europe now that the defeat of Germany appeared imminent.

by Eisenhower to retain command of the U.S. Ninth Army. But he was unhappy about having to return command of the U.S. First Army to Bradley. He complained to Brooke, "[W]e shall take a long time to get anywhere."

He also deplored Patton's practice of ignoring Eisenhower's instructions not to risk exposing his forces to German counterattacks through what seemed to him to be reckless forward thrusts that no general with any understanding of the rules of combat would risk. Advance was supposed to be carefully coordinated clear across the line. He was afraid "that [Eisenhower's] old snags of indecision and vacillation and refusal to consider the military problem fairly and squarely are coming to the front again. . . . One has to preserve a sense of humour these days, otherwise one would go mad."

For purposes of harmony, Eisenhower kept Montgomery informed of his thinking about his refusal to keep the American armies reined in tighter. He told him, "the more Germans we kill west of the Rhine, the fewer there will be to meet us east of the river."

Three coordinated campaigns were organized to serve that purpose. Montgomery's three armies (the British Second, the Candian First, and the U.S. Ninth) were to strike in the north; Bradley's two armies (the U.S. First and Third) would strike in the center; in the south the attack would be by the two armies under Devers (the U.S. Seventh and the French First). Once the Rhineland had been cleared, Montgomery's northern drive would spearhead the advance across the Rhine. With Operation Plunder, his forces would cross the river north of Düsseldorf to plunge deep into Germany.

But while Montgomery prepared for Operation Plunder with his usual meticulousness, an advance unit of Hodges' U.S. First Army not only drove through a gap in crumbling German defenses to reach the Rhine, but found the Ludendorff railway bridge across the river at the town of Remagen still intact and seized it before it could be destroyed by the retreating Germans.

Bradley wanted to move quickly to exploit that breakthrough and secure the first Allied bridgehead east of the Rhine. "Shove everything across it . . . and button up the bridgehead tightly," he ordered. That was contrary to plans. Eisenhower's chief of operations, General Harold Bull, was visiting Bradley's headquarters at the time and dampened Bradley's enthusiasm. "You're not going anywhere down there at Remagen," Bull told him. "You've got a bridge, but it's in the wrong place. It just doesn't fit into the plan. Ike's heart is in your sector but right now his mind is up north."

To Bradley, who well knew it was planned for Montgomery to cross the Rhine first, that was military bureaucracy gone crazy. He contacted Eisenhower by telephone and told him both about taking the bridge and Bull's stopping him from going further. Eisenhower saw things his way. "[G]et across with everything you've got," he told him. "It's the best break we've had. . . . To hell with the planners."

Wishing not to upset Montgomery, Eisenhower took the precaution of "consulting" the field marshal about what was happening. Montgomery made no complaint. It would, he said, draw enemy forces away from the region where his own more massive Rhine crossing was to take place. He was however, less than happy with the continuing rampage of Patton's Third Army. Patton, as determined as Montgomery to blast his way to Berlin first, had pressed forcefully ahead well beyond the limits of his instructions.

After having helped demolish the German Ardennes offensive and then fought his way through to Coblenz on the Rhine, Patton had cleared enemy forces from a good part of the central section of the west bank of the river. Then, on the night of March 22, 1945, a little more than twenty-four hours before Montgomery's Rhine crossing was to be launched, acting without instructions, he upstaged the field marshal by sending his troops across the river south of Mainz. Bradley gave his full approval and Eisenhower showed no signs of objecting. This was his old friend at his aggressive, headline-grabbing best.

With Hodges' First Army established in the Remagen area, the Americans now had two bridgeheads across Germany's last major natural defense line in the west. "For God's sake," Patton told Bradley over the phone, "tell the world we're across. . . .

I want the world to know Third Army made it before Monty
starts across." Bradley's staff took great pleasure in passing
word along, announcing that Patton's troops had crossed the
Rhine, "Without benefit of aerial bombing, ground smoke, artillery preparation, and airborne assistance," all of which were
to be components of Montgomery's river-crossing operation.
"[W]hile the British assault on the river was prepared with
ponderous formality," General Morgan later wrote, "General
Patton's armour roared through the Palatinate and hopped
lightly across the East Bank as and where it suited them."

Hodges' and Patton's troops had both seized their bridgeheads across the Rhine "on the run," without detailed planning, preliminary buildup, or elaborate support. Montgomery,
however, geared up for his crossing almost as if it were another
Normandy landing. He had been thinking about it for months.
He had methodically readied his equipment and reserves. He
believed his planning to be "so good that I shall wait if necessary
four or five days" for weather conditions to be favorable,
though he did not trouble mentioning that possibility to Eisenhower. His attack was to be more than merely a river crossing
and the securing of a bridgehead like the ones Hodges and
Patton had achieved. He was planning an operation that would
be so overwhelming that he would be in a position to go on to
finish off the enemy for good. No replay of the Arnhem fiasco
was to be risked.

He had concentrated more than a quarter of a million troops
and a quarter of million tons of ammunition for Operation Plunder. It was preceded by a ten-day-long massive smokescreen
and the dropping of 50,000 tons of bombs. Two airborne divisions dropped behind enemy lines to lend forward assistance.
More than 35,000 vehicles, including 662 tanks, had been
moved into position for an offensive that could change everything, persuade Eisenhower of the error of his ways, and bring
the war to a rapid conclusion. On the night of March 23, 1945,
on the eve of the crossing, 3,500 guns unleashed a fierce bombardment to pulverize the enemy defenses and communications. All told, it was a remarkable demonstration of how to

mount a major assault, and Montgomery's Rhine crossing was achieved as quickly and as comparatively painlessly as he had predicted.

However, the preparatory bombardment was largely super-fluous, as were most of the other preparations. The whole oper-ation had been premised on the assumption that the Germans were capable of far stronger resistance than they proved to be. At all but a few points along the stretch of land Montgomery's forces controlled, the crossing could have been made with little difficulty at any time over the previous two weeks. Finally accepting that his Ardennes gamble had flopped, Hitler had rushed forces and heavy equipment from west to east to meet a rapidly intensifying Soviet onslaught. Many of his divisions east of the Rhine, decimated and exhausted by their recent experiences and still trying to regroup, no longer qualified to be called divisions. They were starved of troops, ammunition, artillery, and tanks. Among the German prisoners taken by Scottish troops were women soldiers who had only recently been armed with rifles.

With spring the weather cleared, making ideal conditions for river crossing. General Simpson, whose U.S. Ninth Army was still under Montgomery's command, had pleaded with the field marshal for permission to make the crossing. Simpson assured him it would present few problems. His divisions were sitting around doing very little. Simpson's plan did not mean Mont-gomery's Operation Plunder would have to be initiated before the field marshal was ready. But when Plunder was launched, prepared positions across the Rhine would greatly facilitate the more ambitious post-crossing advance Montgomery was planning.

Montgomery wouldn't hear of it. An early crossing did not fit the plan he had been devising with great thoroughness to meet all contingencies. The resourceful Germans had demon-strated in the Ardennes that they were capable of the unex-pected. Bradley, Patton, and Hodges might have been willing to gamble, and Montgomery was pleased they had succeeded. But he was not interested in easy victories that might be of limited significance, and he did not believe they fully understood the risks they had taken or the extent of the far greater achievement he was aiming for. Risk-taking was for amateurs. The results of the first day of his massive Rhine-crossing operation demonstrated the value of doing things right—six divisions were put across the river at a cost of only 1,200 casualties.

Firmly across the Rhine, Montgomery instructed his army commanders to waste no time in making for the Elbe River, sixty miles from Berlin, before the enemy could recover from the punishment inflicted in Operation Plunder. That was contrary to Eisenhower's cautious plan for the Ruhr to be enveloped before further advance was to be undertaken. But Montgomery saw it as the only appropriate course to pursue under the favorable conditions and opportunities he had created. He could not believe that any general, even those at SHAEF with whom he had been required to contend for so long, would fail to understand that. With the preparations he had made and the momentum he had built up, the Elbe could be quickly reached, after which he would speed down the autobahn to Berlin.

The German capital was "the main prize." That was what Eisenhower had told Montgomery the previous September. "[I]t is my desire," he had told him, "to move on Berlin by the most direct and expeditious route, with combined U.S.-British forces . . . all in one coordinated, concerted operation." A SHAEF planning staff memorandum stated, "Our main objective must be the early capture of Berlin, the most important objective in Germany." Bedell Smith believed, "From the day our invasion broke over the beaches of Normandy, the goal of every Allied soldier had been Berlin."

But suddenly it became apparent that Eisenhower had changed his mind. During the closing weeks of the war in Europe, the city had been reduced to peripheral importance in the Supreme Commander's thinking. He told Montgomery it had become "nothing but a geographical location, and I have never been interested in these."

Not only would the field marshal be denied the opportunity to capture Berlin, but Eisenhower informed him that he was to lose the U.S. Ninth Army that he had commanded since the beginning of the German Ardennes offensive and without which his still-flickering hope of playing the major role in the final defeat of Hitler would be finally snuffed out. The Ninth was to revert to Bradley, whose most immediate task would be "mopping up and occupying the Ruhr. . . . The mission of your army group," Eisenhower told Montgomery, "will be to protect Bradley's northern flank." He was to clear the enemy from the north German plain, seize Hamburg and the other north German ports, isolate the German forces in Denmark and Norway, and liberate the Netherlands.

This turnabout in the role he was to play after his massive Rhine crossing made no sense to Montgomery. He said it seemed that in addition to being "unable to evolve a sound plan," SHAEF could not "carry any plan through to its logical conclusion." For Britain, the conquest of northern Germany was of considerable strategic significance. The Red Army's penetration farther west into Europe had to be prevented so that a tolerable postwar European balance of power could be established. But the relegation of Montgomery to what was largely a cleaning-up role was trenchant commentary on Britain's diminished status in the world. Eisenhower's refusal to even consider letting Montgomery proceed to Berlin was conclusive proof.

He cabled Brooke his anguish at this latest development. "I consider," he said, "we are about to make a terrible mistake. The great point now is speed of action, so that we can finish off German war in shortest possible time. . . . It seems doctrine that public opinion wins wars is coming to the fore again." He was right about that. Marshall had complained to Eisenhower about an "overdose of Montgomery" in the press. He continued to emphasize that no British general should be permitted to outshine the Americans in this final stage of the war in Europe.

Eisenhower had no difficulty with that. Away from his British base and from the dignitaries there whose respect, friendship, and hospitality had flattered him, he was anxious to rid himself of the reputation he had among some American generals for going to extremes to accommodate the British. He was also enormously proud of the performance of the U.S. troops. From their clumsy, fumbling start in Tunisia, where he had feared his career as a combat commander would prove exceedingly brief, the image of American fighting men had been transformed into liberators and conquering heroes. And he was their leader. He urged Marshall to come to see them while they were still in action, praising him for having created such an army. But the chief of staff was not one for ceremonial gestures. No doubt he still regretted not having himself been named Supreme Commander.

There were other reasons why Montgomery was being effectively downgraded once more. Eisenhower had no doubt any longer that his reputation as a battle-winning commander was greatly inflated. The experience at Caen, Antwerp, and more recently in the delayed follow-up to the foiled German Ardennes assault and the excessively thorough buildup for the Rhine crossing appeared to provide sufficient evidence for that. General Whitely, Eisenhower's British deputy chief of operations, said the feeling at Allied headquarters "was that if anything was to be done quickly, don't give it to Monty. Monty was the last person Ike would have chosen for a drive on Berlin—Monty would have needed six months to prepare."

In any case, by then Eisenhower had decided to leave Berlin to the Soviets. That was a decision of great historic significance and would have enormous political and diplomatic consequences. But the Supreme Commander did not think in those terms at the time. His mission was to crush the armies of Nazi Germany, and he sought to do that as quickly as possible with the fewest casualties and distractions.

His decision about Berlin came as a surprise to many and a shock to some. Operational factors had led him to change his mind. The previous summer, when the Germans had been routed in Normandy and were in disarray, the war seemed heading for a conclusion by Christmas. But that had been followed by the missed chances of the autumn and the difficulties of the winter. The idea of a decisive surgical strike through enemy lines had lost much of its credibility. In addition, by February 1945, Soviet troops had reached the Oder River and were a mere thirty-five miles from Berlin while the armies of the Western Allies had not yet crossed the Rhine then and were still more than 200 miles from the city. The Soviets appeared to be consolidating their positions before bounding forward to seize the German capital. It seemed to be easily within their grasp.

Bradley, the commander Eisenhower trusted most, advised him it was better first to mop up the German forces cut off in the Ruhr, though that was no longer a crucial undertaking. Bradley thought it might cost the Western Allies 100,000 casualties to take Berlin, "a pretty stiff price to pay for a prestige objective." Besides, another important mission had to be undertaken. Bungled intelligence appeared to confirm Nazi intentions to build a National Redoubt in Bavaria. It was believed that Hitler, having stored quantities of arms, supplies, and equipment, might be able to carry on the war from there for another year or more. That added to Eisenhower's conviction that the capture of Berlin would be a gesture of little military significance to the Allies. Unless instructed otherwise by the Combined Chiefs of Staff or Washington, he was determined to follow a course dictated exclusively by military considerations.

German propagandists had continued with their attempts to drive a wedge between the Western Allies as well as between the Western Allies and the Soviets. They had tried to make capital out of the row over Montgomery's tactless Battle of the Bulge comments. Now, in desperation, they sought to promote anti-Soviet feelings among the Americans and the British. Hitler was convinced that the Western Allies would come to realize that Soviet Communism was a greater danger to them than Nazi Germany now that the Red Army was overrunning Central Europe.

With the destruction of the Third Reich imminent, Churchill had come to agree with the German dictator about that and had grounds for doing so. The Soviets were arousing great mistrust among the Western Allies. Agreements that had been made were being violated—in Romania, for example, where the Red Army had installed a Communist regime, and in Poland, where it was in the process of doing the same.

Whatever Eisenhower's views on such developments, he was determined to resist anything that might offend the Soviets and split the alliance with them when victory was within his grasp. At the February 1945 summit conference at Yalta, it had been decided that Berlin was to be divided among the Allies, but the city had been placed within the area that was to be the Soviet occupation zone of Germany. That seemed to make it pointless to race the Soviets to reach the city or to intrude elsewhere on territory in Germany from which, in accordance with the agreement, American and British troops would have to withdraw at war's end. There was also the danger of accidental clashes and needless deaths when advancing American and British troops came within shooting distance of the advancing Soviets.

The Supreme Commander's strategy for the final destruction of German military strength was to isolate the industrial Ruhr from the rest of Germany and then send Bradley cutting through the middle of Germany toward Dresden to link up with the Russians at clearly specified stop lines. What remained of German resistance in the west would be split apart and mopped up. A secondary advance to deal with Hitler's last-ditch National Redoubt in the south would be made as developments dictated. In the meantime, while covering Bradley's flank Montgomery would proceed with his tasks in the north.

Eisenhower's decision to bypass Berlin appalled Churchill, for whom, appropriately, war was as much a political and diplomatic phenomenon as a military event. Britain had long dreaded the possible insertion of Russian power into the heart of Europe. Because of Hitler and what he had wreaked, that was now to a great extent inevitable no matter what strategy Eisenhower chose to pursue. But to hand the Soviets Berlin as a gift when it probably could have been taken by the Western Allies and used as a postwar bargaining asset against the acquisitive Soviets struck the prime minister as outrageous and absurd.

He appealed to Roosevelt, warning of the dangerous consequences for the postwar world.

The Russian Armies [he told the president] will no doubt overrun all Austria and enter Vienna. If they also take Berlin will
not their impression that they have been the overwhelming
contributor to our common victory be unduly imprinted in their
minds, and may this not lead them into a mood which will
raise grave and formidable difficulties in the future?

But Roosevelt was terminally ill. All decisions related to military matters in Europe were being dealt with by Marshall, who,
like Eisenhower, was a soldier first, not a politician. Marshall
agreed fully with his decision on how to complete the destruction of the German armed forces. Churchill turned to Eisenhower, in effect telling him he did not understand how
important Berlin's capture by the West would be. According to
Kay Summersby, his comments upset the Supreme Commander "quite a bit."

Yet Eisenhower was mistaken about Berlin having little military significance. It remained the capital of Germany. Primary
headquarters and the main control centers of its armed forces
were still there. Most important, Hitler was there as well, issuing orders for the hopeless resistance of his armies, many of
which no longer existed, from his reinforced concrete bunker
beneath his bomb-shattered chancellery. As for the Führer's
National Redoubt in the south, it did not exist, never had, and
never would. It was a fantasy of feverish Nazi minds as the
Third Reich entered its terminal phase.

It was true that the forces of the Soviet Union were no more
than an hour's car drive from Berlin. But there was no certainty
that they were in a better position than the Western armies to
seize the German capital. They were hunkered down beyond
the Oder River, and the Germans were concentrating almost
exclusively on stopping them from going any farther. In the
west German troops were surrendering in great numbers to the
Americans and the British, often whole units at a time. But
Eisenhower did not appreciate the extent of the enemy's collapse on the western front and insisted he would not permit
any move he deemed militarily unwise merely to gain a political
prize.

The British had further reason to be upset by Eisenhower's handling of the situation. He was not authorized to communicate on matters of substance directly with Stalin. Such dealings were supposed to go through the Combined Chiefs of Staff. However, on March 28, 1945, he sent a message to the U.S. Military Mission in Moscow outlining the strategy he intended to pursue in achieving the final destruction of German military power. The message was to be delivered to the Soviet dictator. It informed him that the forces of the Western Allies intended to encircle and destroy the German forces in the Ruhr and to isolate that area from the rest of Germany before directing their main effort toward Kassel and Dresden. That was the same as informing Stalin that a drive by the Western Allies to take Berlin was not under consideration. It was, in effect, an invitation to the Russians to capture the city themselves.

Mistrustful of such generosity, Stalin was convinced the offer of such an unsolicited gift was a trick meant to lull him into complacency about taking the German capital. He informed Eisenhower, who was incapable of being as devious as Stalin suspected, that he agreed that Berlin had "lost its former strategic importance." But he immediately summoned his two senior generals and instructed them to draw up plans to move against the city with a minimum of delay.

Churchill was outraged. Not only had the Supreme Commander failed to consult him about his unprecedented direct contact with the Soviet leader, it also dashed whatever hope the prime minister still entertained of persuading Washington to require Eisenhower to change his mind about Berlin.

But it really didn't matter. Few people in the American capital were much concerned at the time about postwar dangers. The war in Europe had gone on too long. Plans were already in the works to bring the troops home from there. Churchill may have agonized over the Russians taking Prague, Vienna, and Berlin. But such concerns made little impact in the United States, where attention was focused on the showdown with Japan that was still to be faced.

However, the question of who would take Berlin refused to go away. On April 11, when it appeared to have been settled

conclusively, advance units of General Simpson's U.S. Ninth
Army, which was now under Bradley's command and which
had spurted forward two hundred miles in little more than ten
days against little resistance, reached the Elbe near Magdeburg.
Three days later it had a secure bridgehead across the river.
Simpson asked Bradley for permission to storm down the autobahn to take the German capital. He had no doubt he could do
so easily while the Russians were still facing well-organized
and determined resistance to their own advance on the city.

Simpson was not aware of the intensity of the debate over
Berlin or of Eisenhower's decision to pass it by. As a mere army
commander, he had not been informed. No one had anticipated
the rapidity of his advance to the Elbe. His patrols had explored
beyond his bridgehead east of the river and had reported that
the road to Berlin looked open. Simpson later said, "The only
thing that moved faster than [us] those days was a comparatively few fleeing remnants of the battered and broken German
Army." He ordered his staff to prepare an advance on the
German capital and expected to reach it before another twenty-
four hours had passed.

But Bradley stopped him. Instead of advancing further, he
was to clean up his flanks and link up with the Soviets at the
agreed-upon stop line farther south. Bradley later conceded,
"As soldiers we looked naively on [the] British inclination to
complicate the war with political foresight and non-military
objectives."

On April 16, two days after Simpson's troops had crossed the
Elbe to no purpose, the Soviets launched their offensive to take
Berlin, completing its capture three weeks later. Though the
United States, Britain, France, and the Soviet Union subsequently shared occupation of the German capital, the Soviets
considered the Western Allies unwelcome intruders in the city
their troops had taken. In the years that followed, their efforts
to eject them led to the brink of a new war.

General Simpson had not been the only one Eisenhower felt
obliged to rein in. During the last days of April, Patton's Third
Army had advanced as far as the borders of Czechoslovakia
and he wanted to push on to Prague. The British chiefs of staff

urged that he be permitted to do so. Churchill said, "We should shake hands with the Russians as far to the east as possible." But Eisenhower decided not to. With the Russians in position to advance in that region, it would have served no military purpose.

Convinced the final chapter in the conquest of Germany was as preposterously mismanaged as earlier chapters had been, Montgomery later growled, "War is a political instrument; once it is clear that you are going to win, political considerations must influence its further course. It became obvious to me . . . that the way things were being handled was going to have repercussions far beyond the end of the war; it looked to me . . . as if we were going to 'muck it up.' I reckon we did."

CHAPTER 22
Victory

In his underground bunker beneath the bombed ruins of Berlin, Hitler fantasized about the impossible—a reversal of fortunes that would see his forces seize the initiative and drive the Allied invaders from German soil. Poring over battle maps, he ordered armies and divisions that no longer existed to block the enemy advance and go over to the offensive. He ranted that generals incapable of such miracles were traitors and ordered their execution. When Roosevelt died on April 12, 1945, Joseph Goebbels, Hitler's propaganda chief, told him it was a miracle that was meant as a sign that he and his Reich would be saved from defeat.

But the president's death had no effect on the conflict. Marshall had largely assumed control of American policy with regard to the war in Europe weeks before, when Roosevelt's terminal illness had effectively incapacitated him. As was traditional for vice presidents, Harry Truman had been kept poorly briefed on major matters of state. Moving in to the White House, Truman accepted that he was not well enough acquainted with the nuances of the military situation to interfere with Eisenhower's handling of the war in Europe, the end of which was clearly imminent. The Allied armies were continuing to sprint forward, resistance crumbling before them on all sectors of the front.

However, Eisenhower was concerned about the speed of Montgomery's progress in the north. The Russian advance there posed a danger that the Red Army, instead of the Western Allies, would move into position to liberate Denmark and make the Soviet presence felt there as well. There was a measure of contradiction in the Supreme Commander's concern, in view of his earlier lack of interest in seizing what he considered the "political" objective of Berlin.

On April 27, Eisenhower urged Montgomery to realize how important it was to deal quickly with that situation. He also discreetly suggested that Brooke press the field marshal to accelerate his advance. He told the British chief of staff that he was concerned about "the activity of the Russians." He told him, "The fact is that Monty has simply been unable . . . to get his arrangements made to his satisfaction." The implication was that Montgomery was the problem and not the greater than expected resistance his forces were meeting from German infantry newly fed into the line in the north, including service troops, youths, and even young boys armed with bazooka-type anti-tank weapons.

But Montgomery had indeed seemed to have lost a sense of urgency. The war was fizzling out rather than ending in a blaze of glory, and he was bitter. He had no doubt that the Americans had made a mess of things and prolonged the conflict. Despite the fumblings of their generals, they had relegated Britain, which had paid a far heavier price proportionally in the war, to a support role. Aside from the Normandy campaign, he himself had been denied the opportunity of demonstrating how the war in Europe should have been properly fought and won.

But as a British officer with the fate of postwar Europe on his mind, Montgomery was even more aware than Eisenhower of the need to preempt the Russian advance in the north. He caustically told Eisenhower there would have been no need for concern if command of the U.S. Ninth Army had not been taken away from him and handed back to Bradley when he needed it to complete his assignment expeditiously. He said he was dealing with the situation as quickly as possible. In the event, his troops—the British 6th Airborne Division, in this case—captured the town of Wismar, at the gateway to the Jutland peninsula and Denmark, only a few hours before the Russians arrived.

On April 25, 1945, American and Russian troops made contact at the town of Torgau on the Elbe. By April 28, Hitler finally accepted that Germany had lost the war and that he himself was doomed. He learned on that day that Heinrich Himmler, the head of the SS, was in the north trying to negotiate an armistice with the Western Allies through a Swedish intermediary and that there had been an anti-Nazi uprising in Munich, the city from which he had launched his Nazi crusade. The following day, the general commanding the defense of Berlin reported to him that the city was encircled by the Russians and his ammunition to fight them off was virtually exhausted.

On April 30, with Russian troops no more than a few hundred yards away, Hitler took leave of his remaining intimates in his bunker and retired to his bunker apartment with Eva Braun, his mistress of long standing whom he had married in a civil ceremony the day before. There he shot himself, and the new Mrs. Hitler took cyanide. In accordance with instructions he had given, the bodies were taken outside, soaked with gasoline, and burned.

What was left of the German command now sought to salvage what was possible from Germany's catastrophe. The great fear it had was of the Russians, whose homeland their armies had invaded, whose forces they had at first routed, and whose people they had slaughtered. Before committing suicide, Hitler had handed over supreme authority in the Third Reich to Grand Admiral Karl Dönitz, the German Navy's commander-in-chief. Field Marshal Wilhelm Keitel remained commander-in-chief of Germany's armed forces.

On May 3, Keitel dispatched emissaries to Montgomery's headquarters on Lüneburg Heath to surrender all German forces in the north of the country. They were led by Admiral Hans von Friedeburg, who had just succeeded Dönitz as commander-in-chief of the German Navy, and General Eberhardt Kinzel, chief of staff of German ground forces in the north, both of whom would soon commit suicide. When they arrived, Montgomery was in an almost playful mood. An aide said he had been rehearsing for that moment for a long time. He toyed with the Germans, keeping them waiting outside his caravan. When he emerged, he kept them waiting at stiff salute before casually returning it. They were in dramatic-looking military greatcoats. Montgomery was wearing his usual baggy-trous-ered battle dress and his beret.

Keitel's emissaries said they wished to include in the surren-der to Montgomery the three German armies still retreating from the Soviet onslaught to the northeast. They said the Rus-sians were savages and German soldiers captured by them would be sent off to work as slave laborers in Russia. Montgom-ery said the Germans should have thought of that before they invaded the Soviet Union four years earlier. He said those ar-mies would have to surrender to the Soviets, though individual soldiers would be permitted to surrender to his troops.

Keitel's emissaries also asked Montgomery for assurances that German civilians would not be improperly treated. Angrily, the field marshal snapped that such a request seemed strange in view of how little consideration the Germans had extended to the people of British cities bombed by the Luftwaffe at the beginning of the war. Having just visited the newly liberated concentration camp at Belsen and been sickened by what he saw there, he also berated them at length for how people had been cruelly treated and murdered in such camps.

He declared that he would accept nothing less from the Ger-mans than unconditional surrender, backing up his demand by showing them a map of the battle situation along the entire western front. They had not known how thoroughly the Ger-man position had collapsed and were greatly upset by it. But they said they would have to refer the unconditional surrender demand back to Keitel. Montgomery permitted them to do so but ordered his forces to cease all offensive activities. The end had been reached and he wanted his forces to suffer no needless casualties.

The German emissaries returned the next day, May 4, to surrender unconditionally and sign the surrender document. Montgomery invited war correspondents assigned to his head-quarters to witness the ceremony. Two BBC microphones were positioned to hear him read out the Instrument of Surrender. One of the Germans nervously took out a cigarette. Before he could light it, Montgomery glared at him and he put it away. After reading out the surrender terms, he ordered the Germans to sign the document, briskly instructing them in what order they were to do so. (A stone marking the spot where he accepted their surrender was later transferred to England to be set in place on the grounds of Sandhurst Military Academy, in whose chapel there is a stained-glass window in memory of the field marshal.)

It was all over in the north. Montgomery sent messages of praise, congratulations, and thanks to the men who were serving under him. He himself received wide and fulsome praise, including congratulations and an expression of "deepest gratitude" from Eisenhower. Churchill said that the fame of his 21st Army Group, "like that of the Eighth Army, will long shine in history, and other generations besides our own will honour their deeds and above all the character, profound strategy and untiring zeal of their Commander who marched from Egypt through Tripoli, Sicily and southern Italy, and through France, Belgium, Holland and Germany to the Baltic and the Elbe without losing a battle or even a serious action."

But even in those days of elation, Montgomery could not keep from recording his regret at how things had developed. In a memo for his army group log, he wrote of his amazement "at the mistakes we made. The organization for command was always faulty. The Supreme Commander was completely ineffective. . . . The staff at SHAEF were completely out of their depth all the time. . . . [I]f we had run the show properly the war could have been finished [earlier]. The blame for this must rest with the Americans. To balance this it is merely necessary to say one thing, i.e. if the Americans had not come along and lent a hand we would never have won the war at all."

Like Montgomery, Eisenhower was horrified by the what he saw at German labor and prison camps. From intelligence reports he had already had some idea of what had transpired in them, but after a visit to a camp for slave laborers at Ohrdruf, he wrote to a friend that the sights there had to be seen to be believed. There was "visual evidence and verbal testimony of starvation, cruelty and bestiality." Lice-infested corpses of men who had starved to death were stacked in piles. The stink of putrefaction was so great and the sight so horrible that so tough a soldier as Patton declined in horror to complete the tour.

Eisenhower wrote to Marshall that he had gone to see for himself "to be in a position to give *first-hand* evidence of these things if ever, in the future, there develops a tendency to charge these allegations merely to 'propaganda.' " Informed that the people of a nearby town of Gotha claimed to know nothing of what had gone on at the camp, Eisenhower ordered that all of them—including children—be marched there, made to see what had happened, and formed up into work parties to bury the dead. He also issued instructions that all nearby American troops not in the frontline should visit Ohrdruf to see what had transpired there. Shaken upon leaving the camp, he is said to have called out to a GI, "Still having trouble hating them?"

Admiral Dönitz still hoped to maintain resistance to the dreaded Russians in the east while laying down arms in the west so that as many German soldiers and civilians as possible would be able to flee westward across the Elbe to seek sanctuary among the Western armies. At Eisenhower's headquarters in Reims, Admiral von Friedeburg offered a surrender in the west, as he had to Montgomery. But like Montgomery, Eisenhower refused to sanction any German capitulation that was not complete and unconditional. He warned that if the Germans engaged in delaying tactics, he would "break off all negotiations and seal the Western Front preventing by force any further westward movement of German soldiers and civilians."

At 2:41 A.M. on May 7, 1945, in the presence of news correspondents and news cameras, at a hall in the red-bricked Reims
schoolhouse that served as SHAEF's war room, General Alfred
Jodl, Dönitz's senior emissary representing the legally consti-
tuted German authorities, signed the surrender. In attendance
were Bedell Smith, who signed on behalf of the Supreme Commander, other senior SHAEF officers, French General François
Sevez, and Russian General Ivan Susloparoff who had been
invited to witness the event to demonstrate to Stalin that the
Western Allies were not engaged in devious tricks with the
enemy.

Once the surrender documents had been signed, Jodl was
brought to Eisenhower's office, where the chain-smoking Supreme Commander had been waiting for this final fulfillment
of his mission. He asked Jodl if he understood the provisions
of the document he had signed and warned him, "You will,
officially and personally, be held responsible if the terms of this
surrender are violated." The Supreme Commander then cabled
the Combined Chiefs of Staff in Washington that his mission
had been fulfilled.

The war in Europe was over. Congratulations poured in—
from President Truman, Churchill, Brooke, and the leaders of
all the countries that made up the fledgling United Nations.
The message Eisenhower treasured most came from General
Marshall. "You have completed your mission with the greatest
victory in the history of warfare," Marshall told him. "You have
made history . . . for the good of mankind and you have stood
for all we hope for and admire in an officer of the United States
Army."

The Supreme Commander's Victory Order of the Day told
the men and women of the Allied Expeditionary Forces, "The
crusade on which we embarked . . . has reached its glorious
conclusion. . . . Working and fighting together in a single and
indestructible partnership you have achieved a perfection in
unification of air, ground and naval power that will stand as a
model in our time." But Eisenhower had not forgotten the
moments when the unity of the alliance had been far from
perfect. He added a warning in his message to the troops. "Let

us have no part in the profitless quarrels in which other men will inevitably engage as to what country, what service, won the European War."

The quarrel that persisted—and still does among historians—was not so much about which country or service won the war, but how it could have been won more efficiently, more quickly, with fewer casualties and less grief.

CHAPTER 23
In Conclusion

V ast crowds lined the streets of the City of London on June 12, 1945, to give Eisenhower the warmest reception any American had ever received in the British capital. He had gone there en route home to be granted the Freedom of London, only the fifth American ever to receive such an honor. He was received in private audience by the king and queen, another special honor, and was decorated by the king with the Order of Merit, an award restricted by tradition to a mere dozen living individuals.

No American had ever received as triumphant a welcome home as Eisenhower did a few days later. The transport plane that carried him across the Atlantic from Britain was met and escorted to National Airport in Washington by formations of fighter and bomber aircraft. Thousands of people had jammed the airport grounds to cheer as he came down the steps from the plane, and tens of thousands more lined the streets as he rode in procession to the Capitol building to address a joint session of Congress, the first general ever to do so. He told the assembled legislators of his pride in the role he had been permitted to play and paid tribute to the men and women who had served under him in the war.

The following morning, he flew to New York for the city's traditional ticker-tape parade. Three days later, it was the turn of Abilene to pay its respects with the greatest parade in its history; Eisenhower's mother and brothers in attendance. In July he was back in Germany to continue as military governor of the American Zone of the conquered country, the role he had assumed after the surrender.

Like Eisenhower, Montgomery was awarded countless honors in the euphoric postwar days. He was elevated to the peerage, taking the title Viscount Montgomery of Alamein, and was made a Knight of the Garter. In addition to also being made a Freeman of the City of London, he received a similar honor from Edinburgh and almost a score of other British cities. Eisenhower personally presented him with the American Distinguished Service Medal and he was made a Chief Commander of the U.S. Legion of Merit. The French made him a member of their Legion of Honor, as they had Eisenhower. There were awards and honors for him as well from Belgium, the Netherlands, Denmark, Poland, and other countries that had been liberated from the Germans in the war. He was awarded doctorates of law at Oxford and Cambridge. There were speeches galore and countless visits to be made, both at home and abroad.

In the immediate postwar period, Montgomery served as governor of the British Occupation Zone of Germany. At the time, both he and Eisenhower were members of the Allied Control Commission for Germany. They met from time to time, amicably and at ease, mutually respectful, no longer feeling at odds, though the views of their governments on occupation policy differed in some important respects. Indeed, Montgomery generously wrote to Eisenhower, "what a privilege and an honor it has been to serve under you. I owe much to your wise guidance and kindly forebearance. I know my own faults very well and I do not suppose I am an easy subordinate; I like to go my own way. But you have kept me on the rails in difficult and stormy times, and have taught me much. . . . I thank you for all you have done for me."

* * *

There can be no doubt that Montgomery was an extraordinary military leader. But to what effect? In Britain he is still popularly believed to have been one of the great soldiers of modern times. Flashback television documentaries on the war continue to portray him in heroic terms. When the British 7th Armoured Division was sent off on a United Nations peacekeeping mission not long ago, news reports pointed out that the division had been the Desert Rats who had gloriously thrashed Rommel under Montgomery's command in the deserts of North Africa.

He was unquestionably an extraordinary leader of men, especially during his Eighth Army desert days when he led a "brotherhoood in arms." One American general recalled, "Anybody in the British 8th Army, officer or enlisted man . . . if they heard any slur about 'Monty' in a bar or wherever it might be, there was a fist fight right there and then. His troops supported him a thousand percent."

His men had faith in him personally in a way that soldiers rarely trusted their generals. One, who had been a junior officer under his command during the war, recalled him on a dusty road "leaping from his staff car . . . to greet a group of officers or a platoon of soldiers with disarming informality, to tell us his intentions in clear and simple language, make us laugh with some absurd turn of speech, and speed us on our way with fresh hope and assurance of victory."

Montgomery was also unquestionably a supremely well-versed student of logistics and tactics. Not many generals in the war—perhaps none—were more learned than he in the procedures and mechanics of combat. He often demonstrated as much on the field of battle. When things went wrong (or right), he knew almost instinctively how and why. Eisenhower said, "In the study of enemy positions and situations and in the combining of his own armor, artillery, air, and infantry to secure tactical success against the enemy, he is careful, meticulous and certain."

Ironically, that was a big part of his problem as a commander. On the defensive, he was masterful. The enemy had the initiative but was impeccably met with whatever resources Montgomery had at his disposal. However, when he had the initiative and was planning an offensive, he was unable to appreciate how his comprehensive grasp of tactics imposed stifling constraints upon his imagination. Knowing how many troops, guns, and tanks were theoretically required to win a battle and how they should be deployed, he was almost always reluctant to engage the enemy until everything was on hand and in proper order. It was at times a wasteful exercise and often damagingly time-consuming.

The British officer and historian R. W. Thompson believed, "Few men were more enslaved by logistics" than Montgomery. He did not have to be. Had he been subject to the firm orders of a stronger, more experienced commander, his formidable tactical expertise coupled with his grasp of logistics could have been employed to far greater effect.

Much can be said for a general determined not to engage the enemy until the balance of forces is so greatly in his favor that victory is certain. In the last analysis, winning is all that matters in a battle. But for a commander to win when the odds are heavily stacked in his favor is not evidence of unrivaled expertise. Montgomery's military erudition and proficiency were repeatedly nullified by his obsessive caution and because he "lacked the instinct for surprise."

It was a failing that was transmitted to the officers who served under him. Required to act according to his standards and not risk reverses, they sometimes found their own initiative curbed and were thereby denied battlefield opportunities of the kind that many American commanders seized. They were also thereby denied a greater share of recognition and acclaim. Few people even knew the name of Miles Dempsey, though the job he held under Montgomery was equivalent to that held by the famous George Patton under Bradley.

The British historian Basil Liddell Hart believed "allowances must be made for the psychological effect on [Montgomery] of the jealousy aroused by his success, and still more by the extent to which he absorbed the limelight."

He could [said Liddell Hart] hardly fail to be aware of the
biting comments of his fellows and seniors upon what they
termed his conceit, self-advertisement, and undignified ways
of winning popularity among the troops. He must have
known that they were waiting to pounce on any tactical slip
he made. If he had suffered a serious defeat he would have
had a poor chance of survival. In his circumstances he could
afford to miss tactical opportunities but not to make a bad
mistake.

The American historian Martin Blumenson was less charitable. Though calling Montgomery adequate and competent, he
said he was "the most overrated general in the war." In view
of how his achievements contrasted with the adulation he received, this cannot be denied. That this eccentric figure would
be so ecstatically acclaimed was inevitable when he strode forcefully and boastfully into the limelight in the Egyptian desert at
a time when Britain was in desperate need of a victory and of
a military hero. Later, when America's might among the Allies
predominated overwhelmingly in the field, it became all the
more important for British pride and British interests to maintain Montgomery as something he never was and to guard the
idolized image into which he had been molded, with no little
help from himself.

His victories at Alamein and afterward in North Africa were
greatly welcomed. But they were hardly the magnificent combat
triumphs they were cracked up to be. Given the much superior
forces he could field against Rommel at the time, notably in air
power and armor, only an incompetent general could have
done much less. A more aggressive general probably would
have done more by following up the Alamein victory more
energetically. And nothing that he achieved in Sicily or Italy
testified to Montgomery's genius on the battlefield. Up to that
point, only the role he had played in closing the gap in the line
of defense during the Dunkirk evacuation at the beginning of
the war might be said to have served that purpose.

However, the Overlord invasion and campaign in Normandy,
which he commanded, told a different story. There, despite

foolishly ruining his rapport with Eisenhower by issuing a string of misleading reports, his self-defeating cockiness finally had some solid grounding. That battle did not proceed along the lines he had forecast, but in Normandy Allied troops under his direction produced the most significant single victory in the war for the Western Allies. He deserves an exalted place in the annals of modern combat for it, not only for winning, but also for stubbornly holding to his plan despite enormous pressure to deviate from it.

Montgomery's proposal for a subsequent "pencil-line" thrust northeastward while the enemy was still in disarray had much to recommend it. It was bold and imaginative and might have succeeded had he been able to persuade Eisenhower, who no longer trusted him, to allow him to proceed with it. His thwarted intention to drive on to Berlin after he had crossed the Rhine certainly would have succeeded.

Against those must be put his failure to open the port of Antwerp more quickly, as he could have done, so that the Allied drive along the northern route into Germany that he promoted so vigorously could be accelerated. Nor did his hastily conceived and executed plan for the assault at Arnhem, whatever the reasons for its defeat, bestow credit upon him. He performed with great competence during the Battle of the Bulge when the Americans lost control of the situation. But after Normandy, his claim to mastery of the battlefield had more to do with aspiration, theory, and braggadocio than prodigious achievement.

His inability to understand the need to cultivate Eisenhower's respect and friendship was a disastrous failing. Brooke's charge that the Supreme Commander was often "swayed by the last man he talked to" was not without a germ of truth, as Alexander demonstrated in North Africa and Sicily. But Montgomery's determination to confer personally with him as rarely as possible, and often haranguing him with lectures and criticism when they did meet, and in the messages he sent, was insulting and ultimately just plain boring. It made it virtually impossible for him to exercise much influence in the formulation of Allied strategy.

The clarity of his vision sometimes impressed Eisenhower. That might have produced important results for him (and the Allies) at a time when the Supreme Commander was growing ever more confident in his own role and felt increasingly empowered to act decisively without clearing his decisions higher up. But by then, whatever opportunity there had been for Montgomery to retain credibility with Eisenhower had been forfeited, despite the fact that he was best poised to strike the enemy a quick terminal blow. Toward the end, he was no longer even consulted by the Supreme Commander, only informed of what it was thought necessary for him to know.

The same was true with regard to Montgomery's relations with Supreme Allied Headquarters. By virtue of the United States' greater manpower and material contribution to the war effort, SHAEF was dominated by the Americans. But Britain had important strategic and national interests at stake, and Montgomery complained that British officers there "must realize that, in addition to being good Allied chaps, they have definite loyalties to their own side of the house." He expected them to support him in his arguments with "the Yanks." But one British officer protested, "True we were anti-Monty at SHAEF, but he created the situation. No one could get at him. . . . [W]e were appalled by his actions. . . . Used everyone he could against someone else."

If Montgomery had raised fewer hackles and had been able to persuade Eisenhower to give him the wherewithal to build a mightier head of steam when the Germans were in disarray, as their generals later confirmed, he might have proved unstoppable. As it was, Eisenhower was wise not to permit him to remain Allied ground-forces commander after Normandy, and not only because of political factors, important though those were. The field marshal's caution fetish would have made it impossible for the American commanders, conditioned by U.S. Army doctrine always to be on the attack, to serve under him for any length of time. His reluctance to consult with them in a straightforward manner would have had the same effect.

Bradley, who had praised Montgomery for his Normandy strategy, was quickly offended by his conceit and his demands and came to hate him by the end of the war, dismissing him as "a third-rate general" who "never did anything or won any battle that any other general could not have won as well or better." And Bedell Smith, who thought that "for certain types of operations he is without an equal," said Montgomery "always planned a frontal attack and it always bogged down." Smith believed finally that he could not hold a sensible conversation with him.

It is hard to imagine two more contrasting personalities than those of Montgomery and Eisenhower. Everyone, including those who considered Montgomery a superb commander, knew the field marshal was a difficult person who often treated others abominably. But everyone, including Eisenhower's critics, considered "Ike" to be an extremely likable, decent, and honorable man. Even Montgomery called him "a very great human being" who had "the power of drawing the hearts of men towards him as a magnet attracts the bits of metal."

He was emotionally highly strung and often in physical discomfort, but his fiery temper was usually under control. Knowing that "I blaze for an hour" when he got angry, he had "made it a religion never to indulge myself." Only his intimates were aware of his aches and anxieties. He generally respected views that differed from his own and was prepared to examine them without prejudice and often to be influenced by them. Partly for that reason, Brooke and Montgomery held him to be dangerously irresolute and inconsistent.

But there can be no doubt that he performed with great proficiency as managing director of the momentous Allied effort. Horrocks, who called him "a superb coordinator," said, "I do not believe that anyone else in the world could have succeeded in driving that [American-British] team to the end of the road." From an uncertain and apprehensive start, he developed gradually, despite his occasional waverings, into a truly commanding, resolute figure. General Morgan said, "He grew almost as one watched him."

He had to. In a matter of months he had been transformed from an obscure staff officer into someone authorized to make decisions of great historical consequence. He had been required to make important political decisions ever since Algeria, within days of his taking command of troops in combat for the first time in his life. Inexperience, poor guidance by advisers, and the pressures of the moment were responsible for his clumsy handling of the Darlan affair. Mistakes were made in negotiating the Italian surrender but the situation was so complicated, so urgent, and so confused by Washington that they were unavoidable. Nevertheless, he performed better in that episode than might have been expected. Though sometimes humbled by De Gaulle, Eisenhower's dealings with the imperious Free French leader probably produced more satisfactory results than if he had adhered strictly to the stream of instructions issued by the White House and the State Department. But the decision he made not to capture Berlin was a serious mistake, as he later acknowledged.

As for Eisenhower's qualities as a military commander, Brooke said "his greatest asset was a greater share of luck than most of us receive in life." No doubt good fortune did attend him, but certainly his greatest asset was something else—having at his disposal, like Montgomery at Alamein, overwhelmingly greater material resources than the enemy could muster.

However, he was too often distracted from the main task of defeating the Germans in the field by the non-military aspects of his job. All the campaigns in which he was commanding general—in French North Africa, Sicily, southern Italy, and Europe—would have benefitted from closer control and a firmer hand. With regard to the chance of winning the war quickly after Overlord and Normandy, Montgomery was right to complain in anguish that despite "a very good start . . . the Allies . . . got themselves into a most frightful muddle." Most of the responsibility for that has to fall to the Supreme Commander.

After the Normandy breakout, Eisenhower was primarily to blame for allowing his relations with Montgomery to grow complicated and confused. He was advised at SHAEF to "Give him orders instead of arguing; never get into an argument with Monty because you are likely to lose it." He neither argued with Montgomery nor gave him firm orders until the closing phase of the war, when it was too late for them to employ their respective skills dynamically in tandem.

A commander of George Marshall's character and experience would have been more likely to keep his mind focused on the main task. An ideal team at SHAEF would have been Marshall as Supreme Commander and Eisenhower as his chief of staff, a job his experience and qualities would have permitted him to do more effectively. Though Marshall insisted that the Americans not be upstaged by the British on the field of battle, if he himself had been Supreme Commander, Montgomery's considerable talents as a military scientist might have been far better harnessed for an earlier victory over Germany than was finally achieved.

After victory in Europe, Eisenhower served as military governor of the American Zone of occupied Germany for a mere six months. In November 1945, he returned to Washington to succeed Marshall as U.S. Army Chief of Staff. He had dreaded taking on that job, and his forebodings proved justified. He no longer was under the nerve-racking pressures he had endured as Supreme Commander, but it was largely a disagreeable time for him. The United States, the only major combatant nation to emerge from the war stronger than before, was anxiously seeking to adjust to a peacetime existence. The military was peripheral to that task.

Eisenhower's prime task was to superintend the orderly dismemberment of the largest army in American history at a time when the public and Congress demanded that the process be vastly accelerated despite the opening skirmishes of the Cold War with the Soviet Union. His experience of interservice rivalry led him to press for far greater coordination among the army, navy, and air force, but vested interests in the three services frustrated his efforts. After a little more than two years of battling in vain to streamline the American armed forces, he'd had enough.

In February 1948, he resigned as U.S. Chief of Staff to accept one of the many offers he received of prominent positions in civilian life—to become president of Columbia University in New York City. After assuming that role, he was disappointed to discover that he was expected to lend his considerable reputation to the task of fund-raising for the university. Indeed, some of those responsible for his appointment had assumed that this would be his major function as university president. He himself had believed that the job would be largely a sinecure in which he would be able to relax after the years of pressure. He was not comfortable in academia and spent a good deal of time away from the university, playing golf, visiting friends, and just vacationing. He remained a popular public figure and was invited to address audiences across the country.

In 1950, he took a leave of absence from Columbia to become Supreme Commander of the recently formed North Atlantic Treaty Organization, with headquarters in Paris. His task, which he performed with characteristic chairman-of-the-board efficiency, was to mold the member countries into a military alliance capable of withstanding the Soviet threat in Europe. It was not an easy job. Upon his arrival in Paris, he found, "The confusion and the irritations . . . multiplied by the hazy, almost chimerical character of the organization to which I am officially responsible. . . . [T]here is no budget, not even for housekeeping, and there is no clear line to follow in getting . . . things accomplished."

But his ability to get people of divergent interests and different personalities to work together proved extremely useful. He was greatly aided by the intense dread of Soviet Communism and military might among the NATO member nations, and the organization was soon forged into a credible instrument with which to fight the Cold War.

To growing doubts, he continued to deny that he entertained political ambitions. In 1948, while at Columbia University, he had rejected suggestions that he stand as the Republican candidate for president. Nevertheless, some of the officers who had served under him suspected that he could easily be lured onto the political stage. Several prominent businessmen and industrialists who had become his friends considered that he would be eminently qualified to be the next occupant of the White

House after Harry Truman. Many eminent figures in the Republican Party felt the same way. His continuing high-profile popularity was seen as guaranteeing the presidential electoral victory the Republicans had not enjoyed for almost twenty-five years.

While he was fashioning NATO into shape in Europe, the groundwork was laid for his nomination as Republican candidate, which he accepted in 1952 when it was formally offered to him. The United States was again at war, this time in Korea. Eisenhower's Democratic Party opponent, Adlai Stevenson, a man of considerable intelligence and wit, stood no chance against America's most prominent Second World War hero and was easily defeated by the man from Abilene, as he was again four years later.

Like Eisenhower, Montgomery went on to greater rewards after serving as commander of British occupation forces in Germany. When Brooke retired as Chief of the Imperial General Staff a year after the end of the war, Montgomery was chosen to succeed him despite the opposition of some in the War Office who did not hold him in high regard or objected to his eccentricities.

It was not a successful appointment. The new CIGS was not accustomed to holding lengthy give-and-take conferences, being subjected to the views of others, and humoring politicians. He had little enthusiasm for contemplating long-range, politically charged strategy rather than the deployment of divisions and armor and set-piece battles in which armies clashed and one side won and the other side lost. He could no longer be cushioned from disagreeable aspects of the outside world by a cadre of handpicked, reverential junior officers.

Britain was a much different place from what it had been before. The war and its devastations had taken their toll, as had historical evolution. The British Empire that had nurtured Montgomery as a young soldier was in decline. Bits of it had already begun splintering off. The United States and the Soviet Union were now the superpowers. It was difficult for Montgomery to accept the realities of his country's diminished status and role.

Like almost everyone else he did not like the arrival of the
nuclear age, but for reasons of his own. As the Cold War intensified, and mutual atomic destruction appeared to be a genuine
threat, he chose to insist that atomic weapons were overrated.
They did not fit his rules of battle, which involved the deployment of infantry, the thrust of armor, and the support of artillery and air cover. As a general who had always insisted that
preparation for battle be reduced to "essentials," he found the
essentials of combat in the atomic age nothing like he had ever
imagined they could be. He was, however, right and most
others were wrong when he maintained that despite fears in
the West and his own insistence on maintaining strong defenses
in western Europe, the Soviets were too weak to risk going to
war again.

He still was unable to deal harmoniously with equals on military matters. As Chief of the Imperial General Staff, he attempted to lord it over Tedder, who now was RAF Chief of
Staff, and Cunningham, now head of the Royal Navy. Without
bothering to consult them, he sometimes made statements or
took actions with regard to matters that should have been the
province of all the chiefs of staff. He chose to meet with them as
rarely as possible, and sometimes deliberately absented himself
from scheduled chiefs of staff meetings.

The new Labour government that had replaced Churchill and
his Conservatives at war's end contained figures who had
feared that the popular Montgomery might turn into a Napole-
onic demagogue. But the British were not susceptible to the
clarion call of military leaders, and in any case, Montgomery
was issuing none. But he regularly clashed with ministers on
military matters and on the policing of the Empire. He was
unable to accept that terrorists and troublemakers might now
sometimes be considered part of national liberation movements
and that a methodical crackdown by British forces might no
longer suffice in dealing with them. But aside from participating
in occasional House of Lords debates, he pointedly shunned a
political role for himself.

In 1948, Britain, France, and the Benelux nations had formed
the West European Union, a defensive alliance designed to

meet the challenge of Soviet pressure in the east. As the most distinguished soldier in the alliance, Montgomery was appointed chairman of its Commanders-in-Chief Committee. That was preliminary to the formation of the wider and more powerful North Atlantic Treaty Organization to which Montgomery was appointed Deputy Supreme Commander, again serving under Eisenhower though convinced that Eisenhower once more was out of his depth in devising strategy on how to defend Europe if the Cold War turned hot.

But the relationship between them was totally different from what it had been during the war. Eisenhower was now "up in the stratosphere" in a way that Brooke could not have imagined when he first thought of isolating him there during the Tunisia campaign. Not only did he represent the nation through whose generous Marshall Plan subsidies the economies of Western Europe had been saved from collapse, and whose support shielded them from the threat of Soviet domination, but it was no secret at the time that the new NATO commander was likely soon to be a candidate for president of the United States and it was generally believed that he would be elected.

Eisenhower conferred with prime ministers and presidents, employing his influence and organizational skills to weld together the Western military alliance and to ease the process of accepting defeated Germany into it. Montgomery, back closer to the essentials of the science of war, was content to be the planner, studying how the comparative handful of divisions that the NATO nations were prepared to commit to Western defenses could best be deployed against the larger number the Soviets could put in the field. He toured, wrote, lectured, and badgered, pressing for greater military commitment from the NATO countries. He reviewed strategy, training procedures, and combat-readiness with all concerned. To his regret, he came to accept that the West would have to rely on nuclear weapons rather than his precious battlefield tactics if it came to a showdown.

Between 1951 and 1958, Mongomery served under three NATO Supreme Commanders who succeeded Eisenhower. In recognition of the superior military might of the United States in the alliance, all of them were American—Matthew Ridgway, Alfred Gruenther, and Lauris Norstadt. He got along passably well with all except Ridgway, with whom his relations were severely strained.

He remained his arrogant self, to be counted on for occasional, seemingly deliberate tactlessness. After retiring from public office as one of his country's most distinguished figures, he became a self-appointed British ambassador, visiting Russia, China, South Africa, and other countries, conferring with foreign leaders and making sometimes controversial public statements about them to the annoyance and embarrassment of the Foreign Office. However, he remained a greatly honored, highly respected figure. He still drew a crowd whenever he appeared in public. He had written and continued to write extensively about his wartime commands. His comments on a wide range of military and political subjects were solicited and he was often invited to appear on radio and television programs. He was much sought after in distinguished circles and developed a côterie of politically and socially distinguished acquaintances and even developed some friendships among them, though he remained very much a loner, preferring his own company to that of others.

Criticism of some of his comments, and also of his generalship in the war, began to surface in public, particularly in America. He chose not to notice it. Eisenhower did the same. But he did not shun controversy; it was still not in his character to do so. Still trying to convince his former Supreme Commander that the war in Europe should have been fought differently, Montgomery sent him a copy of a lecture he had given on the subject. Eisenhower apparently did not read it—"I will finish it as soon as I get an opportunity," he wrote—but he sent his thanks for the courtesy, adding, "My blood-pressure went up very considerably the other day to read in an American magazine that I 'disliked' you. My first reaction was to write to the editor and tell him what a skunk and a liar he is, but on second thought it seemed to me that to take notice of such a silly falsehood would be simply playing into the hands of some newspaper gossip."

At times Montgomery appeared to have mellowed with age. The cheers of the crowd, the attentions of celebrities, the gratitude of the nation, and the countless honors made him less obsessed with mounting aggressive guard over his own status and reputation. But one of his biographers, an admirer of his wartime achievements, said he retained "a malicious desire to deride, diminish, downgrade the achievements of others." And his conceit remained undiluted. Asked to name the three geatest generals in history, he said, "The other two were Alexander the Great and Napoleon."

Even those who thought highly of Montgomery were astonished by his shabby treatment of General De Guingand. The field marshal generously allowed that he "could not possibly have handled the gigantic task" with which he had been entrusted in the war without the support of his highly efficient, overworked chief of staff. "Freddie" had served him loyally and capably in the desert and Europe. He had saved Montgomery from disgrace when Eisenhower was about to have him relieved of command after the Battle of the Bulge. On several other occasions, he had eased friction between the field marshal and SHAEF. It therefore seemed strange when, at the end of the war, for no apparent reason he barred De Guingand from the surrender-signing ceremony on Lüneburg Heath, the "historic moment" toward which they had striven together ever since Alam Halfa in North Africa, and then failed to make provision for him to be on the reviewing platform for the victory parade in London, though arrangements were made for others to be there.

Worse was to come for De Guingand. He was not well. He had long been of fragile health. Serving under Montgomery had not contributed to his well-being. But when he took sick leave after the war, Montgomery urged him to return to duty. He said he wanted him to become the British Army's Director of Military Intelligence. It was to be preliminary to his becoming Vice Chief of the Imperial General Staff when Montgomery formally assumed the position of CIGS. Because of his poor health, De Guingand was disinclined to take the job. But the offer, which would include the rank of lieutenant general, "a tremendous jump for a junior Major-General, whose permanent rank at that time was only that of a Colonel," was too attractive to turn down. However, when Montgomery did become CIGS, he told De Guingand that he had changed his mind and that another general was to be his deputy.

De Guingand then left the army, but not only did the influential Montgomery offer him no assistance in finding a suitable civilian job with which he could earn a living, he made no effort to have his temporary general's rank made permanent. Instead, De Guingand was to be reduced to his permanent rank of colonel, a matter affecting both his status and his pension. The War Office permitted him to retain the rank of major general only after the outraged Bedell Smith and Eisenhower intervened on his behalf, apparently a matter that Montgomery viewed with total indifference. Still later, he humiliated De Guingand by failing to invite him to a twenty-fifth anniversary commemoration of the battle at Alamein in which his shamefully slighted chief of staff had played a key role.

Why the field marshal treated a man who had served him well and faithfully so abominably is difficult to understand. However badly he might behave with others, he had always been considerate where his own officers and troops were concerned. Many of them testified to his kindness and solicitude. It may be that, by saving Montgomery from possible disgrace when Eisenhower was about to have him relieved of his command in Europe, De Guingand had to be punished. He was a living reminder of a humiliation the field marshal preferred to have wiped from memory.

Montgomery never lost his capacity to offend. In May 1957, he was a guest, at his own request, at President Eisenhower's Gettysburg farm. During that visit, Eisenhower took him on a tour of the nearby battlefields where armies of the Union and the Confederacy had clashed bloodily during the American Civil War a century earlier. On the tour, Montgomery suggested that General Robert E. Lee should have been fired for the way the forces of the Confederacy had been commanded during the battle of Gettysburg, and he urged Eisenhower to agree with him. Never shy of the limelight, he did it so loudly that reporters trailing them would be certain to hear. In view of the high regard and profound affection with which Lee was held in the South, it was ungracious behavior, especially for a foreign visitor, and it was impudent to put the president of the United States in so awkward a position.

Eisenhower was miffed and refused to argue with Montgomery on the subject or say anything at all about it. That was taken as the president's courteous reluctance to take issue with his distinguished guest, especially since Montgomery had extracted from him an invitation to spend the next three days at the White House. It appeared as though he and Montgomery had weathered their wartime differences and that the two old soldiers liked each other personally.

But not for long. A little more than eighteen months later, on January 1, 1959, Eisenhower, who had by then been president for seven years, issued a strange instruction. He wanted letters sent to Bradley and several other American and British generals who had served under him in the war, inviting them to gather at Camp David, the presidential retreat in Maryland.

The object of the gathering would be to discuss what really happened in the liberation of Europe and the conquest of Germany fifteen years earlier. It could not be said that the president had so much time on his hands that he wanted to devote more than a week to chewing over battle tales with a handful of old comrades. Eisenhower wanted the meeting (which, upon reflection, he decided against) because he was once more furious with Montgomery.

The field marshal's memoirs had just been published and had provoked much controversy. The Italians were outraged by the suggestion in the book that their troops were cowards and their generals unreliable. Montgomery was pressured by the British government to offer an "explanation" to the Italian prime minister through the British Foreign Office. The memoirs also included the derisive claim that General Auchinleck, when Commander-in-Chief, Middle East, had planned to retreat in Egypt rather than face Rommel down at Alamein, as Montgomery proceeded to do after Auchinleck was relieved of his command. Auchinleck angrily denied this publicly, and it touched off a heated debate that threatened to find its way into a court of law. Montgomery's publishers felt obliged ultimately to insert a note retracting the disputed claim, though Montgomery himself said he could not see what the fuss was about.

What triggered Eisenhower's fury was Montgomery's public disclosure in his memoirs of how little the field marshal had thought of him as his commander during the war. In contrasting the decisions that were made with what he thought should have been done, it was obvious that he considered the Supreme Commander to have been incompetent as a strategist and responsible for avoidable mistakes that had made prolongation of the war inevitable. He said Eisenhower had pursued a strategy that was "expensive in life," implying thereby that many more American, British, and other Allied troops had been killed than had been necessary to achieve victory.

The book containing those charges had been in the works when Montgomery had enjoyed the president's hospitality at Gettysburg and Washington. He had said nothing about them at the time. But with a display of his extraordinary insensitivity, he sent the White House a copy of the book when it appeared and was surprised by what seemed to him a discourteous lack of response to this friendly gesture. He received not so much as an acknowledgment of the book's receipt. He drew his own conclusion about that. He gloatingly wrote to a former aide, "Apparently Ike has come to realise that he will not go down in history as a great President; he accepts that. But he reckoned his place in history as a 'Captain of War' was secure. My book has demolished that."

Nor was Montgomery content to convey such sentiments in private, or let his writings speak for themselves. During a CBS television interview shortly afterward, he claimed that Eisenhower, though Allied Supreme Commander in the invasion of France, had never been able to understand his plan for defeating the German armies in Normandy, the most crucial battle in the war. He also again criticized Eisenhower's strategy for defeating the Germans and once more suggested that it had been responsible for the needless deaths of thousands of "American boys."

Eisenhower made no public rebuttal, but no secret was made by the White House of the fact that he was incensed. He abandoned his long-held decision to keep to himself what he thought of Montgomery as a soldier. In a letter to Lord Ismay, he wrote of his low regard for his generalship during the war, of his impatience with the Eighth Army's slow advance in Sicily, of Montgomery's failure to fulfill the "great promises that he made during the planning for Overlord about moving quickly . . . beyond Caen," and of "his preposterous proposal to drive on a single pencil-line thrust straight on to Berlin. . . . I cannot forget," Eisenhower told Ismay, "his readiness to belittle associates in those critical moments when the cooperation of all of us was needed."

Among those distressed by the falling out between the two famous warrior chiefs was the ever-tolerant De Guingand, who had always gotten on well with Eisenhower. De Guingand wrote to the president suggesting that the field marshal, who was about to visit Canada, should be invited to visit Eisenhower again for a reconciliation. The president replied that it was not a good idea. To Cornelius Ryan, Eisenhower said, "Montgomery had become so personal in his efforts to make sure that the Americans—and me, in particular—got no credit, that, in fact, we hardly had anything to do with the war, that I finally stopped talking to him."

There was a cool, brief meeting between them at the American embassy in London when President Eisenhower threw a party for his old British comrades in arms. But aside from brief separate appearances on the same television program on the war, the two most famous soldiers of the Western Allies never had anything more to do with each other.

ACKNOWLEDGMENTS

I am much obliged to many people who provided assistance and advice while this study was being researched and written. In the United States, they include Dwight E. Strandberg and other members of the staff of the Dwight D. Eisenhower Library in Abilene, Kansas; David Keough and Richard Sommers at the Military History Institute at Carlisle, Pennsylvania; John Taylor of the Military Reference Branch of the National Archives in Washington, D.C.; and staffs of the Library of Congress in Washington and of the Forty-second Street branch of the New York Public Library.

In London, they include members of the staffs of the Printed Books and Documents sections of the Imperial War Museum; the Public Records Office at Kew, the library of the National Army Museum, the British Library at the British Museum, the Special Collection section of the West Hill Branch of the London Public Library in Wandsworth, the London Library, and the Liddell Hart Centre for Military Archives at King's College, where Kate O'Brien was of particular assistance.

I am grateful also to the late Lieutenant General Sir Ian Jacob, who kindly gave me permission to quote from his diaries, as well as to John Pimlott, historian at the Royal Military Academy at Sandhurst, and to Captain Malachi Doran of Alamein Company at the Academy.

None of the above necessarily share the views expressed in this study and any mistakes are, of course, all my own.

Once again, my wife, Barbara Gelb, provided invaluable moral support and incisive advice.

—NG

ENDNOTES

Abbreviations:

BD—Harry Butcher Diary, Eisenhower Memorial Library, Abilene.

DDE—Pre-presidential Papers, Principal File, Box 53, Eisenhower Memoral Library.

EP—*The Papers of Dwight David Eisenhower: The War Years*. Five Volumes published by Johns Hopkins Press, Baltimore, 1970–1972.

IWM—Montgomery Papers, Imperial War Museum.

L-H—Liddell Hart Centre for Military Archives, King's College, London.

MM—Bernard Montgomery, *Memoirs*, published by Collins in London, 1958.

NA—National Archives, Washington.

OCMH—Office of the Chief of Military History Collection, Military History Institute, Carlisle, Pennsylvania.

OH—Oral History transcript, Eisenhower Memorial Library.

PRO—Public Records Office, Kew, London.

Books by John Eisenhower and David Eisenhower as well as Dwight Eisenhower are noted below (and in the following selected bibliography.) For purposes of simplicity, those identified simply as "Eisenhower" in these endnotes refer to the general's wartime memoirs,

Crusade in Europe. The number before each endnote refers to the page on which the material appears.

Full information on sources cited in brief will be found in the Selected Bibliography.

1. IKE AND MONTY

12. "Damn it": *The New York Times*, November 2, 1958.
12. "There are few cases": De Guingand, *Generals*, p. 192.
12. "a little man on the make": Chalfont, p. 218.
13. "to an exceptional degree": London *Times*, March 27, 1976.
13. "that intensely compacted": Howarth, p. 11.
13. "the greatest field commander": Barnett, p. 266
13. "Nice chap; no general": Gelb, p. 299.
14. "wouldn't go into": OH, Eisenhower.
14. "poring over problems": BD.

2. ORIGINS

22. "Smoking in room": Dwight Eisenhower, *At Ease*, p. 12.
26. "For the first time": MM, p. 20.
26. "developed a streak": Moorehead, p. 33.
26. "There were some": Hugh Thomas, *The Story of Sandhurst*. London: Hutchinson, 1961.

3. WEST POINT TO WAR DEPARTMENT

30. "I was curious about": Dwight Eisenhower, op. cit., p. 24.
33. "missed the boat": Ibid., p. 155.
34. "The tank": Davis, p. 187.
37. "one of the most capable": Ambrose, *Soldier*, p. 77.
40. "minimum of performance": Ferrell, p. 11.
42. "The Chief says": Ibid., p. 39

4. SANDHURST TO DUNKIRK

44. "A great number": Moorehead, p. 44.
44. "as good material": MM, p. 29.
46. "I was not taking": Moorehead, p. 48.
46. "about the Army": MM, 31.
47. "ghosts of the Somme": James Leasor, *War at the Top*. London: Michael Joseph, 1959, p. 329.
47. "as hard as I could": MM, p. 33.
49. "nonsense": Moorehouse, p. 61.
50. "a bit of a bolshevik": Ibid.

50. "thoroughly bad": MM, p. 40.
50. "degrading for us soldiers": Brian Montgomery, p. 182.
51. "entranced. . . .": Morgan, *Peace*, p. 128.
52. "You cannot marry": Brian Montgomery, p. 196.
53. "You cannot make": De Guingand, *Operation*, p. 166.
53. "Which is it to be": Ibid.
54. "unmercifully": Hamilton, Volume I, p. 201.
54. "too much staff work": Moorehead, p. 70.
56. "Definitely above the average": Ibid., p. 84.
58. "My married life": Ibid, p. 91.
59. "He was probably": Horrocks, *Life*, p. 78.
59. "His vigorous": Lord Carver, *Seven Ages of the British Army*.
    London: Weidenfeld and Nicolson, 1984, p. 230.
61. "[T]he British Army": MM, p. 49.
63. "withdraw Monty": Bryant, *Tide*, p. 83.
63. "any further errors": Ibid., p. 82.
63. "he was apt": Ibid., p. 83.
63. "wigging from Brookie": Thompson, *Legend*, p. 79.
63. "I had several": Bryant, op. cit.
66. "a task": Ibid., p. 138.
66. "I thanked heaven": Ibid.
68. "the whole world, including the United States": *Hansard's*, June
    18, 1940.
69. "rather loose criticism": IWM.
69. "one by one": MM, p. 67.
70. "Let them give me some": Ibid., p. 69.
70. "I was disturbed." Lewin, p. 38.

5. TESTING TIME IN WASHINGTON
75. "a cold fish": Brendon, p. 75.
77. "may excuse failure": Eisenhower, p. 25.
77. "We must take risks": Ibid.
77. "Do your best": Ibid.
77. "I must have assistants": Ambrose, *Commander*, p. 6.
78. "Just to give you": EP, p. 33.
79. "In many ways": Ferrell, p. 44.
80. "What a gang to work with": Ibid., p. 48.
81. "They are difficult": Ibid., p. 40.
82. "We were more": OH, Handy.
82. "drop everything else": Ferrell, p. 43.
83. "[I]f we should decide": Eisenhower, p. 31.
84. "Tempers are short": EP, p. 39.
84. "a personal disappointment": Ibid., p. 142.

84. "shut off all business": Ferrell, p. 51.
85. "We've got to go to Europe": EP, p. 66.
86. "With the situation prevailing": Bryant, op. cit., p. 357.
87. "that—at long last": EP, p. 260.
87. "an uneasy feeling": Ibid., p. 315.
87. "It is necessary": Ibid., p. 328.
88. "a tough, intensive grind": Ibid., p. 343.
88. "I'm going to command": Alden Hatch, *Red Carpet for Mamie Eisenhower*. New York: Popular Library, 1954, p. 146.
89. "I'm sorry I'm late": Miller, p. 359.
89. "a decisive type": Ferrell, p. 59.
89. "was furious": Summersby, ibid., p. 25.

6. WHIRLWIND IN SOUTHERN ENGLAND
90. "a distinctly peace-time": Horrocks, *Life*, p. 98.
91. "I am sorry": Moorehead, p. 107.
91. "Sit down, gentlemen": Ibid., p. 99.
92. "Nations have passed away": MM, p. 71.
92. "Let him die": Horrocks, op. cit., p. 98.
92. "Commanders and staff officers": MM, p. 71.
93. "shook away the cobwebs": Lewin, p. 39.
94. "Army commanders": Horrocks, *Life*, p. 99.
95. "Our army is the mockery": David Dilks, editor, *The Diaries of Sir Alexander Cadogan*. London: Cassell, 1971, p. 433.
96. "From what you tell me": Malone, p. 10.
97. "Kick him out at once": Ibid.

7. EISENHOWER EMERGES FROM OBSCURITY
99. "military and economic strength": Davis, p. 309.
100. "considered generally to be": *The New York Times*, June 26, 1942.
100. "a lack of confidence": EP, p. 364.
100. "quite certain": Ibid., p. 360.
100. "no alibis or excuses": Ibid.
100. "What concerned the commanding general": Butcher, p. 4.
101. "I don't know": Ibid., p. 21.
101. "talked informally": *The New York Times*, June 26, 1942.
102. "correspondents with experience": Davis, p. 38.
104. "the fartingest war": Summersby, *Past Forgetting*, p. 43.
105. "Why don't they": Butcher, p. 86.
107. "I cannot tell you": EP, p. 369.
110. "half-baked": Library of Congress, Henry Stimson Diary, reel 7, volume 38.

111. "Russia [he told Marshall]": EP, p. 393.
112. "we might have taken": EP, p. 424.
113. "least harmful diversion": Pogue, *Ordeal*, p. 346
113. "vicissitudes of war": NA, OPD Executive Files, Box 2, Item 7.

8. AFRICA BECKONS MONTGOMERY
115. "The whole thing": MM, p. 77.
118. "seasoned soldiers": Churchill, Volume IV, p. 343.
118. "won't fight": Lord Moran, *Winston Churchill*. London: Constable, 1966, p. 38.
118. "We have a very daring": Hamilton, op. cit., p. 521.
119. ". . . in present circumstances": PRO, CAB 56/92.
119. "before Auchinleck can": Bryant, *Tide*, p. 441.
120. "Rommel, Rommel, Rommel": Diary of Sir Ian Jacob.
120. "I must emphasize": Blaxland, p. 23.
121. "of being able to handle": MM, p. 77.
121. "Montgomery [Churchill wrote]": Churchill, op. cit., p. 420.

9. FORGING OPERATION TORCH
123. "complete control of North Africa": Howe, p. 16.
123. "Our target": Eisenhower, p. 81.
124. "Ordinarily [Eisenhower later wrote]": Ibid., p. 86.
125. "It is so easy": EP, p. 422.
125. "I cannot tell you": David, p. 23.
126. "From General Ike's": Butcher, p. 73.
127. "[W]e didn't know": OH, Handy.
129. "those men will be going in": Clark, p. 61.
129. "Ike personally torn": BD.
130. "drastic measures": Butcher, p. 54.
130. "[I]f the expedition flops": BD.
130. "[T]his business of warfare": EP, p. 617.
131. "We are here": Butcher, p. 42.
133. "I live a hectic day": EP, p. 587.
133. "impatient, tired and nervous": Miller, p. 385.
134. "she took his mind": Ibid., p. 378.
134. "to win over as many": David Eisenhower, p. 342.
135. "listened with a kind": Murphy, p. 136.
136. "sitting ducks": Miller, p. 403.
136. "Ike felt pretty low": Butcher, p. 123.
136. "state of jitters": Ibid., p. 124.
136. "both encouraging and discouraging": EP, p. 627.
137. "As you can well imagine": EP, p. 606.

10. RESHAPING A DESERT ARMY

140. "issuing orders to an Army": MM, p. 103.
141. "Burn the lot": De Guingand, *Generals*, p. 188.
142. "here we will stand": De Guingand, *Operation*, p. 136.
142. "We all felt": Ibid.
142. "he followed the same": Malone, p. 44.
143. "The wise commander": Lewin, p. 80.
144. "One was impressed": Howarth, p. 28.
144. "gaberdine swine": Richardson, *Flashback*, p. 98.
145. "bellyaching": De Guingand, *Operation*, p. 138.
145. "[T]here had grown up": Horrocks, *Life*, p. 120.
146. "gallant band of knights": MM, p. 531.
146. "aren't fighting properly": Howarth, p. 58.
147. "Under that penetrating gaze": Ibid.
147. "for nearly two hours": Churchill, Volume VI, p. 363.
148. "the most abominable bestiality": Howarth, p. 75.
148. "had to . . . admire him": Ibid., p. 123.
148. " 'Monty,' he later recalled": Nigel Nicolson, p. 164.
149. "I couldn't have had": Richardson, *Flashback*, p. 281.
149. "a grand chap": Brooks, p. 267.
150. "As a commander": Howarth, p. 178.
151. "not in a fit condition": Hart, *Rommel Papers*, p. 271.
151. "The whole plan": Lewin, p. 57.
152. "placed particular reliance": Hart, *History*, p. 304.
154. "He knew": Bryant, *Tide*, p. 478.
154. "would result in Rommel": Ibid., p. 505.
155. "The Prime Minister must win": Hamilton, op. cit., p. 746.
155. "stock was rather high": MM, p. 117.

11. EL ALAMEIN

156. "Of course I knew nothing": Richardson, *Flashback*, p. 280.
158. "1. When I assumed": MM, p. 127.
158. "passed just like any other": Lewin, p. 67.
161. "The enemy's superiority": Hart, *Rommel Papers*, p. 310.
161. "The 10th Corps commander": MM, p. 129.
161. "Determined leadership": PRO, WO 214/19.
162. "The tanks *will* go through": Chalfont, p. 187.
163. "What [Churchill asked him]": Bryant, *Tide*, p. 512.
163. "from a desperate feeling": Ibid., p. 513.
164. "has tended to obscure": Hart, *History*, p. 315.
164. "Air raid after air raid": Hart, *Rommel Papers*, p. 317.
164. "It is with trusting confidence": Ibid., p. 321.

165. "Lord Mighty in Battle": IWM, reel 8.
165. "I won't shake hands": Peterson, Edward, *The American Occupation of Germany.* Detroit: Wayne State University Press, 1977, p. 55.
165. "Poor von Thoma": Chalfont, p. 217.
166. "Eighth Army has inflicted": Gilbert, p. 247.
166. "I have defeated the enemy": *Time*, February 1, 1943.
166. "Great News": *Daily Express*, November 5, 1942.
166. "some cracking good news": Hamilton, Volume II, p. 3.
166. "brilliant lieutenant": Gilbert, p. 248.
167. "The enemy has just reached": Lewin, p. 95.
167. "there was no pursuit": Ibid., p. 94.
167. "quite satisfied": Hart, *History*, p. 360.
168. "We never went into battle": Barnett, p. 268.
169. "[W]e have intervals": Lewin, p. 102.
169. "The British commander": Hart, ibid.
169. "lack of resolute decision": Ibid., p. 329.
169. "blown up out of proportion": Hamilton, volume II, p. 403.
169. "Never has there been": Harold Nicolson, *Diaries and Letters*, Volume II. London: Collins, 1967, p. 342.
170. "there is a certain anxiety": Ibid., p. 268.
170. "Before Alamein we never": Churchill, Volume IV, p. 541.

12. TORCH UNDER WAY
171. "Seems to be coming true": Butcher, p. 143.
172. "the most dismal setting": Eisenhower, p. 106.
172. "If I stay underground": *The New York Times*, December 22, 1942.
172. "The eternal darkness": Eisenhower, p. 105.
172. "Never in my wildest dreams": *The New York Times*, ibid.
172. "the Rock of Gibraltar": Butcher, p. 143.
173. "of vital importance": EP, p. 580.
174. "our radios constantly": Eisenhower, p. 110.
174. "I wanted to proceed": Ibid., p. 111.
176. "General Giraud": Ibid., p. 112.
176. "be a spectator": Ibid.
177. "the direct intervention": Brendon, p. 92.
177. "Secrecy in advance": United States Navy Historical Center, Washington, CINCLANT, Serial 0014, January 9, 1943.
179. "I've promised Giraud": EP, p. 677.
181. "can only be": PRO, PREM 3/442/2.
181. "revolting" and "disgusting": Butcher, p. 193.
182. "I have developed": EP, p. 724.

182. "Darlan has been billed": Butcher, p. 173.
182. "kiss Darlan's stern": Ibid., p. 151.
182. "I am simply trying": EP, p. 734.
183. "Foremost": Eisenhower, p. 121.
183. "Many things done": John Eisenhower, p. 66.
184. "until the military situation": Butcher, p. 185.
184. "Fascist organizations": PRO, op. cit.
184. "idealistic as hell": Harold Macmillan, *The Blast of War*. London: Macmillan, 1967, p. 221.
184. "why these long haired": Ibid.
184. "I have been called": EP, p. 1084.
185. "vexatious problems": David, p. 64.
185. "He may think": Pogue, *Organizer*, p. 35.
186. "I kept a firm hand": Blaxland, p. 81.
186. "no mad rush": Ibid., p. 130.
187. "overcautious": Hart, *History*, p. 360.
189. "ill at ease": OH, Coningham.
190. "Though a man": Diary of Sir Ian Jacobs.
190. "Eisenhower seemed": Bryant, *Tide*, p. 527.
190. "like a caged tiger": Butcher, p. 206.
191. "Mud is a silly alibi": Ibid., p. 211.
191. "The boss's neck": Summersby, *Past Forgetting*, p. 93.
191. "eroded Ike's confidence": Bradley, *General's*, p. 124.
191. "walking pneumonia": Ibid.
192. "delegate your international": Ambrose, *Commander*, p. 148.
192. "sudden tragic": EP, p. 861.
193. "had neither the tactical": Bryant, *Tide*, p. 556.
193. "We were pushing": Ibid.
194. "It is my responsibility": EP, p. 944.
194. "overwork himself": Butcher, p. 213.
195. "You must realize": John Eisenhower, op. cit., p. 99.
197. "very alert": Blumenson, *Patton Papers*, p. 171.
197. "bronzed warriors": Bryant, *Tide*, p. 577.
197. "saw several tears": Ibid., p. 578.
197. "After the war": Charles Eade, editor. *The War Speeches of Winston Churchill*, Volume II, London: Cassell, 1952, p. 404.
197. "Your feats will gleam": Blaxland, p. 148.
197. "Since the battle": Playfair, p. 238.
199. "The American troops": Blaxland, p. 193.
199. "Rommel attacked me": Bryant, *Tide*, p. 588.
200. "General situation": Playfair, p. 304.
200. "Am doubtful Anderson": Ibid.
201. "I am disturbed": Pogue, *Organizer*, p. 183.

202. "a certain type of reporter": EP, p. 1019.
202. "that all U.S. personnel": Bradley, *General's*, p. 146.
202. "together as a powerful corps": EP, p. 1090.
203. "we have not played": Butcher, p. 244.
203. "at each other's throats": EP, p. 1020.
203. "just a childish fantasy": Ernest Harmon, *Combat Commander*. Englewood, New Jersey: Prentice-Hall, 1970, p. 130.
203. "In Africa, we learned": Bradley, ibid., p. 159.
204. "Montgomery is of different": Ibid., p. 165.
204. "I like Eisenhower": Hamilton, p. 213.
205. "very much left": Lewin, p. 139.
205. "The pace has been": L-H, Alanbrooke papers.
205. "the final Dunkirk": Playfair, p. 402.
206. "Sink, burn, destroy": Blaxland, p. 258.
206. "It is a strange experience": Lewin, p. 177.
206. "Please send Fortress": Ibid., p. 139.
207. "pray for you every night": *Time*, February 1, 1943.
208. "if I were pretty popular": MM, p. 183.
208. "I'm worried about Monty": *Observer*, August 30, 1992.
208. "In defeat unbeatable": Edward Marsh. *Ambrosia and Small Beer*. London: Longmans, 1964, p. 259.

13. OMENS
210. "utterly cold": Butcher, p. 259.
212. "we will not tolerate": Ambrose, *Commander*, p. 198.
213. "I am quite sure": EP, p. 1212.
213. "the paramount task": PRO, CAB 88/8.
214. "suddenly . . . we nip": D'Este, p. 79.
214. "I am not so": EP, p. 928.
215. "It is clear that": IWM, reel 4.
216. "Montgomery [he observed]": Bryant, *Tide*, p. 640.
217. "General Montgomery is": Ferrell, p. 91.
217. "like an orchestra": IWM, reel 4.
217. "little guidance": Bradley, *General's*, p. 163.
218. "[I]f substantial German": EP, p. 1047.
218. "If [he declared]": Gilbert, p. 379.
219. "begins wrestling with his problems": Butcher, p. 260.
219. "In my youthful days": David, p. 125.
219. "breaks every commonsense rule": Lewin, p. 151.
219. "I am afraid": Tedder, p. 432.
219. "I know well": DDE.
219. "There is some pretty wooly thinking": IWM, op. cit.
220. "I am prepared": MM, p. 175.

221. "Seldom in war": Bradley, *General's*, p. 167.
223. "wondered if his luck": Butcher, p. 294.
225. "George, let me give you some advice": Bradley, *Soldier's*, p. 138.
226. " 'Monty,' the enraged Bradley said": Bradley, *General's*, p. 189.
226. "slowness of the Allied advance": Ambrose, *Commander*, 227.
227. "just marched": Ibid.
229. "Today the Seventh Army": Davis, p. 436.
229. "It's my nerves": Bradley, *Soldier's*, p. 161.
230. "they'll be howling": Miller, p. 532.

14. IMPASSE IN ITALY
233. "best calculated": Ambrose, *Commander*, p. 211.
233. "Would you ever have thought": Butcher, p. 268.
235. "Italy wanted frantically": Eisenhower, p. 202.
235. "the fury of the Italian population": Ambrose, Ibid., p. 255.
236. "I must respectfully": EP, p. 1315.
237. "[W]e hourly expected": Hart, *Hill*, p. 362.
237. "The Italian government": Davis, p. 446.
238. "I think sometimes": EP, p. 795.
238. "tact and diplomacy": *Time*, September 13, 1943.
239. "graveyard": Thompson, *Legend*, p. 231.
240. "full of plans": Macmillan, p. 372.
240. "ability to handle": BD.
241. "I have been given": IWM, reel 4.
241. "to enable": MM, p. 192.
242. "[T]he way the whole party": Hamilton, op. cit., p. 397.
242. "nearly irrational": Bradley, *Soldier's*, p. 199.
242. "his famous conceit": Ibid., p. 206.
242. "I believe [he said later]": OCMH, Eisenhower Oral History transcript.
244. "In the case": Hart, *History*, p. 480.
245. "Monty will move": Butcher, p. 359.
245. "very cautious advance": Ibid., p. 487.
245. "I just arrived in time": Hamilton, op. cit., p. 243.
246. "The going in Italy": Butcher, p. 373.
246. "grieved to think": Ibid., p. 363.
246. "[I]t wearies me": EP, p. 1712.
246. "If the forces employed": Hart, *Hill*, p. 364.
247. "winding up his tail": Butcher, p. 362.
247. "The Germans are": Hart, *History*, p. 494.
248. "[N]one of those": Summersby, *Boss*, p. 107.

248. "by reason of his outstanding": Butcher, p. 372.

249. "Baloney": Miller, p. 558.

249. "I can scarcely imagine": EP, p. 1493.

249. "he would probably be out": Butcher, p. 359.

250. "You and I": Robert Sherwood, *The White House Papers*,
     Volume II. London: Eyre and Spottiswoode, 1949, p. 65.

250. "Nothing has been exactly right": David, p. 159.

252. "a certain amount of experience": Bryant, *Triumph*, p. 106.

252. "I know of no other person": MM, p. 540.

253. "I miss you terribly": David, p. 158.

253. "I am interested in": Ibid., p. 137.

254. "over his strenuous objections": Ibid.

254. "was not fond of Monty": Bryant, *Triumph*, p. 115.

255. "a first class administrative muddle": MM, p. 203.

256. "The initial landing": Ibid., p. 211.

256. "analyse and revise": Lewin, p. 166.

256. "Please look upon him": EP, p. 1625.

257. "I miss you terribly": David, p. 150.

258. "Goddamnit, can't you tell": Summersby, *Past Forgetting*,
     p. 119.

259. "If only things had been different": Ibid., p. 124.

259. "Good night": Ibid., p. 148.

259. "my theater where I can": John Eisenhower, *Strictly Personal*.
     New York: Doubleday, 1974, p. 51.

260. "Don't come back until it's over": Davis, p. 457.

15. PRELUDE TO INVASION

277. " 'The equipment,' he later wrote": Lewin, p. 169.

278. "He had in the months": Eisenhower, p. 253.

278. "I had to hand over": Morgan, *Overture*, p. 178.

279. "When I think of the beaches": Dwight Eisenhower, *At Ease*,
     p. 261.

280. "The COSSAC staff": Morgan, ibid., p. 52.

280. "But for Christ's sake": Ibid., p. 80.

281. "It has a ring of importance": Dwight Eisenhower, ibid.,
     p. 268.

283. "There were many cold feet": Hamilton, op. cit., p. 495.

284. "command of the British Army": Butcher, p. 411.

285. "go off on the end of a limb": Ibid., p. 410.

285. "be the target": Ibid., p. 406.

286. "Much discussion": Ferrell, p. 111.

286. "please make it appear": EP, p. 1693.

287. "noted for his great energy": Pogue, *Supreme Command*, p. 34.

287. "dominant recollection": Morgan, ibid., p. 184.
288. "The main impression": Bryant, *Triumph*, p. 189.
289. "You will enter": Pogue, ibid., p. 53.
292. "I get tired": EP, p. 2521.
292. "It looks like Anvil is doomed": Ambrose, *Soldier*, p. 284.
294. "to be certain": Pogue, ibid., 113.
294. "In the various campaigns": EP, p. 1714.
298. "usually aloof, almost withdrawn": Bradley, *Soldier's*, p. 232.
298. "is merely understatement": DDE.
298. "Plans and preparations": Ismay, p. 351.
299. "Confidence in the high command": Lewin, p. 178.
300. "It would seem to be about time": Ibid., p. 177.
301. "too much earth": Morgan, *Overture*, p. 182.
301. "All my conferences": Miller, p. 597.
301. "Ike looks worn and tired": BD.
301. "I'm having a flare-up": Miller, p. 590.
302. "damned well going to get out": Ibid.
303. "That suits me": Ambrose, *Soldier*, p. 275.
303. "Gentlemen, I am now hardening": OCMH, Box World War
       II—Supreme Command.
303. "realized for the first time": Ibid.

16. OVERLORD
304. "I am very uneasy": Bryant, *Triumph*, p. 205.
304. "do his level best": Wilmot, p. 216.
305. "an illusion, conjured up": Hart, *Hill*, p. 393.
306. "never allow you": MM, p. 328.
307. "the effect of delay": EP, p. 1904.
307. "Success or failure": Ibid., p. 1905.
307. "we have a very insecure": Brown, p. 624.
308. "Our landings": Butcher, p. 525.
309. "bring about the destruction": EP, p. 1913.
309. "General Eisenhower turned": Summersby, *Boss*, p. 135.
310. "To hell with it": Butcher, p. 486.
310. "On the eve of this great adventure": Hamilton, op. cit.,
       p. 615.
312. "I have as yet": EP, p. 1914.
312. "I would like to thank you": Bryant, ibid., p. 206.
314. "a nightmare": Bradley, *Soldier's*, p. 249.
314. "I could see": Butcher, p. 459.
314. "If you saw Omaha Beach": Bryant, ibid., 209.
314. "If things were not going well": Kennedy, p. 330.
314. " . . . parts of the lodgement area": Bryant, ibid.

317. "General situation very good": Hamilton, op. cit., p. 627.
317. "The country here": Lamb, p. 98.
318. "[I]t is great fun": PRO, WO 205/5d.
319. "a Godsend": Miller, p. 631.
319. "little fretful": Ibid., p. 628.

17. NORMANDY
320. "tired and almost listless": Butcher, p. 494.
322. "You can be sure": PRO, op. cit.
322. "Operations . . . proceeding": Lamb, p. 119.
322. "I will continue battling": Ibid, p. 115.
322. "was always uppermost": David Eisenhower, p. 346.
322. "A successful break-in": Lamb, p. 106.
323. "incurably defensive minded": Lewin, p. 206.
323. "had constant trouble": OCMH, Coningham Oral History Transcript.
323. "most people I know": EP, p. 1933.
324. "[A]pparently Monty wants to": BD.
324. "1. . . . we have been": DDE.
325. "I am in high hopes": EP, p. 1934.
325. "When I die": OCMH, Chester Hansen diary.
325. "Chief Big Wind": BD.
325. "quickly and deeply": Weigley, p. 50.
326. "His relations with his staff": Kennedy, p. 346.
326. "One was so often being told": L-H, Carver letter, May 8, 1952.
326. "Of course": D'Este, p. 206.
327. "absolute rubbish": Ambrose, *Supreme Commander*. p. 428.
327. "wonderfully clear and concise": Bryant, *Triumph*, p. 214.
327. "think again": Ibid., p. 219.
327. "I am familiar with your plan": PRO, WO 219/254.
328. "lacked the firmness of will": OCMH, Smith Oral History Transcript.
328. "to get moving": Tedder, p. 557.
328. "More than one": Eisenhower, p. 289.
329. "Monty is a good man": OCMH, Dempsey Oral History Transcript.
329. "I am . . . quite happy": PRO, WO 205/5d.
330. "Monty is beginning to believe": OCMH, Hansen diary.
330. "moves his face briskly": Ibid.
330. "[Churchill] began to abuse Monty": Bryant, ibid., p. 230.
330. "not . . . a single word": Ibid.

330. "interference with the American army": OCMH, Supreme Commander Box.
330. "hold firm near Caen": Bradley, *Soldier's*, p. 264
331. "They were intimately acquainted": Ibid., p. 265.
331. "1,924 kilometers to Caen": OCMH, Hansen diary.
332. "What shall we do?": Churchill, Volume VI, p. 20.
332. "very worried": Hart, *Hill*, p. 415.
332. "was looking back over his shoulder": Ibid.
333. "My whole Eastern flank": DDE.
333. "blue as indigo": Butcher, p. 531.
333. "red as a hot coal": Bradley, ibid., p. 277.
333. "with 7000 tons of bombs": Butcher, ibid.
333. "Open Country": Bradley, ibid., p. 275.
333. "It is always better to do the booming": London *Times*, July 22, 1944.
333. "As a patriotic Briton": Summersby, *Boss*, p. 153.
334. "would have sacked Monty": Bradley, ibid.
334. "the subject we have been discussing": Butcher, p. 536.
334. "[I]t would be folly": OCMH, Hansen diary.
334. "[T]heir confidence": *The New York Times*, August 6, 1944.
335. "to persuade Monty": Bryant, *Triumph*, p. 241.
335. "I am perfectly positive": DDE.
335. "for the clear exposition": Ibid.
335. "I cannot tell you": PRO, WO 219/254.
336. "It fell to the British": Bradley, *Soldier's*, p. 326.

18. GENERALS AT WAR
337. "a blind alley": Butcher, p. 553.
338. "big strong and dominating": Pogue, *Supreme Command*, p. 225.
338. " 'bullying' the British": Butcher, Ibid.
339. "between 40 and 50 divisions": Pogue, ibid., p. 220.
339. "with considerable emotion": Butcher, p. 549.
340. "In two years": Pogue, ibid., p. 226.
341. "grow fat and prosperous": Ibid., p. 228.
341. "Anticipating the Germans": Bradley, *General's*, p. 307.
342. "The equivalent of 5 Panzer Divisions": PRO.
342. "a chance to catch his breath": Weigley, p. 253.
343. "British dominance of the command": Pogue, *Organizer*, p. 424.
343. "It is generally recognized": Ibid.
343. " . . . the Secretary [of War Stimson]": Pogue, ibid., p. 425.

343. "Ike knows nothing about strategy": Bryant, *Triumph*, p. 243.
344. "very clearly to Eisenhower": IWM, reel 12.
344. "two massive, mutually supporting thrusts": Bradley, *General's*, p. 307.
345. "likely to add another three to six months": Bryant, ibid., p. 262.
345. "doing the enemy a favor": Butcher, p. 557.
345. "one of the most disturbing features": Tedder, p. 586.
345. "status equal to Montgomery": PRO, WO 219/1.
345. "demotion": Ibid.
346. "We feel it our duty": *Daily Mirror*, August 17, 1944.
346. "great and personal friend": London *Times*, September 1, 1944.
347. "so coscious of Britain's ebbing manpower": Butcher, p. 534.
348. "We have now reached the stage": IWM, reel 7.
349. "absolutely convinced": *U.S. News & World Report*, October 24, 1958.
349. "The British economy and man-power situation": MM, p. 271.
350. "complete agreement": Hamilton, Volume II, p. 799.
350. "downright crazy": Bradley, *General's*, p. 312.
350. "We would be putting": Ibid., p. 311.
350. "the most fantastic bit of balderdash": OCMH, Smith Oral History Transcript.
350. "Examination of this scheme": NA, RG 165. OPD 1942–44, 201 (A–Z).
350. "Montgomery, principally celebrated": Morgan, *Overture*, p. 198.
351. "What makes me so Goddamn mad": Tedder, p. 631.
351. "Someone must run the land battle for him": MM, p. 268.
352. "seemed to be the chief form of amusement": George Patton, *War As I Knew It*. London: W.H. Allen, 1948.
352. "drive the British back into the sea": Farago, p. 317.
352. "Give people victory": Wilmot, p. 468.
352. "operational coordination": MM, p. 269.
352. "principal offensive mission": EP, p. 2090.
353. "[S]o we got ready": Bradley, ibid., p. 316.
353. "Eisenhower is the best general": Butcher, p. 568.
353. "Monty's plan sprung from his": Bradley, ibid.
356. "The overall situation in the West": Hart, *History*, p. 592.

19. THE WANING OF THE CHASE

357. "outstanding service": MM, p. 270.
358. "signs of victory in the air": EP, p. 2108.

358. "any tendency to be 'sticky' ": Wilmot, p. 470.
359. "cannot hang together": EP, ibid.
359. "[W]e have reached the stage": IWM, reel 7.
359. "completely out of touch": MM, p. 271.
360. "Patience and tolerance": OCMH, Williams Oral History Transcript.
360. "one of the most imaginative": Bradley, *Soldier's*, p. 416.
360. would be "crazy": Summersby, *Boss*, p. 155.
361. its "first priority": EP, p. 2153.
362. "Monty does what he pleases": Blumenson, *Patton Papers*, p. 548.
362. "He was as cocky as ever": Lamb, p. 263.
363. "deep thrust in strength": EP, p. 2146.
364. "defer the clearing out": Eisenhower, p. 336.
364. "white with passion": Morgan, *Overture*, p. 199.
365. "In both the U.S.": Pogue, *Supreme Command*, p. 289.
366. "Ike apparently unable to say": OCMH, Hansen diary.
366. "not possible" for all: Pogue, ibid., p. 290.
367. "I regard it as a great pity": EP, p. 2186.
367. "The envelopment of the Ruhr": Pogue, ibid., p. 294.
367. "your plan 100 per cent": EP, p. 2176.
367. "I cannot agree": Pogue, ibid., p. 293.
368. "completely out of touch": IWM, reel 12.
368. "a lack of grip": Pogue, *Organizer*, p. 475.
368. "very hard for me": Ibid.
368. "The present organization for command": Bradley, *General's*, p. 338.
369. "real issue now at hand": EP, p. 2221.
369. "we have an issue that must be": Ibid., p. 2222.
369. "You will hear no more": DDE.
370. "in order to conserve our strength": Eisenhower, p. 352.
371. " 'harping,' Brooke noted": Bryant, *Triumph*, 324.
371. "have no relation to the practical necessities": Ibid., 334.
371. "entirely detached": Ibid., p. 338.
372. he was "pretty certain": L-H, Alanbrooke Papers, 4, Box 1.
372. "to place before you": David Eisenhower, p. 546.
373. "curious idea that every Army Commander": Bryant, ibid., p. 336.
373. "Ike seems determined": Ibid.
373. " 'Without hesitation,' he advised him": L-H, op. cit.
374. "I proved to him": Bryant, ibid., p. 342.
374. "a strategic reverse": IWM, reel 7.
374. "must not speak": Butcher, p. 607.

375. "hot under the collar": Ibid.
375. "*as we had hoped*": EP, p. 2323.
376. "This was a classic": Bradley, *General's*, 347.
376. "We shall split our resources": IWM, reel 7.
376. "They all arrived": Ibid.

20. THE BULGE

379. "crust of defenses": Pogue, *Supreme Command*, p. 369.
379. "It is possible that a limited scale": Thompson, *Field Marshal*,
     p. 236.
380. "a menace with the young": Hamilton, op, cit., p. 563.
381. "The enemy is at present": Thompson, op. cit., p. 240.
382. "spoiling attack": Bradley, *Soldier's*, p. 455.
383. "Where in hell": Bradley, *General's*, p. 357.
384. "without regard to color or race": EP, p. 2394.
385. "[A] half-million GIs": Bradley, *Soldier's*, p. 467.
386. "The present situation": Eisenhower, p. 382.
386. "may give us the chance": Pogue, op. cit., p. 380.
386. "Hell," he said: Bradley, *General's*, p. 358.
386. ". . . there is a definite lack of grip": Bryant, *Triumph*, 358.
387. ". . . if Monty's were an American command": Bradley,
     Soldier's, p. 476.
387. "very excited and it was difficult": Bryant, ibid., p. 360.
389. "He is a prisoner": Butcher, p. 165.
389. "seemed delighted": Bryant, ibid., p. 361.
389. "like Christ coming": Ibid.
390. "I and my Army": Weigley, p. 615.
390. "Events and enemy actions": Bryant, ibid., 367.
391. "by lecturing and scolding": Bradley, *General's*, p. 369.
391. had "agreed entirely": Bryant, ibid., p. 368.
391. "Monty," Bradley later wrote: Bradley, ibid., p. 370.
391. "The Kraut has stuck his head": OCMH, Hansen diary.
392. "we will fail again": EP, p. 2387.
392. "it will be necessary": MM, p. 318.
392. "it makes me mad": OCMH, op. cit.
392. "slavish hero devotion": Ibid.
393. "very quietly started to explain": De Guingand, *Generals*,
     p. 108.
393. "tired of the whole business": Ibid.
393. "solve the impasse": Ibid.
393. "It was one of the few times": Ibid., p. 111.
394. ". . . understand you are greatly worried": Ibid., p. 112.
394. "I truly appreciate": EP, p. 2389.

394. "are very closely knit": Warren Kimball, editor, *Churchill and Roosevelt*. Volume III. Princeton: Princeton University Press, 1984, p. 498.

394. MONTY'S 'FIRST TEAM' IN: *Daily Express*, January 6, 1945.

395. "According to information": *Daily Mail*, January 8, 1945.

395. "rumblings . . . have now grown": Butcher, p. 625.

395. "As a commander in charge": IWM, reel 12.

396. "bears a great burden": *Washington Post*, January 8, 1945.

396. "General Eisenhower placed me in command": IWM, reel 8.

397. "After what has happened": Bradley, *General's*, p. 383.

397. "I have seen it suggested": *Hansard's*, January 18, 1945.

398. "I have the strong impression": NA, OPD, 384, ETO.

398. "Why is it": Harold Nicolson, op. cit., p. 441.

398. "muzzle, or better still": Brendon, p. 117.

21. THE LONG WINTER

399. "We have reached a stage": L-H, Alanbrooke Papers, 14/2.

399. "succeeded far beyond": David Eisenhower, p. 616.

399. "With their man-power and resources": Bryant, *Triumph*, p. 366.

401. "seize the Rhine crossings": Lewin, p. 246.

401. "fed up with [Churchill]": Lamb, p. 415.

402. "My feeling is this": Pogue, *Organizer*, p. 487.

402. "Super Heavy": Lewin, p. 249.

402. "will not remain as Chief of Staff": EP, p. 2461.

403. "[W]e shall take a long time": Bryant, ibid., p. 387.

403. "that [Eisenhower's] old snags": Ibid.

403. "the more Germans we kill": EP, p. 2438.

403. "Shove everything across it": Bradley, ibid., p. 405.

404. "You're not going anywhere": Ibid., p. 407.

404. "[G]et across with everything": Ibid.

404. precaution of "consulting": Bryant, ibid., p. 429.

404. "For God's sake": Bradley, ibid., p. 412.

405. "Without benefit of aerial bombing": Bradley, *Soldier's*, p. 521.

405. "[W]hile the British assault": Morgan, ibid., p. 205.

405. "on the run": Farago, p. 436.

407. "the main prize": IWM, reel 12.

407. "[I]t is my desire": DDE.

407. "Our main objective": PRO, WO 705/682.

407. "nothing but a geographical location": EP, p. 2568.

408. "mopping up and occupying the Ruhr": EP, p. 2552.

408. "unable to evolve a sound plan": IWM, reel 7.

408. "I consider," he said: Bryant, ibid., p. 447.

408. "was that if anything": Ryan, p. 185.
410. "a pretty stiff price": Bradley, *Soldier's*, p. 535.
412. "The Russian Armies": Pogue, *Supreme Command*, p. 442.
412. "quite a bit": EP, p. 2563.
413. "lost its former strategic importance": Ryan, p. 195.
414. "The only thing that moved faster": *The New York Times*, June 12, 1966.
415. "we should shake hands": EP, p. 2579.
415. "War is a political instrument": MM, p. 332.

22. VICTORY
417. "the activity of the Russians": EP, p. 2650.
420. "deepest gratitude": Ibid., p. 2687.
420. "like that of the Eighth Army": MM, p. 346.
420. "at the mistakes we made": Lamb, p. 394.
421. "visual evidence and verbal testimony": EP, p. 2616.
421. "Still having trouble hating them?": Robert Abzug, *Inside the Vicious Heart*. New York: Oxford University Press, 1985, p. 30.
421. "break off all negotiations": Pogue, ibid., p. 487.
422. "You will, officially and personally": Eisenhower, p. 465.
422. "you have completed your mission": Pogue, *Organizer*, p. 583.
422. "The crusade on which we embarked": Pogue, *Supreme Command*, p. 548.

IN CONCLUSION
425. "what a privilege and an honor": David Eisenhower, p. 819.
426. "Anybody in the British 8th Army": OCMH, Charles Bonesteel Oral History Transcript.
426. "leaping from his staff car": London *Times*, March 27, 1976.
426. "In the study of enemy positions": Eisenhower, p. 232.
427. "Few men were more enslaved": Thompson, *Legend*, p. 181.
427. "lacked the instinct": L-H. Liddell Hart, "Verdict on British Generals."
427. "allowances must be made": Ibid.
428. "the most overrated general": Thompson, *Field Marshal*, p. 322.
429. "swayed by the last man": David Eisenhower, p. 641.
430. "must realize that": Hamilton, p. 781.
430. "True we were anti-Monty": OCMH, OH, Wing Commander Leslie Scarman.
431. "a third-rate general": Lamb, p. 416.
431. "for certain types of operations": Ibid., p. 417.
431. "always planned a frontal attack": OH, Smith, op. cit.

431. "a very great human being": MM, p. 540.

431. "I blaze for an hour": Ferrell, p. 52.

431. "a superb coordinator": Horrocks, *Corps Commander*, p. 8.

431. "He grew almost": Morgan, *Overlord by the Under-Dog-in-Chief*, OCMH, Supreme Command Box.

432. "his greatest asset": Bryant, *Tide*, p. 528.

432. "a very good start": IWM, reel 7.

432. "Give him orders": Lamb, p. 415.

434. "The confusion and the irritations": Brendon, p. 207.

438. "I will finish it": Moorehead, p. 241.

439. "a malicious desire": Hamilton, Volume III, p. 838.

439. "The other two": London *Times*, March 27, 1976.

439. "could not possibly": MM, p. 205.

439. "historic moment": De Guingand, *Generals*, p. 197.

439. "a tremendous jump": Ibid., p. 168.

441. "explanation" to the Italian prime minister: London *Times*, February 20, 1992.

442. "expensive in life": MM, p. 262.

442. "Apparently Ike has come to realize": Hamilton, p. 900.

443. thousands of "American boys": Ibid., p. 901.

443. "great promises that he made": Eisenhower Library, AWF, Names File.

443. "Montgomery had become so personal": Ryan, p. 185.

SELECTED BIBLIOGRAPHY

Ambrose, Stephen. *Eisenhower: The Soldier*. London: Allen & Unwin, 1983.

———. *The Supreme Commander*. London: Cassell, 1971.

Barnett, Corelli. *The Desert Generals*. London: Kimber, 1960.

Blaxland, Gregory. *The Plain Cook and the Great Showman*. London: Kimber, 1977.

Blumenson, Martin. *Breakout and Pursuit*. Washington, D.C.: Center of Military History, United States Army, 1961.

Blumenson, Martin., ed. *The Patton Papers*. Vol. 2. Boston: Houghton Mifflin, 1974.

Bradley, Omar. *A Soldier's Story*. London: Eyre & Spottiswood, 1952.

———. *A General's Life*. New York: Simon and Schuster, 1983.

Brendon, Piers. *Ike*. Secker & Warburg, 1987.

Brooks, Stephen. *Montgomery and the Eight Army*. London, Bodley Head, 1991.

Brown, Anthony Cave. *Bodyguard of Lies*. London: Comet, 1986.

Bryant, Arthur. *The Turn of the Tide*. London: Collins, 1957.

———. *Triumph in the West*. London: Collins, 1959.

Butcher, Harry. *Three Years with Eisenhower*. London: Heinemann, 1946.

Chalfont, Alun. *Montgomery of Alamein*. London: Weidenfeld & Nicolson, 1976.

Chandler, Alfred, Jr., ed. *The Papers of Dwight David Eisenhower.* 5 Volumes. Baltimore: Johns Hopkins, 1970.

Churchill, Winston. *The Second World War.* Volume 6. London: Cassell, 1954.

Clark, Mark. *Calculated Risk.* London: Harrap, 1951.

David, Lester and Irene. *Ike and Mamie.* New York: Putnam, 1981.

Davis, Kenneth. *Soldier of Democracy.* New York: Doubleday, 1946.

D'Este, Carlo. *Decision in Normandy.* London: Collins, 1983.

De Guingand, Francis. *Operation Victory.* London: Hodder & Stoughton, 1947.

———. *Generals At War*, London: Hodder and Stoughton, 164.

Eisenhower, David. *Eisenhower: At War.* London: Collins, 1986.

———. *At Ease.* London: Robert Hale, 1967.

———. *Crusade in Europe.* London: Heinemann, 1948.

Eisenhower, John., ed. *Letters to Mamie.* New York: Doubleday, 1978.

Farago, Ladislas. *Patton.* London: Arthur Barker, 1966.

Ferrell, Robert., ed. *The Eisenhower Diaries.* New York: Norton, 1981.

Gelb, Norman. *Desperate Venture.* New York: Morrow, 1992.

Gilbert, Martin. *Winston. S. Churchill.* Volume VII. London: Heinemann, 1988.

Hamilton, Nigel. *Monty.* 3 Volumes. London: Hamish Hamilton, 1981–86.

Hastings, Max. *Overlord.* London: Michael Joseph, 1984.

Horrocks, Brian. *A Full Life.* London: Leo Cooper, 1974.

———. *Corps Commander.* London: Sidgwick and Jackson, 1977.

Howarth, T.E.B., ed. *Monty at Close Quarters.* New York: Hippocrene, 1985.

Howe, George. *Northwest Africa.* Washington, D.C.: Office of the Chief of Military History, Department of the Army, 1957.

Irving, David. *The War Between the Generals.* London: Allan Lane, 1981.

Ismay, Lord. *Memoirs.* London: Heinemann, 1960.

Kennedy, John. *The Business of War.* London: Hutchinson, 1957.

Lamb, Richard. *Montgomery in Europe.* London: Buchan & Enright, 1983.

Lewin, Ronald. *Montgomery.* London: Batsford, 1971.

Liddell Hart, Basil. *History of the Second World War.* London: Pan Books, 1970.

———. *The Other Side of the Hill.* London: Cassell, 1951.

———. ed. *The Rommel Papers.* London: Hamlyn, 1953.

Lyon, Peter. *Eisenhower.* Boston: Little, Brown, 1974.

Macmillan, Harold. *The Blast of War.* London: Macmillan, 1967.

Malone, Dick. *Missing From the Record.* London: Collins, 1946.

Miller, Merle. *Ike the Soldier.* New York: Putnam, 1987.

Montgomery, Bernard. *Memoirs*. London: Collins, 1958.

Montgomery, Brian. *A Field Marshal in the Family*. London: Constable, 1973.

Moorehead, Alan. *Montgomery*. London: Hamish Hamilton, 1946.

Moran, Lord. *Churchill: The Struggle for Survival*. London: Constable, 1966.

Morgan, Frederick. *Overture to Overlord*. London: Hodder & Stoughton, 1950.

———. *Peace and War*. London: Hodder & Stoughton, 1961.

Murphy, Robert. *Diplomat Among Warriors*. London: Collins, 1964.

Nicolson, Harold. *Diaries and Letters*. Volume II. London: Collins, 1967.

Nicolson, Nigel. *Alex: The Life of Field Marshal Earl Alexander of Tunis*. London: Weidenfeld and Nicolson, 1973.

Playfair, I. S. O. *The Mediterranean and the Middle East*. London: HMSO, 1966.

Pogue, Forrest. *George C. Marshall: Ordeal and Hope*. London: Macgibbon and Kee, 1968.

———. *George C. Marshall: Organizer of Victory*. New York: Viking, 1973.

———. *The Supreme Command*. Washington, D.C.: Office of the Chief of Military History, Department of the Army, 1954.

Richardson, Charles. *Flashback*. London: Kimber, 1985.

———. *Send for Freddie*. London: Kimber, 1987.

Ryan, Cornelius. *The Last Battle*. London: Collins, 1966.

Summersby, Kay. *Eisenhower Was My Boss*. London: Werner Laurie, 1949.

———. *Past Forgetting*. London: Collins, 1977.

Tedder, Lord. *With Prejudice*. London: Cassell, 1966.

Thompson, R. W. *The Montgomery Legend*. London: Allen & Unwin, 1967.

———. *Montgomery, The Field Marshal*. London: Allen & Unwin, 1969.

Weigley, Russell. *Eisenhower's Lieutenants*. London: Sidgwick & Jackson, 1981.

Wilmot, Chester. *The Struggle for Europe*. London: Collins, 1952.

INDEX